Short Stories for Students

National Advisory Board

Short Stories
for Students

Presenting Analysis, Context, and Criticism on Commonly Studied Short Stories

Volume 18

David Galens, Project Editor

GALE®

THOMSON
™
GALE

Detroit • New York • San Diego • San Francisco • Cleveland • New Haven, Conn. • Waterville, Maine • London • Munich

Short Stories for Students, Volume 18

Project Editor
David Galens

Editorial
Anne Marie Hacht, Michelle Kazensky, Ira Mark Milne, Pam Revitzer, Kathy Sauer, Timothy J. Sisler, Jennifer Smith, Carol Ullmann

Research
Michelle Campbell, Sarah Genik, Tamara Nott

Permissions
Debra J. Freitas

Manufacturing
Stacy Melson

Imaging and Multimedia
Lezlie Light, Daniel William Newell, David G. Oblender, Kelly A. Quin, Luke Rademacher

Product Design
Pamela A. E. Galbreath

ISBN 0-7876-4270-3
ISSN 1092-7735

Printed in the United States of America
10 9 8 7 6 5 4 3 2 1

Table of Contents

Why Study Literature At All?

Short Stories for Students is designed to provide readers with information and discussion about a wide range of important contemporary and historical works of short fiction, and it does that job very well. However, I want to use this guest foreword to address a question that it does *not* take up. It is a fundamental question that is often ignored in high school and college English classes as well as research texts, and one that causes frustration among students at all levels, namely—why study literature at all? Isn't it enough to read a story, enjoy it, and go about one's business? My answer (to be expected from a literary professional, I suppose) is no. It is not enough. It is a start; but it is not enough. Here's why.

First, literature is the only part of the educational curriculum that deals directly with the actual world of lived experience. The philosopher Edmund Husserl used the apt German term *die Lebenswelt*, "the living world," to denote this realm. All the other content areas of the modern American educational system avoid the subjective, present reality of everyday life. Science (both the natural and the social varieties) objectifies, the fine arts create and/or perform, history reconstructs. Only literary study persists in posing those questions we all asked before our schooling taught us to give up on them. Only literature gives credibility to personal perceptions, feelings, dreams, and the "stream of consciousness" that is our inner voice. Literature wonders about infinity, wonders why God permits evil, wonders what will happen to us after we die.

Literature admits that we get our hearts broken, that people sometimes cheat and get away with it, that the world is a strange and probably incomprehensible place. Literature, in other words, takes on all the big and small issues of what it means to be human. So my first answer is that of the humanist—we should read literature and study it and take it seriously because it enriches us as human beings. We develop our moral imagination, our capacity to sympathize with other people, and our ability to understand our existence through the experience of fiction.

My second answer is more practical. By studying literature we can learn how to explore and analyze texts. Fiction may be about *die Lebenswelt*, but it is a construct of words put together in a certain order by an artist using the medium of language. By examining and studying those constructions, we can learn about language as a medium. We can become more sophisticated about word associations and connotations, about the manipulation of symbols, and about style and atmosphere. We can grasp how ambiguous language is and how important context and texture is to meaning. In our first encounter with a work of literature, of course, we are not supposed to catch all of these things. We are spellbound, just as the writer wanted us to be. It is as serious students of the writer's art that we begin to see how the tricks are done.

Seeing the tricks, which is another way of saying "developing analytical and close reading skills," is important above and beyond its intrinsic literary educational value. These skills transfer to other fields and enhance critical thinking of any kind. Understanding how language is used to construct texts is powerful knowledge. It makes engineers better problem solvers, lawyers better advocates and courtroom practitioners, politicians better rhetoricians, marketing and advertising agents better sellers, and citizens more aware consumers as well as better participants in democracy. This last point is especially important, because rhetorical skill works both ways—when we learn how language is manipulated in the making of texts the result is that we become less susceptible when language is used to manipulate us.

My third reason is related to the second. When we begin to see literature as created artifacts of language, we become more sensitive to good writing in general. We get a stronger sense of the importance of individual words, even the sounds of words and word combinations. We begin to understand Mark Twain's delicious proverb—"The difference between the right word and the almost right word is the difference between lightning and a lightning bug." Getting beyond the "enjoyment only" stage of literature gets us closer to becoming makers of word art ourselves. I am not saying that studying fiction will turn every student into a Faulkner or a Shakespeare. But it will make us more adaptable and effective writers, even if our art form ends up being the office memo or the corporate annual report.

Studying short stories, then, can help students become better readers, better writers, and even better human beings. But I want to close with a warning. If your study and exploration of the craft, history, context, symbolism, or anything else about a story starts to rob it of the magic you felt when you first read it, it is time to stop. Take a break, study another subject, shoot some hoops, or go for a run. Love of reading is too important to be ruined by school. The early twentieth century writer Willa Cather, in her novel *My Antonia*, has her narrator Jack Burden tell a story that he and Antonia heard from two old Russian immigrants when they were teenagers. These immigrants, Pavel and Peter, told about an incident from their youth back in Russia that the narrator could recall in vivid detail thirty years later. It was a harrowing story of a wedding party starting home in sleds and being chased by starving wolves. Hundreds of wolves attacked the group's sleds one by one as they sped across the snow trying to reach their village. In a horrible revelation, the old Russians revealed that the groom eventually threw his own bride to the wolves to save himself. There was even a hint that one of the old immigrants might have been the groom mentioned in the story. Cather has her narrator conclude with his feelings about the story. "We did not tell Pavel's secret to anyone, but guarded it jealously—as if the wolves of the Ukraine had gathered that night long ago, and the wedding party had been sacrificed, just to give us a painful and peculiar pleasure." That feeling, that painful and peculiar pleasure, is the most important thing about literature. Study and research should enhance that feeling and never be allowed to overwhelm it.

Thomas E. Barden
Professor of English and
Director of Graduate English Studies
The University of Toledo

Introduction

Purpose of the Book

The purpose of *Short Stories for Students* (*SSfS*) is to provide readers with a guide to understanding, enjoying, and studying short stories by giving them easy access to information about the work. Part of Gale's "For Students" Literature line, *SSfS* is specifically designed to meet the curricular needs of high school and undergraduate college students and their teachers, as well as the interests of general readers and researchers considering specific short fiction. While each volume contains entries on "classic" stories frequently studied in classrooms, there are also entries containing hard-to-find information on contemporary stories, including works by multicultural, international, and women writers.

The information covered in each entry includes an introduction to the story and the story's author; a plot summary, to help readers unravel and understand the events in the work; descriptions of important characters, including explanation of a given character's role in the narrative as well as discussion about that character's relationship to other characters in the story; analysis of important themes in the story; and an explanation of important literary techniques and movements as they are demonstrated in the work.

In addition to this material, which helps the readers analyze the story itself, students are also provided with important information on the literary and historical background informing each work. This includes a historical context essay, a box comparing the time or place the story was written to modern Western culture, a critical essay, and excerpts from critical essays on the story or author. A unique feature of *SSfS* is a specially commissioned critical essay on each story, targeted toward the student reader.

To further aid the student in studying and enjoying each story, information on media adaptations is provided (if available), as well as reading suggestions for works of fiction and nonfiction on similar themes and topics. Classroom aids include ideas for research papers and lists of critical sources that provide additional material on the work.

Selection Criteria

The titles for each volume of *SSfS* were selected by surveying numerous sources on teaching literature and analyzing course curricula for various school districts. Some of the sources surveyed include: literature anthologies, *Reading Lists for College-Bound Students: The Books Most Recommended by America's Top Colleges*; *Teaching the Short Story: A Guide to Using Stories from around the World*, by the National Council of Teachers of English (NCTE); and "A Study of High School Literature Anthologies," conducted by Arthur Applebee at the Center for the Learning and Teaching of Literature and sponsored by the National Endowment for the Arts and the Office of Educational Research and Improvement.

Input was also solicited from our advisory board, as well as from educators from various areas. From these discussions, it was determined that each volume should have a mix of "classic" stories (those works commonly taught in literature classes) and contemporary stories for which information is often hard to find. Because of the interest in expanding the canon of literature, an emphasis was also placed on including works by international, multicultural, and women authors. Our advisory board members—educational professionals—helped pare down the list for each volume. Works not selected for the present volume were noted as possibilities for future volumes. As always, the editor welcomes suggestions for titles to be included in future volumes.

How Each Entry Is Organized

Each entry, or chapter, in *SSfS* focuses on one story. Each entry heading lists the title of the story, the author's name, and the date of the story's publication. The following elements are contained in each entry:

- **Introduction:** a brief overview of the story which provides information about its first appearance, its literary standing, any controversies surrounding the work, and major conflicts or themes within the work.

- **Author Biography:** this section includes basic facts about the author's life, and focuses on events and times in the author's life that may have inspired the story in question.

- **Plot Summary:** a description of the events in the story. Lengthy summaries are broken down with subheads.

- **Characters:** an alphabetical listing of the characters who appear in the story. Each character name is followed by a brief to an extensive description of the character's role in the story, as well as discussion of the character's actions, relationships, and possible motivation.

  Characters are listed alphabetically by last name. If a character is unnamed—for instance, the narrator in "The Eatonville Anthology"—the character is listed as "The Narrator" and alphabetized as "Narrator." If a character's first name is the only one given, the name will appear alphabetically by that name.

- **Themes:** a thorough overview of how the topics, themes, and issues are addressed within the story. Each theme discussed appears in a sepa-

rate subhead, and is easily accessed through the boldface entries in the Subject/Theme Index.

- **Style:** this section addresses important style elements of the story, such as setting, point of view, and narration; important literary devices used, such as imagery, foreshadowing, symbolism; and, if applicable, genres to which the work might have belonged, such as Gothicism or Romanticism. Literary terms are explained within the entry, but can also be found in the Glossary.

- **Historical Context:** this section outlines the social, political, and cultural climate *in which the author lived and the work was created.* This section may include descriptions of related historical events, pertinent aspects of daily life in the culture, and the artistic and literary sensibilities of the time in which the work was written. If the story is historical in nature, information regarding the time in which the story is set is also included. Long sections are broken down with helpful subheads.

- **Critical Overview:** this section provides background on the critical reputation of the author and the story, including bannings or any other public controversies surrounding the work. For older works, this section may include a history of how the story was first received and how perceptions of it may have changed over the years; for more recent works, direct quotes from early reviews may also be included.

- **Criticism:** an essay commissioned by *SSfS* which specifically deals with the story and is written specifically for the student audience, as well as excerpts from previously published criticism on the work (if available).

- **Sources:** an alphabetical list of critical material used in compiling the entry, with bibliographical information.

- **Further Reading:** an alphabetical list of other critical sources which may prove useful for the student. It includes bibliographical information and a brief annotation.

In addition, each entry contains the following highlighted sections, set apart from the main text as sidebars:

- **Media Adaptations:** if available, a list of film and television adaptations of the story, including source information. The list also includes stage adaptations, audio recordings, musical adaptations, etc.

- **Topics for Further Study:** a list of potential study questions or research topics dealing with the story. This section includes questions related to other disciplines the student may be studying, such as American history, world history, science, math, government, business, geography, economics, psychology, etc.

- **Compare and Contrast:** an ''at-a-glance'' comparison of the cultural and historical differences between the author's time and culture and late twentieth century or early twenty-first century Western culture. This box includes pertinent parallels between the major scientific, political, and cultural movements of the time or place the story was written, the time or place the story was set (if a historical work), and modern Western culture. Works written after 1990 may not have this box.

- **What Do I Read Next?:** a list of works that might complement the featured story or serve as a contrast to it. This includes works by the same author and others, works of fiction and nonfiction, and works from various genres, cultures, and eras.

Other Features

SSfS includes ''Why Study Literature At All?,'' a foreword by Thomas E. Barden, Professor of English and Director of Graduate English Studies at the University of Toledo. This essay provides a number of very fundamental reasons for studying literature and, therefore, reasons why a book such as *SSfS*, designed to facilitate the study of litererture, is useful.

A Cumulative Author/Title Index lists the authors and titles covered in each volume of the *SSfS* series.

A Cumulative Nationality/Ethnicity Index breaks down the authors and titles covered in each volume of the *SSfS* series by nationality and ethnicity.

A Subject/Theme Index, specific to each volume, provides easy reference for users who may be studying a particular subject or theme rather than a single work. Significant subjects from events to broad themes are included, and the entries pointing to the specific theme discussions in each entry are indicated in **boldface**.

Each entry may include illustrations, including photo of the author, stills from film adaptations (if available), maps, and/or photos of key historical events.

Citing Short Stories for Students

When writing papers, students who quote directly from any volume of *SSfS* may use the following general forms to document their source. These examples are based on MLA style; teachers may request that students adhere to a different style, thus, the following examples may be adapted as needed.

When citing text from *SSfS* that is not attributed to a particular author (for example, the Themes, Style, Historical Context sections, etc.), the following format may be used:

''The Celebrated Jumping Frog of Calavaras County.'' *Short Stories for Students*. Ed. Kathleen Wilson. Vol. 1. Detroit: Gale, 1997. 19–20.

When quoting the specially commissioned essay from *SSfS* (usually the first essay under the Criticism subhead), the following format may be used:

Korb, Rena. Critical Essay on ''Children of the Sea.'' *Short Stories for Students*. Ed. Kathleen Wilson. Vol. 1. Detroit: Gale, 1997. 42.

When quoting a journal or newspaper essay that is reprinted in a volume of *Short Stories for Students*, the following form may be used:

Schmidt, Paul. ''The Deadpan on Simon Wheeler.'' *Southwest Review* Vol. XLI, No. 3 (Summer, 1956), 270–77; excerpted and reprinted in *Short Stories for Students*, Vol. 1, ed. Kathleen Wilson (Detroit: Gale, 1997), pp. 29–31.

When quoting material from a book that is reprinted in a volume of *SSfS,* the following form may be used:

Bell-Villada, Gene H. ''The Master of Short Forms,'' in *Garcia Marquez: The Man and His Work*. University of North Carolina Press, 1990, pp. 119–36; excerpted and reprinted in *Short Stories for Students*, Vol. 1, ed. Kathleen Wilson (Detroit: Gale, 1997), pp. 89–90.

We Welcome Your Suggestions

The editor of *Short Stories for Students* welcomes your comments and ideas. Readers who wish to suggest short stories to appear in future volumes, or who have other suggestions, are cordially invited to contact the editor. You may contact the editor via E-mail at: **ForStudentsEditors@gale.com.** Or write to the editor at:

Editor, *Short Stories for Students*
The Gale Group
27500 Drake Road
Farmington Hills, MI 48331–3535

Literary Chronology

1858: Selma Lagerlöf is born on November 20 on her family's farm estate, Mårbacka, in the province of Värmland, Sweden.

1860: Charlotte Perkins Gilman (born Charlotte Anna Perkins) on July 3 in Hartford, Connecticut.

1862: O. Henry (born William Sidney Porter) is born on September 11 in Greensboro, North Carolina.

1900: Thomas Wolfe is born on October 3 in Asheville, North Carolina.

1906: O. Henry's "Mammon and the Archer" is published.

1908: Selma Lagerlöf's "The Legend of the Christmas Rose" is published.

1909: Charlotte Perkins Gilman's "Three Thanksgivings" is published.

1910: O. Henry dies in New York City.

1917: Arthur C. Clarke is born on December 16 in Minehead, Somersetshire, England.

1924: James Baldwin is born on August 2 in Harlem, New York.

1930: Bruce Jay Friedman is born on April 26.

1933: Philip Roth is born on March 19 in Newark, New Jersey.

1935: Thomas Wolfe's "The Far and the Near" is published.

1935: E. Annie Proulx is born on August 22 in Norwich, Connecticut.

1935: Charlotte Perkins Gilman dies.

1938: Thomas Wolfe dies on September 15 of tubercular meningitis in Baltimore, Maryland.

1940: Selma Lagerlöf dies of a stroke on March 16 at Mårbacka.

1941: Sheila Kohler is born on November 13 in Johannesburg, South Africa.

1942: Terry Bisson is born on February 12 in Hopkins County, Kentucky.

1951: Arthur C. Clarke's "'If I Forget Thee, O Earth . . . '" is published.

1956: Chitra Banerjee Divakaruni is born on July 29 in Calcutta, India.

1957: Peter Høeg is born on May 17 in Cophenhage, Denmark.

1958: Kim Edwards is born on May 4 in Killeen, Texas.

1959: Philip Roth's "The Conversion of the Jews" is published.

1965: James Baldwin's "The Rockpile" is published.

1966: Sherman Alexie is born on October 7 in Spokane, Washington.

1966: Bruce Jay Friedman's "Brazzaville Teen-ager" is published.

1987: James Baldwin dies of stomach cancer on December 1 (some sources say November 30).

1990: Peter Høeg's "Journey into a Dark Heart" is published.

1993: Sherman Alexie's "Because My Father Always Said He Was the Only Indian Who Saw Jimi Hendrix Play 'The Star-Spangled Banner' at Woodstock" is published.

1993: Terry Bisson's "The Toxic Donut" is published.

1997: E. Annie Proulx's "The Half-Skinned Steer" is published.

1997: Kim Edwards's "The Way It Felt to Be Falling" is published.

1998: Sheila Kohler's "Africans" is published.

1998: Chitra Banerjee Divakaruni's "Mrs. Dutta Writes a Letter" is published.

Acknowledgments

The editors wish to thank the copyright holders of the excerpted criticism included in this volume and the permissions managers of many book and magazine publishing companies for assisting us in securing reproduction rights. We are also grateful to the staffs of the Detroit Public Library, the Library of Congress, the University of Detroit Mercy Library, Wayne State University Purdy/Kresge Library Complex, and the University of Michigan Libraries for making their resources available to us. Following is a list of the copyright holders who have granted us permission to reproduce material in this volume of *Short Stories for Students (SSfS)*. Every effort has been made to trace copyright, but if omissions have been made, please let us know.

COPYRIGHTED MATERIALS IN *SSfS*, VOLUME 18, WERE REPRODUCED FROM THE FOLLOWING PERIODICALS:

Critique, v. 44, Fall, 2002. Copyright © 2002 Helen Dwight Reid Educational Foundation. Reproduced with permission of the Helen Dwight Reid Educational Foundation, published by Heldref Publications, 1319 18th Street, NW, Washington, DC 20036–1802.—*English Journal*, v. 90, September, 2000 for "The Landscape of Fiction," by John Noell Moore. Copyright © 2000 by the National Council of Teachers of English. Reproduced by permission of the publisher and the author.—*Journal of the Short Story in English*, Spring, 1999. © Universit' d'Angers, 1999. Reproduced by permission.

COPYRIGHTED MATERIALS IN *SSfS*, VOLUME 18, WERE REPRODUCED FROM THE FOLLOWING BOOKS:

Edstrom, Vivi. From "Short Fiction: The Short Stories Legends, and Short Novels," in *Selma Lagerlöf.* Twayne Publishing, Inc., 1984. Copyright © 1984 by G. K. Hall & Company. All rights reserved. Reproduced by permission.—Evans. Elizabeth. From *Thomas Wolfe.* Frederick Ungar Publishing Co., 1984. Copyright © 1984 Frederick Ungar Publishing Co., Inc. Reproduced by permission.—Harris, Trudier. From "To Be Washed Whiter Than Snow: Going to Meet the Man," in *Black Women in the Fiction of James Baldwin.* University of Tennessee Press, 1985. Copyright © 1985 by Trudier Harris. All rights reserved. Reproduced by permission.—Paterson, Judith, and Guinevera A. Nance. From "Good Girls and Boys Gone Bad," in *Philip Roth.* Frederick Ungar Publishing Co., 1981. Copyright © 1981 by Frederick Ungar Publishing Company, Inc. Reproduced by permission.—Rood, Karen L. From "Close Range: Wyoming Stories," in *Understanding Annie Proulx.* University of South Carolina Press, 2001. © 2001 University of South Carolina. Reproduced by permission.—Schulz, Max F. From "Short Stories," in *Bruce J. Friedman*. Twayne Publishers, Inc., 1974. © 1974 by Twayne Publishers, Inc. All rights reserved. Reproduced by permission.

PHOTOGRAPHS AND ILLUSTRATIONS APPEARING IN *SSfS*, VOLUME 18, WERE

RECEIVED FROM THE FOLLOWING SOURCES:

African Zulu, photograph by Carl Van Haoffman. Corbis-Bettmann. Reproduced by permission.—Atomic bomb blast, photograph. Archive Photos/American Stock. Reproduced by permission.—Baldwin, James, photograph. © Hulton-Deutsch Collection/Corbis. Reproduced by Corbis Corporation.—Clarke, Arthur C., photograph. AP/Wide World Photos. Reproduced by permission.—Einstein, Albert, photograph. AP/Wide World Photos. Reproduced by permission.—Friedman, Bruce Jay, photograph. AP/Wide World Photos. Reproduced by permission.—Front view of Motown Museum, 2648 W. Grand Blvd, Detroit, MI, 1996, photograph by Layne Kennedy. Corbis Corporation. Reproduced by permission.—General Electric's Women's Club, photograph. © Schenectady Museum; Hall of Electrical History Foundation/Corbis. Reproduced by permission.—Gilman, Charlotte Perkins, photograph. The Library of Congress.—Henry, O., photograph. The Library of Congress.—Høeg, Peter, photograph by Marty Reichenthal. AP/Wide World Photos. Reproduced by permission.—Jainschigg, Nick, illustrator. From a cover of *Bears Discover Fire and Other Stories,* by Terry Bisson. Tom Doherty Associates, Inc., 1993. Copyright © 1993 by Terry Bisson. All rights reserved. Reproduced by permission.—Lagerlöf, Selma, photograph. Corbis-Bettmann. Reproduced by permission.—McAllister, Ward, photograph. © Bettmann/Corbis. Reproduced by permission.—Park Circus in Calcutta, India, photograph. © Earl & Nazima Kowall/Corbis. Reproduced by permission.—Proulx, E. Annie, photograph by Jerry Bauer. Jerry Bauer. Reproduced by permission.—Roth, Phillip, photograph. AP/Wide World Photos, Inc. Reproduced by permission.—Ruins of the Abbey of Alvastra, located in Sweden, photograph. © Archivo Iconografico, S.A./Corbis. Reproduced by permission.—Weinberg, Rabbi User, his wife, Fedora, and family arriving in New York, photograph. © Bettmann/Corbis. Reproduced by permission.—Wolfe, Thomas C., photograph. UPI/Corbis-Bettmann. Reproduced by permission.

Contributors

Kate Covintree: Covintree is currently pursuing a master of fine arts degree at Emerson College. Original essay on *Journey into a Dark Heart*.

Timothy Dunham: Dunham holds a bachelor's degree in English literature and a master's degree in communication. Original essay on *Because My Father Always Said He Was the Only Indian Who Saw Jimi Hendrix Play "The Star-Spangled Banner" at Woodstock*.

Douglas Dupler: Dupler has published numerous essays and has taught college English. Original essay on *"If I Forget Thee, O Earth . . ."*.

Curt Guyette: Guyette is a longtime journalist who received a bachelor's degree in English writing from the University of Pittsburgh. Original essay on *The Toxic Donut*.

Charlotte Mayhew: Mayhew is a freelance writer. Original essay on *Three Thanksgivings*.

Candyce Norvell: Norvell is an independent educational writer who specializes in English and literature. Original essays on *Brazzaville Teenager* and *Mrs. Dutta Writes a Letter*.

David Partikian: Partikian is a freelance writer and English instructor. Original essay on *Mammon and the Archer*.

Ryan D. Poquette: Poquette has a bachelor's degree in English and specializes in writing about literature. Entries on *Africans*, *Because My Father Always Said He Was the Only Indian Who Saw Jimi Hendrix Play "The Star-Spangled Banner" at Woodstock*, *Brazzaville Teen-ager*, *The Conversion of the Jews*, *The Far and the Near*, *The Half-Skinned Steer*, *"If I Forget Thee, O Earth . . . ,"* *Journey into a Dark Heart*, *The Legend of the Christmas Rose*, *Mammon and the Archer*, *Mrs. Dutta Writes a Letter*, *The Rockpile*, *Three Thanksgivings*, *The Toxic Donut*, and *The Way It Felt to Be Falling*. Original essays on *Africans*, *Because My Father Always Said He Was the Only Indian Who Saw Jimi Hendrix Play "The Star-Spangled Banner" at Woodstock*, *Brazzaville Teen-ager*, *The Conversion of the Jews*, *The Far and the Near*, *The Half-Skinned Steer*, *"If I Forget Thee, O Earth . . . ,"* *Journey into a Dark Heart*, *The Legend of the Christmas Rose*, *Mammon and the Archer*, *Mrs. Dutta Writes a Letter*, *The Rockpile*, *Three Thanksgivings*, *The Toxic Donut*, and *The Way It Felt to Be Falling*.

Scott Trudell: Trudell is a freelance writer with a bachelor's degree in English literature. Original essay on *The Way It Felt to Be Falling*.

Mark White: White is a Seattle-based publisher and editor. Original essay on *Africans*.

Africans

Sheila Kohler

1998

Sheila Kohler's "Africans" was first published in *Story* magazine in 1998. It received greater exposure when it was published the following year in Kohler's collection of interlinked stories *One Girl: A Novel in Stories*. The book is divided into four sections, each one representing a life stage. "Africans" is included in the largest of the four sections, "Courtship and Marriage." The story, like many of Kohler's works, is set in South Africa, where she grew up. The main theme concerns the betrayal of a woman by her abusive husband, and her ultimate betrayal by her loyal African servant. However, the story, which takes place in the mid- to late-twentieth century, also contains references to apartheid, the legalized racial segregation that took place in South Africa during this time. Apartheid denied blacks many rights, including the right to vote. Kohler published her story four years after Nelson Mandela became South Africa's first black president in the country's first free election. *One Girl: A Novel in Stories* was received well by the critics and inspired *Cracks: A Novel* (1999), which was based on one of the other stories in the collection. "Africans" can be found in *The Best American Short Stories 1999,* which was published by the Houghton Mifflin Company in 1999.

Author Biography

Kohler was born on November 13, 1941, in Johannesburg, South Africa. Although she later immigrated to the United States, her childhood experiences in South Africa would influence much of her writing. In 1988, Kohler's short story "The Mountain" earned an O. Henry Award, and in 1989, Kohler published her first novel, *The Perfect Place*, about a wealthy woman who is forced to remember her traumatic South African past. Over the next five years, Kohler published two books, a collection of short stories entitled *Miracles in America* (1990) and *The House on R. Street: A Novel* (1994). Like much of her fiction, these books are dark stories that deal with physical and psychological abuse as well as sexual issues.

In 1999, Kohler published *One Girl: A Novel in Stories*, a book of interconnected short stories that fall into different stages of life. The book was awarded the 1998 Willa Cather Fiction Prize and featured the story "Africans," which was also included in *The Best American Short Stories 1999*. Kohler's most recent work is *Cracks: A Novel*, which is based on the story "Cracks" from *One Girl: A Novel in Stories*. Kohler lives and works in New York City.

Plot Summary

"Africans" is a story told in recollection. It begins with a lengthy description of the Zulu people, who are the preferred servants of the narrator's mother. The Zulu society is built on loyalty, and the narrator gives several examples from their warrior history to demonstrate this fact. Now, however, following the occupation of South Africa by whites, many Zulus are servants. The narrator says that the Zulu she and her sister preferred was named John Mazaboko. Although John cares for both the narrator and her sister, Mkatie, he has a special relationship with the latter and saved her life on one occasion. He also serves as a teacher and guide to both girls, and they seek him out for advice. Like other male Zulus, John is not above performing any task. After the death of the narrator's father, her mother closes down most of the house and fires all of the servants except John.

The narrator and Mkatie go to a boarding school, and they only see John on holidays. While at school, they are kept busy playing sports, but they are not encouraged to be independent. The narrator remembers back to Mkatie's engagement. John asks questions about her fiancé, and Mkatie says he is an Afrikaner—a white South African who is a descendant of the Boer people. The Boers were farmers of European (mainly Dutch) descent, who were part of the colonization of South Africa by the Dutch East India Company in the seventeenth century. The Boers developed their own language, Afrikaans, which survived the loss of their independence to the British in the early twentieth century. Mkatie is sure that her mother will not approve of her fiancé, which implies that the narrator and her family are British; there was a long-standing tension between the Afrikaners and the British. Mkatie also notes that an ex-girlfriend of her fiancé is against the match, although the woman does not say why.

At her wedding, Mkatie lets her sister know that John will be moving in with Mkatie and her husband in the main house, while their mother will be staying in the cottage. When the narrator next visits her sister, Mkatie tells her that she caught her husband in a homosexual act. While the narrator thinks that Mkatie should have exposed him, Mkatie says that she could not because it would have ruined his career as a doctor. The narrator says that Mkatie's husband is also a pedophile. Her husband makes their son exercise and scrub his skin to improve his looks. Mkatie's husband also makes advances toward their son's friends. Mkatie wants a divorce but is afraid to go to a lawyer because her husband stalks her everywhere.

Many years later, the narrator visits again and notes that her sister is not doing well. Mkatie says that she cannot eat because her husband has started to get violent with her. After this visit, Mkatie takes a vacation in Rome and Instanbul, where she has an affair with a Turk. The Turkish man sends a love letter to Mkatie, which is intercepted by her husband. He is so distraught that he tries to kill himself by cutting his wrists, but Mkatie gets him in the clinic in time to save him. After he recuperates, Mkatie's husband starts to beat the children viciously, especially his son. He tries to beat Mkatie, too, but she is strong when she is angry. The narrator remembers that, during one of these fights, her sister was winning. However, Mkatie's husband calls for help from John, and, after a moment's hesitation, John obeys, betraying his friendship with Mkatie by holding her down while her husband beats her.

Characters

John Mazaboko

John Mazaboko is the favored Zulu servant of Mkatie and the narrator. John betrays Mkatie's trust at the end of the story. Mkatie's mother chooses John as a servant because of his Zulu heritage, which is based on loyalty. John likes spending time with Mkatie and her sister, although most of his time is spent cleaning and doing other menial tasks. When Mkatie's father dies, her mother fires all of the servants except John and retreats into herself, which puts increased pressure on him to run the household. As the years pass, John's extreme focus on work causes him to lose his individuality, and he no longer has the same joy in his relationship with the two women, especially Mkatie. He becomes a machine, doing what he is told and performing whatever task is necessary, including holding down Mkatie while her husband beats her, since he is unable to disobey an order from his male master.

Mkatie

Mkatie is the narrator's sister and lifelong charge of John. When Mkatie goes away to school, she excels in sports but is not encouraged to be ambitious, since most girls are destined to be obedient wives. Mkatie marries a doctor, despite the advice of her mother and her fiancé's ex-girlfriend. During a party she holds for her in-laws, Mkatie discovers her husband in a homosexual act and later tells her sister that he is also exhibiting pedophilic behavior towards her son and his friends. Her husband starts to get violent with her, at one point throwing a glass at her and cutting her lip. Mkatie tries to escape the marriage, first by asking her sister to go to a lawyer for her, then through an affair with a Turkish man. However, when her lover sends her a letter, it is intercepted by her husband, who then tries to kill himself. Mkatie saves him, but he is only more violent towards her because of her affair, and he also starts to beat their children. One day, Mkatie has her husband pinned and thinks she has won. However, her husband orders John to help him, and John obeys, holding a shocked Mkatie down while her husband beats her.

Mkatie's Husband

Mkatie's husband has homosexual tendencies, and Mkatie's discovery of this ignites Mkatie's

Media Adaptations

- *The Best American Short Stories 1999,* which includes the story "Africans," was adapted as an audiobook in 1999. It is available on four audiocassettes from Mariner Books. "Africans" is read by Kohler.

---

affair and leads to his subsequent abuse of his wife and children. When Mkatie first meets her husband, she is excited about the match, although neither her mother nor her fiancé's ex-girlfriend is happy about it. During a party for his family, Mkatie's husband has sex with a man, which Mkatie discovers. From this point on, he turns increasingly violent toward his wife and starts to exhibit pedophilic tendencies towards his son and his son's friends. When he discovers that his wife has had an affair, he tries to kill himself, but Mkatie saves him. After this, he turns even more violent, savagely beating his children, although Mkatie puts up a fight. On one occasion, he calls to John for help and orders John to hold down Mkatie while he beats her with a belt.

Mkatie's Mother

The mother of Mkatie and the narrator spends most of her time in an alcoholic haze, trying to get over her husband's death. In the beginning of the story, Mkatie's mother runs the household, hiring mainly Zulu servants because she knows that they are loyal. However, when her husband dies, she closes down most of the house, fires all of the servants except John, and gets into the habit of drinking until she passes out. When Mkatie gets married, her mother retreats even further, moving to the cottage and letting Mkatie and her husband have the main house and John.

Mkatie's Son

Mkatie's son is the narrator's nephew, and he lives under the threat of abuse from his homosexual father, who also likes to touch his friends when they change to go in the pool.

Narrator

The narrator is Mkatie's sister, who uses her own experiences, as well as information she hears from Mkatie and others, to tell the story. Out of all of their Zulu servants, the narrator and Mkatie like John best, although John has a special relationship with Mkatie. The narrator notes that John has served as a mentor and teacher to her and Mkatie and that they did not see him much while they were at school. When the narrator is married and living overseas with her husband and children, she makes annual visits to see her mother and sister. After her sister marries, the narrator hears increasingly worse stories on her visits. Her sister tells the narrator about her husband's homosexual and pedophilic tendencies as well as his acts of violence towards Mkatie and their children. At the end of the story, the narrator imagines what her sister must have looked like during one specific instance when she was being beaten by her husband—as John was holding her down.

Themes

Betrayal

At the end of the story, John Mazaboko betrays Mkatie's trust by holding her down while her husband beats her. This is far different from the treatment that she has come to expect from John. All of her life, John has proved that he wishes to protect Mkatie. For example, as the narrator notes, he saves Mkatie's life when she is very young. "He was unusually tall, and so strong he was able to catch the ancient armoire when it fell forward and almost crushed my sister as a small child." In addition to protecting Mkatie and the narrator, John has also served as a guide and teacher, showing them how to ride their bicycles and telling them Zulu stories. When Mkatie accidentally breaks her parrot's wing, he puts the bird out of its misery. "He took its pulsing neck between his fingers and wrung it swiftly. 'Better like this,' he told her." Most importantly, John and Mkatie seem to share a connection, a bond that transcends friendship and love. Says the narrator: "Whenever he saw her, he would chuckle as though they shared some secret understanding." As a result, when Mkatie is fighting with her abusive husband, she is shocked when John comes to her husband's aid. "John grasped my sister and held her down. At first she struggled, called out to him, 'What are you doing!'" However, when she sees

that their connection is broken, Mkatie gives up and lets John hold her down while her husband beats her.

Loyalty

Although it may seem strange, John's extreme loyalty to Mkatie's family is the reason why he restrains her in the end. John is a member of the Zulu people in South Africa. As the narrator notes in the beginning, her mother had always "preferred Zulu servants," because they "were obedient, conscientious, and fiercely loyal. Their society was built on loyalty." As noted above, John demonstrates his loyalty to the narrator and her sister, Mkatie, countless times. However, his loyalty to his supervisors is even stronger than his loyalty to the two girls. For example, even though he desires to protect the girls, he feels he must ask permission in certain circumstances. Says the narrator: "Mother said he could not bear to hear us cry when we were babies and would beg the severe Scottish nanny to allow him to hold us in his arms." Although his service to the two girls is enjoyable, his primary service—to the household—is degrading. In one instance, the Scottish nanny complains to John about a smelly cupboard. "Wrinkling her nose, she said, 'It smells Zulu.' He bent down from his great height onto his hands and knees and scrubbed the closet clean." In addition, John is constantly polishing everything in the house, "even the soles of shoes."

Through the decades of loyal service doing menial tasks such as these, John undergoes a transformation. When the narrator is a grown woman and comes to visit Mkatie, she notes the changed appearance of John, who is now the servant of Mkatie and her husband. John has "grown thinner over the years, his face more gaunt, as though he had turned inward and was bent on polishing himself into oblivion. Life in that house had worn away at his spirit." The sole focus of John's life has become his loyalty to his work. In the process, he has become incapable of recognizing or acting on his other emotions, such as his love for Mkatie. Says the narrator: "His eyes had lost that glimmer of humor when he looked at my sister." John's loyalty to Mkatie was based only on love and other emotions, not duty. Without these emotions, all that John is left with is his cultural tradition to be loyal to his master. In the end, although it may be hard to believe, John is being loyal to his master—his male master—by holding down Mkatie. In this male-dominated South African society, Mkatie's husband outranks Mkatie. As a result, when Mkatie's husband gives John a direct order—"'Do what I tell

Topics for Further Study

- Research the similarities and differences between slavery and apartheid and plot these comparisons on a two-column page. Find at least five civilizations from any time in history that have used slaves and try to identify at least one that has implemented apartheid-like conditions. Give a short description of each of these civilizations.

- Find a non-African culture that has been affected by racial segregation. Research this culture and compare it with the South African culture of apartheid in the last half of the twentieth century. Write a script for a conversation between a black South African and a member of this other culture, in which they discuss what their lives are like.

- Research the South African legal system in the mid to late twentieth century and re-enact any of the famous trials of anti-apartheid leaders in this time. For areas in which there is no record of the actual words used in the trial, try to imagine what

might have been said, using your research to support your ideas.

- Research what life was like for a black servant in South Africa from the 1940s to the 1970s and compare this to John's life in the story. Imagine that you are a servant in similar conditions, and write a journal entry describing your typical day.

- At the end of the story, John betrays Mkatie, who then submits to a beating by her husband. Research cases of domestic abuse in South Africa in the 1960s and 1970s, and write a one-page description about what you think would happen next in the story. Use your research to support your ideas.

- Research the travel habits of housewives during the 1960s and 1970s in South Africa and compare this information to Kohler's depiction of Mkatie's solo travels to Rome and Turkey. Discuss freedoms and restrictions that these women faced while traveling abroad.

---

you. Put her on the bed'''—John has no choice but to follow it.

Kohler also includes examples of disloyalty in the story, through the extramarital affairs of Mkatie and her husband. When Mkatie marries her husband, she has no idea that he has homosexual tendencies until she catches him having sex with another man. Mkatie is so distraught at her husband's indiscretions that she eventually chooses to have an affair of her own.

Roles of Women

As noted above, Mkatie holds a secondary rank to her husband, a fact that ultimately results in John helping Mkatie's husband beat her. Mkatie is taught that women in general are considered subservient to men, and are expected to serve very limited roles that are defined by men. For example, Mkatie shows athletic prowess but is not encouraged to excel in sports or pursue her dreams of being a doctor

because "ambition was not considered seemly for Christian girls." In the place of ambition, the girls' school that Mkatie and her sister attend teaches them "meekness," "obedience, diligence, and . . . loyalty." In addition, the narrator notes that there were limited options for women in this time period: "As our headmistress pointed out, most of us were destined to be mothers and wives." Because of this male-centric dynamic, women are not encouraged to speak out against men. When Mkatie is engaged to her husband, Mkatie's mother gets a call from a frantic ex-girlfriend, begging Mkatie's mother not to let Mkatie marry him. As Mkatie notes, "She just kept saying, *Please don't let her marry him.*'" While readers may first take this as a sign that the other woman is jealous of Mkatie, what is more likely is that the woman is trying to protect Mkatie. This other woman most likely knows about Mkatie's future husband's homosexual tendencies or abusive behavior. However, in this male-dominated society, the woman would not feel comfortable speaking out against him directly and might, in fact, feel unsafe doing so.

Sex

Sex has a negative in this story. In the very beginning, the narrator says that one of the reasons why her mother preferred male Zulu servants was that they "did not fall pregnant." In addition, the narrator references one famous Zulu warrior who required all of his followers "to remain celibate until they were forty." When John, a Zulu himself, accidentally runs into a naked Mkatie as she is coming out of the shower, the narrator notes that he "lifted his eyes to the ceiling and gasped in horror." One of the biggest taboos is premarital sex. The girls at the narrator's boarding school are normally not encouraged to compete, for fear that it will make them independent and rebellious in their relationships with men. However, a bigger fear is the loss of their virtue, and so the girls do compete in sports as a way "to combat sexual urges." The story's two extramarital affairs are also depicted as negative. When Mkatie discovers her husband "on the floor, embracing another man," she is horrified. However, Mkatie chooses not to expose him because, as she notes to the narrator, "'He would have been ruined, struck off the doctor rolls.'" Homosexuality is one of the strongest sexual taboos in this society. Instead of exposing her husband's homosexual act, Mkatie has her own taboo affair with a man in Turkey. The narrator notes: "When my sister arrived back home, her husband found a letter from the Turkish lover and cut his wrists." Although his suicide attempt is unsuccessful, it prompts the subsequent abuse of Mkatie and their children, which in turn leads to the story's negative ending.

Style

Point of View

The story uses a first-person narrator, Mkatie's sister. In first-person narratives, the story is told from the point of view of one character, who gives readers information based on what the narrator has seen or heard. In this case, the narrator talks about her sister's life. Throughout the story, the narrator seems very dispassionate, merely reporting events. Even the most emotionally charged scenes, such as the narrator's retelling of Mkatie's husband's pedophilic acts, are described in plain, understated

terms. The narrator says: "My sister's husband made their boy exercise in the morning to keep slim. He had him do sit-ups and scrub his fair skin with a loofah in the bath." In another example, the narrator describes the condition of her sister's deteriorating marriage: "By then my sister was keeping the shutters down and sleeping for hours in the afternoons." These simple statements have large implications, but the narrator leaves readers to draw their own conclusions.

However, at the end, the narrator switches tactics, suddenly turning from straight reportage to a passionate, in-depth description of the scene in which Mkatie is beaten. This abrupt change is designed to increase readers' sense of surprise and their sympathy for Mkatie. Says the narrator, "I imagine her lying on the blue silk counterpane, her face swollen as if she has soaked up water." This is a very lyrical description of Mkatie's face and is the first of many. The narrator also discusses the flush "that spreads over her cheeks like a stain," her "small chin" that "trembles," and eyes that are "as soft a blue as the silk beneath her." This is imagery that is imagined by the narrator, and it all builds up to the last sentence. Says the narrator: "The white *baas* takes off his belt and beats her across her legs, her breasts, her face." The narrator uses the contrast between the very personal, sympathetic description of Mkatie and the generic description of Mkatie's husband as the "white *baas*" to shock readers. This shock intensifies through the methodical style of the beating, which starts out bad, hitting "her legs," gets worse, hitting "her breasts," and finally gets to the worst part of all, "her face"—the same face that was just described in sympathetic detail by the narrator.

Setting

The physical setting is very important to the story. "Africans" takes place in South Africa, where the Zulus are a native people. Since the plot hinges on the effects of John's Zulu heritage, the story would not be as effective in any other location. There is an established history between the Zulu and white people in South Africa, and this story draws on that history. The temporal setting is equally as important. The story takes place over a long period of time, a fact that the narrator comments on near the end of the story, when she is trying to keep the specific details of her annual visits straight. "All those visits, year after year, have run into one another." Using a long period of time to tell the story is an effective method, because it shows the long-term effects of too much loyalty without humanity by demonstrating John's part in the beating of his once-beloved Mkatie.

Imagery

The story makes use of many images, the majority of which suggest ideas of war and violence—a suitable imagery for the tumultuous South Africa setting. In some cases, these images of violence are very clear, as in the description of the Zulu warrior culture from the past. "There was the cruel Shaka, who armed his men with short stabbing spears," says the narrator. The use of the word "stabbing" especially calls to mind images of violence. In addition, when the narrator talks about how Mkatie's husband starts to abuse his children, she notes that he "beat the children with a belt, especially the boy, broke his bones. He beat the eldest girl unconscious." Even John's mercy killing of Mkatie's parrot is described in violent terms: "He took its pulsing neck between his fingers and wrung it swiftly."

Kohler also uses many images of blood in the story, starting, once again, with the description of the brutal Zulu kings, "who conquered much territory in a series of bloody wars." In addition, Mkatie recounts an incident where she found her husband planting cabbages in the middle of the night. His response is violent and bloody: "He had thrown a glass at her, cutting her lip, the blood streaming down her chin." In fact, Mkatie's husband himself provides one of the bloodiest images, when he tries to commit suicide. Says the narrator: "All the children stood in a hushed circle with John at the bottom of the stairs and watched the blood running down their father's hands."

In other cases, the violence and war imagery is subtler, such as when the narrator describes bottles of champagne at a party, "which were lined up like soldiers on a field of damask." Following this description, the narrator makes note of John's "white uniform and the red sash with the tassel." At an earlier point in the story, the narrator associates this red tassel with John's Zulu warrior heritage, while describing what male Zulu servants wear. Says the narrator: "Red sashes ran slantwise across their chests from shoulder to waist and ended in tassels that dangled on their hips like decorations of valor." At one point, even the ground outside the servants' quarters is described as "red." Collectively, this use of the color red, a color commonly associated with violence and war, serves to underscore the brutal nature of the story.

Foreshadowing

Like her narration and some of her imagery, Kohler's use of foreshadowing—giving clues to future events—is very subtle in this story. When readers get to the end of the story, they may be shocked when John betrays his friendship with Mkatie. However, Kohler does offer some indications in the story that John might do this. In the beginning, John is a mentor to the two girls, who treat him like a mentor, not a black servant. When Mkatie is an adult, John tries to maintain this relationship but is slowly shut out by Mkatie. This starts even while Mkatie is away at school. Says the narrator: "My sister dreamed that she had passed John on the stairs without knowing who he was." Later, after school, Mkatie tells John and the narrator that she is going to marry a doctor. "'You said you wanted to be a doctor, Mkatie,' John reminded her, and chuckled." John is trying to give Mkatie advice, showing her that she has set aside her own goals, but Mkatie completely ignores John's comment and goes on talking. At the end of this conversation, "John stared down at the toothbrush in his hand," recognizing that he is only a servant and that his advice and opinions no longer matter. This shunning of John continues throughout the story. John is not invited to Mkatie's wedding and is not consulted when Mkatie decides that he will move in and perform housekeeping for her and her new husband. John begins to focus only on work and following orders. As a result, when Mkatie's husband tries to kill himself, John is powerless to stop it. "John clucked his tongue and shook his head and did what he was asked to do." By the end of the story, when Mkatie's husband tells John—"'Do what I tell you. Put her on the bed.'"—John is once again powerless to do anything but obey.

Historical Context

The First Free Elections in South Africa

"Africans" was first published in 1998, four years after the first one-person, one-vote, nonracial free election in South Africa. In this election, Nelson Mandela, a black South African who had been imprisoned for twenty-seven years on political

Compare & Contrast

- **1940s and 1950s:** In 1948, Daniel Malan and the National Party institute apartheid, a legalized system of separation and oppression, which gives preference to white—especially Afrikaner—interests.

  1960s and 1970s: The disenfranchising effects of apartheid galvanize South African resistance groups, some of which exchange their nonviolent approaches for a move to militant opposition. The South African government kills or imprisons many resistance leaders, including Nelson Mandela, the head of the African National Congress, who in 1964 is sentenced to life in prison. In 1977, Steve Biko, the originator of the Black Consciousness resistance movement, dies from massive head injuries inflicted during his interrogation by the police.

  Today: Following the release of Nelson Mandela in 1990, Mandela successfully wins the presidency in 1994 and serves until 1999. During his presidency, Mandela takes the first steps to reverse the effects of apartheid, but tensions remain between some ethnic groups.

- **1940s and 1950s:** Hendrik Verwoerd, a pro-Afrikaner extremist, is appointed minister of affairs in the South African government in 1950. The ruthless policies that he introduces quickly distinguish him as an icon of apartheid. When he experiences opposition from the Native Representative Council on his plan to place Bantu education under his auspices—thereby limiting blacks' ability to educate themselves enough to challenge the government—Verwoerd works quickly to abolish the council.

  1960s and 1970s: Verwoerd's zeal becomes even greater during his rule as South Africa's prime minister from 1958 to 1966. Despite international condemnation, Verwoerd, who becomes known as *Die Rots* (The Rock), brutally crushes resistance efforts and orchestrates the separation of South Africa from the United Kingdom. In 1966, Verwoerd is stabbed to death by a light-skinned, multiracial parliamentary member who is passing as a white man.

  Today: Wilhelm Verwoerd Jr., the grandson of Hendrik Verwoerd, shocks his family and Afrikaner countrymen as well as the world, when he becomes a member of the multiracial African National Congress in 1992. During the late 1990s, he works for the Truth and Reconciliation Commission (TRC) to help research, write, and edit the official TRC report on the lasting legacy of his grandfather's apartheid policies.

- **1940s and 1950s:** With the exception of the Dutch Reformed churches—the main church of Afrikaners—most white Christian leaders in South Africa denounce the introduction of apartheid.

  1960s and 1970s: In 1961, the Dutch Reformed Church withdraws from the World Council of Churches. In an effort to give biblical justification to its government's apartheid system, the church commissions several studies. Nevertheless, apartheid becomes a controversial issue within the Dutch Reformed churches.

  Today: Following a reversal of thinking in the 1980s, the Dutch Reformed church now denounces its former pro-apartheid stance and condemns apartheid as a sin.

---

charges, was elected president. This event occurred after centuries of racial unrest and inequality in South Africa, which culminated in the twentieth century in the institution of apartheid, a strict system of racial segregation and oppression that came into being in the 1940s.

World War II and the Beginning of Apartheid

Racial segregation and discrimination had existed in one form or another in South Africa for hundreds of years. However, it was not until the 1940s that these practices were formalized into a complete system. When World War II broke out in 1939, South Africa, as an official member of the British empire, took up arms with the Allies against German forces in Africa. However, many Afrikaners—who had relied on German support during their fight for independence in the South African War (1899–1902)—did not support this move. In addition to Germany's prior support, many Afrikaners identified heavily with Germany's pro-Nazi, white supremacist policies. As a result, several Afrikaners split off from the South African government into a new political party, known as the Herenigde (Reunited) National Party, or HNP. At the same time, despite the attempts of segregationists to separate the races, the wartime production effort rapidly increased the number of nonwhite workers, especially blacks, in the cities. This influx of urban blacks, coupled with the rise of militant, nonwhite trade unions that were partly inspired by the Communist Party, alarmed whites.

The HNP tapped into this public fear. In the 1948 election, while the incumbent United Party structured its campaign on the idea that segregation of the races was impossible, the HNP won on a platform of apartheid, a word that means "apartness" in Afrikaans, the Dutch-based language of Afrikaners. Although the HNP lost the popular vote, it won the electoral college vote. Because of the weak victory of the HNP, later known simply as the National Party, the new prime minister, Daniel Malan, rapidly introduced apartheid legislation that would show immediate improvement in the lives of whites. In this way, his party could ensure its win of the next election.

Early Apartheid Legislation

In the late 1940s and early 1950s, the Malan government passed several legislative acts designed to increase the power and privilege of whites, segregate the races, and remove the ability of nonwhites to fight these changes. These included the 1949 Prohibition of Mixed Marriages Act and the 1950 Immorality Act, which collectively prevented interracial marriage or sexual relations. However, two other laws passed in 1950 had the greatest long-term effect. The Population Registration Act classified all South Africans as one of three categories—white, colored (mixed race), or native (black Africans; later referred to as Bantu)—while the Group Areas Act segregated urban business and residential areas by race and gave the best land to whites. The civil rights of nonwhites were increasingly limited or ignored, and, as the years passed, the overwhelm-

ing majority of South African land was given to whites. By law, nonwhites were required to remain separate from their white masters. While this idea worked in theory, in practice it did not make sense. Even though white South Africans owned most of the land and controlled the economy, they were still a minority in numbers, heavily outnumbered by blacks, whom they needed as cheap labor in their homes and businesses.

The African Resistance to Apartheid

Despite their oppression and the systematic removal of their rights, nonwhites fought back through resistance organizations like the multiracial African National Congress (ANC), which included some whites as members. These organizations used methods of opposition, such as strikes and boycotts, which were often met with violent consequences from the government. In 1959, several ANC members left to form a strictly black resistance organization, the Pan-Africanist Congress (PAC), which, in 1960, began to organize many public protests. On March 21, 1960, at one of the first of these demonstrations, thousands of blacks gathered peacefully outside a police station in Sharpeville to protest South Africa's pass laws, which required nonwhites to carry—and be prepared to present to any authority figure at any time—a set of detailed documents. These included a photograph, racial classification, fingerprints, and government-sanctioned rights of movement within the country. As a constant reminder of their white oppressors, these passes were a sensitive issue with many blacks, who were often harassed—even in their homes—by whites. The protesting blacks arrived at Sharpeville's police station without passes, attempting to be arrested en masse in an effort to clog the South African prison system while at the same time weakening South Africa's workforce by their absence. The Sharpeville demonstration turned violent when the police, nervous at the prospect of a black uprising, opened fire on the protesters. Almost 70 blacks were killed and more than 180 were injured.

International Censure

The Sharpeville incident focused worldwide attention on South Africa's apartheid system. In 1960, South Africa was banned from the Olympics, and in 1961, to the shock and dismay of white South African leaders, Albert John Lutuli, a Zulu chieftain and then-president of the ANC, was awarded the Nobel Peace Prize for his nonviolent efforts in the struggle against the apartheid system. However, international censure did not faze South Africa, whose government voted in 1961 to become an independent republic, separate from the British Commonwealth. The government continued to intimidate and harass nonwhite residents, especially activists. As David Goodman notes in his 1999 book, *Fault Lines: Journeys into the New South Africa:* "Local police had sweeping authority in the black townships, and they routinely harassed, brutalized, and even killed activists at will." Other incidents, including the mass killing of protesters in Soweto in 1976 and the murder of popular resistance leader Steven Biko in 1977, further helped to increase international pressure on South Africa, which eventually began to feel the strain of economic and other sanctions.

Critical Overview

"Africans" was included in 1999 in Kohler's *One Girl: A Novel in Stories*, a book that was not heavily reviewed. However, those who did review the book reacted positively. Some reviewers discuss the definition of the book and decide that it is more short-story collection than novel, despite the book's title. Says the reviewer for *Publishers Weekly,* "This collection is a novel only in the most metaphorical sense, but that suits a book in which so much is accomplished by implication and suggestion." Likewise, in her review of the book for the *New York Times,* Sarah Saffian notes: "This is ultimately a story collection and not a novel . . . because while the threads running through do intertwine, her story lines are left tantalizingly unresolved."

Reviewers also note Kohler's skilled use of language. The *Publishers Weekly* reviewer calls the language "lush" and says that it "belies a sense of menace." Saffian calls Kohler's language "spare and haunting," saying that her "descriptions sing in their lyrical precision; at turns crisp and languid, they are always sensual, and often sexual." Reviewers also identify Kohler's use of narration to reveal the story. In her review of the book for *Library Journal,* Barbara Hoffert says that "these stories are told glancingly, without the burden of too many facts, allowing the complexity and occasional harshness of human interaction to come through." Likewise, Saffian says that Kohler "spools out information gradually, selecting what to reveal and what to keep hidden." On a similar note, Hoffert notes that, while "Kohler is not explicitly political in her writing . . . by capturing the power plays that define

human relationships, she suggests the brutality of regimes like apartheid South Africa."

Most discuss the book as a whole, although some talk about "Africans" in particular. Hoffert gives the story a brief mention, focusing on Mkatie as "a wife shocked to discover her husband in another man's embrace and thereafter subject to his abuse." The *Publishers Weekly* reviewer gives "Africans" the biggest praise, calling it "the collection's strongest story."

Criticism

Ryan D. Poquette

Poquette has a bachelor's degree in English and specializes in writing about literature. In the following essay, Poquette discusses Kohler's political and historical subtext in "Africans."

Kohler's "Africans" is actually two stories. On the surface, it is a powerful story about the betrayal of a white woman by her beloved African servant. However, for those who are familiar with the complex political history of South Africa, it yields much more. In her review of *One Girl: A Novel in Stories* for *Library Journal,* Barbara Hoffert notes: "Kohler is not explicitly political in her writing, yet implicitly, by capturing the power plays that define human relationships, she suggests the brutality of regimes like apartheid South Africa." In fact, upon further analysis, one can see that Kohler does much more than suggest the brutality of apartheid. Through the story's subtext, Kohler examines the crippling effects of apartheid through the study of John and his oppressed life.

So, how does one dig through the layers of the story to find this political subtext? The surface story provides several openings, but they may not be apparent to readers at first, given the narrative structure of the story. The narrator tells Mkatie's story in a series of flashbacks, starting with their early childhood and working forward in time, narrating the story in small, self-contained episodes. This episodic narration speeds up the pacing of the story, which makes it harder for readers to slow down and see the historical clues.

However, when one deliberately slows down and starts to examine the story in-depth, its emphasis on South Africa's political history becomes apparent. In the very first sentence, the narrator

Zulu people, shown here, are described as the preferred servant of South Africa in Kohler's ''Africans''

says: ''Mother preferred Zulu servants.'' Right away, Kohler offers a depiction of history as compared to current events. The Zulu people, who were once mighty warriors, are now servants as a result of colonization of South Africa by white settlers. For those not familiar with the Zulu warrior heritage, Kohler gives historical background, disguised as an introduction to the character of John Mazaboko. The historical instruction begins with the second sentence: ''She said they had been disciplined warriors.'' They had been warriors, but this is part of their long-lost history; now they are servants.

This is the first of many historical events that, on the surface, appear to be there only to advance the plot but which actually have deeper political implications when viewed as subtext. In fact, Kohler goes to great lengths to establish the importance of history. From her starting point of the Zulu nation, which prospered in the 1800s, she tells a story that ends in the second half of the twentieth century. This is a long time span for such a short story, especially one that, at first, seems to deal only with the life of one small family. Even the generic title of the story, ''Africans,'' suggests that there is a broader historical context to the story. The title could be referring to any, or all, of the South African groups

that are featured in the story—whites, blacks, or Afrikaners—since they all reside in Africa.

If history is so important to Kohler, why make it subtext? The answer appears to lie in one of the narrator's lines. When the narrator is describing her experience at the boarding school, she says: ''we read nineteenth-century authors and studied history that stopped before the First World War, which was considered too recent to be taught objectively.'' While this statement may at first appear to be an indication that the narrator's school is merely behind the times, the implications go deeper than that. At this point in the story, the narrator and Mkatie are attending school during South Africa's apartheid years. One of the Afrikaner government's tactics during these years was to sugarcoat the more questionable aspects of apartheid in an effort to gain more support. By not teaching their schoolgirls about recent history—which is saturated with black oppression—the boarding school is using a similar tactic.

As the story progresses, the initial discussion of the mighty Zulu warrior society serves as a constant contrast to the present condition of Zulus like John. In Shaka's warrior society, Zulu loyalty was tested

What Do I Read Next?

- Chinua Achebe is one of the most acclaimed novelists from Nigeria, a republic in West Africa. Achebe published his first novel, *Things Fall Apart,* in 1958, two years before Nigeria's declaration of independence from Great Britain. The novel, which Achebe wrote in English so that it would receive greater exposure, details the culture of the Ibo society at the end of the nineteenth century and shows the chaotic effects of colonialism.

- (Harold) Athol Fugard, a white South African who grew up in the 1930s and 1940s, attempted to resist the racist tendencies practiced by many other whites at this time. However, at one point, he made his black servants call him Master Harold and even spit in the face of one servant who had always treated him like a friend. Fugard, who grew up to become one of South Africa's most noted anti-apartheid writers, later dramatized the spitting incident in his play, *''Master Harold'' . . . and the Boys* (1982).

- Kohler's *Cracks: A Novel* (1999) is an expansion of the short story ''Cracks'' from *One Girl: A Novel in Stories.* The story takes place in a South African boarding school. The book uses multiple middle-age narrators, including one named after the author. They collectively tell the tale in a series of flashbacks, in which they remember the horrible acts they committed in an effort to gain favor with their swimming coach.

- Kohler's first novel, *The Perfect Place* (1989), tells the story of a wealthy middle-aged woman whose lover forces her to dredge up harrowing memories from her childhood in South Africa.

- Rian Malan's family name is notorious, since one of his relatives institutionalized apartheid in 1948. Malan, an Afrikaner crime reporter, rebelled against his heritage and became a black sympathizer in his youth; however, when the violence in South Africa escalated in the 1970s, he left to avoid having to carry a gun for either side. In 1985, Malan returned to South Africa and began to re-investigate crime stories he had written about in the 1970s. In his book *My Traitor's Heart: A South African Exile Returns to Face His Country, His Tribe, and His Conscience* (1990), Malan discusses many of these violent stories, giving readers a brutal view of the effects of apartheid.

- Nelson Mandela, a black leader of the African National Congress (a banned anti-apartheid organization), was sentenced to spend life in prison in 1964. As violence in South Africa increased in the 1970s and 1980s and the worldwide community began to condemn apartheid, Mandela's status as a political prisoner increased, and both local and international groups demanded his release. After he was finally released in 1990, he won the Nobel Peace Prize in 1993, and, in 1994, during South Africa's first free elections, he was elected president. In *Long Walk to Freedom: The Autobiography of Nelson Mandela* (1994), he tells the story of his tribal childhood, his political involvement, his imprisonment, and his life since his release.

- Mark Mathabane grew up in a black ghetto outside Johannesburg, South Africa, where he and his family were subjected to crushing poverty, starvation, gang violence, and mistreatment by the police. Despite these conditions, Mathabane beat the odds, taught himself English, graduated at the top of his class, and earned a tennis scholarship to Limestone College in South Carolina. In his autobiography, *Kaffir Boy: The True Story of a Black Youth's Coming of Age in Apartheid South Africa* (1986), Mathabane details the horrors of his early life in South Africa.

in many ways: by making soldiers travel "barefoot for greater speed and mobility," making them "remain celibate until they were forty," and, in some cases, making them "walk off a cliff." All of these tasks, even the self-sacrificial acts, have noble connotations, which have disappeared from modern-day life for a servant Zulu. John's cultural tradition taught him to be extremely loyal, which in the past would have been used to mold him into a better warrior, but which today is exploited for menial tasks. In fact, on one occasion, he must clean a smelly cupboard, directly following an ethnic slur on his heritage by the Scottish nanny: "Wrinkling her nose, she said, 'It smells Zulu.' He bent down from his great height onto his hands and knees and scrubbed the closet clean."

This is not the only time that John bends down in the story—another sign of his conquered status. His head is also "bent" when he polishes silver. In fact, when John sees the narrator's little girl, he bows down before her as if she is royalty. "'*Nkosazana*,' he said, addressing my daughter with the Zulu title of honor and bowing his head, holding her hand." Through invocations like this, one never loses sight of John's Zulu heritage in the story. In some cases, the narrator even references John in masculine, warrior-like ways, although they inevitably have domestic associations. For example: "He was unusually tall, and so strong he was able to catch the ancient armoire when it fell forward and almost crushed my sister as a small child." John's strength, a quality that would serve him well in tribal war, is here being used to save the child of his white master.

In another instance, the servant uniform worn by John and other Zulus is described in distinctly war-like terms. "Red slashes ran slantwise across their chests from shoulder to waist and ended in tassels that dangled on their hips like decorations of valor." However, this flashy uniform is only meant to please their white masters' desire that servants look presentable when "they served at table." Even John's attempts at passing on his cultural heritage fail. When they are little girls, the narrator and Mkatie hear stories from John, such as one about "the Tokolosh, the evil spirit who lived in the fish pond at the bottom of the garden." If John were able to live with his own family, he would pass these stories down to his own children, spreading his culture to the next generation. However, when the two white girls grow up to be women, they promptly dismiss John and his advice, so his stories ulti-

> "If she chose, Mkatie could go to a lawyer for a divorce or have her husband's homosexuality exposed. When John is not around, she can also fight back against her husband. For John, these are not options."

mately fall on deaf ears, and he is unable to pass on his traditions.

In the end, however, Kohler's two stories—the top layer and the subtext—act as mirror images to each other. Both stories examine the effects of oppression. In the top layer, Mkatie chooses marriage over her initial plan to be a doctor and becomes increasingly more dependent on and fearful of her Afrikaner husband. In fact, when the narrator is discussing their experiences at school, she hints at the connection between Mkatie and John. Says the narrator: "We were taught meekness—for the meek would inherit the earth—as well as obedience, diligence, and, like the Zulus, loyalty."

However, there is an important distinction between the plights of Mkatie and John. If she chose, Mkatie could go to a lawyer for a divorce or have her husband's homosexuality exposed. When John is not around, she can also fight back against her husband. For John, these are not options. Because of the laws of apartheid, John is destined to be a servant until he dies. Even the fact that he must call Mkatie's husband "*baas*" reinforces his subservient status. As David Goodman explains in his 1999 book, *Fault Lines: Journeys into the New South Africa:* "Whites insisted that blacks address them as *baas* (boss) in perpetual acknowledgement of their mastery." For John, it does not matter by the end of the story, anyway, since his individual spirit has been burned out of him through years of menial service. In the end, the oppressive nature of the apartheid regime turns him into a robot, incapable of doing anything but adhering to his duties.

Source: Ryan D. Poquette, Critical Essay on "Africans," in *Short Stories for Students,* Gale, 2003.

Mark White

White is a Seattle-based publisher and editor. In this essay, White argues that Kohler's story must be read both literally and allegorically.

"Africans," by South African writer Sheila Kohler, is, at its heart, an allegory of power relations between individuals in a colonial setting. While the story can be appreciated on the level of its narrower, literal meaning, its characters and the struggles they wage are representative, to varying degrees, of the struggles of any colonial setting in the world where power was afforded and institutionally prescribed along the lines of race, ethnicity, and gender. For a full appreciation of "Africans," one must read the story both literally and allegorically.

To understand the story's literal dimensions, one must first have a general knowledge of South Africa's system of apartheid and the way that system impacts Kohler's characters.

"Africans" is narrated by a white South African woman who is recollecting a series of events that take place over a period of years and that are related to her sister, her sister's husband, and John Mazaboko, a family servant. Mazaboko, a man of Zulu heritage (one of the several ethnic groups that comprise the country's black population), has been with the family since the narrator's childhood and is described in glowing terms as a father figure to the narrator and her sister. The narration opens in the years following World War II, just as the South African government was embarking on what was one of the most ambitious policies of racial segregation the world had yet seen. "Apartheid," which comes from the Dutch and literally means "separateness," went far beyond the Jim Crow laws of the pre-civil rights United States and was perhaps second only to Nazi Germany's racial policies in the breadth and scope of its racial goals.

As this narration opens, South Africans are being legally forced to register according to their race ("white," "black," or "colored"), and laws are being passed that sanction "white-only" jobs, prohibit interracial marriages, and force blacks to carry "passes" on their persons that dictate where and under what conditions they are allowed to travel or work. So-called "homelands" are being established for specific ethnicities of the black population; a person of Zulu heritage such as Mazaboko, for instance, would very likely be relegated by law to living in the KwaZulu Natal homeland, with a fine or imprisonment being the penalty for traveling outside of that area without the proper paperwork. In Mazaboko's particular case, however, because he is a domestic servant, his paperwork would allow him the "freedom" to live in white areas during the terms of his employment; losing that job would most likely mean losing that "privilege."

Despite blacks being the overwhelming majority of the population during apartheid's four-decade rule, they had no voting rights, and the vast majority of them lived in abject poverty. Economic and political power was held by whites of British and Dutch origin. This situation provided South African business with cheap labor, and it provided most white South African families of even working class means with extremely cheap servants for their households or farms.

As the story progresses, apartheid plays a growing and increasingly ominous role behind the story's scenes, and it will have a tremendous impact in the way Mazaboko conducts himself in the story.

The family's economic background also plays a determining role in the characters' lives, particularly the lives of the sisters. Although there is no direct discussion of the family's economic status, readers are given several hints that it is of at least upper middle-class standing: the narrator and her sister are educated in English-style boarding schools, and when the narrator's sister is married, we are told that the mother complained that the man's family was "common."

The sister's fiancé is, in fact, an Afrikaner. Afrikaners are South Africans of Dutch descent, and most are farmers or members of the working class, known for their religious and political conservatism and most noted for their staunch support of the apartheid system.

Kohler assumes a knowledge of these various social constructs, and during the discussion the narrator, her sister, and Mazaboko have about the sister's fiancé, Kohler relies on this knowledge as she foretells the story's ultimate conflict.

The sister has just described her future husband's ethnic and economic background when the narrator asks her, "What is he like?"

"Frank," the sister responds, and with a hint of what looms before all of them, she adds, "Brutally frank. It's refreshing. Do you know what I mean?"

The narrator nods her head at this, and she describes Mazaboko's response as simply "star[ing] down at the toothbrush in his hand."

Without an understanding of apartheid, one could not grasp the sense of fatalism inherent in Mazaboko's gesture. While the narrator has certainly made a strong case for the servant's "loyalty" in the opening paragraphs of the story, even if that case is largely based on white stereotypes of Zulus, and while one wouldn't necessarily question the man's commitment to the family or to his job, the fact is that with the sister's impending marriage, Mazaboko knows that he'll be sent to work for the sister and her new husband, and he also knows that while working in the service of any white family is one thing, being relegated to the service of an Afrikaner, and a "brutally frank" one at that, will be quite another. Mazaboko's life is about to change, and all he can do if he wants to retain the "security" of his position is to act the "loyal" servant that he is and accept the changes without question.

As it turns out, it is not only Mazaboko's life that is about to undergo a radical transformation; shortly after her marriage, the sister discovers her husband has strong homosexual and pedophilic predilections that he acts upon. Her initial response is to protect her husband from public scrutiny; analogous to Mazaboko's response, she remains silent, for if she speaks out, her husband's professional standing, and by extension her own social status and economic well-being, will be destroyed.

As the story progresses, Kohler steadily builds around her characters a box constructed of the hardwoods of economic, racial, and sexual determinism. Mazaboko, described by the narrator several years into the sister's marriage as a much thinner man with a "face more gaunt" and a spirit that has been "torn away" by his service to that household, has chosen to accept his fate and continue with the sister and her husband. Similarly, the sister, who was taught "meekness" as young school girl, and who was told by her headmistress that she and her classmates were "destined to be mothers and wives," suffers in silence. The narrator sparingly describes the sister during this time as "keeping the shutters down and sleeping for hours in the afternoons."

But when the husband's cruelty turns physical, the sister steps outside of Kohler's box and acts in her own defense, and for a brief moment, in the story's climactic scene, she is able to gain an upper hand. Unfortunately for her, Mazaboko knows perfectly well where his future meals will come from, and when he is forced by his master to choose between the powerless white woman he helped to

> To understand the story's literal dimensions, one must first have a general knowledge of South Africa's system of apartheid and the way that system impacts Kohler's characters."

raise from birth and the white man who will break him without a second thought if given the chance, Mazaboko reluctantly chooses the husband. Spending his "golden years" destitute in the streets or worse is not an appealing thought.

While this analysis of "Africans" is predicated on an understanding of the apartheid system, this story could easily have been set, with some minor revisions, in virtually any colonial setting. Apartheid was but one extension of the colonial rule that Africa, and much of the Third World, suffered under through the eighteenth, nineteenth, and mid-twentieth centuries. *Colonial rule* means the process by which (mainly European) powers, or *colonialists,* took economic and political control of local populations primarily through military means and enforced laws that helped them retain their power. Political and economic advantages were often prescribed along racial and ethnic lines; virtually every colonial power was "white," while the colonized were universally "non-white." Every country that was colonized had countless "Mazabokos," along with variations of all the issues and conflicts expressed in "Africans." In Africa, these dynamics of power began to shift starting in the 1950s, and apartheid, which was finally abolished in 1990s, was one of the final colonial hold-outs.

In the final scene in "Africans," Kohler has constructed the archetypal struggle for power at the height of colonial rule between the relatively powerless white woman, the seemingly omniscient white man, and the virtually helpless black man.

So what exactly is Kohler saying? Is she stating that it's a "man's world," and that males, regardless of their race, have power over women? Or is she suggesting that it's more particularly a "white man's world,'' and that to survive, black men must continually compromise, even at the expense of the ones they love and are loyal to? Or is her view more narrow than either of these summations: should ''Africans'' be read less allegorically and more literally as a reminiscence of one particular South African's experiences?

As to the story's larger meaning, it would be wise to start with the title for an answer. If the story were meant to be particularized to this narrator's experiences, Kohler would have chosen a more specific title such as ''My Sister and John Mazaboko.'' Even the title ''South Africans'' would narrow its meaning to a greater extent, but the title ''Africans'' is a very clear indication that at the very least Kohler intended that the story's full meaning be read far beyond the attributes her narrator is able to give it and beyond the boundaries of South Africa itself.

More evidence that points towards an allegorical reading is the fact that none of the characters, with the exception of Mazaboko, is named: the narrator, the sister, the husband, their children, and the mother all remain nameless throughout the story and have all effectively become representatives of their roles in society. And Mazaboko, by virtue of the in-depth introduction of his Zulu heritage that Kohler give us, comes to represent the displaced and exploited black African in this allegory: a man steeped in heritage but who can only reach back for that heritage to serve the white household, or the white colonialist. Colonial powers relied heavily on their ''Mazabokos'' to help strengthen their hold on power.

As for the questions of interpretation, the answers can be found in the story's final scene. As the husband is being overpowered by the sister, he calls out to his servant for help. Mazaboko responds ''swiftly and silently,'' as usual, but when he enters the room, he stops. Kohler makes a point to emphasize Mazaboko's hesitation before he continues to the bed.

It is not insignificant that Mazaboko, a man, assists the husband in beating the woman, just as it is not insignificant that the narrator and her sister attended a boarding school where the girls were educated to become good ''mothers and wives.'' The world Kohler is describing is clearly a ''man's world,'' but Mazaboko's hesitation, coupled with the earlier descriptions of him becoming ''gaunt'' and ''spiritless'' as a result of his service to the sister and her husband, point to a more definite conclusion that the world which she is describing is, above everything else, a ''white man's world.''

''Africans'' takes place in a time and place that no longer exists; apartheid is gone, and ours is a *postcolonial* world. What Kohler has done in this story is to distill, in a few brief pages, the essence of what characters caught up in colonialism experienced in their struggles to survive.

Source: Mark White, Critical Essay on ''Africans,'' in *Short Stories for Students*, Gale, 2003.

Sources

Goodman, David, ''Victorious Victim,'' in *Fault Lines: Journeys into the New South Africa*, University of California Press, 1999, pp. 34, 38.

Hoffert, Barbara, Review of *One Girl: A Novel in Stories*, in *Library Journal*, Vol. 124, No. 18, November 1, 1999, p. 124.

Kohler, Sheila, ''Africans,'' in *The Best American Short Stories 1999*, Houghton Mifflin Company, 1999, pp. 216–22, originally published in *One Girl: A Novel in Stories*, Helicon Nine Editions, 1999, pp. 101–9.

Review of *One Girl: A Novel in Stories*, in *Publishers Weekly*, Vol. 246, No. 37, September 13, 1999, p. 58.

Saffian, Sarah, Review of *One Girl: A Novel in Stories*, in the *New York Times*, Books in Brief, November 21, 1999, Section 7, p. 74.

Further Reading

Hurford, Elaine, *Southern Africa Revealed: South Africa, Namibia, Botswana, Zimbabwe, and Mozambique*, Bookworld Services, 2000.

Hurford's photographic journal of southern Africa includes photos of the distinctive landscapes, wildlife, and cultures in the five title nations. Each section also includes a short history of the region.

Kanfer, Stefan, *The Last Empire: De Beers, Diamonds, and the World*, Noonday Press, 1995.

In the late nineteenth century, diamond and gold discoveries in South Africa forever changed the landscape, economy, and culture. People came from all over the world seeking their fortunes and increasing the spread of colonialism in South Africa, and Africans flocked to the mines to find work. As production methods became more sophisticated, corporations were formed to attract international investors. The biggest of these, the De Beers Consolidated Mines, helped reinforce the types of racial segregation among its workforce that would set the stage for twentieth-century apartheid. Kanfer gives the history of De

Beers which today controls a percentage of the world-wide sale of diamonds.

Lyman, Princeton N., *Partner to History: The U.S. Role in South Africa's Transition to Democracy,* United States Institute of Peace, 2002.

Lyman, who was the United States ambassador to South Africa from 1992 to 1995, discusses the intricate process that was required to convert the apartheid state to a democracy. In particular, Lyman explains how the United States used its influence and resources to help assure that this was a peaceful transition.

Morris, Donald R., *The Washing of the Spears: The Rise of the Zulu Nation under Shaka and Its Fall in the Zulu War of 1879,* Da Capo Press, 1998.

Morris gives a history of the Zulu Nation, from its rise in the early nineteenth century to the crumbling of the Zulu empire during the late nineteenth century. The book details many battle scenes and features many illustrations.

Welsh, Frank, *South Africa: A Narrative History,* Kodansha International, 1999.

Welsh gives a history of South Africa from the arrival of the first white settlers to the end of Nelson Mandela's presidency. The book covers the famous events, such as the Great Trek and the Boer War, but also covers lesser-known events that have had a historical impact on the development of South Africa. Welsh draws on previously unpublished source material and his own background in international business to help tell the story.

Because My Father Always Said He Was the Only Indian Who Saw Jimi Hendrix Play "The Star-Spangled Banner" at Woodstock

Sherman Alexie

1993

"Because My Father Always Said He Was the Only Indian Who Saw Jimi Hendrix Play 'The Star-Spangled Banner' at Woodstock" was first published in Sherman Alexie's 1993 short story collection, *The Lone Ranger and Tonto Fistfight in Heaven.* Although Alexie, a Spokane/Coeur d'Alene Indian, had previously published three books, this collection gave him much greater exposure and was a critical and popular success. In 1998, when Alexie adapted part of the collection into a movie entitled *Smoke Signals*, the book—and Alexie—received even more exposure. Alexie is one of many late twentieth-century Native-American authors who have found acceptance with the general public in recent years. Many feel this literary renaissance was sparked by N. Scott Momaday's Pulitzer Prize-winning 1968 novel, *House Made of Dawn,* which details the alienation of the modern Native American in American society.

Like many of Alexie's works, the stories in this collection all take place on or around the Spokane Indian Reservation in Washington State, where Alexie grew up, and detail the many hardships that Native Americans face on reservations. In addition, many of the stories draw upon characters created in Alexie's earlier works. In "Because My Father Always Said He Was the Only Indian Who Saw Jimi Hendrix Play 'The Star-Spangled Banner' at Woodstock," one of these characters, Victor, recalls his father's separation from the family through several forms of escape. The story addresses the

turbulent nature of reservation relationships, the widespread use of alcohol among Native Americans, and the power of music. Most importantly, the story underscores the struggle to survive against the loss of cultural identity. The story can be found in the paperback version of *The Lone Ranger and Tonto Fistfight in Heaven*, which was published by HarperPerennial in 1994.

Author Biography

Alexie was born on October 7, 1966, in Spokane, Washington. A Spokane/Coeur d'Alene Indian, Alexie grew up in Wellpinit, Washington, on the Spokane Indian Reservation. At birth, Alexie was diagnosed with hydrocephalus—an abnormal swelling of the brain and head due to excess fluid—and he underwent brain surgery at six months. The hydrocephalus gave Alexie an enlarged skull, which prompted merciless teasing by other children on the reservation. As a result, Alexie spent most of his time alone, reading in the Wellpinit School Library.

Alexie's father, an alcoholic, was frequently absent from home, while Alexie's mother worked as a clerk at the Wellpinit Trading Post and sewed quilts to support Alexie and his five siblings. Alexie transferred to a mostly white high school in Rearden—thirty miles off the reservation—to get the credits he needed to attend college. Alexie was accepted by the high school community and became captain of the basketball team and class president. He graduated with honors in 1985 and was awarded a scholarship to Gonzaga University in Spokane. However, the pressure to fit in led him to abuse alcohol for the first time in his life. In 1987, he dropped out and moved to Seattle, where he worked busing tables. The same year, he gave up drinking and enrolled at Washington State University, where he took a poetry class taught by Alex Kuo. After reading Alexie's first poem, Kuo told Alexie that he should be a writer. Inspired, Alexie produced several poems and short stories by the time he graduated in 1991. In 1992, he published his first two books, a poetry collection entitled *I Would Steal Horses* and a poetry and short fiction collection entitled *The Business of Fancydancing*. The latter was named the 1992 Notable Book of the Year by the *New York Times Book Review*.

In 1993, Alexie proved to be even more prolific, publishing three books: a poetry collection entitled *First Indian on the Moon*; a poetry col-

lection entitled *Old Shirts & New Skins*; and a collection of short stories entitled *The Lone Ranger and Tonto Fistfight in Heaven*. The last title, which includes the story ''Because My Father Always Said He Was the Only Indian Who Saw Jimi Hendrix Play 'The Star-Spangled Banner' at Woodstock,'' attracted the attention of both critics and readers. The book received even greater exposure when Alexie used part of it as the basis for his screenplay for the film *Smoke Signals* (1998). In 1995, Alexie published his first novel, *Reservation Blues*, which won the American Book Award the following year. Alexie's recent works include a short-story collection entitled *The Toughest Indian in the World* (2000) and a collection of poetry and short stories entitled *One Stick Song* (2000). In addition to his published writing, Alexie is also noted for his performances, particularly his poetry readings. In June 2001, Alexie became the first four-time winner of the World Heavyweight Championship Poetry Bout, an annual challenge held in Taos, New Mexico. Alexie still lives and works in Wellpinit.

Plot Summary

''Because My Father Always Said He Was the Only Indian Who Saw Jimi Hendrix Play 'The Star-Spangled Banner' at Woodstock'' begins with the narrator, Victor, remembering his father. Victor's father quickly becomes the focal point of the story, as Victor explains how his father went to prison after beating up a National Guard private at a peace demonstration. The event was heavily documented, since Victor's father was a Native American. Victor recalls how, even though somebody new was killed every day in prison, his father was able to escape any serious confrontations. After he was released, Victor's father hitchhiked to Woodstock, where he saw Jimi Hendrix play ''The Star-Spangled Banner.''

Victor notes that, twenty years later, his father had played his Jimi Hendrix tape with the live song on it over and over again. He also notes the ritual that he and his father had followed when playing the tape. When Victor would hear his father come in late at night from drinking, Victor would start the tape. His father would listen for a little while, then pass out at the kitchen table, while Victor would fall asleep under the table by his father's feet. Victor notes that his father felt guilty about this ritual and so in the mornings would try to make it up to Victor by telling him stories. Sometimes these stories centered on Victor's mother, whom his father remembers as very beautiful. In fact, Victor notes that as the years went by and his parents' relationship deteriorated, Victor's father remembered his wife as increasingly more beautiful.

Victor notes how his parents had a violent relationship, which was often based on nights of heavy drinking and making love. Victor talks more about his relationship with his father, citing one memory in particular, a drive home from a basketball game in blizzard-like conditions. Jimi Hendrix's version of "The Star-Spangled Banner" comes on the radio, inspiring Victor to talk to his father—something they did not often do. After the song is over, Victor tells his father that he is sad that his generation has not had a real war to fight. His father tells him that he is lucky and that there is only war and peace in life, with nothing in between.

On another occasion, Victor's father tells him about the first time that he danced with Victor's mother, a conversation that leads his father into talking about how kids in Victor's generation know nothing about romance or music. Victor remembers how he used to stay awake at night listening to his parents making love, a concept that is alien to his white friends. Victor thinks that this positive experience makes up for the negative experience of watching his parents fight all the time. Victor notes that sometimes he would listen to his parents making love while dreaming about his father at Woodstock and says that he has seen footage of the music festival. However, Victor also admits that he still does not know what it was like for his father.

Victor recalls how his father drove them to Seattle a few years back to visit Jimi Hendrix's grave. While his father idolizes Hendrix, his mother is derogatory towards Hendrix's drug-related death. This disagreement turns into a fight, and Victor notes that, in contemporary Native-American marriages, fights get more destructive as the relationship falls apart. With the increasing number of fights, Victor's father buys a motorcycle as a means of escape from his life. While the bike helps his father cut down on his drinking, it also closes him off even more from his family. One night, Victor's father wrecks the bike and almost dies in the accident. Victor's mother supports her husband while he gets well, but after that she returns to her old life as a traditional Native-American dancer.

Victor talks about his father's ability to alter his memories and says that this is something he has learned from his father. Victor remembers how his father moved away and how his mother raised him after that. Victor talks to his mother, asking her why his father left, and she says that Victor's father would rather be alone than hang around other people. After he leaves, Victor catches his mother looking through old photographs and realizes that she misses his father but that she does not want him back. Victor starts listening to blues music and thinks that he can identify with how his father felt at Woodstock.

One night, Victor imagines his father pulling up on his motorcycle and asking Victor if he wants to go for a ride. Victor realizes that it is not real but goes along with the illusion, anyway. He goes outside to wait for his father, and when his mother comes outside to fetch him from the cold night, he says that he knows his father is coming back. Victor's mother wraps him in a blanket and goes back to sleep. Victor stays up all night waiting and imagining, then finally goes back inside to have breakfast with his mother.

Characters

Victor

Victor is the narrator, who talks about the events that lead to his father leaving him and his mother. Victor has grown up in a household defined by sex and violence. When he was young, his father went to prison for two years for beating up a National Guard private at a peace demonstration. When his father returns, Victor watches his parents fight constantly, which is a negative experience, although it is canceled out in his mind by the positive experience of listening to his parents make love. Victor has difficulty communicating with his father, who has a hard time opening up. However, Jimi Hendrix's version of "The Star-Spangled Banner," as well as other music, becomes a medium through which Victor is able to talk to his father. In one conversation with his father, Victor says that he wishes that his generation had a war to fight. His father says he is lucky that they are in peacetime, especially since Native Americans should not be fighting for a country that has been killing them from its very beginning.

Victor's father often talks about his past relationship with Victor's mother, which he remembers fondly. However, Victor's mother tells her son a different story. Victor realizes that his father remembers the past as he would have liked it to be, not as it was, and that his father has passed this belief in false memories and the imaginary to Victor. When Victor's father ultimately leaves, Victor has trouble remembering the exact way that it happened. After his father leaves, Victor listens to a lot of music, especially the blues. One night, when Victor is missing his father the most, he imagines his father's motorcycle pulling up to their house to take him for a ride. Although he knows it is not real, Victor goes along with the illusion and waits on the porch all night for his father. In the morning, he goes inside and shares a breakfast with his mother.

Victor's Father

Victor's father lives his life in the past, which eventually drives him away from Victor and his mother. Victor's father has lived a hard life. When he was young, he attended a peace demonstration, where he ended up beating a National Guard private. This action earned him two years in prison, where he was constantly under the threat of being killed or molested. After getting out of prison, Victor's father hitchhiked to Woodstock to see Jimi Hendrix play "The Star-Spangled Banner." Based upon this experience, Jimi Hendrix becomes the most important person in his life. After his many nights of drinking, Victor's father comes home to listen to Hendrix until he passes out. Music is one of the few ways that Victor's father is able to open up to Victor, and when he does, he tells Victor that kids his age do not understand romance or music. However, Victor's mother lets Victor know that his father is not good at either romance or music.

The relationship between Victor's parents is volatile—based mainly on drunken parties and lovemaking—although Victor's father remembers it as being better in the past. In fact, Victor notes that his father has the ability to remember things as they should have been, not as they really were. Because of this, as the relationship with his wife deteriorates, Victor's father remembers her as being increasingly more beautiful in the past. This inability to let go of false memories, as well as his inability to open up to his family, eventually pushes Victor's father away from the family. When Victor's father buys a motorcycle, this situation gets even worse, because he now has a means of literally escaping his home life. He rides his motorcycle until he crashes it, and after he recovers, he leaves Victor and his mother. He travels to various locations in the West and sends

Media Adaptations

- Alexie's official website, www.Fallsapart.com, features a wide variety of resources on the author, including a biography, interviews, information on his books and films, and details about his current projects.

- Several stories from *The Lone Ranger and Tonto Fistfight in Heaven,* especially "This Is What It Means to Say Phoenix, Arizona," were drawn on for the film adaptation *Smoke Signals.* The film, written by Alexie, was billed as the first film with an all-Native-American cast and crew. It was produced by ShadowCatcher Entertainment and released by Miramax Films in 1998. The film, which featured Adam Beach in the role of Victor, won the 1998 Sundance Film Festival's audience award. It was published as a screenplay by Talk Miramax Books in 1998 and was released on VHS and DVD from Miramax Home Entertainment in 2001.

frequent postcards to Victor, although the frequency lessens with time.

Victor's Mother

Victor's mother used to be a traditional Native-American dancer. She met her husband at a party where they were the only two Native Americans. Although Victor's father has fond memories of their time together, his mother tells Victor that his father was always half crazy. She says that their best times were when he fell into a drunken sleep while they were making love. Victor's parents have little in common beyond their drunken parties and lovemaking. They fight constantly, which eventually drives them apart. When Victor's father ultimately leaves them, Victor and his mother try to go on with their lives, but they both miss Victor's father and look through old pictures of him. When Victor goes on the porch one cold night to wait for his father to come back, Victor's mother covers Victor in a blanket and leaves him to his thoughts. In the morning, Victor's mother shares a breakfast with her son.

Themes

War

The story describes both physical and cultural wars. Victor references actual wars, such as Vietnam, when he remembers how his father beat a guard at a peace demonstration. In the photograph of the event, Victor notes his father's warlike appearance, saying, "my father is dressed in bell-bottoms and flowered shirt, his hair in braids, with red peace symbols splashed across his face like war paint." Later, when Victor tells his father that "my generation of Indian boys ain't ever had no real war to fight," Victor's father says that he is "lucky" that there are no wars going on and that there is only "war and peace with nothing in between." Victor's father also questions Victor's desire to fight for a country that has "been trying to kill Indians since the very beginning." Victor notes that cultural wars take place off the reservation, too, such as when his father goes to prison for beating the guard. "Although his prison sentence effectively kept him out of the war, my father went through a different kind of war behind bars." In prison, Victor's father, like everybody else, lives under the constant threat of being killed by someone from a different culture. As he notes to Victor: "We'd hear about somebody getting it in the shower or wherever and the word would go down the line. Just one word. Just the color of his skin."

Reservation Relationships

In the story, Victor describes what relationships are like on a reservation. One of the biggest social problems on reservations is alcoholism, and both of Victor's parents are heavy drinkers. Says Victor, "My mother and father would get drunk and leave parties abruptly to go home and make love." Alcohol and sex form the foundation of their marriage, which is destructive and unstable. Says Victor, "their love was passionate, unpredictable, and selfish." Victor also compares modern Native-American marriages on reservations to traditional Native-American marriages. "A hundred years ago, an Indian marriage was broken easily. The woman or man just packed up all their possessions and left the tipi." However, since early settlers first started intruding on Native-American lands, Native Americans have become focused on cultural and physical survival. As a result, when a modern Native-American marriage deteriorates, "it's even more destructive and painful than usual," as Victor notes. This is because modern Indians tend to "fight their way to the end, holding onto the last good thing, because our whole lives have to do with survival."

The Power of Music

Music serves many purposes in the story. For Victor's father, music becomes an escape from his daily reality, especially when it is coupled with alcohol. For example, Victor notes how his father listens to his tape of Jimi Hendrix's "The Star-Spangled Banner" repeatedly while drinking. Says Victor, "He'd sit by the stereo with a cooler of beer beside him and cry, laugh, call me over and hold me tight in his arms." Later in the story, Victor's father buys a motorcycle and attaches "an old cassette player to the gas tank so he could listen to music." The motorcycle and music are an effective combination for escaping his situation, so much so that Victor's father "stopped drinking as much" and "didn't do much of anything except ride that bike and listen to music." Music also becomes a means of communication between Victor and his father, who has a hard time opening up. Says Victor, "Music turned my father into a reservation philosopher. Music had powerful medicine."

In particular, Jimi Hendrix's version of "The Star-Spangled Banner" becomes a catalyst for getting Victor and his father to talk about Victor's mother, war, and what it means to be a Native American. Says Victor, "Those were the kinds of conversations that Jimi Hendrix forced us to have. I guess every song has a special meaning for someone somewhere." Music also becomes a passion for Victor, who sees it both as a means of gaining insight into life and as a way of understanding his father. At one point, Victor notes why he wanted to play the guitar. Says Victor, "I just wanted to touch the strings, to hold the guitar tight against my body, invent a chord, and come closer to what Jimi knew, to what my father knew." Even after Victor's father has left the family, music is a way for Victor to connect with him. Victor listens to the blues and thinks: "That must have been how my father felt when he heard Jimi Hendrix. When he stood there in the rain at Woodstock."

Topics for Further Study

- Choose another culture in history that has been affected by colonization. Compare this civilization to the Native-American civilization, paying particular attention to the effects on the culture's identity and ability to govern itself.

- Choose one Native American who grew up on a reservation—besides Alexie—who has become a success. Compare this person's life story to Alexie's life story, focusing on any social factors that helped lead to each person's success.

- On a map of the current United States, plot the various methods that were used to acquire each area from Native Americans, including a date and description at the site of each major land acquisition. On a separate map, outline each current, federally funded Native-American res-

ervation, including the date it was founded and a short description. Compare the two maps.

- Choose an actual band member who played at Woodstock, research this person's life, and put yourself in this person's place at the music festival. Write a journal entry that sums up one day of your Woodstock experience, using your research to support your ideas.

- Jimi Hendrix became famous and died within a very short time. Research other young, twentieth-century music stars, actors, or other celebrities who have died from alcohol or drug abuse, and discuss any trends among these deaths. Finally, discuss efforts that are being made both within the entertainment community and by outsiders to prevent these deaths.

Style

Point of View

The story is told from the first person point of view, a fact established by the use of the word "my" in the first sentence of the story: "During the sixties, my father was the perfect hippie, since all the hippies were trying to be Indians." In first person works, the story is narrated by one of the characters, who gives the reader his or her view of the events in the work. first person narratives like this one are very personal. Since Victor talks to readers directly—instead of having his thoughts and feelings related to the reader through an outside, third person narrator—readers feel closer to Victor.

Setting

As Victor remembers his father's life and experiences, the setting changes several times. These setting changes are not arbitrary. Each time, the setting is important to the narrative. When the story begins, Victor is remembering his father's arrest at a Vietnam peace demonstration. His experiences in

Walla Walla State Penitentiary, the next setting that Victor describes, are important because they highlight the war theme of the story. Also, because he survives his prison experience, Victor's father is inspired to go to the Woodstock Festival. Says Victor, he "got out of prison just in time to hitchhike to Woodstock to watch Jimi Hendrix play 'The Star-Spangled Banner.'" This experience instills a deep love of Hendrix and his song in Victor's father, and becomes the controlling force in his life—and by extension, in Victor's life.

Victor remembers one of the rituals in their relationship, which involved playing Hendrix's version of "The Star-Spangled Banner" for his father when he came home from a night of drinking. Says Victor, "My father would weep, attempt to hum along with Jimi, and then pass out with his head on the kitchen table." Meanwhile, Victor "would fall asleep under the table" and stay with his father until the morning. Even the reservation setting where Victor grows up plays an important role in the story. Victor's father feels the need to escape his reservation life—and his family—and tries to do so through music and alcohol. In fact, Victor directly associates alcohol problems with reservation life at one point, when he is describing what it was like the night he thought his father might come back for him. Says Victor, "It was so quiet, a reservation kind of quiet, where you can hear somebody drinking whiskey on the rocks three miles away."

Personification

In the story, Jimi Hendrix's music becomes a living force in the lives of Victor and his father. In this way, Alexie uses personification, a literary technique by which a non-human object or idea—in this case Hendrix's recorded music—is described as having human qualities. Says Victor, "Jimi Hendrix and my father became drinking buddies. Jimi Hendrix waited for my father to come home after a long night of drinking." This is technically impossible, since music is not alive and so does not have human consciousness—a necessary prerequisite to being able to "wait" for anything. On another occasion, Hendrix's music helps ensure that Victor and his father get home safely in near-blizzard conditions. Victor and his father are driving on treacherous roads, when suddenly Hendrix's version of "The Star-Spangled Banner," the favorite song of Victor's father, comes on the radio. Says Victor, "My father smiled, turned the volume up, and we rode down the highway while Jimi led the way like a snowplow."

Victor notes that his father idolizes Hendrix so much that, at one point, he "packed up the family and the three of us drove to Seattle to visit Jimi Hendrix's grave." This unnatural obsession with Hendrix helps to further isolate Victor's father from his family, which eventually leads to the divorce between Victor's parents. Victor asks his mother, "Was it because of Jimi Hendrix?" Victor's mother notes that Hendrix did play a part in the divorce: "This might be the only marriage broken up by a dead guitar player."

Historical Context

The Persian Gulf War

The Persian Gulf War, also known simply as the Gulf War, began on August 2, 1990, when Iraq invaded Kuwait—presumably in an attempt to steal the small country's large oil supply. Although the United Nations Security Council imposed economic sanctions on Iraq, Saddam Hussein, Iraq's leader, continued to increase his military forces in Kuwait. On August 6, the United States and its allies began to occupy nearby Saudi Arabia to prevent an attack on the Saudi oil supply. This combined military buildup was known as Operation Desert Shield. On November 29, the United Nations Security Council gave Hussein a deadline of January 15, 1991, to peacefully withdraw his forces. At the same time, the Security Council authorized the use of force by the United States and its allies if Hussein did not comply. Hussein ignored the deadline, and on January 18, Operation Desert Storm was launched. Under the leadership of United States General Norman Schwarzkopf, the United States and its allies began a sustained aerial assault on Iraq and effectively destroyed Iraq's military forces; government and military installations; transportation and communication networks; and oil refineries. On February 24, the allies launched Operation Desert Sabre, a ground assault from Saudi Arabia into Kuwait and southern Iraq that faced relatively little resistance. On February 28, President George Bush called a cease-fire.

Native Americans in the Early 1990s

The 1990 United States census revealed that roughly two million Native Americans were living in the country, an increase of more than 40 percent since 1980. This increase made Native Americans one of the fastest-growing ethnic groups, even though they were still less than 1 percent of the United States population. More than 60 percent of Native Americans lived in urban areas such as Los Angeles, although most were in the habit of returning to reservations for annual visits. The census also revealed some disturbing facts about the social problems that many Native Americans continued to face, including lack of education, poverty, and alcoholism. Of the more than one million Native Americans who were twenty-five years or older, roughly 65 percent had finished high school, while less than 10 percent had completed a bachelor's degree or higher level of education. In addition, Native Americans were the poorest population group in the United States. More than 27 percent of Native-American families were living below the poverty level. The median household income for all Native Americans was less than twenty thousand dollars per year, while on reservations, it was even lower—thirteen thousand dollars per year. However, one of the biggest social problems, especially on reservations, was alcoholism. Native-American alcoholism rates were three times as high as those in

Compare
&
Contrast

- **Late 1960s:** The Woodstock Music and Art Fair, one of the most famous rock festivals in history, is held August 15–17, 1969, on a farm in Bethel, New York. It is organized by four inexperienced promoters, who encounter massive problems when the festival draws ten times more people than they expected, taxing the available food, water, and medical resources. Still, despite these and other problems such as drug overdoses, most remember Woodstock fondly, and it quickly becomes a legend.

  Today: Two Woodstock revivals—one on the twenty-fifth anniversary in 1994 and one in 1999—are also memorable, but for different reasons. The first revival features better organization, while at the second, a riot breaks out. However, both fail to live up to the legend of the original.

- **Late 1960s:** In 1969, a group of Native Americans calling themselves the Indians of All Tribes seizes Alcatraz, the island-based prison in San Francisco Bay that has been closed since 1963. The group intends to turn the decaying prison facility into a Native-American university, cultural center, and museum. They claim that this is within their rights, because an 1868 Sioux treaty says they can occupy government surplus land like Alcatraz. They offer to buy the island for twenty-four dollars—the same price that white settlers paid to Native Americans for Manhattan island three centuries ago. They occupy Alcatraz peacefully for twenty months, ignoring requests by the federal government to leave, until they are removed by federal marshals in 1971.

  Today: Since its inception in 1972, the Golden Gate National Recreation Area—the largest urban park in the world—has administered control over Alcatraz. There are few attempts to renovate or repair the facility, in which some areas are still unsafe and closed off to the public. Despite this fact, Alcatraz is attracting almost one million visitors annually by the mid-1990s.

- **Late 1960s:** N. Scott Momaday, a Native-American author, wins the Pulitzer Prize for fiction in 1969 for his novel *House Made of Dawn.* The novel depicts the difficulties Native Americans face when trying to fit in among other Americans, and it helps spark an increase in fiction and nonfiction writing by and about Native Americans.

  Today: Alexie is one of many Native-American authors who have earned critical and popular success with works that depict the plight of the modern Native American. Other authors include Louise Erdrich and Leslie Marmon Silko.

---

the rest of the United States, and occurrences of fetal alcohol syndrome births were also high.

Native-American Activism

Two hot issues in Native-American activism in the early 1990s were the protection of burial lands and artifacts and the preservation of religious freedom. In the 1980s, federal agencies such as museums retained Native-American human remains and sacred artifacts, when many spiritual leaders preferred that these items be laid to rest in the earth. Concerned Native-American organizations lobbied heavily to have these burial items returned to them.

In 1990, these groups scored a victory when Congress passed the Native American Graves Protection and Repatriation Act (NAGPRA). The act required all universities, museums, and other agencies that received federal funds to inventory any Native-American bones, human remains, and sacred artifacts that they held. In addition, these agencies were required to notify the tribal governments that they held these artifacts and to return any or all of these items to the respective tribal governments upon request.

The passing of this act signaled a victory for Native Americans on a culturally important issue.

However, in the area of religious freedom, Native Americans were dealt two significant setbacks by the United States Supreme Court in the late 1980s and early 1990s. In 1978, Congress had passed the American Indian Freedom of Religion Act, which stated that the federal government would work to protect Native Americans' right to practice their traditional, tribal religions. This included giving Native Americans access to sacred sites on federal lands. However, in 1988, in *Lyng v. Northwest Indian Cemetery Protective Association,* the Supreme Court ruled that the National Forest Service could build a road that passed through sacred Native-American sites on federal lands.

In addition, in 1990s *Employment Division, Department of Human Resources of Oregon v. Smith,* the Supreme Court ruled that individual states could outlaw religious practices of the Native American Church. This shocked many Native Americans, since they had thought these practices were federally protected by the 1978 American Indian Freedom of Religion Act as well as by the First Amendment. The issue at stake was the use of peyote, a stimulant drug. Two Native-American drug counselors had been fired for using the drug in a legally sanctioned Native American Church ritual and had been denied unemployment compensation by the state of Oregon since the use of peyote violated state law.

Critical Overview

When *The Lone Ranger and Tonto Fistfight in Heaven* was published by the Atlantic Monthly Press in 1993, it was the first of Alexie's books to be published by a major press. The book has been received well by audiences, and most critics give it high marks, too. Some critics note that the book shares themes that are common in Alexie's first three books. Says Susan B. Brill, in her 1997 entry on Alexie in the *Dictionary of Literary Biography:* "Survival is perhaps the omnipresent theme of these four books." On a similar note, in her Winter 2000/2001 *Ploughshares* article, Lynn Cline notes that Alexie's work "carries the weight of five centuries of colonization, retelling the American Indian struggle to survive, painting a clear, compelling, and often painful portrait of modern Indian life."

Specific critical discussion on *The Lone Ranger and Tonto Fistfight in Heaven* is often marked by a definition of what the book actually is. Many label the book a collection of short stories, but critics like Alan R. Velie believe that it is not so easily classified. Says Velie, in his 1994 review of the book for *World Literature Today,* it is "somewhere between a novel and a collection of short stories." Regardless of how people classify it, the book has greatly increased Alexie's esteem in many critics' eyes. Velie praises Alexie, saying that the book "establishes him not only as one of the best of the Indian writers but as one of the most promising of the new generation of American writers."

A reviewer for *Kirkus Reviews* notes in 1993 that, in the book, "The history of defeat is ever-present; every attempt to hold onto cultural tradition aches with poignancy." Velie is one of many reviewers who notes the characters' feelings of "despair, guilt, and helplessness," a factor of life on the reservation, where people often "give up on life and lapse into unemployment and alcoholism." Several critics note that Alexie employs characters that he created in his earlier works. However, in her 1994 review of the book for *Western American Literature,* Andrea-Bess Baxter says that, although Alexie is covering old ground, "this work is more personal, autobiographical at times." Since *The Lone Ranger and Tonto Fistfight in Heaven* was one of five books that Alexie published within two years, it is not surprising that some of the books share common themes and characters. However, not all critics appreciate this. In fact, one critic, Reynolds Price, thinks that Alexie's rapid output is affecting his quality. Price, in his 1993 review of *The Lone Ranger and Tonto Fistfight in Heaven* for the *New York Times Book Review,* notes: "There is very little plot in any of them—plot in the sense of consecutive action with emotional outcome." Price asks: "Has Sherman Alexie moved too fast for his present strength?"

Very few critics have singled out "Because My Father Always Said He Was the Only Indian Who Saw Jimi Hendrix Play 'The Star-Spangled Banner' at Woodstock." However, of those who have commented specifically on the story, the reviews have been positive. In his 1993 review of the book for the *Review of Contemporary Fiction,* Brian Schneider praises Alexie's narrative voice in the story, saying that it "resonates . . . with a passion that sees the irony in the flower power movement's co-opting of mostly American Indian values.'' Finally, Leslie Marmon Silko, an acclaimed Native-American author, notes in a 1995 *Nation* article that the story is her ''favorite'' in the collection.

Criticism

Ryan D. Poquette

Poquette has a bachelor's degree in English and specializes in writing about literature. In the following essay, Poquette discusses Alexie's use of point of view to underscore the message of cultural struggle in ''Because My Father Always Said He Was the Only Indian Who Saw Jimi Hendrix Play 'The Star-Spangled Banner' at Woodstock.''

In her article about Alexie for *Ploughshares,* Lynn Cline notes: ''His work carries the weight of five centuries of colonization, retelling the American Indian struggle to survive, painting a clear, compelling, and often painful portrait of modern Indian life.'' As a modern Native-American child, Victor, the narrator, feels the effects of this colonization, too. Like most children, Victor relies on the examples set by his parents to provide him with the cultural instruction he needs to survive in the world. Unfortunately, his parents represent two extremes, making it difficult for him to form any solid beliefs. In fact, at one point when discussing his parents' genetic contributions to his makeup, he says he ''was born a goofy reservation mixed drink.'' Although this specific example is referring to the alcoholic nature of his parents, it also serves to underscore Victor's mixed cultural education. While Victor is exposed to Native-American traditions through his mother, his father abandons tradition in favor of addictive American influences.

When Victor's mother is mentioned in the story, there is often a reference to her traditional Native-American background. Victor's father recognizes the traditional qualities of his wife, and often tells stories about her to his son. On one occasion, his father remembers the first time he met her. ''I thought she was so beautiful. I figured she was the kind of woman who could make buffalo walk on up to her and give up their lives.'' In addition to associating Victor's mother with a traditional buffalo hunt, Victor's father also notes her former status as a Native-American dancer. Says Victor's father, ''I remember your mother when she was the best traditional dancer in the world.'' In fact, when Victor's father is in the hospital, his mother sings ''Indian tunes under her breath, in time with the hum of the machines hooked into my father.'' Victor's mother is most happy when she is involved with Native-American traditions, such as her dancing. As soon as her husband does not need her to stay with him in the hospital, ''she went back to the life she had created. She traveled to powwows, started to dance again.''

When he is a young man, Victor's father also tries to maintain his Native-American identity and values, by demonstrating at a Vietnam antiwar event. However, since he looks like a hippie and ''all the hippies were trying to be Indians,'' his attempts at asserting his Native-American identity are thwarted. As Victor notes, ''Because of that, how could anyone recognize that my father was trying to make a social statement?'' In his review of the short-story collection for the *Review of Contemporary Fiction,* Brian Schneider cites this event as an example of the power of ''Alexie's narrative voice,'' which ''sees the irony in the flower power movement's co-opting of mostly American Indian values.'' When Victor's father beats up a National Guard private, he is sent to prison for two years. When he gets out, he goes to Woodstock, where he really begins to be assimilated into the American culture.

While his father is at Woodstock, Victor notes that: ''My mother was at home with me, both of us waiting for my father to find his way back home to the reservation.'' However, once he has gone to prison, Victor's father has found his way *off* the reservation—at least in a figurative sense—for the rest of his life. From the time he leaves prison, he begins trying to escape his reality through American influences, the first of which is the trip to Woodstock to hear distinctly American rock music. In fact, his choice of Hendrix's ''The Star-Spangled Banner'' is symbolic. ''The Star-Spangled Banner'' is America's national anthem, and represents the solidarity of the country. When people sing the anthem, it is generally to express their pride and support for their country and government. As a young man, Victor's father is rebellious, and lashes out against icons of the government, such as the National Guard private.

What Do I Read Next?

- Like many of his works, Alexie's *The Business of Fancydancing* (1992), a collection of poems and short stories, depicts life on the Spokane Indian Reservation. In this collection, Alexie created characters and addressed themes that he has visited again in subsequent works.

- Alexie's first novel, *Reservation Blues* (1995), once again features characters that Alexie made famous in his earlier collections, including Victor from "Because My Father Always Said He Was the Only Indian Who Saw Jimi Hendrix Play 'The Star-Spangled Banner' at Woodstock." The story details the experiences of Coyote Springs, an all-Native-American, Catholic rock band from the Spokane Indian Reservation, which gets its big break after the band members acquire the guitar of blues legend Robert Johnson.

- When Alexie was in his influential poetry class at Washington State University, his professor, Alex Kuo, suggested that he read *Songs from This Earth on Turtle's Back* (1983). The book, an anthology of Native-American poetry edited by Joseph Bruchac, inspired Alexie to write his first poem.

- In 1984, Louise Erdrich, a woman of Chippewa Indian and German-American heritage, published her book *Love Medicine*. Although some have labeled it a novel, others consider it a collection of interlinked short stories like *The Lone Ranger and Tonto Fistfight in Heaven*. The multiple-narrator book tells the stories of two Native-American families living in and around a reservation. Erdrich issued an expanded version of the book, which is the first in a series, in 1993.

- Much of Alexie's fiction and poetry draws upon experiences from his own life. Alexie has also written autobiographical essays. In *Here First: Autobiographical Essays by Native American Writers* (2000), editors Arnold Krupat and Brian Swann collect essays from Alexie and more than twenty other writers.

- N. Scott Momaday's Pulitzer Prize–winning novel, *House Made of Dawn* (1968), is commonly acknowledged as the work that sparked the modern renaissance in Native-American literature. The novel tells the story of Abel, a Native American who returns home from fighting in World War II and has trouble adjusting to life in the modern Anglo world.

His prison experience changes his tune, literally, and he soon starts to be assimilated into many aspects of American culture, starting with his endless replaying of Hendrix's "The Star-Spangled Banner."

He also drinks large quantities of alcohol, which is another effect of assimilation. As Fred Beauvais notes in a 1998 article for *Alcohol Health & Research World*, Native Americans did not have access to strong alcohol prior to European colonization. Says Beauvais: "The distillation of more potent and thus more abusable forms of alcohol was unknown." Besides providing Native Americans with access to alcohol, Beauvais notes that colonists also set a bad example. Says Beauvais: "Extreme intoxication was common among the colonists and provided a powerful model for the social use of alcohol among the inexperienced Indian populations." Like his music, Victor's father uses alcohol as a form of escape from his life. On a typical night, he will "come home after a long night of drinking" to listen to Hendrix until he passes out in a drunken sleep.

By modeling alcoholism as a way of life, Victor's father is increasing the chance that Victor will become one of the many Native Americans who learn this addictive behavior from their parents. However, when he is sober, Victor's father becomes more responsible, and tries to save his son from harm by educating him politically. For example, during one conversation, Victor's father talks about the commercial quality of the Persian Gulf War, which he says only benefited the rich. Says Victor's father: "Should have called it Dessert Storm because it just made the fat cats get fatter." Victor's father also speaks out about the historical mistreatment of Native Americans by the United States. He discourages Victor's youthful desire to fight a war by asking him: "why the hell would you want to fight a war for this country? It's been trying to kill Indians since the very beginning."

However, despite these occasional discussions in which Victor's father rebels against the United States, for the most part he has agreed to his assimilation. He tells Victor that Native-American children have been hearing drums so long that "you think that's all you need. Hell, son, even an Indian needs a piano or guitar or saxophone now and again." The acceptance of all of these American instruments is a further sign that Victor's father is no longer fighting hard to maintain his cultural identity as a Native American. Victor notes as much when he remarks that, although his father "was the drummer" in his high school band, "I guess he'd burned out on those. Now, he was like the universal defender of the guitar." As the reviewer for *Kirkus Reviews* notes of the short-story collection: "The history of defeat is ever-present; every attempt to hold onto cultural tradition aches with poignancy."

Victor's father's dependence on music, alcohol, and other American influences eventually separates him from his wife and son. In addition, when his marriage starts to fall apart, Victor's father does not follow tradition. As Victor notes, "A hundred years ago, an Indian marriage was broken easily. The woman or man just packed up all their possessions and left the tipi." However, times have changed. When modern Native-American relationships start to deteriorate, Victor notes that "Indians fight their way to the end, holding onto the last good thing, because our whole lives have to do with survival." At a certain point, the fighting gets so bad that Victor's father buys a motorcycle, and uses it to totally get away from the situation. Says Victor: "With that bike, he learned something new about running away. He stopped talking as much, stopped drinking as much. He didn't do much of anything except ride that bike and listen to music."

In addition to escaping his life through music, alcohol, or riding his motorcycle, Victor's father has also gained the ability to change his negative memories. As Victor puts it: "If you don't like the things you remember, then all you have to do is

> When a colonized culture loses its heritage, it dies, as emphasized by the profound silence. All that is left over is the negative effect of assimilation, which in this case is represented by the sound of a person drinking alone in the dark."

change the memories." For example, as the relationship between Victor's parents falls apart, Victor's father remembers his mother as increasingly more beautiful. Says Victor, "By the time the divorce was final, my mother was quite possibly the most beautiful woman who ever lived." Victor's mother usually gives her son a different story than what he hears from his father. At one point, Victor's father tells him that Victor's generation does not know anything about music or romance. However, when Victor's mother describes her husband's failed attempts at playing the guitar, she demonstrates that he is also bad at romance. Says Victor's mother, "His eyes got all squeezed up and his face turned all red. He kind of looked that way when he kissed me, too." Victor notes that his father's example has taught him how to change his own memories. This becomes evident when Victor discusses the separation from his father. He describes the event from three different points of view: his father's memory, his own memory, and his mother's memory. He is confused as to which version really happened, which is understandable, gives the mixed-culture environment in which he has grown up. When his father leaves, Victor notes that, while "white fathers" have been abandoning their children forever, "Indian men have just learned how. That's how assimilation can work."

In the story, Victor grows up in an environment where he is subjected to both his mother's traditional Native-American values and his father's addiction to American influences. However, the latter are much more prominent. The mentions of Victor's father and his problems far outweigh his father's failed attempts to preserve his cultural heritage as well as any traditional associations with Victor's mother. In the end, Alexie is trying to show how, with each successive generation, the Native-American identity can be eroded some more, as children learn destructive American habits for themselves. In fact, it is fitting that Alexie focuses part of his story on Victor's memory, since if this cultural erosion trend continues, the Native-American identity could become a memory itself. Alexie seems to suggest this idea at the very end of the story, when Victor goes outside his house to wait for his father, who he has imagined is coming to get him. Says Victor: "It was so quiet, a reservation kind of quiet, where you can hear somebody drinking whiskey on the rocks three miles away." When a colonized culture loses its heritage, it dies, as emphasized by the profound silence. All that is left over is the negative effect of assimilation, which in this case is represented by the sound of a person drinking alone in the dark. As Alan R. Velie notes in his review of the collection in *World Literature Today:* "A major theme of the book is the feeling of despair, guilt, and helplessness that overcomes Indians as they and their friends and relatives give up on life and lapse into unemployment and alcoholism."

Source: Ryan D. Poquette, Critical Essay on "Because My Father Always Said He Was the Only Indian Who Saw Jimi Hendrix Play 'The Star-Spangled Banner' at Woodstock," in *Short Stories for Students,* Gale, 2003.

Timothy Dunham

Dunham holds a bachelor's degree in English literature and a master's degree in communication. In the following essay, Dunham considers Alexie's story in relation to the impact of assimilation on Indian culture.

In Alexie's "Because My Father Always Said He Was the Only Indian Who Saw Jimi Hendrix Play 'The Star-Spangled Banner' at Woodstock," the narrator, Victor, uses the word "assimilation" to describe how attributes of one culture are adopted by another culture, often resulting in the destruction of the culture adopting them. He states:

> On a reservation, Indian men who abandon their children are treated worse than white fathers who do the same thing. It's because white men have been doing that forever and Indian men have just learned how. That's how assimilation can work.

"Because My Father Always Said He Was the Only Indian Who Saw Jimi Hendrix Play 'The Star-Spangled Banner' at Woodstock" is Victor's account of how assimilation works in his family. He

shows how his father's fascination with American popular culture—namely his obsession with pop music icon Jimi Hendrix—tears apart his family and undermines the values of his Indian culture.

Alexie begins the story by making a statement about assimilation with Victor's very first sentence: "During the sixties, my father was the perfect hippie, since all the hippies were trying to be Indians." The irony here is that Victor's father was not the perfect hippie. He had long hair, wore bell-bottoms, smoked pot, dropped acid, loved rock and roll, and protested the United States' involvement in Vietnam, but he did not stand for peace. He was a warrior at heart, and the first thing Victor relates about him is how he severely beat a National Guard private with a rifle at a peace rally. Such an opening is significant because it creates a powerful image that introduces the reader to the story's main theme: failure to assimilate in an appropriate manner has destructive consequences.

As a result of that incident, Victor says, his father was arrested and sent to prison, but he got out just in time to hitchhike to Woodstock, where he witnessed a musical performance that changed him forever: Jimi Hendrix playing "The Star-Spangled Banner." His father tells him that it was just what he needed at that point in his life: "After all the s——— I'd been through, I figured Jimi must have known I was there in the crowd to play something like that. It was exactly how I felt." Victor claims that he "[doesn't] have any clue about what it meant for [his] father to be the only Indian who saw Jimi Hendrix play at Woodstock" and understands its significance only in terms of the consequences of his father's resulting obsession with Hendrix.

One consequence is frequent arguments between his parents. Although Victor does not recount every argument, the reader is led to believe that most of them had to do with Jimi Hendrix. The particular argument that Victor speaks about occurred during a family trip to Hendrix's grave in Seattle. Commenting on the untimely nature of Hendrix's death, his father said, "Only the good die young," to which his mother replied, "No, only the crazy people choke to death on their own vomit." The ensuing dispute was not unlike the many others that Victor witnesses in his parents' marriage. As he says, "I was used to these battles."

Another consequence is his father's inward retreat, at first characterized by lone bouts of heavy drinking and later by frequent disappearances from the house. Victor remembers how his mother once tried to explain his father's behavior to him: "Your father just likes being alone more than he likes being with other people. Even me and you." But, this explanation is not entirely accurate. As Victor recalls, even when his father wanted to be alone, Jimi was always somebody he liked to be with. They began as "drinking buddies," with his father spending long evenings laughing, crying, and drinking beer while listening to Jimi play "The Star-Spangled Banner" on the stereo. They ended as traveling companions, with his father's desire to drink giving way to a new desire: getting away for hours, even days, on his new motorcycle with an old tape player strapped to the gas tank.

The final consequence is his parents' divorce and the subsequent abandonment by his father. At the time of his father's near fatal motorcycle accident, Victor relates, his mother had already decided she did not want to be married to him anymore. She had had enough of the arguing, the drunkenness, and the disappearances. She visited him in the hospital and helped nurse him back to health by quietly singing Indian tunes to him, but after he recovered, they separated for good. Understanding what happened, Victor asks his mother, "Was it because of Jimi Hendrix?," to which she replies, "Part of it, yeah. This might be the only marriage broken up by a dead guitar player." What is interesting about his mother's reply is that she only lays part of the blame on Hendrix. The remainder of the blame rests with both his father and mother.

Victor's father is to blame for the manner in which he responds to Jimi Hendrix's performance of "The Star-Spangled Banner" at Woodstock. This is not to say that his feelings at the time were inappropriate. They were, in fact, warranted and entirely justifiable. After all, here was Jimi Hendrix playing the American national anthem at an event where patriotism was less than fashionable and during a time when racial and political unrest were greater than at any point in America's history. And there was Victor's father, living like an outcast in what was once the land of his fathers, heir to prejudice and years of inequitable government polices, able to identify, better than most, with Jimi Hendrix's soulful rendition of the American national anthem. But, instead of inspiring him to live a richer and more meaningful life and encouraging him to bravely face the challenges of living in a racially polarized world, it impaired his ability to live at all, causing him to retreat into his own world. As he tells Victor, "I ain't interested in what's real. I'm interested in how things should be."

> **"** But, because of his own appreciation of Hendrix, Victor comes to the conclusion that assimilation is something far more complex than simply adopting white men's bad behavior."

Unfortunately for Victor's father, it never occurs to him that he could be a force for positive change in the world, that he could help make things the way they should be. Like much of the music of the 1960s, "The Star-Spangled Banner" at Woodstock was a "call to arms," a rallying cry for people such as Victor's father to fight for justice in an unjust world. Victor's father, however, chose to surrender rather than fight. This, too, is how assimilation can work. "The Star-Spangled Banner" at Woodstock should have motivated him to help make a difference in the world, but instead it alienated him from the world. "The Star-Spangled Banner" at Woodstock should have energized him to help make the world a better place, but instead it immobilized him, making him unfit for service to the world and his family.

As a result of having to live with her husband's immobilizing obsession with Hendrix, his mother retreats to the life she knew when she was younger. She travels to powwows and begins to dance again. She immerses herself in the music, customs, and traditions of her native culture. In so doing, she finds a refuge from the destructive effects of the foreign culture that violated the sanctity of her home with motorcycles and guitars. Her response to Hendrix, then, is a rejection of assimilation and, hence, a rejection of her husband. Such is her part in the breakup of their marriage.

Interestingly enough, Victor is never trapped between the two distinctly different worlds in which his parents lived. He is a loving son who looks at both sides with sympathy and compassion. Victor sees how his father's obsession with Hendrix breaks apart his family. He also sees how his mother's rejection of white American pop culture—with Jimi Hendrix ironically included—contributes to the breakup. But, because of his own appreciation of Hendrix, Victor comes to the conclusion that assimilation is something far more complex than simply adopting white men's bad behavior.

After his father leaves for good, Victor draws comfort from the music of Jimi Hendrix and Robert Johnson. He says, "On those nights I missed him most I listened to music. Not always Jimi Hendrix. Usually I listened to the blues. Robert Johnson mostly." On one particular night, Victor imagines that he hears his father's motorcycle outside and his father yelling, "Victor, let's go for a ride." He goes out and finds the driveway empty, so he stands on the porch all night and imagines he hears motorcycles and guitars. The fact that Victor can derive comfort from these sounds is significant because it is a response unlike what his father's would have been. Instead of causing him despair, these sounds offer the hope that maybe someday his father will return home. These sounds of American pop culture are an inspiration for this Indian boy to go on; so when the sun comes up and shines brightly, he knows that it is time to go inside and have breakfast with his mother. This, too, is how assimilation can work. This is how assimilation should work.

Source: Timothy Dunham, Critical Essay on ''Because My Father Always Said He Was the Only Indian Who Saw Jimi Hendrix Play 'The Star-Spangled Banner' at Woodstock,'' in *Short Stories for Students,* Gale, 2003.

Jerome DeNuccio

In the following essay, DeNuccio examines a selection of stories from Alexie's collection, looking closely at how the Native-American characters "wage daily battle against small humiliations and perennial hurts."

The Spokane Indian characters in Sherman Alexie's short story collection *The Lone Ranger and Tonto Fistfight in Heaven* wage daily battle against small humiliations and perennial hurts. Situated on a reservation where the Department of Housing and Urban Development (HUD) houses, the Bureau of Indian Affairs (BIA) trucks, and commodity foods continually mirror paternalism and dependency, and where ''tribal ties'' and a cohesive ''sense of community'' have waned, Alexie's characters confront the dilemma of how to be ''real Indians,'' of how to find ''their true names, their adult names,'' of how to find a warrior dignity and courage when it is ''too late to be warriors in the old way,'' of how to ameliorate what Adrian C. Louis has termed ''the ghost-pain of history''—that haunting sense of personal and cultural loss that generates a paralyzing sense of ineffectuality. They struggle to cope with passivity, cynicism, and despair to find healing for the pain that turns into self-pity and the anger that turns into self-loathing.

One of Alexie's characters, Thomas Builds-the-Fire, a Spokane storyteller, articulates a useful image for understanding the distress and anguish these characters experience: *''There are things you should learn,''* he tells Victor and Junior, two young Spokanes who either narrate or are featured in 18 of the collection's 22 stories. ''Your past is a skeleton walking one step behind you, and your future is a skeleton walking one step in front of you.'' Indians, thus, are always *''trapped in the now.''* But the skeletons are ''not necessarily evil, unless you let them be.'' Because ''these skeletons are made of memories, dreams, and voices,'' and because they are ''wrapped up in the now,'' it becomes imperative to ''keep moving, keep walking, in step with your skeletons.'' To stop or slow down, to ''slow dance'' with one's skeletons, risks being caught ''in the in-between, between touching and becoming,'' the immediately felt and the potentially experienced. Such a situation severs the necessary relation between the structure of experience that at any one moment has shaped each life and the structure of ongoing time to which that life must continuously adapt and in which it develops. Keeping in step is not easy, however, for ''your skeletons will talk to you, tell you to sit down and take a rest, [. . .] make you promises, tell you all the things you want to hear.'' They can ''dress up'' as seductive women, as a best friend offering a drink, as parents offering gifts. But, ''no matter what they do,'' Thomas warns, ''keep walking, keep moving.''

Thomas's image of the skeletons suggests that Indian subjectivity is dialogic, an interplay of perspectives and points of view that Bakhtin describes as ''a plurality of unmerged consciousness.'' The self is positioned in a social space replete with memories, dreams, and voices that invite attention and response, that must be accommodated and negotiated if the self as an individual and a tribal subject is to emerge. Such negotiation, although paramount, is never easy. Memories, dreams, and voices form a dense network of social significations. They bear traces, are mediated by social relations and cultural dynamics, are inflected by family, friends, lovers, traditions, mass media, history. The term *Indian* names a subject position traversed by competing claims, saturated by multiple insinuations, the confusion or mastering force of which can induce a capitulation that Thomas identifies as failing to keep "in step with your skeletons." Such capitulation forecloses choice, and the result is often self-sabotage. Commenting on what appears to a white state trooper as an unmotivated suicide by a successful tribal member, Junior notes that "when we look in the mirror, see the history of our tribe in our eyes, taste failure in the tap water, and shake with old tears, we understand completely." To "keep moving, keep walking, in step with your skeletons," then, suggests the necessity of listening to *and answering* the multiple voices that clamor for attention, a process of accommodation *and negotiation* that resists totalization and keeps the self "unconsummated" and "yet-to-be" (*Art and Answerability . . .*), moving always toward "becoming" rather than trapped "between touching and becoming," moving so that some coherent story of the self can be discovered. Thomas's image of the skeletons resonates throughout the collection's 22 stories, precisely because so many characters have fallen out of step and, thus, are suspended, passively and destructively, in a seemingly incoherent present.

Appropriately enough, the collection's opening story, "Every Little Hurricane," displays the provenance of those elements that problematize Indian subjectivity. Significantly, Alexie sets the story at a New Year's Eve party ushering in 1976, the bicentennial year. Nine-year-old Victor, whose parents are hosting the party, awakens to what he thinks is a hurricane but is really a metaphor Alexie uses to represent Victor's experience of the intensifying anger and painful memories, unleashed by alcohol, that circulate among the Indian partygoers. Victor's father, for instance, remembers his father being spit on at a Spokane bus stop; his mother remembers being involuntarily sterilized by an Indian Health Service (IHS) doctor after Victor's birth; his uncles Adolph and Arnold fight savagely because each reminds the other of childhood poverty so great that they hid crackers in their bedroom so they wouldn't have to go to bed hungry. Lying in his basement bedroom, Victor thinks he sees the ceiling lower "with the weight of each Indian's pain, until it was just inches from [his] nose." As the adults' drunken rage fills the house, it blends with and feeds Victor's own nightmare fears of drowning in the rain, of alcoholic "fluids swallowing him." for at the age of five he had witnessed at a powwow an Indian man drown after passing out and falling "facedown into the water collected in a tire track." "Even at five," the narrator notes, "Victor understood what that

> **"** Without a viable counterbalance of Spokane culture--a point Alexie implies by setting his opening story on the eve of America's bicentennial festivities--the self appears finalized, unmodifiable because personal history appears consumed by the totalizing narrative of History."

meant, how it defined nearly everything." Seeking the comfort of physical connection, he lies between his unconscious parents, and, putting a hand on each of their stomachs, feels "enough hunger in both, enough movement, enough geography and history, enough of everything to destroy the reservations." As this image suggests, the confluence of past currents of suffering meet in Victor.

Given the intensity of the pain that presses upon Indian subjectivity, it is not surprising that the adults and their children get caught "in the in-between, between touching and becoming." The now of felt experience becomes ceaseless repetition of what has been. Without a viable counterbalance of Spokane culture—a point Alexie implies by setting his opening story on the eve of America's bicentennial festivities—the self appears finalized, unmodifiable because personal history appears consumed by the totalizing narrative of History. There is no sense of particularity, of difference that prevents the self from being absorbed into the larger culture's dominant narrative, no way to position the self so that its story unfolds within, not into, ongoing time, no "outsidedness" (*Speech Genres . . .*) where the choice to keep moving in step with one's skeletons keeps the impinging or "touching" now provisionally open to "becoming."

Victor's father, for example, has stopped walking in step with his skeletons altogether by retreating into an idealized moment twenty years earlier. Active in the Vietnam War protest movement and jailed for assaulting a National Guardsman, Victor's father endures two years of racial warfare in prison. On his release, he hitchhikes to Woodstock, arriving just in time to hear Jimi Hendrix's performance of "The Star-Spangled Banner." "'After all the [sh——] I'd been through,'" he tells Victor, "'I figured Jimi must have known I was there in the crowd to play something like that. It was exactly how I felt.'" Twenty years later, he still plays the song and dissolves into tears in memory of a pure moment of connection and understanding, from which he views all his subsequent life as a declension. At thirteen, Victor finds he cannot penetrate his father's self-imposed exile from the painful memories of those twenty years and, thus, Victor loses the potentially usable experiences, the realized knowledge, those twenty years contain. David Murray has noted that "the absent or failed father," a common feature in Indian texts, often symbolizes "the rupture and absence of guidelines from the past, and consequent alienation from a cultural heritage." "'I ain't interested in what's real,'" Victor's father tells him. "'I'm interested in how things should be.'" What Victor learns from his father is a strategy that shields him from pain but surrenders the connectedness to events that opens them to meaning: "instead of remembering the bad things, remember what happened immediately before. That's what I learned from my father."

Consequently, the struggle to sort through fractious memories, dreams, and voices dogs Victor into young adulthood. In the story "A Drug Called Tradition" Big Mom, the Spokane Tribe's spiritual leader, gives Victor a small drum as a "pager" to summon her in times of need. Victor doubts the drum's efficacy and admits he has never used it. Yet, even after Big Mom dies, he keeps it "really close," because it is "the only religion I have," and "I think if I played it a little, it might fill up the whole world." Victor is situated at a boundary between cultural rejection and cultural connection, torn between skepticism toward the heritage of traditional spirituality and the desire to retain that heritage as a possible source of plenitude to "fill up" a world seemingly bereft of continuity. Much the same irresolution marks his relationship with the storytelling Thomas, whom he has bullied since childhood and whose stories he ignores, precisely because, for Victor, those stories register cultural loss. Yet, Victor admits, when Thomas "stopped looking at me, I was hurt. How do you explain that?"

The story "All I Wanted To Do Was Dance" opens with Victor drunk and reeling wildly on a barroom dancefloor. Suddenly, he sees "the faces of his past. He recognized Niel Armstrong and Christopher Columbus, his mother and father, James Dean, Sal Mineo, Natalie Wood." He then recalls himself as a young boy, "fancydancing in the same outfit his father wore as a child." Looking "into the crowd for approval," he sees his mother and father, "both drunk" and staggering, the "other kind of dancing" that "was nothing new." The continuous history of Euro-American dominance, emblematize by Columbus and Armstrong, coupled with the shameful spectacle of his parents, have invalidated fancydancing as a culturally specific signifying practice by which he can position himself within a localized system of meaning. In its place Hollywood supplies a mass-mediated construction, the rebel without a cause, a subject position at once disenfranchising and inauthentic.

Similarly, a bewildering mix of personal experience, memory, dream, and history affects Junior in "The Lone Ranger and Tonto Fistfight in Heaven." Living in Seattle and involved in a loving but contentious relationship with a white kindergarten teacher, Junior dreams she is "a missionary's wife" and he is "a minor war chief" who is her clandestine lover. Her husband discovers their relationship and shoots him. "Disembodied," Junior watches as his murder provokes massive and bloody warfare between several tribes of Indians and the U.S. Cavalry. Junior's "most vivid image of that dream," however, is three mounted soldiers playing "polo with a dead Indian woman's head," an image he at first considers "a product of my anger and imagination," but which he subsequently discovers in histories of war in "the Old West" and journalistic accounts of atrocities "in places like El Salvador." This blurring of internal and external, wherein private nightmare is simultaneously public record disseminated across space and time, terrifies Junior. He finds himself both inside and outside his own experience, caught in the seam between past and present, agent and object, at once the author of a unique narrative expressing his own "anger and imagination" and an authored character in an old and ongoing story of racial hatred. The dream is and is not his own; he is himself and a historical clone. Moreover, the dream redoubles this ambiguity: killed early on, he haunts the scene, a disembodied witness of the carnage his sexual relationship with the white woman has produced. At some level, then, Junior experiences his cross-racial relationship as transgressive, a betrayal, perhaps, of tribal hopes that, as "a smart kid" and "former college student,'' he would provide the model for a ''new kind of warrior.''

Returning to the reservation, Junior attempts to reestablish a connection with his personal past through basketball: ''I'd been a good player in high school, nearly great. [. . .] I liked the way the ball felt in my hands and the way my feet felt inside my shoes.'' The pleasure of recapturing his skill is short-lived, however; the entire history of Indian-white relations repeats itself on the night he is ''ready to play for real.'' After some initial success, the white son of the reservation BIA chief takes control of the game away from Junior. ''He was better that day,'' Junior admits, ''and every other day.'' The basketball court, like the battlefield he dreamed of in Seattle, becomes for Junior a scene of failure and betrayal. The ''BIA kid needed to be beaten by an Indian,'' and the watching tribal members have invested their hopes in him, ''one of their old and dusty heroes.'' The white boy, however, ''played Indian ball, fast and loose,'' and, having appropriated the Indian style, Junior knows he is ''better than all the Indians there.''

The next day Junior drives to Spokane and takes a job ''typing and answering phones'' for a ''high school exchange program.'' The racial anonymity he finds as a detached telephone voice is compromised when his Seattle lover calls. ''The connection was good,'' Junior notes, an ironic counterpoint to the lack of emotional clarity characterizing their conversation.

> ''What's going to happen to us?'' I asked her and wished I had the answer for myself.
>
> ''I don't know,'' she said. ''I want to change the world.''

The desire to direct change is not an option for Junior; as his dream and the basketball game have demonstrated, he can only experience its consequences. His relationship with his white lover, he realizes, is riven by an unbridgeable racial difference that distributes unequally the capacity for, even the imagining of, performative agency. The woman he remembers, ''whose ghost has haunted'' him, is, irreconcilably, a ''real person'' he can never know, a person whose otherness remains irreducible.

At their worst, the contending memories, voices, and dreams reach a kind of critical mass that impels Victor and Junior to racial abjection. In ''Amusements,'' Victor comes across a fellow tribesman, Dirty Joe, lying in a drunken stupor on a carnival midway. In an attempt to dissociate himself from a sight that evokes the contemptuous laughter of passing white tourists, Victor plays a practical joke on Dirty Joe by putting him on a roller coaster. When a crowd of whites gathers, their ''open mouths grown large and deafening'' with laughter, Victor suddenly realizes his complicity with those whites in a long history of cultural degradation. He has been, he sees, a ''court jester'' who has poured ''Thunderbird wine into the Holy Grail,'' a freak like ''the Fat Lady'' and ''the Dog-Faced Boy''—an ''Indian who offered up another Indian like some treaty.'' Victor recognizes, in other words, that he has reduced himself from speaking subject of his own discourse to sign in official discourse, effectually removing himself from his own history. His complicity is a cultural forgetting or dismembering that, according to ethnologist Robert Cantwell, permits ''parts and pieces of social identity'' to signify only insofar as they comport with and consolidate the cultural myths of society at large. ''[L]ike some treaty,'' then, Victor's betrayal of Dirty Joe, multiplied by many others many times, has contributed to ''the folding shut of the good part of [the] past.''

Junior, too, realizes the complicity involved in his denial of Indian identity. While in college he attended a basketball game after partying with a group of whites from his dormitory. One of the players on the opposing team is a twenty-eight-year-old who has overcome his inner-city Los Angeles upbringing and a stint in prison. Junior realizes that he and the basketball player ''had a whole lot in common. Much more in common than I had with those white boys I was drunk with.'' Nevertheless, he joins in the vicious taunting that greets the player's entrance on the court, an act that in its replication of white bigotry and in its defiance of shared experience actually constitutes self-subversion. Little wonder, then, that Junior describes his time in the city in terms of debilitating ineffectuality: '''It's like a bad dream you never wake up from. [. . .] Standing completely still on an escalator that will not move, but I didn't have the courage to climb the stairs by myself.''' Like Victor, Junior is immobilized by the kind of double consciousness W. E. B. Dubois describes as ''the sense of always looking at one's self through the eyes of others, of measuring one's soul by the tape of a world that looks on in amused contempt and pity.''

Alexie's Indian characters are caught, as Bakhtin puts it, in the ''framework of *other people's* words'' about them, a framework that can ''finalize and deaden'' the self. But Alexie also demonstrates that in his characters ''there is always something that only [they themselves] can reveal, in a free act of self-consciousness and discourse, something that does not submit to an externalizing second-hand definition'' (*Problems . . .*). And Alexie again uses the Spokane storyteller Thomas Builds-the-Fire to explain this resistant something.

> We are all given one thing by which our lives are measured, one determination. Mine are the stories which can change or not change the world. It doesn't matter which as long as I continue to tell the stories. [. . .] They are all I have. It's all I can do.

Thomas's ''one determination'' posits subjectivity as both determined and particular, given, and its own measure of value. There is a personal narrative that unfolds within the larger culture's master narrative, which situates an individual subjectivity within the cultural topography and keeps it in step with the skeletons of past and future. For Thomas, only recognizing and choosing to follow that ''one determination'' matters. Thomas himself is widely ignored by his tribe, yet he tells his stories, stories that he does not author but that come to him from the culturally specific ground to which he is connected and which his storytelling articulates. What Thomas transmits, then, is the persistence and adaptability of Spokane signifying practices.

Indeed, those of Alexie's characters in step with their skeletons have in common a connection, or a re-connection, to tribal tradition. Victor's Aunt Nezzy, by donning the ''heaviest beaded dress'' she has made and finding ''the strength to take the first step, then another quick one,'' overcomes 30 years of casual cruelty by her family and the memory of being hoodwinked into a tubal ligation by an IHS administrator. Nezzy then ''heard drums, she heard singing, she danced. Dancing that way, she knew things were beginning to change''; for, as she had earlier predicted, the woman ''who can carry the weight of this dress on her back [. . .] will save us all.'' Victor's mother, after her husband's desertion, ''traveled to powwows, started to dance again. She was a champion traditional dancer when she was younger.'' Having revived her traditional dancing ability enables her to provide a countering nurture to the emptiness caused by her husband's abandonment, not just for herself, but for thirteen-year-old Victor as well. After a night spent futilely waiting for his father's return, Victor ''knew it was time to go back inside to my mother. She made breakfast for both of us and we ate until we were full.'' Uncle Moses responds to the ''unplanned kindness'' of his young friend Arnold by telling it to him as a story, thereby creating, as the title of the story indicates, a ''good story,'' one to be repeated—as the narrator

himself is doing—and that, like Moses's house, ''would stand even years after Moses died,'' to nourish ''the tribal imagination'' and ''ensure survival.'' The twenty-year-old narrator of ''Jesus Christ's Half-Brother Is Alive and Well on the Spokane Indian Reservation'' accedes to tradition by accepting responsibility for an infant whose life he has saved. Raising young James saves the narrator as well. He learns that ''we should be living for each other instead [of dying] for each other,'' and that such solicitude generates an ethic of reciprocal care: ''I know when I am old and sick and ready to die that James will wash my body and take care of my wastes. He'll carry me from HUD house to sweathouse and he will clean my wounds. And he will talk and teach me something new every day.''

Victor and Junior both manage to find their ''one determination'' and, thereby, negotiate the contentious memories, dreams, and voices that attenuate their lives. In ''All I Wanted To Do Is Dance,'' Victor has returned ''home'' to the reservation from the city and a failed romance with a white woman, an experience, he says, that seemed like ''being lost in the desert for forty years.'' Despondent and drinking heavily, he meets a Cherokee who tells him that ''the difference between a real Indian and a fake Indian'' is that ''a real Indian got blisters on his feet;'' a ''fake Indian got blisters on his ass.'' The allusion to the 1,200-mile Trail of Tears, a literal wandering in the desert more profoundly painful than the self-pity occasioned by a lost love, is not lost on Victor. He realizes that fancydancing—all he ever really wanted to do—also blisters the feet. His ''one determination'' authenticates him as a ''real Indian.'' The story concludes, aptly enough, on a crest of conjunctions, progressive verbs, and modals that suggest possibility will become probability:

> And he was walking down this road and tomorrow maybe he would be walking down another road and maybe tomorrow he would be dancing. Victor might be dancing.
>
> Yes, Victor would be dancing.

And, presumably, getting blisters!

Junior gets a new name that, in its honest acknowledgment of ''the worst thing I ever did''— his hateful taunting of the inner-city Los Angeles basketball player—reconciles him to and releases him from that guilt-laden memory and the larger personal failures it has come to emblematize. ''I was special,'' Junior explains, ''a former college student, a smart kid. I was one of those Indians who was supposed to make it. [. . .] I was the new kind of warrior.'' Instead, Junior left college, fled the city, and left behind a son whom he is allowed to see only six days a month. Junior's new name is given by Norma Many Horses, a widely respected ''cultural lifeguard,'' according to Junior, ''watching out for those of us that were so close to drowning.'' After revealing his secret to Norma, Junior notes that ''she treated me differently for about a year,'' and he assumes she ''wouldn't ever forgive me.'' She does, however, and signals her forgiveness by giving Junior a ''new Indian name'': Pete Rose. ''[Y]ou two got a whole lot in common,'' she explains. After all his ''greatness, he's only remembered for the bad stuff'' and ''[t]hat ain't right.'' Sometime later, Norma seeks Junior out:

> ''Pete Rose,'' she said. ''They just voted to keep you out of the Hall of Fame. I'm sorry. But I still love you.''
>
> ''Yeah, I know, Norma. I love you, too.''

Where Junior had previously denied, out of self-abnegating shame, someone with whom he had ''a whole lot in common,'' he now acknowledges a commonality of experience that frankly concedes not just his error, but also its ineradicability, its permanence a part of his psychological terrain. Although it is unfair that an entire life is marked by ''the bad stuff,'' accepting such a condition requires courage and breaks the cycle by which past failures are repeated in the present. In giving him a ''true'' name, an ''adult'' name—the lack of which Thomas identified as ''the problem with Indians these days,'' Norma, the ''cultural lifeguard,'' has taught Junior what he thought he could never learn—forgiveness— and opened for him the possibility of an identity he thought he had forfeited—a ''new kind of warrior.''

It is important to see that in linking Thomas's ''one determination'' to a localized cultural practice Alexie is not advocating a simple return to some traditional tribal past. Such a return ignores Thomas's point that the past and future are ''wrapped up in the now,'' It is a retreat into cultural monologism that, politically, serves bureaucratic interests because, pragmatically, it disjoins past and present, thereby avoiding the necessity, or even the inclination, of situating oneself in relation to modem day realities, to ''the now'' Moreover, a traditional tribal past simply no longer exists. It has been co-opted, and that co-optation has altered Indian subjectivity. Alexie's frequent use of ''five hundred years'' as a sort of grammatical intensifier makes clear that history has redefined what being Indian means. Victor points to a hybridization that has

attenuated biological identity and vitiated cultural identity: ''all the years have changed more than the shape of our blood and eyes. We wear fear like a turquoise choker, like a familiar shawl''

The pun on ''choker'' figures all too well a point Adrian C. Louis makes in his novel *Skins:* Indians have ''learned to oppress themselves.'' Likewise, Junior reflects on ''pain, how each of us constructs our past to justify what we feel now. How each successive pain distorts the preceding'' to the point where nothing is ''aboriginal or recognizable.'' Having internalized the otherness by which they have historically been defined, Indians become like the transistor radio that the narrator of the story ''Distances'' finds. Though ''no imperfection'' is evident on its exterior, it does not work. The problem, he suggests, ''the mistakes,'' are ''inside, where you couldn't see, couldn't reach.'' Or, like the diabetes Junior has inherited from his father, five hundred years of history have ceased working ''like a criminal, breaking and entering,'' instead, for Indians in the late 20th century, it works ''just like a lover, hurting you from the inside.''

The apparently naturalized historical forces that have decentered and determined Indian subjectivity certainly compromise the ability to discern and to choose to affirm the ''one determination'' that Thomas opposes to the derailing skeletons of past and future. Yet, those of Alexie's characters who refuse to stop, who stay in step, do manage to see ''inside,'' do manage to conduct a clarifying introspection, do choose to align themselves with some still viable traditional practice that prevents ''the folding shut of the good part of [their] past'' and that works through and in time as a usable ground for identity construction, that establishes the self as a structure of relation between past, present, and future. Indeed, Thomas teaches Victor this lesson in the aptly named story ''This Is What It Means to Say Phoenix, Arizona.'' Feeling that ''[h]e owed Thomas something'' for helping fund their trip to Phoenix to claim the cremated remains of his father, Victor offers Thomas half his father's ashes. Thomas accepts the gift and tells a story:

> ''I'm going to travel to Spokane Falls one last time and toss these ashes into the water. And your father will rise like a salmon, leap over the bridge, over me, and find his way home. It will be beautiful. His teeth will shine like silver, like a rainbow. He will rise, Victor, he will rise.''
>
> Victor had in mind a similar method of disposing of the ashes but acknowledges,

"[. . .] I didn't imagine my father looking anything like a salmon. I thought it'd be like cleaning the attic or something. Like letting things go after they've stopped having any use."

"Nothing stops, cousin," Thomas said, "nothing stops."

Thomas demonstrates to Victor the power of Spokane myth to synthesize the twin domains of private and tribal experience and reveals the boundary that Victor has imposed between them as a restriction, not constituent, of identity. Thomas challenges Victor's belief that he can sweep his father from memory, abandon the father, who abandoned him. Thomas's story inserts Victor's father in a process-laden narrative that assigns cultural significance to a father whom Victor had considered obsolescent and dispensable. In effect, then, Thomas's story forces Victor to reread and, thus, reinterpret his father as a cultural tie, a point of continuity with the past, a fusion of "historical memory and subjectivity" (Said . . .) that never "stops," that, like the mythic phoenix, will always "rise," a continual story of self emerging "from the ash of older stories."

Stories, then, teach survival. They *re*-member, bridging the rupture created by "what we have lost," reconnecting time to aspect, past and present to progressive and perfective. Talking stories yields something "aboriginal and recognizable," something, as Thomas says, "by which our lives are measured." In the story "Family Portrait," Junior, contemplating his hands, is led to an acute realization of cultural loss:

> Years ago, the hands might have held the spear that held the salmon that held the dream of the tribe. Years ago, the hands might have touched the hands of the dark-skinned men who touched medicine and the magic of ordinary gods.

He then recalls a story his father told about "the first television he ever saw." It had "just one channel and all it showed was a woman sitting on top of the same television. Over and over until it hurt your eyes and head." That image, persistently reflexive, depicts the kind of storytelling Alexie himself enacts: an unsparing examination of what is gone and what remains. That, Junior declares, is "how we find our history." And repossess it, too, for although such storytelling must, of necessity, measure "heartbreak" and "fear," it also becomes the means "by which we measure the beginning of all our lives," the means "by which we measure all our stories, until we understand that one story"—the official historiography—"can never be all."

Like the television that continuously frames the image it continuously represents, broadcasting in the present its backward gaze, Alexie's storytelling links "now" with "then," Indian lives with "five hundred years of convenient lies," repeatedly, for though "it hurt[s] your eyes and head" it speaks survival.

Source: Jerome DeNuccio, "Slow Dancing with Skeletons: Sherman Alexie's *The Lone Ranger and Tonto Fistfight in Heaven*," in *Critique*, Vol. 44, No. 1, Fall 2002, pp. 86–96.

Sources

Alexie, Sherman, "Because My Father Always Said He Was the Only Indian Who Saw Jimi Hendrix Play 'The Star-Spangled Banner' at Woodstock," in *The Lone Ranger and Tonto Fistfight in Heaven,* Atlantic Monthly Press, 1993, pp. 24–36.

Baxter, Andrea-Bess, Review of *Old Shirts and New Skins, First Indian on the Moon,* and *The Lone Ranger and Tonto Fistfight in Heaven,* in *Western American Literature,* Vol. 29, No. 3, November 1994, pp. 277–80.

Beauvais, Fred, "American Indians and Alcohol," in *Alcohol Health and Research World,* Vol. 22, No. 4, 1998, p. 253.

Brill, Susan B., "Sherman Alexie," in *Dictionary of Literary Biography,* Vol. 175: *Native American Writers of the United States,* Gale Research, 1997, pp. 3–10.

Cline, Lynn, "About Sherman Alexie," in *Ploughshares,* Vol. 26, No. 4, Winter 2000–2001, pp. 197–202.

Price, Reynolds, "One Indian Doesn't Tell Another," in the *New York Times Book Review,* October 17, 1993, pp. 15–16.

Review of *The Lone Ranger and Tonto Fistfight in Heaven,* in *Kirkus Reviews,* July 1, 1993.

Schneider, Brian, Review of *The Lone Ranger and Tonto Fistfight in Heaven,* in the *Review of Contemporary Fiction,* Vol. 13, No. 3, Fall 1993, pp. 237–38.

Silko, Leslie Marmon, "Big Bingo," in the *Nation,* Vol. 260, No. 23, June 12, 1995, pp. 856–58, 860.

Velie, Alan R., Review of *The Lone Ranger and Tonto Fistfight in Heaven,* in *World Literature Today,* Vol. 68, No. 2, Spring 1994, p. 407.

Further Reading

Allen, Paula Gunn, *Off the Reservation: Reflections on Boundary-Busting, Border-Crossing Loose Cannons,* Beacon Press, 1999.
    In this collection of essays, Allen examines the boundaries between Anglo and Native-American cultures from a feminine perspective, critiquing many of the conventions of Western society in the process.

McDermott, John, and Eddie Kramer, *Hendrix: Setting the Record Straight,* Warner Books, 1992.

This book is the definitive account of Hendrix's music career. Written entirely from first person accounts—including the recollections of Kramer, Hendrix's influential producer—the book gives in-depth, behind-the-scenes coverage of the rock legend.

Nies, Judith, *Native American History: A Chronology of a Culture's Vast Achievements and Their Links to World Events,* Ballantine Books, 1996.

Nies gives a thorough timeline of the major events in Native-American history. Using a two-column format, she places these events next to the other world events from the same year, giving readers a context within which to place the Native-American events. The book covers prehistoric times until 1996, and each major time period is prefaced by a short overview.

Peat, F. David, *Lighting the Seventh Fire: The Spiritual Ways, Healing, and Science of the Native American,* Birch Lane Press, 1994.

Peat, a physicist and author, first came in contact with the scientific beliefs of Native Americans in the 1980s. In this book, he gives a complete overview of science in the Native-American culture, including ceremonies of renewal, sacred mathematics, healing and disease, time, and language.

Rosenman, Joel, John Roberts, and Robert Pilpel, *Young Men with Unlimited Capital: The Story of Woodstock,* Scrivenery Press, 1999.

Although the Woodstock Music and Art Fair of 1969 has become a landmark event of an age, many people are unaware that the festival was generated through an advertisement placed by Rosenman and Roberts in the *New York Times.* This book gives a behind-the-scenes look at the creation of Woodstock and at the event itself, which spawned a number of complaints, lawsuits, a death, births, medical emergencies, and other unforeseen problems for the festival organizers.

Thornton, Russel, ed., *Studying Native America: Problems and Prospects,* University of Wisconsin Press, 1999.

Thornton, a Cherokee Indian and professor of anthropology at the University of California, Los Angeles, collects a number of essays by various contributors. The essays concern the various issues involved in developing Native-American studies programs that are culturally and historically accurate. Most contributors address the fact that traditional academic methods do not always work for Native-American studies.

Brazzaville Teen-ager

Bruce Jay Friedman

1966

Bruce Jay Friedman's "Brazzaville Teen-ager" was first published in the author's 1966 short-story collection, *Black Angels*. "Brazzaville Teen-ager" differs from most of Friedman's works, which emphasize the Jewishness of their characters. In this story, the ethnicity of the protagonist, Gunther, as well as of the other characters, remains undefined. Most of Friedman's fiction, including this story, has been characterized as black humor, a twentieth-century term coined by Friedman himself. Black comedies tend to involve neurotic, inept characters in modern settings, where they face comic and often absurd predicaments. In "Brazzaville Teen-ager," Gunther, a young man who is unable to communicate with his stoic father, feels he has a chance to break this communication barrier when his father gets seriously ill. Gunther believes that if he performs an illogical, embarrassing act—in this case, getting his boss to sing backup for a doo-wop band—it will help his father recover.

The doo-wop band was one of many forms of popular music in the 1960s, which also included the Motown sound, rhythm and blues, and rock and roll. The 1960s was also a serious era, as the United States became increasingly involved in Vietnam. The story mentions one such conflict, in the doo-wop song, "Brazzaville Teen-ager," where a teen accompanies his father into the war-torn Republic of Congo. Gunther's efforts to reconnect with his father ultimately fail, leading some critics to believe that the story is pointless. Friedman does use the

story to explore the ideas of miscommunication, fear, and irrationality, and seems to imply that serious situations cannot be solved through frivolous solutions. The story can be found in the paperback version of *The Collected Short Fiction of Bruce Jay Friedman*, which was published by Grove Press in 1997.

Author Biography

Friedman was born in New York City on April 26, 1930, and grew up in the Bronx. He wrote a column for his high school newspaper, which sparked his interest in writing. In 1951, he graduated from the University of Missouri with a bachelor's degree in journalism, then joined the United States Air Force. As an officer, he worked as a correspondent, feature writer, and photographer for the Air Force magazine, *Air Training*. He also wrote his first two short stories, including ''Wonderful Golden Rule Days,'' which was his first story published in a commercial periodical. In 1954, a year after he left the military, Friedman began working for Magazine Management Company in New York, where he eventually became editor for three men's magazines. In 1962, Friedman published his first novel, *Stern*, which was a critical—if not popular—success. The next year, Friedman published *Far from the City of Class and Other Stories*, which collected ten years of his short stories, including the two he wrote while in the Air Force. In 1966, he published his second short-story collection, *Black Angels*, which included the story ''Brazzaville Teen-ager.''

Besides his novels and short stories, Friedman has been successful in many other types of writing. In 1968, he wrote his first play, *Scuba Duba: A Tense Comedy*, which was a smash hit Off-Broadway that ran for two years. In 1978, Friedman published his first book of nonfiction essays, *The Lonely Guy's Book of Life*. The book was adapted into the film *The Lonely Guy* in 1984 and became a cult favorite. In addition to his own works that have been adapted, Friedman has also written original screenplays, including *Stir Crazy* (1980). His recent works include a novel, *A Father's Kisses* (1996), and two nonfiction works: *The Slightly Older Guy* (1995) and *Even the Rhinos Were Nymphos: Best Nonfiction* (2000). Friedman currently lives and works in New York.

Bruce Jay Friedman

Plot Summary

Friedman's ''Brazzaville Teen-ager'' begins with an introduction of Gunther, a young man who has always expected that his father would open up to him only in dire circumstances. When his father gets sick with an unknown, potentially fatal disease and is confined in a hospital harness, Gunther puts this theory to the test. However, as always, his father is very stoic, giving indifferent, unemotional answers to all of Gunther's questions, even those concerning the prospect of his death. Gunther leaves and decides that he can help his father recover if he does something outrageous, an embarrassing act that will sacrifice Gunther's self-esteem. Gunther goes in to work the next day and confronts his boss, Hartman, of whom he is terrified. Gunther explains that his dad is ill and says that if his boss will sing backup for a doo-wop band, for a new single that is about to be recorded, it will help Gunther's father get better. Hartman is understandably confused at Gunther's logic and kicks him out of his office.

That night, Gunther is driving around Manhattan and finds himself driving out to Hartman's estate, where he interrupts a dinner. Hartman takes Gunther into a side room, where Gunther pleads with his boss again to do the backup singing.

Hartman's wife interrupts them and convinces her husband to help Gunther. The next day, Gunther uses his lunch hour to talk to Conrad Jaggers, a young record company president whom Gunther had met in a bar. Gunther convinces Jaggers to let Hartman be a backup singer on "Brazzaville Teen-ager," a new single that Jaggers had mentioned over drinks. Later that day, Hartman shows up to do the backup singing, and Jaggers asks him to try to sing like a little boy. Despite this potentially humiliating experience, Hartman admits on the ride back that he enjoyed himself somewhat. Gunther sees a man flipping pancakes in a restaurant window and convinces an initially unwilling Hartman to flip a round of pancakes. Gunther thinks this extra insurance will definitely help his father get better. Gunther's father does get better, but he is as stoic as ever. Gunther helps his father back to his apartment, where he tries and fails to start a serious conversation. After Gunther has seen his father safely into his apartment, he starts taking the elevator down to the lobby. He stops the elevator and screams up at his father, frustrated that even his embarrassing acts did not break the communication barrier between him and his father.

Characters

Gunther

Gunther is a young man who assumes that either his father's potentially fatal disease or Gunther's attempts to help him cure it will finally get his stoic father to open up to him. Unfortunately, neither assumption is correct. Gunther has long hoped that he could find a way to get his father to talk to him about life and has daydreamed that it might happen on his father's deathbed. However, when he visits his suffering father in the hospital, his father is still nonchalant about everything, even about the immense pain he is suffering and what appears to be his impending death. Gunther thinks that if he overcomes his fears and does something illogical and potentially harmful, his sacrifice might help his father get better. As a result, Gunther asks his boss, of whom he is terrified, to be a backup singer on a doo-wop record. After convincing his boss to do this, he also asks him to flip some pancakes at a restaurant. Following these acts, Gunther's father gets better, but he is as stoic as ever, and the two remain distant in their communications.

Gunther's Father

Gunther's father is struck with an unknown, possibly fatal disease that keeps him in the hospital for weeks. Even this affliction is not enough to change his trademark stoicism.

Mr. Hartman

Hartman is Gunther's boss. He is a man whose calm, steady gaze inspires fear in his employees, including Gunther. Hartman goes along with Gunther's crazy request to sing backup for a fledgling doo-wop band's new single. Against his better judgment, he also agrees to flip some pancakes in a restaurant.

Hartman's Wife

Hartman's wife encourages her husband to go along with Gunther's crazy stunts.

Conrad Jaggers

Conrad Jaggers is a young record company president who meets Gunther in a bar, where he tells him about the "Brazzaville Teen-ager" recording. Gunther convinces Jaggers to include Hartman as one of the backup singers for the record.

Themes

Communication

In the story, Friedman explores the idea of communication in both personal and professional relationships. Gunther's father is very stoic, refusing to open up about how he is really feeling even when he is potentially on his deathbed. When Gunther visits his father in the hospital and asks how he is feeling, his father says simply, "It's no picnic." Gunther knows that his father is in excruciating pain, yet this is all his father says. For Gunther's father, this lack of communication appears to be a lifestyle choice. This is frustrating for Gunther, who wants to communicate with his father but does not know how to ask his father anything other than everyday questions. Gunther's father is not the only person Gunther has trouble communicating with, however. When Gunther is speaking to his boss, he tells his boss about this lifelong communication barrier between Gunther and his father, which also underscores the difficulty that Gunther has communicating with his boss. ''Hell, I've talked more intimately with you, Mr. Hartman, and you know how I've kept my distance in the last eight years.'' The only time in the story that Gunther is able to let his guard down and really communicate with somebody else is when alcohol is involved. He meets Conrad Jaggers at a bar, and they strike up a great, relaxed conversation. When Gunther goes to visit Jaggers in his busy office, the atmosphere is changed, and Gunther realizes that it will be difficult ''to get back on the footing they had so quickly established at the bar, three in the morning, two fellows drifting quickly into a kind of cabaret intimacy.''

Illogic

When Gunther is searching for a way to help his father get better, he seizes on a highly illogical idea. Gunther believes that if he ''were to debase himself, to do something painful beyond belief, the most embarrassing act he could imagine, only then would his dad recover.'' This is not a very rational idea, something that Gunther himself admits to Hartman after he explains his plan, asking ''Can we forget the logic part for just a second?'' Hartman ends up going along with Gunther's absurd plan, which ultimately consists of Hartman performing two acts: singing backup for a doo-wop band and flipping a round of pancakes in a restaurant window. Gunther's illogical beliefs are not just limited to his father's situation. At one point, the narrator notes the following about another one of Gunther's quirks: ''For no special reason, he owned a car in the city and had to pay a huge monthly garage bill for it. To get his money's worth, he took it out for pointless drives at night.''

Fear

Most of the characters in the story appear to have little or no fear, while they inspire fear in Gunther in some way. Gunther's father is depicted as the ultimate tough guy, somebody with a ''lifelong cool'' who does not even express fear over what looks like his upcoming death. He states: ''To tell you the truth, I think I'm finished.'' Gunther is so afraid of his father that, in the hospital, before he asks his father how he is feeling, ''Gunther pulled up a chair, not too close.'' Gunther is afraid to get

Media Adaptations

- Friedman's 1966 short story ''A Change of Plan'' was adapted as a film entitled *The Heartbreak Kid.* The film was directed by Elaine May, featured Charles Grodin and Cybill Shepherd, and was released by Twentieth Century Fox in 1972. It is available on DVD and VHS from Anchor Bay Entertainment.

- Friedman's 1978 collection of essays, *The Lonely Guy's Book of Life,* was adapted as a film entitled *The Lonely Guy.* The film, which was directed by Arthur Hiller, featured Steve Martin, Charles Grodin, Merv Griffin, and Dr. Joyce Brothers. It was released by Universal Studios in 1984 and is available on DVD from Universal and on VHS from Goodtimes Home Video.

- Friedman's novel *Stern* (1962) was adapted as an abridged audiobook by Jewish Contemporary Classics, Inc., in 2000. It is read by Adam Grupper.

close to his father, even when his father is stretched out in an elaborate hospital contraption. In fact, Gunther thinks that if his father knew about the obscene questions Gunther wanted to ask him, ''his father would somehow get out of the contraptions and smack him in the mouth.'' Hartman also appears to have no fears. He bravely sings his part in the doo-wop recording and flips the pancakes without expressing any fear or anxiety over performing these unfamiliar acts. On the other hand, Gunther, like most of Hartman's employees, ''feared the man.'' Gunther comes ''to work an hour early each morning so there would be no chance of a time-clock slipup.'' Even Hartman's ''calm reaction'' after Gunther's absurd request sends ''Gunther into panic.'' While Gunther overcomes his fears of his boss by begging him to fulfill Gunther's illogical request, Gunther never does overcome his fear of his father. In fact, at the end of the story, he attempts to get his father to open up but says only, ''Dad.'' When Gunther's dad turns around ''suddenly as

Topics for Further Study

- Choose one doo-wop or Motown group that was popular in the 1960s and write a short profile about this group.

- In the story, Gunther performs pointless acts to try to save his father, leading some critics to call the story itself meaningless. Find another creative work from any medium that you find meaningless or difficult to understand. Research the history of this work and discuss whether this was the intention of the artist or artists.

- Research how many record singles in each musical category were released during the 1960s and the 1990s. Compare the two time periods on a chart or graph, by category.

- Research any song from the 1960s until now that has capitalized on a war or other military conflict, like the song ''Brazzaville Teen-ager'' does in the story. Research the historical context of this song and create a sample compact-disc-single insert that both advertises the single and gives the historical background of the song.

- In the story, Gunther's father is struck with an unknown disease, which he thinks will be fatal. Research any of the rare or incurable diseases that are known to occur today. Write a short report on this disease, including its history, known symptoms, and any methods that are being used to treat it.

though he had guessed Gunther's dirty thoughts and might throw a decrepit punch,'' Gunther drops his question, afraid to continue.

Style

Black Humor

Friedman himself is credited with coining the term black humor, which has evolved into a genre in which most of his fiction works are categorized. That said, however, most acknowledge that this is an ambiguous genre. Even Friedman refuses to clarify what a black comedy does or should contain. Still, black comedies share at least a few similar characteristics. They generally take place in a modern setting, like the New York setting in the story. The settings of many black comedies also have nightmarish qualities. The only such setting in the story is the African conflict in Brazzaville, which is not given much prominence, at least on the surface. Black comedies often feature frustrated attempts at communication, like Gunther's attempts to speak to

his father in the story. Often, black comedies feature predicaments that are absurd, like Gunther's plan to save his father by having his boss sing backup for a doo-wop band. Finally, they often feature shock endings that contradict readers' expectations. One may wonder what is so comical about these characteristics, which often lead to depressing, or at least cynical, stories. Writers of black comedies expect that their audiences will laugh at the pathetic quality of their characters and the characters' absurd actions, which ultimately tend not to lead to satisfying resolutions.

Antihero

Black comedies also tend to contain antiheroes, protagonists that have widely different, and sometimes opposite, characteristics from those associated with traditional heroes. Traditional heroes are often good, brave, and confident, while antiheroes can be evil, fearful, and neurotic, to name just a few qualities. In Gunther's case, he is not evil, but he is both fearful and neurotic. Despite these characteristics, which may seem inherently negative, some antiheroes can have redeeming qualities that help readers identify with them better. In Gunther's case, however, even his one major redeeming quality is tarnished. Gunther has absurd, illogical beliefs that inspire a reader to mock his pathetic exploits, but at first he appears to be sacrificing himself for the purpose of helping his father recover—a noble act. By the end of the story, readers realize that Gunther's real purpose is to try to get his father to open up to him about the sordid parts of his personal life. "Had he ever stolen anything? ... What about broads? Was Mom the first he'd ever slept with? Had he ever gone to a cathouse?" Gunther is so frustrated at his inability to acquire this private information that he gets mad at his father and does not care anymore about his father's recovery.

Shock Ending

Friedman is known for his endings that deliberately shock readers in one of two ways. Either they illuminate the absurdity of the human condition through Friedman's insightful commentary or they baffle readers through their pointlessness. "Brazzaville Teen-ager" is an example of the latter type. Throughout the story, readers are exposed to Gunther's illogical ideas and actions, which leave little hope that they will do any good in healing his father's inexplicable and probably fatal disease. However, near the end, readers get a surprise when they find out that Gunther's father is recovering: "A week later, Gunther arrived at the hospital to help his father pack." The narrator goes on to describe Gunther's father's improved condition, saying that "color had appeared in his cheeks and he had put on a few pounds." At this point, the reader might expect that Gunther's crazy plan worked and that he and his father are finally going to reconcile. This is where Friedman introduces the shock. The communication barrier still holds between the two men, and Gunther has not gained enough confidence through his illogically brave acts to even try to break through it. The story ends on a baffling note. Gunther helps his father to his apartment, then waits until he is out of earshot before yelling at his father for not acknowledging the sacrifices Gunther had to make to help him get better.

Historical Context

Rock and Roll

In the story, Gunther convinces his boss to be a backup singer for a doo-wop band. In the 1960s,

doo-wop was just one of many popular music styles that dominated the social scene. This pop-music phenomenon began with the introduction of rock and roll in the mid-1950s. Rock and roll had its roots in country music and rhythm and blues, and its first practitioners were African-American vocal groups that incorporated gospel-style harmonies. However, in such a racially segregated culture, most large record companies, owned and operated by whites, initially shunned rock and roll as an African-American fad. This changed with the immense popularity of Elvis Presley, a white singer from Tupelo, Mississippi. Presley's energetic voice, use of many vocal styles, and overt sexuality quickly won over ostensibly repressed white teens—much to the chagrin of parents and religious groups. Since Presley's voice had an African-American quality to it, white fans also started to buy more records by African-American rock-and-roll musicians, and the racial lines of music began to blur.

Doo-Wop

Like most popular music in this era, doo-wop was a combination of styles, in this case rhythm and blues and rock and roll. Doo-wop songs featured a lead singer with a group of backup singers, who made the sounds that gave the music its name. In addition, the lyrics themselves often featured a detailed narrative, telling a story that generally had to do with love. Doo-wop began in the 1950s in urban areas, where many young African-American singers could not afford the musical instruments used in other types of popular music. Doo-wop songs placed the emphasis on vocal harmony, so they required little or no instrumental accompaniment. This cut production costs, which allowed many small record companies to produce doo-wop records.

The Motown Sound

One of the biggest success stories of this era was Motown Records, which was founded in a Detroit basement in 1959 by Berry Gordy, Jr., a professional boxer turned record-store owner. The company eventually grew to become the largest African-American owned company in the United States. The name, "Motown," a shortened version of motor town—after Detroit's nickname, the Motor City—eventually expanded to encompass any song or musical act that embodied the qualities of those at Motown Records. The Motown sound, like doo-wop, generally consisted of a lead singer with a

Compare & Contrast

- **1960s:** Doo-wop and the Motown sound are two African-American musical styles that find acceptance with white American teens.

  Today: A variety of musical styles—including rock, pop, alternative, rap, rhythm and blues, and punk—and performers—including whites, African Americans, and Latin Americans—find acceptance with American teens of all races and ethnicities.

- **1960s:** Large record companies dominate the American recording industry, forcing smaller companies like Motown Records to work harder to assert themselves and make sales.

  Today: The American recording industry is undergoing massive changes, as it tries to deal with the changing face of technology. While the Internet gives record companies and their distributors greater flexibility in selling albums, it also gives private individuals the ability to distribute songs for free to other Internet users, thus threatening large record companies' profits.

- **1960s:** The United States escalates its military involvement in Vietnam in an effort to stop the spread of communism in Asia.

  Today: Following the terrorist attacks on New York City and Washington, D.C., in September 2001, the United States escalates its military involvement in the Middle East in an effort to stop the spread of terrorism.

---

harmonizing backup group. In fact, doo-wop was one of several musical styles incorporated into the Motown sound, which also borrowed from rock and roll, rhythm and blues, gospel, and jazz. Unlike doo-wop, Motown music generally featured a full orchestral accompaniment. Motown achieved success early in the 1960s as a result of Gordy's high standards, connections to talented African-American songwriters like Smokey Robinson, a talented pool of singers such as Stevie Wonder and Marvin Gaye, and Gordy's unerring ability to pick hit songs.

The Beatles and the British Invasion

One of the biggest stories in popular music in the twentieth century was the Beatles, a group of four musicians from Liverpool, England. In 1964, they made their debut in the United States with eleven hit songs—six of which reached number one on the charts—and a film, *A Hard Day's Night.* The music of the Beatles borrowed from the conventions of rhythm and blues to create their unique style of positive, catchy rock and roll. The Beatles' extreme popularity, known as Beatlemania, led the way for other British bands, including the Rolling Stones, in a cultural phenomenon known as the British Invasion.

Critical Overview

Not much has been written specifically about ''Brazzaville Teen-ager.'' In her 2001 entry on Friedman for *Dictionary of Literary Biography,* Brandy Brown Walker notes Gunther's wild attempts to save his father's life, but says that the illogic of Gunther's ''reasoning is typical of Friedman's non-sequitur stories'' and that the story's ending is ''rather anticlimactic and as pointless as the stunts themselves.'' On the other hand, in his 1973 article for *Studies in Short Fiction,* Stuart Lewis takes the story seriously and analyzes Friedman's ritualistic use of the ''doo-wahs'' and 'yeh, yeh, yehs'' as a ''magic chant,'' like those found in traditional rituals.

Despite the lack of specific criticism on the story, it does share characteristics with other Friedman works, so many general critiques apply. For example, in her 1978 entry on Friedman for *Dictionary of Literary Biography,* Karen Rood says the following about Friedman's protagonists: ''As losers who try to cast themselves as movie versions of romantic heroes, they seek the solutions to their problems in dramatic, simple, often physical acts.'' Rood also

The doo-wop sounds of Motown in the 1960s provide the setting for Friedman's "Brazzaville Teen-ager"

notes that "personal relationships within his family are especially sterile. His father is incapable of imparting manly wisdom, talking instead of such simple matters as his daily routine." Likewise, in his 1997 review of *The Collected Short Fiction of Bruce Jay Friedman* for *Studies in Short Fiction,* Sanford Pinsker notes that "Friedman's characters are born losers, as nervous as they are neurotic."

Walker says that *Black Angels,* the collection in which the story first appeared, "exemplifies Friedman's trademark style of black humor, including themes of frustrated human communication and

shock endings that twist reader expectations and thwart any resolution for characters within the story." In his assessment of the collection for the Winter 1966–67 issue of the *Hudson Review,* J. Mitchell Morse praises the work, but not as a literary endeavor. Says Morse: "Friedman doesn't aim high. He fully achieves his low ambition. He isn't satirizing . . . anything . . . he's just being generally contemptuous." Thirty years later, in his 1995 review of *The Collected Short Fiction of Bruce Jay Friedman* for *Booklist,* Brad Hooper also praises Friedman's short stories as popular fiction. Says Hooper: "Readers who feel short stories are too high-flown—too literary, arcane, and serious—will find counterbalance in Friedman." However, David Gates disagrees. In his 1995 review of the collection for *Newsweek,* Gates notes: "The return to print of some of Friedman's best work is a bona fide literary event." Gates sees literary merit in many of the stories, which deal with "shame, anxiety, self-delusion and miscommunication."

Criticism

Ryan D. Poquette

Poquette has a bachelor's degree in English and specializes in writing about literature. In the following essay, Poquette investigates and denounces the general assumption that the static endings of stories like Friedman's are pointless.

Many of Friedman's works have a reputation of being silly, absurd, and sometimes pointless. At first glance, "Brazzaville Teen-ager" seems to lack a point as well. Gunther chooses absurd and self-destructive ways of helping his father get well and healing their relationship. In the end, while his father does get better, they remain as distant as ever, and Gunther ends the story frustrated. As Brandy Brown Walker notes in her entry on Friedman for *Dictionary of Literary Biography:* "The ending . . . is not a triumphant celebration of how irrational behavior that risks sacrificial self-destruction can result in happiness and fulfillment, but rather anticlimactic and as pointless as the stunts themselves." Although not much has been written about this specific story, many critics seem comfortable placing the majority of Friedman's works into one of two categories, both of which use a shock ending that either makes a profound statement or baffles the reader with its pointlessness. While the static ending of "Brazzaville Teen-ager" does seem at first to be pointless, there is a method to Friedman's madness. By examining Friedman's juxtaposition of serious and frivolous ideas and situations, readers can grasp his intended message.

"Brazzaville Teen-ager" is a story told in pairs. Throughout the story, Friedman juxtaposes serious ideas and situations with frivolous counterparts, bouncing back and forth between the two extremes. In the beginning, Gunther notes his long-held romantic notion that the communication barrier between his father would be broken on his father's deathbed. In Gunther's mind, the fantasy plays out like this:

> . . . he and his father would clutch at each other in a sicklied fusion of sweetness and truth, the older man dropping his lifelong cool, finally spilling the beans, telling Gunther what it was all about.

When envisioning this fantasy, one can almost hear the rising swell of a background orchestra, as if this is a climactic scene in a movie. Indeed, as Karen Rood notes of Friedman's protagonists in her entry on the author for *Dictionary of Literary Biography:* "As losers who try to cast themselves as movie versions of romantic heroes, they seek the solutions to their problems in dramatic, simple, often physical acts." However, the next scene cuts through the romance of this fantasy with a gritty, realistic portrait of suffering and potential death. "Two weeks before, the old man had suddenly collapsed into himself, accordion-style, pinching off nerves. Undreamed of pain. A classic new high. He had to be kept stretched out indefinitely." The doctors are unsure what has caused this affliction, but as Gunther's father says: "It's bad, very bad. It's one of those things where they don't know. . . . To tell you the truth, I think I'm finished."

Gunther notes his father's deteriorating condition, and he stops for a moment, reflecting on the seriousness of the situation. He knows that there are practical methods of helping his father recover but is alarmed by his father's swollen knuckles: "there were force-feedings. You could get back the weight. The knuckles were the tip-off, though. Once knuckles got out of hand, you were washed up." Faced with his father's impending death, Gunther forms a plan that he hopes will cure his father. At the same time, as Walker notes, Gunther's ultimate goal seems to be to break the communication barrier between the two men. In any case, like Gunther's romantic deathbed fantasy, this new idea is frivolous. After Gunther leaves the hospital, "the idea came to him that only if he, Gunther, were to debase himself, to do something painful beyond belief, the most embarrassing act he could imagine, only then would his dad recover."

Within this illogical plan, Gunther takes his frivolous notions a step further by picking a trivial vehicle for his plan—a doo-wop song. He feels that if he can get his boss—of whom he is terrified—to sing the background "doo-wah, doo-wahs and the second-chorus yeh, yeh, yehs," he will have tipped the cosmic scale in his father's favor. However, while 1960s doo-wop songs in general tended to be romantic and frivolous, this particular song,

What Do I Read Next?

- Readers of "Brazzaville Teen-ager" might question whether the author intended the story to have a point. For those who like pointless questions, David Borgenicht's *The Little Book of Stupid Questions: 300 Hilarious, Bold, Embarrassing, Personal, and Basically Pointless Queries* (1999) will not disappoint.

- William Boyd's novel *Brazzaville Beach* (1991) tells the story of Hope, a young Englishwoman who seeks solitude on the coast of Africa following traumatic personal and professional experiences. Her professional experiences entailed her work at an animal research center in Africa, in a region that is surrounded by guerrilla war.

- Friedman's novel *A Mother's Kisses* (1964) tells the story of Joseph and his oppressive Jewish mother. The two share an unusually close mother-son relationship, which smothers Joseph and affects his ability to lead an independent life. While Joseph resents his mother at times, he finds it hard to leave the familiarity of their relationship. Unlike "Brazzaville Teen-ager" but consistent with most of Friedman's novels, *A Mother's Kisses* emphasizes the Jewishness of the characters.

- Friedman worked the first part of his career as a journalist, and much of his nonfiction was characterized by the same view of the world as that found in many of his stories. In *Even the Rhinos Were Nymphos: Best Nonfiction* (2000), Friedman offers his unique insight on a wide range of topics, including the film industry, Japan, author Mario Puzo, butlers, and cigars.

"Brazzaville Teen-ager," touches on a very serious topic: "It's about a young boy whose father is a mercenary and gets sent to the Congo." In 1960, six years before Friedman wrote this story, the area that is now known as the Republic of Congo received its independence from its European colonizers. As Martin Gilbert says in his book, *A History of the Twentieth Century,* Vol. 3, *1952–1999:* "The transfer of power was accompanied by violent attacks by units of the Congolese army on Europeans, including rape, and looting." Gilbert notes that in the following years, the situation only got worse: "The struggles for power in the Congo, and the disruption caused by civil war, led to famine on a scale that horrified the United Nations observers sent in to advise."

Yet the fictional song "Brazzaville Teen-ager" does not explore or comment on these horrors. Instead, the song uses the tragic situation only as a platform for launching a plaintive love ballad. While the teenager is with his father in the Congo, he "writes this letter back to his girl in the States, talking about how great it was surfing and holding hands and now here he is in Brazzaville." In *Studies in Short Fiction,* Stuart Lewis notes the song's "commercialization and vulgarization" of this serious conflict. In fact, as Gunther notes to his boss, Hartman: "If this goes, the idea is to come up with an album of teen-agers at the world's trouble spots."

The actual recording of the song also introduces a situation that is both serious and frivolous. Conrad Jaggers is the president of a small but successful record company, which is planning on recording "Brazzaville Teen-ager" a week after Jaggers tells Gunther about it in a bar. The recording industry, then and now, is a highly competitive, cutthroat business, and the choice of singers—even backup singers—is a serious matter. If someone has the wrong type of voice, it can throw off the recording. This is especially true in a doo-wop band, which emphasizes harmony. Despite this fact, Gunther expects Jaggers to let Hartman, an unknown, sing backup, potentially creating a bad recording, just because Jaggers enjoyed talking to Gunther at the bar. This is a frivolous expectation, one that is fulfilled by Jaggers's own frivolous decision-mak-

> " By juxtaposing these two frivolous characters in their respective serious situations, Friedman is noting the effect of 1960s popular culture on young people who have been bombarded by romantic examples of how to solve problematic situations."

ing behavior. Jaggers puts "his head on the table," says "Yogi," and then meditates for thirty seconds before giving his answer. "'Done,' he said. 'Like you say, two guys at a bar, one asks the other a favor. Operate that way and you never go wrong.'"

Even Gunther's expectations of his father touch on both serious and frivolous ideas. Gunther is desperate to have his father open up to him, which is a serious issue of communication, one faced by many parents and their children. However, for the most part, the type of knowledge that Gunther desires is not his dad's serious "philosophy" on life, as Gunther briefly claims in the beginning. Instead, what he really wants to know is extremely private information about his father's life, "stories of extramarital rascality, the straight dope on how much dough he had to the penny, was Mom any good in the hay." In addition to Gunther's desire for this trivial, and in many cases lewd, information, Gunther's anger at his father is also frivolous. At the end of the story, he leaves his father in his apartment, unable to ask the questions he wants to ask. As he is riding the elevator "he pulled the emergency switch and screamed up the shaft, 'You son of a b——, do you know what I had to go through to get you on your g—— feet?'" The fact is, his father does not know, because Gunther has neglected to tell him. Even though Gunther's acts appear absurd to most people and may not have been the reason that his father got better, Gunther's actions do require a sacrifice on his part. Had he told his father about how he conquered his fears, his father might have appreciated his son's heartfelt, if misguided, attempts to save him. However, since Gunther lives

in a romantic world, he does not want to have to tell his father; he just wants his illogical plan to magically work—like it might in a movie.

In the end, the juxtapositions of serious and frivolous ideas and situations and the static ending have a greater purpose than just unsettling the reader; they underscore a trend in 1960s society. Like Gunther, the Brazzaville teenager in the song is unable to free himself from his romantic notions long enough to properly assess the serious situation going on around him. By juxtaposing these two frivolous characters in their respective serious situations, Friedman is noting the effect of 1960s popular culture on young people who have been bombarded by romantic examples of how to solve problematic situations. Says Rood:

> Friedman's protagonists try to deal with the complexities of modern, urban society, not with the full force of their intellectual and emotional powers, but by playing oversimplified roles which the mass media have foisted upon them.

In the 1960s, when the story was written, teenagers had to face many complex and serious issues. These included one of the biggest and most-publicized stories of the decade, the bloody war in Vietnam—which is only hinted at in the story by the struggle in Brazzaville. However, as the ending of the story indicates, those who try to solve these serious problems through frivolous means only end up frustrated. In such situations, there can be no resolution. Thus, the story itself has no resolution.

Source: Ryan D. Poquette, Critical Essay on "Brazzaville Teen-ager," in *Short Stories for Students,* Gale, 2003.

Candyce Norvell

Norvell is an independent educational writer who specializes in English and literature. In this essay, Norvell discusses what sets Friedman's story apart from most contemporary literary fiction.

One of the things that sets Bruce Jay Friedman apart from most of his contemporaries is the richness of his writing. Much current American literary fiction is minimalist, to use a neutral term, or barren, to use a not-so-neutral one. In an article in the July/August 2001 issue of the *Atlantic Monthly,* B. R. Myers wrote what many readers and at least a few critics had been thinking. Myers's article begins:

> Nothing gives me the feeling of having been born several decades too late quite like the modern "literary" bestseller. Give me a time-tested masterpiece or what critics patronizingly call a fun read—*Sister*

Carrie or just plain *Carrie*. Give me anything, in fact, as long as it doesn't have a recent prize jury's seal of approval on the front and a clutch of previous raves on the back. In the bookstore I'll sometimes sample what all the fuss is about, but one glance at the affected prose—''furious dabs of tulips stuttering,'' say, or ''in the dark before the day yet was''—and I'm hightailing it to the friendly black spines of the Penguin Classics.

The article is entitled ''A Reader's Manifesto: An Attack on the Growing Pretentiousness of American Literary Prose,'' and it stirred up so much passionate comment that Myers has since expanded it into a book. In his long article, Myers focuses on five much-ballyhooed authors (Annie Proulx, Cormac McCarthy, Don DeLillo, Paul Auster, and David Guterson) and uses samples of their prose to make a powerful case that the emperors and empresses of contemporary literary fiction have no clothes. (Toni Morrison and Rick Moody also receive disapproving mentions.) A writer who has a story to tell and tells it well, Myers declares, is sure to be labeled an author of mere genre fiction; to earn the rank of literary author, a writer must produce what Myers calls ''self-conscious, writerly prose'' that is not actually about anything.

Fans of Friedman will not be surprised to learn that his name is absent from Myers's list of literary offenders. Unlike Proulx, Guterson, and a host of others, Friedman can be counted on to write stories that are about something; stories that have content and structure, texture and depth. The short story ''Brazzaville Teen-ager'' is a parade example of what sets Friedman apart from—and above—his contemporaries. In less than six and one-half pages, Friedman gives readers more than some writers do in a full-length novel.

''Brazzaville Teen-ager'' is not only about something, it is about something important: the relationship between father and son. More specifically, the story is about a son's desperate attempt to connect with his emotionally distant father. While not all fathers are emotionally distant, virtually all men can relate to the struggle of Gunther, the son in Friedman's story. Nearly every woman knows at least one man like Gunther. Friedman has chosen a subject with universal relevance, and he uses both humor and pathos to remind readers that Gunther's struggle is, at least in some degree, every man's struggle. The title gives the impression that the story is about a young African, but it is not. Gunther lives in New York City. Friedman drops the names of other far-flung locales—Berlin, Nairobi, Vienna— as one way of establishing the universality of his

> **"Gunther's life has revolved around this thing he wants from his father, and only for one fleeting second did the father ever have a slight suspicion of the thing's existence."**

tale. Readers understand that this story could be set in any place where there are sons and fathers.

Having begun with a significant and universal subject, Friedman uses a combination of insight and humor to communicate his perspective on it. Friedman has something specific to say about this subject, another thing that sets him apart from his peers. He does not hold himself or his readers at a distance from his subject. His tone is not arch or condescending or even coolly neutral. He has compassion for Gunther, and he wants his readers to share it. *It is so hard to be a young man desperately trying to pry wisdom and love from a father who stays resolutely shut up inside himself,* Friedman seems to say. *It is hysterically funny, you see, but it is also deeply moving.*

Gunther's attempts to engage his father are absurd, and there is a strong current of hysteria in the story. But, Friedman reports Gunther's ridiculous machinations as if they were the feats of Hercules. Gunther is trying so hard, and the fact that what he is trying to do is absurd does not negate his courage and perseverance. Friedman shows readers both Gunther's fear and his determination to plow ahead in spite of it. When Gunther is on the verge of giving up his quest, Friedman writes:

> At least I came out with it, Gunther thought. . . . His contentment lasted only momentarily and before long, he was stifled, out of breath. Hands other than his seem to sweep the car into a U-turn and out he drove to Westchester.

Friedman's story has a subject. It has a point of view. And, he conveys these in well-crafted prose that is designed to bring readers face to face with both the comedy and the tragedy of life. Friedman uses language in a way that is fresh and inventive but never nonsensical or self-conscious. He wants readers to focus on and understand the story and what it means, and to feel the struggle of his protagonist. Describing Gunther trying to think of a way to save his father, Friedman writes, ''Grimly, he shopped along the noisy streets of his mind. The instant the plan formed, he wanted to tear it from his head.'' This is much, much more than words strung together in an unexpected way. This is both funny and painful, because every reader knows exactly how Gunther feels, and feels for him. What human being has not, at least once, realized that he had to do a certain thing and then wished that he had never realized it? Friedman's interest here is in his character and his readers, not in calling attention to the inscrutable ways in which he can manipulate the English language, and that makes him something of a throwback.

Even the absurd elements of ''Brazzaville Teen-ager'' are profoundly comprehensible. Gunther's mission is absurd; Hartman's two performances—one in the recording studio, the other in the diner—cannot possibly cure Gunther's father. But, readers understand what this means: Any feat that any son accomplishes in an effort to connect with a closed, distant father is an exercise in absurdity, because it is destined to fail. Yet, the effort is not to be despised. Sons will always throw themselves into such doomed missions, risking all, because they must. It is the nature of being a young, male human, and there is nothing to be done about it, any more than a salmon can alter its fate of returning to its birthplace to spawn and die. It is the way of things.

The way of things is painful and sad, but in Friedman's world, the way of things is also funny. This, too, sets him apart. While most of his literary contemporaries find life bleak and unredeemable, Friedman finds it bleak and redeemed by laughter. *Bring on the tragedies,* he seems to say. *Watch me turn them into comedies with a few taps on my keyboard.* And while the rest of the pack often settles its gaze on the worst bits of humanity—from the merely unsavory to the truly disturbing—Friedman prefers to find the hero in even deeply flawed characters.

The hero of ''Brazzaville Teen-ager'' is almost, but not quite, ruled by fear. Friedman does not hide or minimize the fear; readers see it in Gunther's every action and interaction. He is afraid of his father. As he muses about outrageous questions he would like to ask his father, the narrator notes, ''Let him dare to ask one of these; his father would

somehow get out of the contraptions and smack him in the mouth.'' Gunther is afraid of Mr. Hartman, a wealthy, powerful man ''with steady bomber-pilot eyes.'' Everybody is afraid of Hartman, readers learn (''The boss's quiet gaze had sent others in the office writhing into colitis attacks.''), but they can also assume that only Gunther comes to work an hour early every day just in case the time clock should go haywire. Gunther is even afraid of record executive Conrad Jaggers, who seems to be about Gunther's age and with whom Gunther has struck up a friendship in a bar. In the bar, they had been peers, but when he goes to Jaggers's impressive office as part of his mission, ''Gunther momentarily lost his nerve.''

In other hands, Gunther might become a symbol of man's cowardliness and impotence. While Friedman acknowledges the weakness, he does not let it define Gunther. Gunther always loses his nerve, but only momentarily. He always screws up his courage and goes on against all odds, the way most ordinary men get through life. All adults know the horrors that life is capable of; there are twenty-four-hour news stations to keep everyone apprised of the latest of them. Yet, nearly everyone gets out of bed every morning and runs to embrace life anyway. The fact that fear is a constant companion is not what makes ordinary people vile; it is what makes them heroes, according to Friedman. How refreshing.

Given Friedman's ''half full'' approach to humanity, it is not surprising that ''Brazzaville Teen-ager'' has plenty of conflict but no real villain. Gunther's father is his adversary, but he is not a bad man. He tells Gunther that the doctors who are trying to help him are nice. He is convinced that he will die of his illness, but he shows no fear. Of course, his lack of emotion is just what drives Gunther to absurdity, but stoicism is hardly a despicable quality. Gunther's father is not purposely withholding anything from his son. He simply cannot seem to grasp what it is that Gunther wants from him, as Friedman conveys clearly in the story's penultimate scene. Gunther's impossible quest has somehow succeeded. Gunther's father has recovered, and the son is taking the father back to the old man's apartment. Having jerked his father back from the brink of death, having won for himself one last chance to connect with his father on more than a superficial level, Gunther is desperate to initiate a no-holds-barred, man-to-man conversation. He makes a feeble attempt but then tells his father that it is ''nothing.'' ''I thought you wanted something,'' his father says. "For a second there it sounded like it, but what the hell, everyone's wrong sometimes. The top men in the country."

With this comment the comedy and the tragedy of the tale reach a simultaneous crescendo. Gunther and the reader know that Gunther's best opportunity has just passed forever. That is tragic. But both parties also grasp the hilarity of the father's total lack of comprehension. Gunther's life has revolved around this thing he wants from his father, and only for one fleeting second did the father ever have a slight suspicion of the thing's existence. Humans frustrate and hurt each other out of lack of understanding more often than out of meanness.

Even the much-feared Mr. Hartman is a man of some kindness and patience. He says that he has never fired anyone "on the spot," and this is believable. He concludes that Gunther is a lunatic, but not only does he not fire him, he goes along with the lunacy. He does this at least in part to please his wife. In Hartman's case, it is the power the man wields, and not the man himself, that inspires fear. Harman may have "steady bomber-pilot eyes," but he is a teddy bear in executive's clothing.

This, then, is humanity, life, and literature according to Bruce Jay Friedman. Undoubtedly, *Atlantic Monthly* writer B. R. Myers would find it far preferable to the versions offered up by Proulx, McCarthy, DeLillo, Auster, Guterson, et al. He is not the only one.

Source: Candyce Norvell, Critical Essay on "Brazzaville Teen-ager," in *Short Stories for Students,* Gale, 2003.

Max F. Schulz

In the following essay excerpt, Schulz examines symbolism in the psychological relationship between Gunther and his father in "Brazzaville Teen-ager," asserting that Gunther is "risking sacrificial self-destruction as a way of realizing a closer blood union with his father."

Friedman's second collection of short stories, *Black Angels*, appeared in 1966. All but one of its sixteen stories had been published the preceding four years and most showed a marked improvement over those of *Far from the City of Class.* These stories in the second collection neatly divide into fantasy and realism. Friedman is basically a social critic, as indicated by his articles in *Esquire* and *The Saturday Evening Post* on such subjects as Raquel Welch and the definitive chickie, Joe Frazier in his training camp, Adam Clayton Powell on Bimini, the Phila-delphia disc jockey Jerry Blavat at a dance session, and the Chicago detectives Valesares and Sullivan on a homicide case. He continued into the mid-1960's to ignore the stale cold-war horrors of the East-West confrontation, for his compulsions directed him to examine instead our more immediately felt life of platitudes, neuroses, and patented anodynes which he finds too horrible at times to contemplate other than when refracted through the Surrealistic blur of fantasy. Like his novels, the most thoughtful of these short stories have dual psychosocial tracks.

The best of the fantasies is the title story, "Black Angels." Its hero, Stefano, is a harried suburbanite; a free-lance writer of technical manuals, he has moved into a house beyond his means and, like Stern, finds the upkeep of the grounds a cyclical nightmare. On an impulse, desperate to find a gardener cheaper than his present one, Stefano checks the advertisement of a gardener named Please Try Us; and he receives a preposterously low estimate. Tingling with both guilt and glee, Stefano quickly hires Please Try Us, a quartet of stolid Negroes who work in stifling heat "in checkered shirts and heavy pants, two with fedoras impossibly balanced on the backs of their great shaved heads." In the next two months, for ridiculously low fees and for American cheese sandwiches given them by the conscience-stricken Stefano, they clean up the yard, fertilize the beds, shave the lawns, plant new trees, paint the house with four coats, waterproof the basement, clean out the attic, sand and shellac the floors. Stefano's property shines and is now a showplace that slows down passing cars.

At this level of the story, Stefano acts out the wish fulfillment of the suburbanite who teeters anxiously between paycheck and monthly bills. But he has an even more upsetting problem than the height of this lawn: his wife has run away with an assistant director of daytime television and has taken their ten-year-old son with her. Stefano—lonely, unsuccessful in his quest for dates with young girls, weary of "Over 28" dances—is heartsore and in need of friendly counseling, if not psychoanalytic treatment. One night, over a beer, he tells a lot of his troubles to the head Negro gardener, who listens quietly and then stuns Stefano every now and then with an ambiguous, noncommittal question, like "You think you any good?" or "How long she gone?" that jolts him into a healthy re-evaluation of his situation. Pleased with the results, Stefano asks the Negro what he would charge an hour to listen to him a couple of times a week to pose

'Brazzaville Teen-ager,' while evoking the frenzied, hallucinated social scene of the other fantasies, explores the psychosocial trauma of coming of age in America, a thematic preoccupation of Friedman in his novels, his plays, and his many Realistic short stories."

occasionally a haymaker question. The Negro's fee of four hundred dollars floors Stefano, but his need for psychological comfort is so great that he engages the handyman on the spot. The story ends with Stefano's rambles about the similarity between his wife and his mother, while the gardener settles back in a couch, pad and pencil in hand, taking notes like a professional for the remaining minutes of the hour.

The shriek in "Black Angels" at the high price of getting one human being to listen to another is a variation on the recurrent situation in Friedman's fiction of people's confronting one another physically but failing to acknowledge the other's presence orally. This situation acquires sinister overtones, like so many of Roald Dahl's stories, when Friedman portrays his people as ready to take advantage of another's weaknesses only to discover that the chance-in-a-lifetime has a *quid pro quo* rider attached to it. At the same time that "Black Angels" looks squarely at the hidden traumas of suburbia, it glances obliquely at the fraudulent industry which has become rich on suburban ills. Many of the recent fantasies uncover the emotional quicksand that lies beneath the deceptively solid surface of some of our proudest and shabbiest national fixations. The hysteria of the stock market, parodied in "The Investor," is a witty instance of his hallucination version of our world.

Another story, "The Hero," satirizes the public's blind worship of a hero—any hero however grotesque and however imaginary or exploited his

deeds. A boy, who doglike goes for and bites all flying feet as a result of a football head injury, becomes an overnight national hero when he loses his life while clinging with a death's grip to the fleeing heel of an assassin of The Most Important Man in the Territory. The boy's vulgarian aunt (and reluctant guardian) reaps a deluge of gifts, testimonials, and money—both movable and unmovable property, to paraphrase Wemmick in Dicken's *Great Expectations.* A coarse harridan, she is identified in the eyes of the public with her nephew and is soon receiving their accolades as if she had been the hero. She is asked to comment on national and international questions, to address patriotic rallies, and to run for political office.

"The Hero" is a parody of the aftermath of the J. F. Kennedy assassination when the wife of the murdered police officer trying to apprehend Lee Harvey Oswald, reaped over a million dollars from well-meaning citizens as reward for what had been at best a negative or unsuccessful act of heroism. "The Night Boxing Ended" takes a hard look at the covert wish beyond the savage words of mayhem and abuse shouted as advice to boxers from the audience. Warming up, one such heckler at a heavyweight affair graduates from screaming insults about the fighter's nationality, which delights the fight mob, to chanting "KILL THE BASTARD . . . KICK HIS BALLS, PUNCH HIS EYES OUT. KNOCK HIS HEAD OFF, KNOCK HIS HEAD OFF." The instruction the other fighter obligingly follows by blasting his opponent's head into the sixth-row ringside "in the style of a baseball hit off the end of a cracked bat . . . with a certain amount of zip to it." The heckler was heard to say something like "attaboy" as he slumped in his seat.

The final macabre touch of the story is that the whole incident represents for the narrator "no big deal," merely his "saying goodbye, officially, to Uncle Roger." For several years when the narrator was a boy, his uncle had taken him each Friday night to the fights. Then, when his uncle went into a hospital, he telephoned his nephew at the office twice a week. On one of these calls the nephew had been unable to talk at the time. Unfortunately, Uncle Roger "died in less than an hour," never giving "anyone a chance to say goodbye," which worried the narrator for years. Thus, the farewell to boxing becomes symbolically a wake for the uncle, a purging of grief, the ceremonial dismemberment of the scapegoat boxer giving tragic distance not only to public but also to private guilt.

"The Mission" laughs at the fetish with which we lugubriously honor the tradition of supplying the condemned man in Death Row with a last meal of his choice, even if it means chasing half way around the world for the ingredients and for the chef capable of preparing them. In this instance, the condemned man requests "Casserole of Sharpes—grysbok tongue with mushrooms in *béchamel* sauce." "The Mission," however, is not a one-cylindered sketch, with a single theme and a single twist to the narrative; instead, it is another instance of Friedman's mastery of dual-track storytelling. The Death Row context is introduced only in the final paragraph; until then, "The Mission" purports to be a parody of the screenland superman, of the tight-lipped, little-man miracle worker, popularized by Alan Ladd.

Friedman's fascination with show business provides the bases of two other fantasies, one of the best in *Black Angels*, "Brazzaville Teen-ager," and one, "Show Biz Connections," whose central situation had already been used in the earlier story "The Big Six." "Show Biz Connections" is a not too successful attempt to update the fable of the lion and the mouse, or of Aladdin and the genie, into what could almost be the script for a Broadway musical version of how time machines should be used. As reward for pulling a thorn out of a distinguished-looking stranger's foot, Mr. Kreevy, "a shambling, Lincolnesque man," is thrown among women about to die through some disaster. His genie-benefactor thus explains the reward:

> "What I've got for you involves women, and what I've seen of those charming little ways for yours, and those socks you wear, you need this like life itself. . . You appear to them and suddenly they don't mind these cute little ways of yours the way they would if they met you under different circumstances. You're the last man they'll ever have a shot at. Are you getting the picture? You show up, they know it's all over and *bam*, you're all set. As soon as you finish up I whiswk you out of there. *You* don't die, just them."

The inevitable *quid pro quo* interrupts Mr. Kreevy's larks when he wishes to return with one of the ladies, a redheaded actress with dazzling hips. The mysterious gentleman with the thorn in his foot agrees after many threats to bring her back, but the catch is that someone must stay behind to die—and that someone is Mr. Kreevy. As African natives come for him, the oldster and the redhead "twinkle off into the sun"; and the redhead's dazzling hips provide Mr. Kreevy with his last sight on this earth. What piquancy the story has derives from the flavor of the genie-benefactor's language, a "show-biz" patter about the "class operation" that he runs,

which contrasts roguishly with his Edwardian appearance.

"Brazzaville Teen-ager," while evoking the frenzied, hallucinated social scene of the other fantasies, explores the psychosocial trauma of coming of age in America, a thematic preoccupation of Friedman in his novels, his plays, and his many Realistic short stories. The youth Gunther—distressed by the inherent gulf that separates father and son—dreams of a death-bed scene which would unite them. In it, the older man discloses at last, man to man, the answers to all Gunther's prurient questions about his father's sexual life—"Could he still get it up at his age? What about broads. Was Mom the first he'd ever slept with? Had he ever gone to a cathouse? Which way did he like it best, straight or tricky stuff?"—as if sexual confidence was somehow the key to their apartness. During a mysterious collapse of the old man into himself, "accordion-style, pinching off nerves," Gunther grimly conceives the idea that he must "do something painful beyond belief, the most embarrassing act he could imagine"—but only then would his dad recover. He is driven to cadge his boss, whom he deathly fears, into performing wild promotional stunts.

Gunther is, in effect, risking sacrificial self-destruction as a way of realizing a closer blood union with his father. He bullies his employer into supplying the "doo-wah, doo-wah and yeh, yeh, yeh background" at a recording session of Little Sigmund and the Flipouts. The song, "Brazzaville Teen-ager," is about a teen-ager who accompanies his mercenary soldier father to the Congo. Homesick, nostalgically recalling how great it had been surfing and holding hands. In its lyrics and in its association with the high decibel world of hi-fi and discotheque, the song evokes in another dimension, if it does not exactly parallel, the troubled madness and adolescent yearning of Gunther's world.

When his father recovers, Gunther finds that the inalienable gulf between them has not lessened. No confidences ensue. Despite the father's near squeak with death, the two continue to address each other in the inspired language of triviality:

> "Dad," said Gunther.

> "What's that?" the old man said, whirling suddenly as though he had guessed Gunther's dirty thoughts and might throw a decrepit punch.

> "Nothing," said Gunther.

> "I thought you wanted something. For a second there it sounded like it, but what the hell, everyone's wrong sometimes. The top men in the country."

The less explicitly fantastic stories often remind one of the tales of Raold Dahl. The same ill-defined smell of danger, the same distant whiff of the sinister, and the same dimly antagonistic people appear in both men's work. The transformation of the English author's tone and setting into an American voice and milieu is, however, bonafide. Whereas Dahl portrays most frequently the English upper-middle class at home and abroad, Friedman concentrates on the mass-produced product of urban America. Whereas Dahl's characters play for keeps a deadly game of get-the-other-fellow, Friedman's characters try to play the game but never quite succeed. Dahl is attracted to the story possibilities of such gadgetry and special situations as computers, wine tasting, picture restoration, and dog racing; Friedman, while intrigued by such ridiculous occupations as sectional-couch making, shoulder-pad cutting, and the myriad peripheral jobs in show business, is stung into creativity by his contemplation of human obsessions, impulses, and undefined family antagonisms.

Source: Max F. Schulz, "Short Stories," in *Bruce J. Friedman,* Twayne Publishers, 1974, pp. 78–101.

Sources

Friedman, Bruce Jay, "Brazzaville Teen-ager," in *The Collected Short Fiction of Bruce Jay Friedman,* Grove Press, 1997, pp. 9–15.

Gates, David, "The Bruce Is Loose," in *Newsweek,* November 6, 1995, p. 88.

Gilbert, Martin, *A History of the Twentieth Century,* Vol. 3, *1952–1999,* Perennial, 2000, pp. 226–27.

Hooper, Brad, Review of *The Collected Short Fiction of Bruce Jay Friedman,* in *Booklist,* Vol. 92, No. 4, October 15, 1995, p. 384.

Lewis, Stuart, "Myth and Ritual in the Short Fiction of Bruce Jay Friedman," in *Studies in Short Fiction,* Vol. 10, No. 4, Fall 1973, p. 416.

Morse, J. Mitchell, Review of *Black Angels,* in the *Hudson Review,* Vol. 19, No. 4, Winter 1966–1967, pp. 677–78.

Myers, B. R., "A Reader's Manifesto: An Attack on the Growing Pretentiousness of American Literary Prose," in the *Atlantic Monthly,* July–August 2001.

Pinsker, Sanford, Review of *The Collected Short Fiction of Bruce Jay Friedman,* in *Studies in Short Fiction,* Vol. 34, No. 1, Winter 1997, pp. 121–22.

Rood, Karen, "Bruce Jay Friedman," in *Dictionary of Literary Biography,* Vol. 2: *American Novelists Since World War II, First Series,* edited by Jeffrey Helterman, Gale Research, 1978, pp. 157–62.

Walker, Brandy Brown, "Bruce Jay Friedman," in *Dictionary of Literary Biography,* Vol. 244: *American Short-Story Writers Since World War II, Fourth Series,* edited by Patrick Meanor, Gale, 2001, pp. 107–18.

Further Reading

Dudley, William, ed., *The 1960s,* America's Decades series, Greenhaven Press, 2000.
   Like other books in the America's Decades series, this book offers a brief overview of the history and culture of America in a particular ten-year period. The book covers several topics, including popular music, the space race, the Civil Rights movement, and overseas conflicts like the Vietnam War.

George, Nelson, *Where Did Our Love Go?: The Rise and Fall of the Motown Sound,* St. Martin's Press, 1985.
   George gives a comprehensive account of Motown's development, from the sociological factors that ultimately forced Berry Gordy Jr.'s family to move to Detroit, to Gordy's sale of Motown's distribution rights in the 1980s. George draws on several first-person accounts from industry insiders to chronicle Gordy's struggle to launch and sustain Motown, offering plenty of behind-the-scenes anecdotes along the way. The book also includes a comprehensive chart that gives information on Motown's greatest hits.

Gribin, Anthony J., and Matthew M. Schiff, *The Complete Book of Doo-Wop,* 2d ed., Krause Publications, 2000.
   This book provides a detailed history of doo-wop music from the 1950s to the early 1970s. It features definitions, photos, sheet-music covers, prices for the most popular albums, fun facts, anecdotes, and quizzes. This book is a great introduction to the history and culture of doo-wop music.

Schulz, Max F., *Bruce Jay Friedman,* Twayne, 1974.
   Schulz offers an in-depth, critical discussion of the first half of Friedman's life and career, including the period in which he wrote "Brazzaville Teen-ager."

The Conversion of the Jews

Philip Roth's ''The Conversion of the Jews'' was first published in 1959 in his first book, *Goodbye, Columbus, and Five Short Stories*. The book's novella and five short stories offended many Jewish Americans, who quickly lashed out at Roth for his unflattering depictions of Jewish Americans. However, most non-Jewish critics loved the book, and it received a 1960 National Book Award, an impressive achievement for a short-story collection, much less one from a new author. This polarized sentiment about Roth's works has persisted throughout his career, making him both controversial and adored. For critics who like Roth's writing, ''The Conversion of the Jews'' is viewed as a seminal story, which includes themes he has since examined in many other works.

The title of the story is derived from ''To His Coy Mistress,'' a seventeenth-century poem by British poet Andrew Marvell in which the poet refers to the conversion of the Jews that some Christians believe will take place before the Last Judgment. The story was written and takes place in the 1950s, following the Holocaust of World War II, a time in which many Jews immigrated to the United States from Europe. Most Jews embraced assimilation into American culture but still attempted to maintain some degree of cultural solidarity. In the story, Ozzie Freedman, a Jewish teenager, questions the hypocrisy that he witnesses as a result of this solidarity and devotion to Jewish formalism. His rabbi's efforts to suppress Ozzie ultimately lead

Philip Roth

1959

to Ozzie's escape onto the synagogue roof, where he achieves religious freedom by forcing the Jewish community to convert to Christianity. This story can be found in *American Short Story Masterpieces,* which was published by Laurel in 1987.

Author Biography

Roth was born in Newark, New Jersey, on March 19, 1933, into a working-class Jewish family. He attended Rutgers University (1950–1951), then transferred to Bucknell University, where he received his bachelor's degree in English in 1954. He received his master's degree in English from the University of Chicago in 1955; then he briefly joined the United States Army. However, within a year, he was discharged because of a back injury and returned to the University of Chicago. He did two years of doctoral work (1956–1957), working as an instructor at the same time. In 1957, he withdrew from the doctoral program, traveled for a summer in Europe, then moved to New York City. His experiences growing up as a Jewish American in a largely Jewish community have influenced many of his works, including his first work, *Goodbye, Columbus, and Five Short Stories* (1959), which included ''The Conversion of the Jews.'' The book was awarded a National Book Award for fiction in 1960.

Over the next four decades, Roth published more than twenty books, including novels, two autobiographies, and a collection of essays. One book in particular, *Reading Myself and Others* (1975), addresses many of the controversial issues that surround Roth's satirical attacks on Jewish Americans. The book also addresses another controversy surrounding Roth's writing, the fact that he has repeatedly changed his style throughout his career. While most writers with long careers generally hone their writing skills in a certain style of writing, Roth has used a wide range of fiction styles, from tightly plotted novels to wildly experimental fables. In the past ten years, Roth has published six novels, including *Sabbath's Theater* (1995), which won a National Book Award for fiction the same year; *American Pastoral* (1997), which won both a National Book Award for fiction and the Pulitzer Prize for fiction in the same year; and *The Dying Animal* (2001). Roth lives and works in New York.

Plot Summary

''The Conversion of the Jews'' starts with a theological conversation between Ozzie Freedman and his friend, Itzie Lieberman, two Jewish teenagers. Ozzie recounts an argument that he had that day with Rabbi Binder in Hebrew school at their synagogue, or Jewish place of worship. The rabbi had denounced the virgin birth of Jesus as impossible. Ozzie was confused because he had been taught to believe that God was all-powerful, which would mean that He could create a divine birth if He chose. Ozzie pushes the issue, and Rabbi Binder says he needs to speak with Ozzie's mother. This is the third time that Ozzie's widowed mother will have to come speak to the rabbi about Ozzie's religious questions. (The first two times were sparked by Ozzie's rebellion against the belief that Jews are the chosen people.) That night, Ozzie delays telling his mother about his day, waiting patiently while his mother performs her Sabbath candle-lighting ritual. Afterwards, he tells his mother why she needs to go meet with the rabbi the next day, and she slaps his face for the first time in his life.

The next day, during free-discussion time, Ozzie asks his previous question about why God cannot do anything He chooses to do, then he insults the rabbi by attacking his knowledge of God. The rabbi smacks Ozzie's face, giving him a bloody nose. Ozzie curses the rabbi and escapes to the roof of the synagogue. Yakov Blotnik, the old custodian at the synagogue, calls the fire department, thinking that the firemen will get Ozzie off the roof as they once did a cat. The fire engines arrive, drawing a larger crowd in the process. A fireman asks Ozzie if he is going to jump, and Ozzie says he will, and then he runs around to different parts of the roof, making the firemen follow him on the ground with their safety net. The rabbi gets down on his knees and pleads with Ozzie not to jump, while Ozzie's friends tell him to jump. Amid this commotion, Ozzie's mother arrives and pleads with Ozzie not to jump. Ozzie carefully considers whether he should commit suicide. He tells everybody to kneel, and they do, assuming the Gentile, or non-Jewish, posture of prayer. Ozzie makes the rabbi and the assembled crowd say that they believe God can do anything, including making a child without intercourse, and that they believe in Jesus Christ. After this, Ozzie starts to cry, and he makes his mother and the rabbi say that they will not ever hit anybody over religious matters, like they did him. The entire crowd repeats this statement, then Ozzie jumps safely off the roof into the firemen's net.

Characters

Rabbi Marvin Binder

Rabbi Binder is Ozzie's teacher at the Hebrew school who constantly punishes Ozzie for his religious questions, which the rabbi sees as deliberately insolent behavior. The rabbi believes in order and does not like to have his explanations questioned. When Ozzie asks him about the possibility of Jesus Christ's virgin birth, the rabbi says that Jesus was an historical figure, not a divine one. Ozzie says the rabbi knows nothing about God, and Rabbi Binder tries to lightly slap Ozzie on the face, but ends up giving Ozzie a bloody nose. Ozzie curses the rabbi and escapes onto the roof. The rabbi tries to be firm with Ozzie, commanding him to come down off the roof. This does not work and, at several points, it looks like Ozzie is going to fall or jump off the roof to his death. The rabbi falls to his knees, pleading with Ozzie to come down, then crying. At Ozzie's request, he says that he believes God can make a child without intercourse, he believes in Jesus Christ, and he will never hit anybody again over a religious matter.

Yakov Blotnik

Yakov Blotnik is the synagogue's aged custodian, who calls the fire department. He is only interested in whether situations are good or bad for Jews. Ozzie believes that Blotnik's constant praying is meaningless, since Blotnik appears not even to know the meaning of what he is saying anymore.

Mrs. Freedman

Mrs. Freedman is Ozzie Freedman's widowed mother. Mrs. Freedman is a devout Jew and reverently observes Jewish rituals such as the Sabbath. She is distressed that she has to keep going to see Rabbi Binder about Ozzie's behavior and slaps Ozzie's face after he tells her she must do so again. This is the first time that she has slapped Ozzie. When Mrs. Freedman comes to the synagogue for her appointment with the rabbi, she sees Ozzie on the roof and pleads with him not to jump. At Ozzie's

Philip Roth

request, she gets down on her knees and says that she believes God can make a child without intercourse, she believes in Jesus Christ, and she will never hit anybody again over a religious matter.

Oscar Freedman

Oscar Freedman is a thirteen-year-old Jewish boy whose persistent questions about the validity of Judaism eventually lead him to escape the classroom and go onto the synagogue roof. Oscar, known throughout most of the story as Ozzie, is an earnest young man who wants to understand his religion. As a result, he reads the Hebrew book very slowly, trying to comprehend each word, and questions his religion in ways that others do not dare. These actions constantly get Ozzie in trouble with Rabbi Binder, who feels that Ozzie is being deliberately insolent. Ozzie is particularly troubled by the fact that Jews do not acknowledge the possibility of Jesus' divine birth, even though Jews believe that God is all-powerful. Ozzie persists in his question about this issue, and then he says that Rabbi Binder knows nothing about God. The rabbi hits Ozzie, who then curses Rabbi Binder. Ozzie escapes onto the synagogue roof and ignores the rabbi's commands to come down. The fire department comes, and Ozzie makes them move back and forth, shad-

Media Adaptations

- *Goodbye, Columbus, and Five Other Short Stories* was adapted as an unabridged audio file by Audio Literature. It is available on the Web at www.audible.com and features several narrators, including Theodore Bikel and Harlan Ellison.

- *Goodbye, Columbus* was released by Paramount Pictures in 1969 as a feature film entitled *Goodbye Columbus*. The film, which was directed by Larry Peerce, featured Richard Benjamin, Ali MacGraw, and Jack Klugman. It is available on VHS from Paramount Home Video.

owing his movements as he runs from one end of the roof to the other, threatening to jump. While Rabbi Binder pleads with Ozzie to come down safely, Itzie Lieberman and the other children chant for Ozzie to jump and kill himself. Ozzie threatens to commit suicide unless his mother kneels. Then, Ozzie makes the largely Jewish crowd kneel, admit that God can make a child without intercourse, and profess their belief in Jesus Christ. After this mass conversion, Ozzie starts to cry and makes them promise that they will never hit anybody over a religious matter. Finally, he jumps safely into the firemen's net.

Itzie Lieberman

Itzie Lieberman, Ozzie's best friend, initially criticizes Ozzie's outspoken behavior but later encourages Ozzie to jump off the synagogue roof. In class, while Ozzie persists in asking Rabbi Binder about the possibility of Jesus' virgin birth, Itzie is content with making gestures behind the rabbi's back. However, after Ozzie goes up on the synagogue roof, Itzie becomes more outspoken. While the rabbi pleads with Ozzie not to jump, Itzie starts chanting for Ozzie to jump and kill himself, inspiring other children to chant as well.

Ozzie

See Oscar Freedman

Themes

Hypocrisy

Ozzie is a truth-seeker who does not deal well with factual inconsistencies, especially in his religion. He is passionate about Judaism and deeply respectful of its beliefs and rituals. When his mother lights candles on the Sabbath, he picks the ringing phone off the hook but does not answer it; instead, he holds it ''muffled to his chest.'' He does not want anything to disturb his mother's ritual: ''When his mother lit candles Ozzie felt there should be no noise; even breathing, if you could manage it, should be softened.'' However, as much as he strives to be a respectful Jew, he has problems claiming allegiance with any religion that supports hypocrisy—the act of claiming to be something that one is not or believing in something that one knows is not true. Ozzie knows that Jews believe in the all-powerful nature of God. As a result, he is surprised when the Jewish elders to whom he looks for guidance—his mother and his rabbi—fail to acknowledge even the possibility of Jesus' divine birth. Ozzie is even more shocked when his mother and rabbi hit him as a result of his attempts to point out this hypocrisy.

Ozzie sees evidence of this hypocrisy in other areas of the Jewish life. He notices Yakov Blotnik, the seventy-one-year-old custodian, who constantly mumbles prayers to himself that he does not seem to understand. Ozzie believes that it is more important to understand one's prayers than to mouth them ritualistically without understanding. Ozzie follows the same belief when he reads slowly from the Hebrew book in order to increase his comprehension. But doing so gets him in trouble with Rabbi Binder: ''Ozzie said he could read faster but that if he did he was sure not to understand what he was reading.'' However, the rabbi does not care whether Ozzie can understand. As far as the rabbi is concerned, the important thing is that Ozzie follows the rules.

Freedom

When Ozzie asks questions about his religion, he is not trying to be ''deliberately simple-minded and a wise guy,'' as the rabbi assumes. He is earnestly trying to understand his religion. Nevertheless, in his quest for truth, he comes up against a restrictive wall of religious authority, represented mainly by Rabbi Binder. On the surface, the rabbi encourages students to ask him questions. However,

Topics for Further Study

- Christianity has a long history of attempting to convert non-Christians. Jews, on the other hand, do not usually try to convert others to their religion, although converts are generally welcome. Research the steps required to convert to Judaism and create a diagram that depicts these steps. Include relevant artwork, photos, quotes, or other sources that illustrate each of these steps.

- Choose any example from history in which a mass of people was converted to Christianity, either by choice or against their will. Write a short overview of this event, discussing where and when this mass conversion took place, whether the converted people had a choice in their conversion, and what long-term effects the event had.

- Using a standard calendar, plot all of the Christian and Jewish holidays. Write a short description of each holiday, including its history and traditional rituals. Also, discuss the differences between a standard calendar and the Jewish calendar.

- Research the Jewish bar mitzvah ceremony. Imagine being a Jewish boy or girl going through your own bar or bat mitzvah. Write a journal entry that describes what the bar or bat mitzvah is like, using research to support your ideas.

---

the students also witness the rabbi's "soul-battering" of Ozzie after Ozzie tries to question the idea of reading faster at the expense of comprehension. For them, the rabbi's actions speak louder than his words: "Consequently when free-discussion time rolled around none of the students felt too free." The students do not ask any questions, and the silence is filled only with Blotnik's rote, uninspired prayers. This detail underscores the fact that what Rabbi Binder really wants is conformity. Blotnik is an obedient Jew, one who adheres totally to his faith. Roth states: "For Yakov Blotnik life had fractionated itself simply: things were either good-for-the-Jews or no-good-for-the-Jews." When he witnesses Ozzie up on the roof, Blotnik surveys the situation and sees that nobody outside of the synagogue is watching, so "it-wasn't-so-bad-for-the-Jews. But the boy had to come down immediately, before anybody saw." Blotnik is concerned more with his religion's reputation or image than with Ozzie's safety.

However, Ozzie has no intention of coming down from the roof, at least not right away. He escapes to the roof to get away from his rabbi but soon realizes that his position on the roof gives him great power. When Rabbi Binder commands Ozzie to come down, Ozzie can see that the rabbi is bluffing, because he has no way of making Ozzie follow his order. "It was the attitude of a dictator, but one—the eyes confessed all—whose personal valet had spit neatly in his face." When Ozzie realizes that he is in charge, not the rabbi, he starts "to feel the meaning of the word control: he felt Peace and he felt Power." Once Ozzie realizes that the crowd also thinks he is going to kill himself, and the rabbi and his mother do not want him to do so, he gains even more power. He uses the freedom of his newfound power to once again address his question about the possibility of Jesus' virgin birth. This time, he takes it one step further, by forcing the assembled crowd—including the rabbi, his mother, and even Blotnik—to say they believe God can do anything, they believe in the possibility of a virgin birth, and they believe in Jesus. By forcing the crowd to acknowledge his beliefs, Ozzie beats the system of religious authority and achieves the freedom that he has been seeking.

Irreverence

The story raises the issue of what constitutes irreverence, or lack of respect, for one's religion. Characters in the story variously interpret the concept. The rabbi thinks that Ozzie's questions are deliberately disrespectful. He is shocked when Ozzie, frustrated that he is not getting answers, tells him: "You don't know! You don't know anything about God!" He is even more astounded when Ozzie curses him after he smacks Ozzie for this comment. "Ozzie screamed, 'You bastard, you bastard!' and broke for the classroom door." For Rabbi Binder, these are all clear signs of irreverence. As for Ozzie, he does not think his questions are irreverent, since he is asking them out of a genuine desire to understand. However, even Ozzie is surprised that he has cursed his rabbi and wonders whether he is still himself—"For a thirteen-year-old who had just labeled his religious leader a bastard, twice, it was not an improper question." However, upon further examination, Ozzie believes that he is not being irreverent. On the contrary, he feels that, by taking a stand against religious hypocrisy, he is more reverent than his rabbi or any other conformist Jew. In fact, he feels so comfortable with his actions that he briefly considers the possibility of jumping off the roof and dying for his cause. Finally, there is the case of Itzie, who is deliberately irreverent but who practices a passive form of disrespect. Itzie has seen Ozzie's outspoken behavior get him in trouble to the point where Ozzie's mother has to come talk to the rabbi. Itzie, who is irreverent for the thrill of misbehaving not because he has serious issues with his faith, does not think getting in trouble is worth it. "Itzie preferred to keep *his* mother in the kitchen; he settled for behind-the-back subtleties such as gestures, faces, snarls and other less delicate barnyard noises."

Style

Satire

Satire is a form of criticism that makes its point through biting irony and ridicule. Satire can be more effective than direct discussion because satire leaves a lasting image. In the story, Roth's satirical target is Jewish formalism in the 1950s, particularly in Jewish communities like the one depicted in the story. In this community, Jews take to ludicrous and dispassionate extremes the belief that they are God's chosen ones. For example, Ozzie's mother studies a

newspaper article describing a plane crash and only declares the accident a tragedy when she sees that eight of the victims have distinctly Jewish names. Roth satirizes this Jewish community in other ways, too, such as in Rabbi Binder's insistence that Ozzie read fast from the Hebrew book, even though he does not understand the words. Of course, the ultimate satire is the fact that the rabbi, a representative of Jewish religious authority, refuses to acknowledge the possibility of a virgin birth, even though this refusal means denying the fact that his Jewish God is all-powerful.

Imagery

Unlike the Jewish community in the story, which Roth portrays as very closed-minded, Ozzie is an independent thinker who views his world in an expressive way. Nothing is boring for Ozzie. His mind, which depicts even simple acts and situations as vivid images, influences the narration. The imagery in the story is particularly expressive when it applies to Ozzie's religious beliefs. For example, he likes watching his mother perform the ritual of lighting candles: "When his mother lit the candles she would move her two arms slowly towards her, dragging them through the air, as though persuading people whose minds were half made up." Ozzie is enthralled by the spiritual nature of this simple yet meaningful ceremony. The power of this image makes him think that his mother will support his religious inquiry into the possible divine birth of Jesus. Says the narrator, "when she lit candles she looked like . . . a woman who knew momentarily that God could do anything." For this reason, he is crushed when his mother hits him for asking his question in class.

Ozzie thinks he is going to receive an even harsher punishment from the rabbi when he curses him and escapes onto the synagogue's roof. Ozzie locks the trap door and sits on it to prevent the rabbi from coming after him. However, Ozzie is still tied to the traditional Jewish belief that one should never disrespect a rabbi, and so he imagines violent consequences. As the narrator notes, "any instant he was certain that Rabbi Binder's shoulder would fling it open, splintering the wood into shrapnel and catapulting his body into the sky." When this does not happen, Ozzie begins to realize that his religion is not as powerful as he had assumed. Although this gives him a sense of power, it also puts him in a state of confusion, since he does not know where to go for guidance for serious issues such as whether he should die for his religious beliefs. In one of the most expressive images in the story, Ozzie looks to the heavens for answers: "Yearningly, Ozzie wished he could rip open the sky, plunge his hands through, and pull out the sun; and on the sun, like a coin, would be stamped JUMP or DON'T JUMP."

Symbolism

Some of the images in the story also have symbolic meanings. A symbol is a physical object, action, or gesture that represents an abstract concept, without losing its original identity. A symbol can be local, with a meaning that is dependent upon the context of the story. It can also be universal, with a meaning that remains the same regardless of its context. The most prominent examples of local symbols in the story are the last names of Ozzie and the rabbi. Ozzie's last name is "Freedman," which symbolizes his quest for religious freedom, in which his rebellion makes him a freed man. His main opponent is Rabbi "Binder," who constantly tries to restrict Ozzie's religious inquiries and bind him to formal Jewish doctrine.

The story also contains several universal symbols. One that evolves throughout the story is connected to the crowd of Jewish children that gathers on the street outside the synagogue to watch Ozzie on the roof. When Ozzie first observes this crowd, the narrator describes it as follows: "In little jagged starlike clusters his friends stood around Rabbi Binder." Whenever a star is used in conjunction with Jews or Judaism, it usually refers to the Magen of David. This six-pointed star, which is located on the flag of Israel—the world's only Jewish state—is a recognized symbol of Jewish solidarity. When the children form themselves into star-shaped groups around the rabbi, the shape suggests the idea of cultural unity. However, as Ozzie realizes that he has the power to rebel against his religion, the children in the crowd follow his example, starting with Itzie. "Itzie broke off his point of the star and courageously, with the inspiration not of a wise guy but of a disciple, stood alone." The use of the word "disciple," a term generally used to refer to the followers of Jesus in his lifetime, underscores even more the religious significance of Itzie's defiant gesture. As more children follow suit, the star disintegrates, a clear symbol of religious rebellion.

Historical Context

The Attempted Annihilation of the Jews

To understand the historical context of the 1950s, when Roth wrote the story and when the story takes place, one must first look at the mass killing known as the Holocaust. During World War II (1939–1945), the German Nazi regime carried out a plan of genocide known as The Final Solution. The Nazis intended to wipe out European Jewry. They nearly succeeded. Prior to World War II, approximately nine million Jews lived in Europe. Of these, roughly six million Jews, or two-thirds, had died by the war's end.

The Migration of the Jews

Following the defeat of the Nazis, many European Jews could no longer face life in Europe and became part of a mass migration to other countries. In 1948, the Jewish state of Israel, the first Jewish state in nearly two thousand years, was formed in Palestine. Some European Jews chose to migrate to this new Jewish homeland. However, Israel was economically disadvantaged and experienced near-constant hostility from its Arab neighbors, so it was not an attractive choice for many European Jews, who had just been through a war. For those who did not go to Israel, a new opportunity presented itself in the United States. Jews had been living there since its founding, but anti-Semitism was prevalent in the States until and even during World War II. When the gruesome details of the Holocaust came to light, American anti-Semitic feelings dissipated.

The Assimilation of the Jews

Now that Jews were more welcome in the United States, they came in large numbers in the late 1940s and the 1950s, eager to take advantage of American freedom and other opportunities. The Jewish community as a whole, recognizing that Jewish prosperity in the States hinged on the ability to blend in, encouraged assimilation into American culture. The segregation of distinctly Jewish communities, which had been practiced in Europe, was now seen as a barrier to success. The rapid development of U.S. suburbs after World War II helped Jews assimilate rapidly. Except in certain neighborhoods where anti-Semitic tensions still existed, Jews

Compare & Contrast

- **1950s:** Following the Holocaust during World War II, which kills an estimated six million Jews, many European Jews emigrate to other countries such as Israel and the United States. In 1957, due to this migration, the United States attains the world's largest Jewish population.

  Today: The majority of the world's estimated thirteen million Jews live in either the United States, which hosts almost six million Jews, or Israel, which hosts almost five million Jews.

- **1950s:** Most American Jews encourage assimilation with American culture as a way to get ahead and make a better life for themselves.

Today: The biggest problem facing American Jewry is the loss of its Jewish identity as a result of assimilation into American culture. Judaism, like other major religions, is in a state of flux as it attempts to reconcile secular issues with religious traditions.

- **1950s:** Intermarriage is frowned upon, and a mere 6 percent of Jewish marriages are to non-Jews.

  Today: More than 50 percent of all Jewish marriages are to non-Jews.

---

moved next door to non-Jewish neighbors and formed multi-faith friendships.

The Education of the Jews

One area in which Jews, especially children, were rapidly assimilated was in their education. Traditionally, Jews receive extensive education in their faith from both their parents and the community. To help their children fit in as Americans, many Jewish parents sent their children to public schools. As a result, most Jewish children received their Jewish education in Hebrew school, a supplementary schooling that took place in the afternoons after the public schools let out.

Critical Overview

Roth's critical reputation for "The Conversion of the Jews" is the same as for the rest of his works: sharply divided. Sanford Pinsker sums it up best in his 1984 entry on Roth for the *Dictionary of Liter-*

ary Biography: "His readers tend to have strong attachment to one end or the other of the evaluative yardstick, which is to say, people either love his fiction or they hate it. Gray areas are rare indeed." This trend began with Roth's first book, *Goodbye, Columbus, and Five Short Stories.* Much of the Jewish community, critics and readers alike, were shocked and outraged at Roth's negative or unflattering depictions of American Jews. As Pinsker says, the book "made it clear that Roth was a force to be reckoned with." Pinsker also notes that the book "changed the ground rules by which one wrote about American-Jewish life."

Most critics who like Roth's work have also liked "The Conversion of the Jews." Many of them note the story's use of themes that Roth revisits in much of his work. Even those who do not like the story, like Peter L. Cooper, agree that it is one of Roth's seminal works. In his 1991 entry on Roth for *American Writers,* Cooper notes: "Although marred by a simplistic treatment of good and bad, a strained resolution, and a heavy-handed underscoring of 'message,' the story presents issues that pervade the later work." As Judith Paterson Jones and Guinevera A. Nance note in their 1981 book, *Philip Roth,* these issues include "the difficulties of communication in a world in which materialism has replaced spirituality'' and ''representation of the individual in a society that values 'normality' and conformity more than the development of the individual.''

Of course, these are generic themes. Many critics are more specific and note Roth's application of these themes to Jewish life, which has continued to outrage much of the Jewish-American community. However, as Naseeb Shaheen notes in his 1976 article for *Studies in Short Fiction,* this negative criticism has not affected sales. Says Shaheen, ''the fact that his works on Jewish themes have been by far the most successful of all his works indicates where his genius truly lies.'' As Roth has come under repeated fire from the Jewish community, some critics who like Roth's work have explored answers to Jews' questions about why Roth would depict them in such a manner. In his overview of ''The Conversion of the Jews'' in *Reference Guide to Short Fiction,* Steven Goldleaf answers the question, posed by members of the Jewish community, of why Roth would portray Jewish people ''as small-minded bigots who suppress Ozzie's inquiries.'' Goldleaf responds: ''The reason is the same for both Roth's affront and for Ozzie's: because, by restricting free discussion, the community harms itself while claiming to defend itself.''

Likewise, in their 1990 book, *Understanding Philip Roth,* Murray Baumgarten and Barbara Gottfried offer some historical background of actual events in the Jewish community at the time, which support Roth's satirical attacks in the story: ''Like many Jewish communal leaders in the 1950s Rabbi Binder spends the greater part of his energies in separating what is Jewish from what is non-Jewish.'' Shaheen agrees, noting specifically the inability of Rabbi Binder and others in the story to acknowledge the possibility of Jesus' virgin birth. Says Shaheen in 1976, two decades after the story was written: ''The tenacity with which this conviction is held in some Jewish circles is disquieting.''

Criticism

Ryan D. Poquette

Poquette has a bachelor's degree in English and specializes in writing about literature. In the

Jews immigrated to America in large numbers in the 1950s when ''The Conversion of the Jews'' was written and takes place

following essay, Poquette discusses Roth's use of foils and religious imagery.

Ozzie is quickly identified as the moral voice in Philip Roth's ''The Conversion of the Jews.'' He is respectful of Jewish ceremonies, he is quick to point out hypocrisies that he sees committed by his Jewish community, and he refuses to be silenced in his quest for the truth. However, in addition to these noble characteristics, Roth also uses foils and religious imagery to emphasize Ozzie's superior morality and strength of conviction.

A foil is a character who contrasts strongly with another character to make the second character seem more prominent in a specific way. In this story, several characters are deliberately depicted as weak in their morals or religious convictions, which makes Ozzie appear even stronger in these areas. Since these foils are all Jewish, Roth has taken fire from some Jewish readers at their negative portrayal. Says Steven Goldleaf in his overview of the story for the *Reference Guide to Short Fiction:* The

What Do I Read Next?

- Saul Bellow's *The Adventures of Augie March* (1953) concerns the title character, a young Jewish American in a working-class Chicago neighborhood, who is forced to embark upon a number of odd jobs during the Great Depression. Despite all of his negative experiences, Augie fights to remain optimistic and attempts to make sense of the world by seeking a worthwhile fate.

- Since the Holocaust, a number of prominent Catholic and Protestant religious leaders have made public statements expressing remorse at the Christian mistreatment of Jews and have also expressed the desire to recognize the validity of Judaism. *Christianity in Jewish Terms* (2000), a collection of essays by Tikva Frymer-Kensky and more than thirty other Jewish and Christian scholars, opens a dialogue about the similarities and differences between the two faiths.

- The essays in Richard J. Israel's *The Kosher Pig: And Other Curiosities of Modern Jewish Life* (1993) explore the difficulty of adhering to traditional Jewish beliefs and practices in a modern world. Israel explores his many topics with humor and insight and offers such eclectic tips as how to survive a Yom Kippur fast with the least amount of discomfort and how to keep a *yarmulke*—or skullcap—on a bald head.

- In Bernard Malamud's *The Assistant* (1957), Frankie Alpine, an Italian-American street thug, gets a job working for a humble Jewish-American grocer, Morris Bober. Morris cannot modernize his traditional Jewish beliefs, even though his inability to change threatens his family's economic survival. Meanwhile, Frankie falls in love with Morris's daughter and is forced to question his own moral and religious beliefs.

- In Roth's novel *The Ghost Writer* (1979), Nathan Zuckerman is a young Jewish-American author who is in love with the literary classics. Zuckerman's father does not see the value in his son's story, which portrays Jews in a negative fashion, and Zuckerman seeks out his literary idol, E. I. Lonoff, for guidance. During an evening at Lonoff's rural home, Zuckerman explores the complex nature of a writer's moral responsibility to both art and society.

- In *Reading Myself and Others* (1975), Roth collects a number of his previously published articles and essays. These include commentary on his works, his reasons for writing about Jews in ways that are sometimes viewed as disparaging by members of the Jewish community, and various aspects of Roth's life.

---

story "offends its audience by addressing a serious theme in terms of low-comic characters."

Indeed, Ozzie's counterparts in the story are a motley bunch of characters. The rabbi, who is positioned as Ozzie's nemesis, is so bent on denying the legitimacy of the Christian faith that he is willing to deny the legitimacy of his own faith in the process. Judaism advocates the belief in an all-powerful God, one who can do anything. If one applies this belief to the virgin birth of Jesus, as Ozzie does, then Jesus' divine birth would be possible. Yet, the rabbi stubbornly refuses to agree with this logic. This is only the first of many moral paradoxes in the rabbi's ministry. He also gives Ozzie a "soul-battering" for reading from the Hebrew book too slowly. Ozzie tries to explain that "he could read faster but that if he did he was sure not to understand what he was reading." However, the rabbi is not interested in whether Ozzie understands. He only wants him to show progress in his reading speed. Finally, the rabbi outwardly encourages people to discuss any Jewish question with him but makes it clear through examples like Ozzie's punishment that what he really wants is conformity.

Ozzie's friend, Itzie, demonstrates both a lack of religious conviction and a questionable morality.

Ozzie is extremely impressed with the fact that God created heaven and earth in six days, especially God's ability to make light: "the light especially, that's what always gets me, that He could make the light." Itzie, however, does not have Ozzie's degree of reverence. "Itzie's appreciation was honest but unimaginative; it was as though God had just pitched a one-hitter." Itzie's behavior demonstrates that he is childish and mostly interested in creating disorder, which eventually affects his morality. When Ozzie and Itzie start talking about the possibility of Jesus' virgin birth, Itzie is very crass and uses sexual slang: "'To have a baby you gotta get laid,' Itzie theologized. 'Mary hadda get laid.'" Ozzie, on the other hand, is trying to keep the conversation at an academic level and so uses the neutral term "intercourse" instead. Even this inspires a juvenile response in Itzie. "For a moment it appeared that Itzie had put the theological question aside. '[Binder] said that, intercourse?'" The thought makes Itzie smile, and he focuses on the idea of intercourse for the rest of the conversation. Itzie exhibits this same childishness when Ozzie is on the roof, although this time it affects his morality. When Itzie first breaks off from the rabbi, it appears to be a courageous move. He soon proves that he is really only interested in creating disorder, even at the expense of his friend's life. He is the first to tell Ozzie to jump and kill himself, and he incites the rest of the children to try to get Ozzie to jump, too.

Ozzie's mother is another paradoxical character. Although she observes the Sabbath and is stronger in her religious convictions than most of the other foils in the story, she still exhibits some disturbing moral quirks. Ozzie witnesses his mother and grandmother looking through the paper after a plane crash to count the Jewish names. Since his mother finds eight names, "she said the plane crash was a 'tragedy.'" Ozzie is sickened by the thought that the fifty-eight deaths on the plane are not enough to make the crash a tragedy in his mother's mind.

The most comical foil in the story is Yakov Blotnik, the seventy-one-year-old custodian. Yakov is completely clueless about his surroundings, "unaware that it was four o'clock or six o'clock, Monday or Wednesday." Yakov's religious conviction is equally clueless. He is the ultimate example of the effects of blind devotion to doctrine and ritual without understanding. He has been mumbling his Jewish prayers to himself for so many years that Ozzie suspects he has "memorized the prayers and forgotten all about God." Yakov has lost all objectivity outside of his limited sphere of Jewish exist-

> " Roth is turning Ozzie into a Christ figure. Both Christ and Ozzie were born Jews. Both had the utmost reverence for the Jewish God. Both spoke out against religious hypocrisy in the Jewish faith. Both succeeded in converting a number of Jews to Christianity."

ence. For Yakov, the public reputation of the Jews takes precedence over understanding what he is praying about or anything else for that matter, including the physical safety of one of the Jewish community's members. As a result, life events are defined only as whether they are good or bad for Jews. When Ozzie first goes up on the roof, Yakov panics, thinking that if he does not get the boy down, somebody will see and the Jews will look bad. Yakov calls the fire department, like he did in the past to get a cat off the roof. Because he does not think that Ozzie will be any different than the cat, he is befuddled when Ozzie runs around the roof. As Yakov notes to himself: "It wasn't like this with the cat." Instead of worrying about Ozzie's safety, Yakov is still more focused on the potential for bad publicity, since a crowd has gathered to watch the event: "In the excitement no one had paid the crowd much heed, except, of course, Yakov Blotnik, who swung from the doorknob counting heads."

In addition to the foils, Roth also includes a number of descriptions and images that underscore Ozzie's depiction as a superior religious person. When Ozzie tells off his rabbi, he does so in "a loud, toneless sound that had the timbre of something stored inside for about six days." By deliberately choosing six as the number of days for this description, Roth is referring to the six days in which God made heaven and earth, which is mentioned earlier in the story. By associating Ozzie with God in this way, it helps to make Ozzie appear more holy. Other references in the story add to this positive depiction of Ozzie. When the rabbi asks him if he is ready for the rabbi to count to three, Ozzie realizes that a divine change has come over him. "Ozzie nodded his head yes, although he had no intention in the world—the lower one or the celestial one he'd just entered—of coming down even if Rabbi Binder should give him a million." Noting that Ozzie has entered a "celestial" world once again makes him seem holier than everybody else. Another image of his holiness comes at the end of the story, when Ozzie jumps safely off the building, "right into the center of the yellow net that glowed in the evening's edge like an overgrown halo." By giving Ozzie a symbolic halo, Roth elevates Ozzie even higher.

In fact, throughout the story, Roth elevates Ozzie to a higher place than the other characters, physically by placing him on the roof and spiritually by making him seem so holy in comparison to the other characters. In fact, what Roth is doing becomes apparent if one follows this elevation idea along to its natural conclusion: Roth is turning Ozzie into a Christ figure. Both Christ and Ozzie were born Jews. Both had the utmost reverence for the Jewish God. Both spoke out against religious hypocrisy in the Jewish faith. Both succeeded in converting a number of Jews to Christianity. By making Ozzie into a Christ figure, Roth sharpens the edge of his satirical sword even more. Now, he is doing more than just symbolically converting Jews to Christianity. He is doing it through a boy who evokes an image of Christianity's most revered figure, Jesus—the same figure whose divine birth the Jewish characters in the story refuse to acknowledge.

Source: Ryan D. Poquette, Critical Essay on "The Conversion of the Jews," in *Short Stories for Students,* Gale, 2003.

Theoharis C. Theoharis

In the following essay, Theoharis explores Ozzie's questions about and confrontation with Judaism in "The Conversion of the Jews."

The term "other" can express a relation of simple opposition—the reverse, "the other side of the coin," or a relation of simple identity—the additional, "the other penny." Very often, though, the relation presented by the 'other' involves a complex and dynamic fusion of opposition and identity. Literature and philosophy and religion may reasonably be thought of as attempts to disclose the laws by which that fusion works, to make its energy our own. The natural sciences and the humanistic disciplines have long given the name "conversion" to the process by which opposition yields up identity. For centuries the phrase "conversion of the Jews" has been a trope for the pragmatically unlikely, the tragically impossible, the heroically resisted, the idealistically sought for event. Andrew Marvell plays wittily on all these meanings in his carpe diem love lyric "To his Coy Mistress." If the two had "World enough, and Time," the speaker promises gallantly, he would woo her indefinitely while she could, if she "please, refuse/Till the Conversion of the *Jews.*" The complex reversal invoked and forestalled by axiomatic reference to the "conversion of the Jews," is, of course, the acceptance by the Jews of Christ's, and Christianity's claim that Jesus is the fusion raising all oppositions into redemptive identity, that he is God for us and with us, our life, whether we are for him or not, our joy if we are. Two faiths separated by a common dogma, monotheism, Christianity and Judaism are locked in a simple credal opposition—God is One, that One is Three. God is not only the unmultiplied other, but most crucially the unassimilable and unassimilating other for Jews; from Jesus forward, he is another one of us, any one of us, all of us, for Christians. The history of the Jews in Christian times has been a struggle with assimilation. They are the paradigmatic "other," always struggling with the simple and complex meaning of being different, and always bringing Christians to struggle with the same problem. Christians have carried out the struggle violently, almost entirely antagonistically, and mostly unsuccessfully; Jews have prevailed by suffering stubbornly and righteously past the Christian campaign of assimilation through annihilation. Wittily, elegantly, and with elemental humanistic dignity, Philip Roth takes all these matters up in the story of obdurate Ozzie Freedman's unconventionally righteous preparation for his Bar Mitzvah.

Ozzie, like Socrates, confronts the false necessities of his world by persistently exceeding them. As Roth puts it, "What Ozzie wanted to know was always different." During afternoon Hebrew school, which Roth depicts with genially burlesque comedy, Ozzie has wanted to know something different three times. Each desire has ended in the dreaded summons of his mother to the Rabbi's office. The first time he required Rabbi Binder to resolve the contradiction between his instruction that the Jews are God's chosen people and the Declaration of Independence's claim that all men are created equal. When Binder offered a distinction between political and spiritual identities, Ozzie discounted it, insisting that what he wanted to know was something different. The implication Roth makes here is that Ozzie wanted to know why the Rabbi made the incoherent statement to begin with, not how he can get himself out of it, why, in other words, being Jewish can never mean being created equal. The second question is similar: why did his mother single out the eight Jewish deaths in a plane crash as tragic, ignoring the rest. To Binder's inadequate citation of cultural unity, Ozzie responds not only that he wanted to know something different, but when pressed to accept it, blurts out that he wishes all fifty-eight victims had been Jews. Mrs. Freedman is summoned again. The exasperated response again annuls the privilege of Jewish "difference," substituting a comically punitive, absurd compassion, a Marx brother's quip, along with the anger— if they all had been Jews, his cracked logic runs, there would be less of what Ozzie cannot understand and more compassion.

The third connundrum is the worst, and centers on the dividing line of Christianity and Judaism: the human and divine status of Jesus. If God is omnipotent, Ozzie asks, how can Binder claim that he could not father Jesus on Mary without intercourse? Roth makes much of the snickering comedy attending thirteen year-old male inquiry into this subject, as in this exchange: "'Sure its impossible. That stuff's all bull. To have a baby you gotta get laid,' Itzie theologized. 'Mary hadda get laid.'" As the story begins, Ozzie has not yet responded to Binder's evasive restatement that the historicity of Jesus excludes his divine status, except to say again that he wants to know something different. The implied object of inquiry here is how can being Jewish, an identity established in righteous worship of an omnipotent God, require a stiffnecked limitation of that omnipotence. The bulk of the action takes place on Wednesday afternoon, the day his mother has to come and account a third time to Binder for her son's insubordinate recalcitrance. Ozzie has told her why she's been summoned again, and her response, over Sabbath supper, has been to slap his face.

Before she arrives Ozzie and Binder have a blowout, in which Ozzie challenges the Rabbi with the question, "Why can't He make anything He wants to make?," and then assaults him with the rebellious insult "You don't know! You don't know anything about God!" Binder responds with an accidental blow to Ozzie's nose; a nosebleed, and a chase ensue, and the scene ends with Ozzie on the roof of the synagogue, and the other boys, with Binder, on the sidewalk staring up at him. Binder commands Ozzie to descend, unavailingly, at which

> "Ozzie's prophetic compelling of the crowd to confess belief in Jesus Christ is pure bravado, the exuberance of an Alexander in short pants, and certainly not an acceptance on their part or on his of Christian dogma or worship."

point the dotty caretaker of the synagogue calls the fire department to get Ozzie off the roof, because he once got a cat off his roof that way. Going to the roof to flee repudiated and discredited religious instruction, Ozzie starts his real initiation into manhood. Accordingly, he's confused about what he's done, initially. The first question, Is it me up here?, yields quickly to a subtler pair—is the question Is it me on the roof, or Is it me who called Binder a Bastard? The split inquiry presents the split status of the boy straining to become the man in Ozzie, and the division is quickly dispelled once his identity as defier is established by Binder's command that he descend immediately. Establishing him as Ozzie, the command ironically fills him with a feeling of peace and power. The first strain toward adulthood is finished, and the irenic potency it bestows will swell soon into comic resolution of Christian and Jewish theological and cultural difference as Ozzie compels, in his peculiar way, childrens' and adults' submission to his righteousness, his difference.

Enter the firemen. Roth turns the escalating circumstances deftly thematic by having Binder opportunistically respond to the fireman's appropriate but mistaken questions Is the kid nuts, Is he going to jump? with the terrified lie "Yes, Yes, I think so. . .He's been threatening to. . ." Ozzie registers Binder's cowardly fraud, and responds to the matter of fact fireman's challenge . . . jump or don't jump. "But don't waste our time, willya?" by playing with the power incompetent and indifferent adults have just accidentally and formally bestowed on him. The moment is a comic masterpiece, and teasingly ethnic, sounding what Joyce in *Ulysses* calls the Jewish ''accent of the ecstasy of catastrophe'' in a sequence of events that fractures and preserves the formal logic of cause and effect. To torment the Rabbi, impress his friends, lord it over the firemen, and match the new man he's becoming to the boy he still is, Ozzie calls back, ''I'm going to jump.'' He runs back and forth on the roof, feigning to jump from one side and the other, pulling the crowd with him like a puppet-master. A competition then ensues, as Itzie, who's caught on to the anarchic power Ozzie wields, counters Binder's ''Please don't jump,'' with his call for Ozzie to do so, a call taken up by all the other boys. Eventually they reduce Binder to tears, in a triumph of the adolescent will.

Enter, at precisely that moment, the mother. When she asks Binder what Ozzie's doing on the roof, the Rabbi stays mute with humiliated fear and anguish. To her plea that Binder get Ozzie down from the roof and prevent him from accidentally killing himself, the Rabbi pleads impotence, explaining to Mrs. Freedman that Ozzie wants to kill himself to please the boys urging him to do so. The mother finishes the cleric's logic by calling her son down: ''Don't be a martyr, my baby.'' Binder repeats this last plea to Ozzie, and the boys immediately turn the infantilizing parental counsel to their advantage. Following Itzie's lead they all shout out in chorus to their heroic rebel leader to gawhead and ''Be a Martin, be a Martin. . .'' Their ignorance of what they're asking, comically indicated by their changing of the sacred role into a common name, signals that Ozzie's championing of Jesus has reached a new ironic level in the story.

The scene Roth evokes here is from the three temptations Jesus undergoes in the wilderness before he starts his ministry. Matthew 4, 5–7:

> Then the devil taketh him up into the holy city, and setteth him on a pinnacle of the temple, And saith unto him, If thou be the Son of God, cast thyself down: for it is written, He shall give his angels charge concerning thee: and in *their* hands they shall bear thee up, lest at any time thou dash thy foot against a stone. Jesus said unto him, It is written again, Thou shalt not tempt the Lord thy God.

The logic of the story casts Binder as the original tempter here. He put Ozzie onto the pinnacle of the synagogue, and first put the idea of jumping into Ozzie's head. The boys have usurped and transformed that unintended seduction. The Rabbi doesn't want the martyrdom at all, unlike Satan; the boys do, but not exactly for Satan's reason. Unlike the Biblical seducer, they have the

angels immediately at hand, those put upon firemen, and they are boys, and therefore can't belief in death and so don't envision or require any self-destruction in Ozzie's self-aggrandizing leap. The parental figures do, of course, see that death is really possible now, despite the firemen. Here Roth makes his criticism of Christian culture: its worship of martyrdom may too much resemble an incoherent adolescent frenzy delusionally aspiring to utopian and vain rebellion.

And where is Ozzie in all this? He's finally realized how strange the boys' request for him to jump is. The question he now poses to himself is no longer Is it me that counts up here on the roof, but ''Is it us? . . . Is it us?.'' The issue, in other words, is cultural. Ozzie wonders if he can create an order of values for his fellows if he jumps. He asks himself if the singing would turn to dancing at his leap, if the jumping would stop anything in the culture of the parents or the boys. He has a fantasy of plucking a coin from the sun with an inscription do or don't written on it, and then hallucinates that each part of his body is taking a vote, independently of his will, on what he should do. The sum makes the decision for him, but not as he expected. The late afternoon gets suddenly darker, and the voices are subdued by the oncoming night. Ozzie makes his mother, the Rabbi, the boys, the caretaker and the firemen with their net all kneel. In this omnipotent posture he forces Binder to go through a catechism that ends with the Rabbi saying ''God . . . can make a child without intercourse.'' The mother the caretaker and the boys and the firemen are then all forced to make the same confession to Ozzie, who then requires the multitude to confess singly and then in chorus that they believe in Jesus Christ. There is yet a triumph to compel. Ozzie turns an exhausted, weepy voice, his boy's voice which Roth says has the sound of an exhausted bell-wringer's, to his mother, tells her she shouldn't hit him, or anybody ever about God, and when she asks him to come down, makes her promise first that she'll ''never hit anybody about God.'' Although he's only asked the grey-haired madonna (Ozzie's earthly father is teasingly symbolically absent from the story through death) everyone kneeling in the street makes the promise. Roth ends Ozzie's impossible performance this way.

> Once again there was silence.

> ''I can come down now, Mamma,'' the boy on the roof finally said. He turned his head both ways as though checking the traffic lights. ''Now I can come down. . .'' And he did, right into the center of the

yellow net that glowed in the evening's edge like an overgrown halo.

Both senses of "other"—the reverse and the additional—which were invoked at the beginning of this essay play through Ozzie's conversion of the Jews. He has compelled Binder to tell him the different thing he wanted to know, to reverse himself and admit that Jewish exclusiveness cannot bind God. This much is righteousness and converts Jews not to Christianity, but back to the ethos of loving and exemplary obedience to God which their status as "chosen" was meant to secure when it was first announced to Abraham. Ozzie's prophetic compelling of the crowd to confess belief in Jesus Christ is pure bravado, the exuberance of an Alexander in short pants, and certainly not an acceptance on their part or on his of Christian dogma or worship. Indeed the whole scene is a burlesque of both. Roth's comic reduction of salvation through martyrdom makes that much perfectly clear. But something Christian is required by the boy of his people, something Christians have consistently proved to be exemplary failures in, something Christians were told by Jesus himself was the basis of the law and the prophets. In his commandment that no one violate their neighbor for God's sake, Ozzie condenses what Jesus in Mark 12, 29–31 cites to demonstrate his authority as a religious teacher against the scribes, the Binders of his day, who view him as a subversive interloper.

> And Jesus answered him, The first of all the commandments is, Hear, O Israel; The Lord our God in one Lord: And thou shalt love the Lord thy God with all thy heart, and with all thy soul, and with all thy mind, and with all thy strength: this is the first commandment. And the second is like, namely this, Thou shalt love thy neighbour as thyself.

Jesus claims, and Christians believe, that he not only obeys and preaches these commandments, but exemplifies them uniquely by instantiating, in his living presence, the God who set them forth to establish the proper relation of human life to him. God is now no longer the reverse of you, but another one of you, and loving him should be all that more compelling, immediate, and pure. This fusion of otherness as difference and as similarity in the logic of the Incarnation is the conversion Jesus urged on his contemporary Jews. Ozzie also feels himself to be an exemplary instantiation of God's power and peace, and the mixture of delusion and insight on his part may very well be Roth's final word in the story on Christ's mentality. But the ethos of the Incarnation is certainly included in the broken-hearted injunction Ozzie closes the story with. Thou shalt

love thy neighbor as thyself Jesus says is like the first commandment, thou shalt love thy God exclusively and exhaustively. The identification here of exclusive and exhaustive love is the theological basis for the humanism, Christian in one aspect, Jewish in another, of Ozzie's belief, to which he converts the Jews, that "You should never hit anybody about God." Exclusive love of God means exhaustive love of humankind. Exclusive and exhaustive love are two sides of the one Jewish coin, and of the additional Christian coin, and of the coin that is Judeao-Christian. In Ozzie Freedman's glorious tantrum on the pinnacle of a synagogue, Philip Roth comically condenses a strife over Jewish "otherness" that has in many ways defined the Christian world as much as it has the Jewish one. Ozzie is able to turn martyrdom as a resolution of that strife into a boyman's righteous game. Whoever has meditated on the cross might profit much from imagining the look on Ozzie's face as he leaps into the firemen's net that Roth has made this new man's halo.

Source: Theoharis C. Theoharis, "'For with God All Things Are Possible': Philip Roth's 'The Conversion of the Jews,'" in *Journal of the Short Story in English,* No. 32, Spring 1999, pp. 69–75.

Judith Paterson Jones and Guinevera A. Nance

In the following essay excerpt, Jones and Nance explore the struggles of individuals against conformist society in "The Conversion of the Jews" and other stories in Roth's Goodbye, Columbus *collection.*

Goodbye, Columbus contains not only the title piece but also five of Roth's short stories. Among these, "Epstein," "The Conversion of the Jews," and "Eli the Fanatic" are thematically consonant with the novella in their concern with the conflicts associated with love, the family, and the difficulties of communication in a world in which materialism has replaced spirituality. These stories also introduce another theme that will pervade Roth's later books and which exists, submerged, in *Goodbye, Columbus.* This theme emanates from Roth's representation of the individual in a society that values "normality" and conformity more than the development of the individual. In the essay in which he maintains that choosing is the "primary occupation" of protagonists like Neil Klugman and Brenda Patimkin, Roth goes on to make choosing the principal activity of the characters in his short stories as well. He says:

> The soul-battered Ozzie
> is literally driven to
> defiance out of frustration
> when he is forced either to
> deny his own perceptions and
> be 'good' or to deny the
> teachings of religion and
> family and be 'bad.'"

Then there are the central characters in the stories published along with *Goodbye, Columbus,* "Defender of the Faith," "The Conversion of the Jews," "Epstein," "Eli, the Fanatic," and "You Can't Tell a Man by the Song He Sings," each of whom is seen making a conscious, deliberate, even willful choice *beyond* the boundary lines of his life, and just so as to give expression to what in his spirit will not be grimly determined, by others, or even by what he had himself taken to be his own nature.

All the major characters in these short stories, in the process of resisting the dominion of others over their lives, must also resist their own previous acceptance of the roles that the family, society, and the people they love have said they should play. As always, the struggle for the Roth protagonist is complicated by the duality of an enemy that is at the same time internal and external.

Of the three stories, "Epstein" connects most closely to the dual themes of family restraint and the conflict of the individual identity with the social expectations he and those around him have imbibed. A stalwart father and successful first-generation American businessman, Lou Epstein feels at fifty-nine that "everything is being taken away from him." His son Herbie, who was to have been heir to the Epstein Paper Bag Company, is dead of polio; his rosy-complexioned baby Sheila has grown into a pimply, fat socialist who curses him for being a capitalist; and his once beautiful and sexually adventurous wife, Goldie, has become an unappetizing cooking and cleaning machine with pendulous breasts, who smells like Bab-O.

One night, Epstein's discovery of his nephew passionately making love on the living room floor with the girl from across the street, Linda Kaufman,

finally jolts him into realizing the full extent of his impoverishment and leads him to an emotional and sexual involvement with Ida Kaufman, Linda's widowed mother. The result is comedy that borders on the tragic. Epstein develops a rash that he fears indicates syphilis; and in a comic scene in which everyone in the house winds up in Epstein's and Goldie's bedroom, Goldie declares that she wants a divorce. Displaced from his bedroom and from his usual duties as husband and father, Epstein seeks refuge in Ida Kaufman's house, where he has a heart attack. In the final scene, Goldie asserts her prerogative as Lou's wife and rides beside him in the ambulance, urging him to come to his senses and live a normal life.

Like many of the fathers in Roth's fiction, Epstein has accepted fully the responsibilities of citizenship, marriage, and parenthood but has missed out on pleasure. He has lived a sensible, structured life of conformity to the images his culture has taught him. Pleading his case to his nephew, Michael, after he has been banished from his own bedroom, Epstein offers the rationale that has governed his life: "All my life I tried. I swear it, I should drop dead on the spot, if all my life I didn't try to do right, to give my family what I didn't have. . ." The irony of this statement is fully realized in the double meaning of Epstein's attempting to give what he "didn't have." The surface meaning is, of course, that Epstein has tried to provide for his family those material possessions which he had not had. But the submerged implication is that Epstein tried to give his family what he did not have to give. He has tried to give them a self duty-bound to accept the loss of his dreams—to be a "good" father and a "good" husband despite the little he receives in return. The affair with Ida, however, causes him to confront an uncharacteristic side of himself—a side that is passionate and, more significant, adulterous. As Roth points out in one of his essays, Epstein's adultery does not "square with the man's own conception of himself." Having acted in a way contrary to what he had perceived to be his own nature, Epstein sounds like so many of Roth's characters when they exceed the limits of the image that they and others have of them: "I don't even feel any more like Lou Epstein."

If Lou sees his actions as uncharacteristic, his wife regards them as positively aberrant. Ordered, meticulous, and resolute, Goldie is associated repeatedly in the story with cleanliness, restriction, and normality. When she is told by the doctor in the ambulance that Lou can recover if he will forgo trying to act like a boy and live a life normal for sixty, Goldie repeats his message as if it were an incantation: ''You hear the doctor, Lou. All you got to do is live a normal life.'' Much of the pathos of this story turns on the meaning of the normal life. Experiencing it as attrition and restriction, Lou has, for a time, attempted to free himself; but, as Roth says in synopsizing the story, ''in the end, Epstein . . . is caught—caught by his family, and caught and struck down by exhaustion, decay, and disappointment, against all of which he had set out to make a final struggle.'' The extent to which Epstein is caught is evident in the last lines of the story. The doctor assures Goldie that he can cure Epstein's rash ''so it'll never come back,'' and Epstein's grim future is forecast in his words.

''Epstein'' is one of Roth's short stories that has attracted considerable hostility from the Jewish community. It has drawn charges of anti-Semitism against Roth and has been condemned for presenting a negative picture of Jews in America. In defending himself and the story against readers who resent the presentation of an adulterous Jew, Roth reasonably asserts that his interest is principally in the man Epstein, not the Jew, and that his focus on a man who is an adulterer is intended primarily to reveal the condition of the man. That the adulterous man is a Jew seems, in itself, to set up the kind of internal conflict Roth wishes to explore in a character who ''acts counter to what he considers to be his 'best self,' or what others assume it to be, or would like it to be.'' Part of Epstein's sense of his ''best self'' is inextricably tied up with the religious and cultural fact of his being Jewish, with all the attitudes toward marriage, the family, and adultery that socialization implies; and it is with his acting contrary to that image of himself that Roth the fictionist becomes engaged.

This emphasis upon fidelity to ''characterological'' truth rather than moralistic truth leads Roth to make some important distinctions between the apologist and the artist and between moralism and literature. He maintains that it is not the purpose of fiction to ''affirm the principles and beliefs that everybody seems to hold'' but rather to free our feelings from societal restrictions so that we may respond to imaginative experience without the compulsion to judge in the same way that we would in everyday experience, where we might be expected to act on our judgments. ''Ceasing for a while to be upright citizens,'' Roth suggests, ''we drop into another layer of consciousness. And this expansion of moral consciousness, this exploration of moral fantasy, is of considerable value to man and to society.''

In ''The Conversion of the Jews,'' written when Roth was twenty-three, moral fantasy and moral fable are intertwined. As in ''Epstein,'' Roth explores the dilemma of the individual caught by his family and in conflict with the constraints of his immediate environment, but this story is less realistically rooted than ''Epstein.'' Elsewhere, Roth calls it a ''daydream'' and describes it in a way that suggests its fabulous qualities: ''A good boy named Freedman brings to his knees a bad rabbi named Binder (and various other overlords) and then takes wing from the synagogue into the vastness of space.'' On a less mythical level, the story deals with religious myopia, cultural limitation, and power. Ozzie Freedman, a young student in the Hebrew school of Rabbi Binder, comes into conflict with his teacher when the rabbi contends that Jesus was historical but not divine and that a virgin birth defies biological possibility. Building on the logic that God was omnipotent in making what he wished, when he wished, during the six days of the Creation, Ozzie reasons that surely God could ''let a woman have a baby without having intercourse.''

Binder's insistence on a major difference between Judaism and Christianity—that Christ was human but not God—and Ozzie's refusal to deny that God could make anything he chose leads to a physical confrontation in the classroom. For the second time, Ozzie is struck in the face over the issue of God's omnipotence and Christ's divinity. When his mother had learned why he was once again in trouble with the ''authorities,'' she had hit Ozzie across the face ''for the first time in their life together.'' When Rabbi Binder strikes Ozzie, the boy flees to the roof of the building, after calling his teacher a bastard. Amazed at the extent of his defiance, Ozzie Freedman on the roof of the synagogue confronts an unrealized side of his nature and, at the same time, comes to discover the meaning of power. Because the crowd below, which eventually includes the rabbi, his fellow students, his mother, and the fire department, construes Ozzie's taking refuge on the roof as a threat that he will jump, Ozzie turns their fears against them and begins to control the crowd by threatening to jump. Seeing Rabbi Binder on his knees in an unprecedented pose of supplication, Ozzie realizes the full extent of his power and makes everyone kneel in ''the Gentile posture of prayer.'' He begins to catechize the rabbi and then his mother, making them both admit that God can ''make a child without intercourse,'' and, finally, he extracts from everyone in the crowd a verbalization that they believe in Jesus Christ.

Having accomplished at least a ritualistic, if not actual, conversion of the Jews, Ozzie directs his final demand to his mother—a promise that she will never ''hit anybody about God.'' The religious symbolism that pervades the story and the positiveness with which Roth obviously intends to present Ozzie Freedman are accentuated in the concluding line, when Ozzie jumps ''right into the center of the yellow net that glowed in the evening's edge like an overgrown halo.''

On the level at which ''The Conversion of the Jews'' reads like a fable, with Ozzie *Freed*man's personifying the urge for individualistic freedom and Rabbi *Binder* the social and religious constrictions which seek to bind that freedom, the story suggests that defiance is heroic when one's soul is in jeopardy. It also illustrates in a general way, through its focus on the particular constraints imposed by the Jewish community, that the sustaining influences of family and culture are also often the most powerful forces working to inhibit the spiritual and psychological development of the individual. The soul-battered Ozzie is literally driven to defiance out of frustration when he is forced either to deny his own perceptions and be ''good'' or to deny the teachings of religion and family and be ''bad.'' Such a double bind leaves him with no clear-cut options.

Bernard F. Rodgers, Jr., has suggested that a parallel exists between Ozzie's position and that of the young Roth during and after the writing of *Goodbye, Columbus*. He sees ''The Conversion of the Jews'' functioning as

> an effective metaphor for the pressures of the Jewish community which combine with the self-righteousness of its young author to prompt the satiric thrust of *Goodbye, Columbus* itself. Rabbi Binder, Mrs. Freedman, and Yakov Blotnik personify all that Roth was determined to reject in the attitudes of the Jewish environment which had surrounded him for the first eighteen years of his life; and Ozzie Freedman's adolescent revolt against their xenophobia and closed-mindedness, their constant concern for ''what-is-good-for-the-Jews,'' reflects Roth's own artistic revolt.

Although in approaching the story metaphorically Rodgers makes some questionable assumptions about Roth's intention—that he was ''determined'' to reject portions of his early Jewish environment, for example—he appropriately suggests that the piece is grounded in personal experi-

ence. Roth's comments on the story indicate that he wrote from what he knew. He says that it ''reveals at its most innocent stage of development a budding concern with the oppressiveness of family feeling and with the binding ideas of religious exclusiveness which I had experienced firsthand in ordinary American-Jewish life.'' Out of this early personal knowledge of constraint, Roth has proceeded to construct a diversity of fictional worlds in which the characters attempt to work through a dispute over control between themselves and some outside authority; thus ''The Conversion of the Jews'' occupies an important place in Roth's career—as the first indication of a concern that becomes pervasive.

''Eli, the Fanatic'' bridges the predominant themes of ''Epstein'' and ''The Conversion of the Jews'' on the one hand and *Goodbye, Columbus* on the other. It recalls ''Epstein'' in its presentation of an uncertain and somewhat pathetic man in conflict with what he and others around him regard as normal, and it extends the ''what-is-good-for-the-Jews'' attitude of ''The Conversion of the Jews'' in a way that becomes ironic in light of the previous story. It also anticipates Roth's emphasis in *Goodbye, Columbus* on the moral and spiritual vacuousness of the assimilated, suburban Jew whose pursuit of the materialistic American Dream has cut him off from the sustaining aspects of Jewish culture and tradition.

Eli Peck, the ''fanatic'' in this story whose title ironically takes the perspective of those opposed to him, is a successful Jewish lawyer living in the secular suburb of Woodenton (Wooden Town), He and his Jewish friends have been assimilated into the once exclusively gentile community by distinguishing themselves as little as possible from the Gentiles—by seeking to become largely inconspicuous as Jews. They manage successfully to secure a peaceful coexistence out of this compromise until a group of Orthodox Jews—displaced persons from Germany—establish a ''yeshivah'' in the community and disturb the security of the assimilated Jews by being in dress and manner conspicuously Jewish. Particularly offended by one of the emissaries from the school who comes into town dressed in an antiquated black suit and a talmudic hat, whom they refer to as the ''greenie,'' the Americanized Jews hire Eli Peek to use the law in ridding them of these reminders of their own difference from the rest of the community—of their Jewishness. Eli's commission as the spokesman for this Jewish constituency brings him into contact with Leo Tzuref, the director of the yeshivah, and the mysterious greenie; and from that point the story focuses predominantly on Eli Peck's strange involvement with the yeshivah and his progressive identification with the greenie until, finally, he is dressed in the greenie's rabbinical garb and becomes his "Doppel-ganger," or double. At the conclusion of the story, Eli, considered insane by his friends and family, has taken on the characteristics of religions fanaticism that had previously been associated only with the dispossessed Orthodox Jews living on the edge of Woodenton.

The story begins with Eli in conflict with Jewish orthodoxy and ends with him in conflict with modern, assimilated Jewishness. Initially, in speaking for the progressive upper-middle-class Jews of Woodenton, Eli urges Leo Tzuref and his companions to conform to the customs of the community, pointing out that the amity which Jews and Gentiles have established has necessitated that each relinquish "some of their more extreme practices in order not to threaten or offend the other." Ironically, he builds his case for conformity to these remnants of Hitlerian Germany on the notion that if Jews in prewar Europe had been less obviously Jewish—had not given offense to those in power by differentiating themselves from the "norm"—the persecution of the Jews might not have occurred. On the continuum from the "normal" to the "abnormal," the progressive Jews of Woodenton obviously stand in relation to the Orthodox Jews as the Gentiles in restrictive communities have generally stood in relation to assimilated Jews. The Gentiles have required of the Jews that they conform to traditional, normal American practices in order to live peacefully in the community, and these Americanized Jews, in their turn, require of the yeshivah members that they conform to the standards of their segment of the society in order to live satisfactorily with the Jewish community.

Seen from this perspective, the "what-is-good-for-the-Jews" motif of "The Conversion of the Jews" takes on ironic overtones in his story. In both instances, that which is good for the Jews is whatever protects the Jew from the disapproval of the "goyim"—usually inconspicuousness. In "The Conversion of the Jews," Yakov Blotnik is concerned with Ozzie Freeman's making a spectacle of himself on the roof of the synagogue, and in "Eli, the Fanatic," the assimilated Jews are concerned with the traditional Jews' making a spectacle of their religious distinctiveness.

There are significant differences, however, in the way the two stories deal with what may be called "Jewishness." In "The Conversion of the Jews," Ozzie's intellectual progressiveness is at odds with religious exclusiveness, and Roth treats his resistance to the restrictions of Jewish dogma sympathetically. His unwillingness to conform to what others want him to believe, although perhaps not good for the Jews, is represented as being good for him. In "Eli, the Fanatic," Eli's progressive acculturation is initially at odds with religious orthodoxy, and Roth treats his and the Jewish community's antipathy for Jewish exclusiveness, or distinctiveness, unsympathetically. His and his neighbors' insistence that the refugees from the yeshivah conform to their secular way of life, although perhaps good for the Jews, is represented as being insupportably restrictive and ultimately not good for the very sensitive Eli. In his own way, the unstable Eli Peck is as much an identity in flux, seeking to ground itself in an individuality of its own choosing, as the adolescent Ozzie Freedman; and when his compromised modern Jewishness comes up against uncompromising traditional Jewishness, he seems to lose his balance.

Whether Eli actually loses his balance or gains it at last depends entirely upon the perspective one chooses; and Roth has constructed the story deftly so that it supports either conclusion. What the Jewish community and Eli's family regard as insanity, Eli experiences as revelation. And because the story is clearly about identity and the standards that define it as normal or abnormal, the question of how Eli Peck is finally to be regarded is ironically consistent with the principal issue of the story. To call him insane because his behavior is inconsistent with social expectations, or to call him whole because he embraces a severed portion of his past and comes to know who he is, implies something about the perspective of the judge. At the beginning of the story, speaking for legalism and compromise in his initial encounter with Leo Tzuref, Eli is clearly associated with the Americanized Jewish community, which desires to rid itself of an obtrusive reminder of its nonmaterialistic, non-American, immoderate past. Asked by Tzuref to distinguish his position from that of the community, Eli responds, "I am them, they are me, Mr. Tzuref." He is, then, by the standards of his neighbors, sane—normal. But what Eli comes slowly to realize is that he must say of his relationship to the yeshivah the same as he has said of his relationship to the Jewish-American community: "I am them, they are me." As he begins to acknowledge his kinship with the "fanatical" Jews, his neighbors determine that he is insane.

Both the literal and the symbolic indications of Eli's identification with the Orthodox Jews and with Jewish orthodoxy revolve around clothes. Clothing, in fact, is a central metaphor in the two predominant conflicts in the story—the Jewish community's conflict with the yeshivah and Eli's internal conflict between secular and religious Jewishness. The relation of clothing and identity emerges when Tzuref responds to Eli's insistence that the greenie wear modern attire by saying, "The suit the gentleman wears is all he's got." It becomes clear that Tzuref is referring to the rabbi's identity, his connection with his past, and not to his clothes. The clothes are all that he has of what he was. Later, the connection between appearance and identity reaches its culmination when Eli and the greenie exchange clothing. Putting on the discarded clothing that the greenie has left on his doorstep, Eli feels himself transformed into a Jew. When his suburban neighbor, busy with the meaningful task of painting the rocks in her yard pink, tells him that there is a Jew at his door, Eli responds, "That's me." And when he goes up the hill to the yeshivah dressed in the greenie's garb and encounters the greenie clothed in his own best green suit, Eli at first has the notion that he is two people and then that "he was one person wearing two suits." To Eli, the intermingling of the two identities is so complete that for a moment "his hands went out to button down the collar of his shirt that somebody else was wearing." The "Doppel-gänger" motif here indicates that in facing the "fanatic," the rabbinist who stands for the unassimilated Jewish tradition, Eli also confronts a part of himself—that part of his identity represented in his religious and cultural heritage.

When the rabbi, without uttering a word, points down the hill to the town of Woodenton, Eli has a revelation. It is the awareness toward which he has been moving throughout the story—the recognition that he is connected with the Jews of the yeshivah in a way that his fellow American Jews deny. His earlier words, "I am them, they are me," now refer to Old-World Jews rather than modern Jews. Like Moses descending from the mountain with a holy commission, Eli walks down the hill into Woodenton and among those who were his people. For the first time Eli seems to know who he is and to feel that he has the ability to choose. He worries for a moment that he has chosen to be crazy but then decides that it is when a person fails to choose that he is actually crazy. Therefore, he makes a conscious decision to

remain in his rabbinical garb as he goes to the hospital to see his newborn son, whose birth happens to coincide with Eli's spiritual rebirth.

The story ends with the hospital attendants humoring Eli long enough to tear off his jacket and give him a sedating shot that "calmed his soul, but did not touch it down where the blackness had reached." Since Eli has associated blackness with the clothes of the rabbi, and Roth has constructed the story so that clothing stands symbolically for identity, the conclusion implies that the spiritual assimilation Eli has achieved remains untouched by sedation. In the sense that normality in this story means moderation, compromise, and alienation from the religious and cultural past, Eli will never be normal again.

In this story, as in "Epstein" and "The Conversion of the Jews," Roth explores the conflicts between conformity and identity, between the individual and his social environment, and the conflict within the individual as he makes a choice that challenges not only what others would like him to be but also his own sense of his "best self." In the introduction of these themes, the stories in the *Goodbye, Columbus* volume are auguries of the predominant issues to emerge in Roth's novels. Throughout his fiction, Roth is preoccupied with the moral imperatives that a person imposes on himself and their relationship to the dictates of family, culture, and religion. In the absence of heroes of epic proportion, he draws protagonists characteristically modern in the sense that their battleground is the self and their struggles are with the forces that shape, and attempt to impose limitations upon, that identity.

Source: Judith Paterson Jones and Guinevera A. Nance, "Good Girls and Boys Gone Bad," in *Philip Roth,* Frederick Ungar Publishing Co., 1981, pp. 9–86.

Sources

Baumgarten, Murray, and Barbara Gottfried, *Understanding Philip Roth,* University of South Carolina Press, 1990, p. 45.

Cooper, Peter L., "Philip Roth," in *American Writers,* Supplement 3, Vol. 2, Charles Scribner's Sons, 1991, pp. 401–29.

Goldleaf, Steven, "'The Conversion of the Jews': Overview," in *Reference Guide to Short Fiction,* 1st ed., edited by Noelle Watson, St. James Press, 1994.

Jones, Judith Paterson, and Guinevera A. Nance, ''Good Girls and Boys Gone Bad,'' in *Philip Roth,* Frederick Ungar Publishing Company, 1981, pp. 9–85.

Pinsker, Sanford, ''Philip Roth,'' in *Dictionary of Literary Biography,* Vol. 28: *Twentieth-Century American-Jewish Fiction Writers,* edited by Daniel Walden, Gale Research, 1984, pp. 264–75.

Roth, Philip, ''The Conversion of the Jews,'' in *American Short Story Masterpieces,* edited by Raymond Carver and Tom Jenks, Laurel, 1987, pp. 440–55, originally published in *Goodbye, Columbus, and Five Short Stories,* Houghton, 1959.

Shaheen, Naseeb, ''Binder Unbound, or, How Not to Convert the Jews,'' in *Studies in Short Fiction,* Vol. 13, No. 3, Summer 1976, pp. 376–78.

Further Reading

Brodkin, Karen, *How Jews Became White Folks: And What That Says about Race in America,* Rutgers University Press, 1998.

> Brodkin explores her own racial status as a Jewish American and discusses how Jews have shifted from the non-white to the white category in the American social consciousness. She also applies this discussion to the greater issue of how racial-ethnic backgrounds help to define social identities in the United States.

Cooper, Alan, *Philip Roth and the Jews,* State University of New York Press, 1996.

> Cooper examines and dispels the common impression that Roth is either a self-hating Jew or a writer bent on making fun of the Jewish community. Cooper reviews Roth's life and works and compares the author's experiences to the experiences of Jewish Americans in general.

Dershowitz, Alan M., *The Vanishing American Jew: In Search of Jewish Identity for the Next Century,* Little, Brown and Company, 1997.

> Dershowitz says that modern Jewish Americans face a different challenge than previous generations, which fought against an anti-Semitic attitude that has largely disappeared. Instead, today's Jewish Americans, who have been widely assimilated into American culture, stand to lose their Jewish identity through the increase in intermarriage and the lapse of Jewish practices. Dershowitz proposes some steps to ensure that a permanent loss of identity does not happen.

Heilman, Samuel C., *Portrait of American Jews: The Last Half of the Twentieth Century,* University of Washington Press, 1995.

> Heilman draws from his dual background as sociologist and Jewish Studies professor to demonstrate the sociological changes that have taken place in the Jewish-American community since the 1950s.

Robinson, George, *Essential Judaism: A Complete Guide to Beliefs, Customs, and Rituals,* Pocket Books, 2000.

> Robinson offers an up-to-date, one-volume overview of Jewish practices and beliefs. Written in an accessible style, the book includes several sidebars that highlight specific aspects of Judaism, answer the most commonly asked questions, and explore current controversies.

The Far and the Near

Thomas Wolfe

1935

Thomas Wolfe's short story "The Far and the Near" was first published in *Cosmopolitan* magazine in 1935 and was reprinted later that year in Wolfe's first short-story collection, *From Death to Morning*. For a writer known by his long, sprawling novels such as *Look Homeward, Angel: A Story of the Buried Life* and *Of Time and the River*, this ultra-short short story is a rare occurrence. While Wolfe's novels have often fallen under criticism for their excessive autobiographical sources, the influence of their editors, and Wolfe's wordy style, many critics in the last half of the twentieth century began to praise Wolfe for his short fiction. "The Far and the Near" details the story of a railroad engineer in the 1930s who passes a certain cottage every day for more than twenty years, waving to the women who live there but never actually meeting them or seeing them up close. Upon his retirement, he goes to see the women, but they treat him badly and destroy the idyllic vision that he has built up around them. Within its few pages, Wolfe's short story emphasizes the potentially devastating effects on a person who is forced to confront the reality behind a vision. Since the work was written during the Great Depression, the loss of hope that takes place in the story would have been extremely familiar to Wolfe's audience. The story can be found in the paperback edition of *The Complete Short Stories of Thomas Wolfe*, which was published by Collier Books in 1989.

Author Biography

Thomas Wolfe was born on October 3, 1900, in Asheville, North Carolina, a resort community. Wolfe was a good student at the local elementary school, and in 1912 he was sent to a private school. At the ripe age of fifteen, he entered the University of North Carolina at Chapel Hill. In 1919, one of Wolfe's plays, *The Return of Buck Gavin: The Tragedy of a Mountain Outlaw*, was staged by the Carolina Playmakers, with Wolfe playing the lead role. Wolfe graduated in 1920, and, emboldened by his initial success in the theater, he entered Harvard University the same year, where he studied playwriting.

In 1922, Wolfe graduated from Harvard with his master's degree, although he remained in Cambridge, Massachusetts, writing plays and unsuccessfully trying to sell them. In 1924, he started teaching English at Washington Square College of New York University, a position that he held on and off until 1930. In 1924, he also traveled to Europe, returning the next year. On his voyage home, he met Aline Bernstein, a married woman nineteen years his senior, with whom he started a long affair. The two stayed together in England during Wolfe's 1926 trip and shared a New York apartment when they both returned to the United States. His first novel, *Look Homeward, Angel: A Story of the Buried Life*, was published in 1929. For this first publication, Wolfe and Maxwell Perkins, an editor at Charles Scribner's Sons, worked closely together. In 1930, Wolfe gave up his teaching post, ended his affair with Mrs. Bernstein, and traveled to Europe again. In 1935, he published his second novel, *Of Time and the River: A Legend of Man's Hunger in His Youth*. The same year, he published his first short-story collection, *From Death to Morning*, which included the story "The Far and the Near."

In 1935, Wolfe published *The Story of a Novel*, an essay detailing his writing methods and theories. In a review of the essay, Bernard DeVoto attacked all of Wolfe's work, stating that Wolfe depended upon the heavy editing of Perkins. As a result, Wolfe eventually left Scribner's, signing with Harper's in 1937. However, he was unable to publish any more works before he died of tubercular meningitis in Baltimore, Maryland, on September 15, 1938. Following his death, Wolfe's editor at Harper's, Edward C. Aswell, set about creating distinct volumes out of the massive amount of manuscripts, notes, and outlines that Wolfe had left with him. From this assortment, Aswell created several works,

Thomas Wolfe

including two novels—*The Web and the Rock* (1939) and *You Can't Go Home Again* (1940)—and a short story collection, *The Hills Beyond* (1941). In 2001, the original, unedited manuscript (according to its editors) of *Look Homeward, Angel: A Story of the Buried Life* was published as *O Lost: The Story of the Buried Life*.

Plot Summary

Wolfe's "The Far and the Near" starts out with a description of a little town, which contains a small cottage on its outskirts. The cottage appears clean and comfortable. Every day, just after two o'clock in the afternoon, an express train passes by the house. For more than twenty years, the train engineer blows his whistle, prompting a woman inside the house to come out on her porch and wave to him. Over this time, the woman's little girl grows up, and she joins her mother in waving to the engineer. The engineer grows old during this time and sees a lot of tragedy during his service for the railroad, including four fatal accidents on the tracks in front of him. Throughout all of this tragedy, however, he remains focused on the vision of the cottage and the two women, an image that he thinks is beautiful and unchangeable. He has a father's love towards the two women and, after so many thousands of trips past their cottage, feels that he knows the women's lives completely.

As a result, he resolves to visit the women on the day he retires, to tell them what a profound effect they have had on his life. When that day comes, he walks from the train station into the small town. As he walks through the town, he is unsure of his decision, because the town seems so unfamiliar—much different from how it has looked from his train cab. When he gets to the women's cottage, he is even more unsure, but he decides to go through with it. When he meets the woman, she is instantly suspicious of him, and the train engineer is sorry that he has come. The woman whom he has idealized all of those years appears different, and her harsh voice is not what he expected. He explains who he is and why he has come, and the woman reluctantly invites him inside and calls for her daughter. The engineer sits down with both women in an ugly parlor and awkwardly talks to them while they fix him with hostile looks. Finally, the engineer leaves, and he is shaken from his experience. He is distraught because the one aspect of his life that he thought was pure and beautiful is stained. With this revelation, he realizes that he has lost all hope and that he will never be able to see the good in life again.

Characters

The Train Engineer

The train engineer is the protagonist of the story, whose idealistic vision is shattered when he sees the reality behind it. Every day for twenty years, the engineer's express train passes a cottage on the outskirts of a little town. Each time, he blows the train's whistle, and the woman in the cottage comes out and waves at him. As the years pass, he watches her little girl grow into a woman, who joins her mother to wave at the engineer. He has never met either of the women but feels he knows all about them and their lives. In fact, the beauty of his vision of the women is so strong that he relies on it to get him through hard times—including the four fatal accidents he witnesses when people get stuck on the train tracks in front of him. He resolves to go visit the women when he retires, to tell them about the impact they have had on his life. However, when he goes to do this, it is not the idealistic trip that he had

envisioned. The town is unfamiliar, and the women are hostile and suspicious, even when he explains who he is. In addition, the women look different—older and more haggard—than how they appeared from the engineer's train cab. Still, he forges ahead, and by the time he leaves the women, he is shocked and disappointed and has lost his hope and his ability to see the good in life.

The Woman in the Cottage

The woman in the cottage waves to the train engineer every day for twenty years but is very hostile to him when he comes to visit her. Although she is comfortable with waving to the engineer when there is a safe distance between them, she is suspicious of him when he comes to her cottage. As a result, she and her daughter—who has grown up with the daily waving ritual—are on guard against the engineer, and the conversation is awkward. Her unexpected hostility shatters the engineer's idealistic vision.

The Woman's Daughter

The woman's daughter grows up in the cottage by the railroad tracks, where she joins her mother in the daily waving ritual to the train engineer. When the engineer sits down to talk to the two women, the daughter is as guarded and suspicious as her mother.

Themes

Appearances

For more than twenty years, the engineer blows his train whistle every day as he passes the cottage, and ''every day, as soon as she heard this signal, a woman had appeared on the back porch of the little house and waved to him.'' Although he has seen the woman—and later the two women—do this from afar, the engineer nevertheless allows his mind to fill in the gaps about how the women might appear up close. In his mind, he crafts these assumptions about the women's appearance into an idealistic vision, in which he feels very connected to them. The narrator reports, ''He felt for them and for the little house in which they lived such tenderness as a man might feel for his own children.'' As the years pass, this vision builds in strength, until the engineer feels that he knows "their lives completely, to every hour and moment of the day." However, when he meets the women face to face, his vision is shattered. The reality is that, even though the two women have waved to him from afar, up close they are suspicious and fearful of him. Also, while he has imagined their beauty, when he comes face to face with the woman who owns the cottage, he sees that her face is "harsh and pinched and meager," and her flesh sags "wearily in sallow folds." When the engineer finally leaves the house of the two women, he realizes as he is walking away that he has allowed himself to be fooled by a distant appearance. Now, he can see "the strange and unsuspected visage of the earth which had always been within a stone's throw of him, and which he had never seen or known."

Happiness

While he is under the spell of his false vision, the engineer is truly happy: "The sight of the little house and of these two women gave him the most extraordinary happiness he had ever known." When he prepares to go visit the two women, he is even more happy, because he will finally be able to tell them how their "lives had been so wrought into his own." In turn, he thinks they will be happy to see him and that they will welcome him as a friend. While he is working as a train engineer, he never has the opportunity to go and visit the women, and so the ultimate realization of his vision—meeting the women—remains a goal. While this goal is not met and he still has the desire to go see them, he is happy. However, once he leaves the safety of the train and its distance from the women, his happiness is quickly undermined. He is overcome by a "sense of bewilderment and confusion" as he walks through the town. Nothing lives up to his idealistic vision, and his happiness diminishes with each disappointment, from his confusing journey through the town to the hostile treatment by the two women.

Regret

Although the engineer is confused when he walks through the town, he pushes on, thinking that the situation will improve when he gets to the cottage. However, the engineer starts to regret his journey as soon as the woman in the cottage opens the door: "And instantly, with a sense of bitter loss and grief, he was sorry he had come." Still, the engineer tries to talk to the women, determined to overcome "the horror of regret, confusion, disbelief

Media Adaptations

- Wolfe's *From Death to Morning,* which includes "The Far and the Near," was adapted as an unabridged audiobook in 1997. It is available from Books on Tape, Inc.

- Wolfe's *Look Homeward, Angel: A Story of the Buried Life* was adapted as an audiobook in 1995 under the title *Look Homeward, Angel.* It is available in two parts from Books on Tape, Inc.

- Wolfe's *Of Time and the River: A Legend of Man's Hunger in His Youth* was adapted as an audiobook in 1996 under the title *Of Time and the River.* It is available in two parts from Books on Tape, Inc.

that surged up in his spirit." After he leaves the cottage, this sense of regret has physical effects, as the man suddenly loses his strength—which his vision provided him—and realizes that he is old and frail. "His heart, which had been brave and confident when it looked along the familiar vista of the rails, was now sick with doubt and horror." Even more crushing is the realization that his vision has been a lie and that his former happiness is gone forever. He knows "that all the magic of that bright lost way, the vista of that shining line, the imagined corner of that small good universe of hope's desire, could never be got again."

Style

Mood

For roughly the first half of the story, Wolfe paints an idealistic picture of a railroad engineer who has built up a silent relationship with two women. The reader is led to believe that this is going to be a positive story, since even negative events like the deaths the engineer has witnessed are tem-

Topics for Further Study

- Research the various documentation that explores how Wolfe and his editors created his books and stories. Find another author—from any point in history—who has been accused of having overzealous editors and compare this author's life to Wolfe's life.

- Research the various railroads that were operational in the 1930s. Plot all of these railway lines on a map of the United States. For each railway line, use photos, illustrations, or any other form of visual representation to depict the types of trains that were run on each line. Also, provide a short description for each railroad, which details what its primary use was and how the Great Depression affected its business.

- Research the history of the toy train industry and discuss how it began. Compare the decline in the use of railroads to sales figures for their toy equivalent and discuss any apparent trends. Then, write a short report on the state of the toy-train industry today.

- In the story, the engineer witnesses several deaths on the railroad tracks during his many years of service, although he is initially able to cope with them through his optimism. Research the psychology of death and dying and discuss at least two coping mechanisms that people may use after they have witnessed a violent death.

pered by his idyllic vision. However, a little more than halfway through, the mood. or emotional quality of the story, starts to change: ''Everything was as strange to him as if he had never seen this town before.'' From this point on, the reader's awareness of the changing mood increases as the engineer's ''perplexity of . . . spirit'' increases. When the engineer gets to the cottage and sees the woman's face, he—along with the reader—realizes that his idyllic vision is a lie. As the story progresses to its negative ending, the reader empathizes with the engineer's feelings of regret, sadness, and disappointment.

Setting

The physical setting is extremely important in this story. The setting is established with the first line: ''On the outskirts of a little town upon a rise of land that swept back from the railway there was a tidy little cottage.'' The cottage is located by the tracks, but it is ''swept back from the railway.'' This distance shields the engineer from the reality of the two women's appearance and thus becomes the means by which his mind creates the idyllic vision. If the cottage were located close to the tracks, the engineer would see the true appearance of the

women. Also, the distance serves as a safety buffer for the two women. The women are comfortable waving to the engineer when he is far away but are suspicious of him when he is up close. If the setting were slightly different and their cottage were located close to the train, the two women might not have felt comfortable waving to the engineer. On a similar note, the cottage is located at a bend in the tracks, where each day, the train ''swept past with a powerful swaying motion of the engine, a low smooth rumble of its heavy cars upon pressed steel, and then it vanished into the cut.'' During this brief time, the engineer and the women only have a few moments to view each other. Just like the distance factor, the time factor plays a part in helping to build the engineer's vision. If he had had more time to observe the women as he passed by, he might have a more accurate picture of the two women, which would also decrease his chances of blindly following a self-made illusion.

Another aspect of the setting, the cottage's distance from the train station, is important in the story. The cottage is ''on the outskirts'' of town, while the train station is located in town. As a result, on the day he retires and gets off at the train station, he must walk through the town to reach the cottage. As noted above, it is during this walk that the engineer gets an increasing sense of apprehension. If the cottage were located close to the train station, the engineer would not have to walk as far, and Wolfe would not have the time he needs in the story to slowly build the negative mood.

One last aspect of the setting deserves mention. The town is located either in a northern or a mountainous region, since the narrator talks about the "wintry gray across the brown and frosted stubble of the earth." The fact that the town experiences seasons is important to the engineer's perception of the women because he has "seen them in a thousand lights, a hundred weathers," and thinks that this diversity gives him a greater understanding of their lives. Since they appear the same in his idyllic vision, no matter what the weather conditions, it becomes proof to his mind that they must be as he imagines them.

Tragedy

In his many years working for the railroad, the engineer witnesses several tragedies, including four fatal accidents. "He had known all the grief . . . the peril, and the labor such a man could know." However, despite all of this tragedy, the engineer maintains his happiness and his optimistic view of life, as a result of "the vision of the little house and the women waving to him." The vision becomes a coping strategy by which the engineer is able to look past the tragedy. He sees the women as the one aspect of his life that is "beautiful and enduring, something beyond all change." Unfortunately, the engineer's determination to realize this vision proves to be his tragic flaw—the personal quality that leads to his downfall. The engineer is sure that his vision will play out exactly as he imagines it. When he gets to the town, it is unfamiliar and strange, but he pushes on nevertheless, determined to see the two women. Had the engineer given up on his goal to see the women once the town failed to live up to his vision, he would have preserved his fond memory of the women through blissful ignorance. He does not back down from this resolve, however, even when the gate to the cottage appears unfamiliar, the woman opens the door and the engineer is obviously unwelcome, and the two women sit "bewildered" while he talks. At any point, he could have left and tried to salvage some of his memories, or at least his dignity. Instead, by "fighting stubbornly" against his apprehensive feelings, "his act of hope and tenderness" ultimately feels like a shameful one, and at the end of the story, he must live with the tragedy of tainted memories and a failed dream.

Historical Context

Following a revitalization that had taken place in the economic good times of the 1920s, the railroads were well equipped to handle the 1930s—or so they thought. Unfortunately, several factors led to the bankrupting of many railroad companies. Chief among these factors was the severe national economic downturn that the country experienced in the 1930s, called the Great Depression. Although the exact causes of this economic catastrophe are still debated, most historians give at least some blame to the stock market crash of 1929. The Great Depression bankrupted many individuals and sent the unemployment rate skyrocketing to a high of more than 23 percent. Hunger and poverty became common in many areas of the country. Some families who lived by railroad tracks were so desperate that they sent their children to search for dropped coal from passing trains so that they could heat their homes and operate their cooking appliances. As widespread panic and despair gripped the nation, the suicide rate rose, and millions of families migrated to other areas of the country, only to find that those areas were just as bad—if not worse. Dislocated families set up makeshift shelters on vacant lots in cities and towns. These collections of makeshift dwellings became known as Hoovervilles, after President Hoover, whom many blamed for the Depression.

Businesses were affected, too, including the railroad industry. Railroad traffic—both freight and passenger—plummeted, and many railroads went out of business. When they did, their rail lines were often taken over by other railroad companies that were more financially stable. However, even these companies faced many challenges. As the decade progressed, railroads faced increasing competition from other transportation industries, including automobiles, trucks, buses, and airplanes. Collectively, these industries threatened both freight and passenger transportation on railroads. To make matters worse, many of these industries were supported by government funds and were not burdened by heavy regulations, while the railroads were privately owned and still heavily regulated—a side effect of earlier

Compare & Contrast

- **1930s:** The United States is in the midst of the Great Depression. The unemployment rate reaches more than 23 percent, and poverty and hunger are common in many areas.

  Today: The United States is in the midst of an economic downturn. The unemployment rate rises from a thirty-two-year low of 4 percent in 2000 to hover in the 5 to 6 percent range in 2002.

- **1930s:** Following the widespread adoption of trucks in the United States in the 1920s, the railroads lose business on their freight trains.

  Today: Although the railroads' percentage of domestic freight traffic has decreased at a relatively steady rate since World War II, their higher percentage of freight traffic than trucks has been maintained.

- **1930s:** During the Great Depression, many railroads fall into bankruptcy. Those that survive do so in part because of their adoption of new technologies, such as the diesel locomotive, which help make the trains faster and more efficient.

  Today: In the United States, subways and passenger trains are popular options for daily commuting, although subways exist only in large cities such as New York, Boston, and Chicago. In Western Europe and Japan, however, railroads are experiencing a renaissance, thanks in part to the availability of technologically advanced, high-speed trains.

government involvement. The fact that railroads were privately owned led to another inherent problem in the industry. Railroads required a lot of maintenance, such as replacing track, and railroad owners were on their own to cover these expenses. The railroads that did survive were innovative, using new technologies such as the diesel locomotive, a faster and more efficient locomotive that was first introduced at the end of the previous decade. Railroads also courted passengers by using improved passenger cars, many of which were air conditioned, and by slashing the ticket fares.

Critical Overview

Like much of Thomas Wolfe's short fiction, the stories in *From Death to Morning*, including "The Far and the Near," were formed from leftover material that did not fit into his novels—in this case, 1935's *Of Time and the River*. Although the novel sold well, the collection of stories did not. In addition, as Ladell Payne notes in his 1991 entry on Wolfe for the *Dictionary of Literary Biography*, although Wolfe was famous in 1935, "he also was stung by the criticism that he was too wordy, too autobiographical, and too dependent upon Perkins." Payne is referring to Maxwell Perkins, Wolfe's editor at Charles Scribner's & Sons.

These three criticisms were brought up again the next year by Bernard DeVoto. In his now-famous piece for the *Saturday Review of Literature*, "Genius Is Not Enough," DeVoto used the review of Wolfe's essay *The Story of a Novel* as an opportunity to discredit Wolfe himself. "Mr. Wolfe is astonishingly immature," says DeVoto, adding that Wolfe has not mastered "the psychic material out of which a novel is made nor the technique of writing fiction." In addition, DeVoto says that if Wolfe "gave us less identification and more understanding," people would stop "calling him autobiographical." Finally, DeVoto criticized the influence of Perkins and the other editorial staff who helped Wolfe with his novels, calling them "the assembly line at Scribner's."

Although others had brought up these concerns before, most acknowledge that DeVoto's influential review helped guide criticism of Wolfe in general for much of the twentieth century. As Terry Roberts notes in his 2000 article for the *Southern Literary Journal,* DeVoto's essay "set the tone for critics ever since who wished to establish their own intellectual superiority by attacking Wolfe in print." Despite this fact, however, Wolfe did regain some critical favor. In his 1970 article for the *South Atlantic Quarterly,* Martin Wank notes one of the first events that helped inspire this revival: the 1953 publication of *The Enigma of Thomas Wolfe,* a collection of critical essays. Wank notes that this collection was followed by several other biographical and critical works on Wolfe. One of these was B. R. McElderry, Jr.'s 1964 *Thomas Wolfe.* In this work, McElderry notes that, amidst all of the negative critical attention given to Wolfe's longer works, not much has been said about his short fiction. Says McElderry: "The detailed study of these shorter pieces, their precise relation to the novels, and to such manuscripts as survive, has not been carried very far."

Over the next decade, more critics started to notice Wolfe's stories, although the attention was not always positive. In his 1947 book, *Thomas Wolfe,* Herbert J. Muller notes of Wolfe's *From Death to Morning* that it "is a collection of short pieces which, with a few exceptions, add little to his stature or to our understanding of him." Muller also says that many stories seem incomplete and singles out "The Far and the Near," saying that it is "a bare outline for a potentially good short story." Others disagree. In his 1974 entry on Wolfe for *American Writers,* C. Hugh Holman, a noted Wolfe scholar, says that *From Death to Morning* "has never received the attention it deserves." Holman also notes that, contrary to the belief that Wolfe's works lacked structure, "he showed a control and an objectivity in his short stories and his short novels that effectively belie the charge of formlessness."

For the short stories, this positive criticism has continued to increase. In her 1981 entry on Wolfe for the *Dictionary of Literary Biography,* Leslie Field notes that *From Death to Morning* "contains many fine pieces." In his 1983 article for *Thomas Wolfe: A Harvard Perspective,* James Boyer cites the quality of Wolfe's story collection, saying that this quality is largely due to the influence of his agent at the time, Elizabeth Nowell. Boyer singles out Wolfe's "The Cottage by the Tracks" (the original title of "The Far and the Near"). As Boyer notes, stories like this "represent units complete in themselves." In her 1984 book, *Thomas Wolfe,*

Elizabeth Evans calls "The Far and the Near" "a sentimental story" and notes how the destruction of the engineer's "idyllic scene" leaves him "disappointed and lonely, since the reality of the unfriendly cottage inhabitants precludes his hopes of friendship with them and indeed ruins his memory." With the 1987 publication of *The Complete Short Stories of Thomas Wolfe,* Wolfe's short stories received even more attention.

Although Wolfe's overall literary reputation is still in question, several critics, like Roberts, continue to focus on Wolfe's short fiction. As Roberts notes:

> in the short fiction he wrote during the nine brief years between the publication of *Look Homeward, Angel* and his death, Wolfe managed to turn almost all of the critical stereotypes about his work inside-out.

Criticism

Ryan D. Poquette

Poquette has a bachelor's degree in English and specializes in writing about literature. In the following essay, Poquette discusses Wolfe's pervasive use of opposites in "The Far and the Near."

The story title "The Far and the Near" presents two diametrically opposed concepts. In fact, if readers examine the title of the collection in which the story was included, *From Death to Morning,* they find two more opposite concepts. When death is associated with a time of day, it is usually night. Likewise, when morning is used to represent a life stage, it usually symbolizes birth. As C. Hugh Holman notes in his entry on Wolfe for *American Writers,* most of Wolfe's books featured opposites in their titles in either a suggestive or an overt way. Holman notes that this had to do with Wolfe's view on life: "Thomas Wolfe grappled in frustrated and demonic fury with what he called 'the strange and bitter miracle of life,' a miracle which he saw in patterns of opposites." This obsession with opposites is also evident in the content of Wolfe's tales themselves. "The Far and the Near" is a particularly vivid example of Wolfe's use of opposites. In the story, Wolfe employs distinct contrasts in imagery and word choice to increase the effectiveness of the story's mood shift.

What Do I Read Next?

- Unlike ''The Far and the Near,'' which features an unnamed railroad engineer, the majority of Wolfe's longer works employ autobiographical characters, like Eugene Gant. Wolfe's first novel about Gant, *Look Homeward, Angel: A Story of the Buried Life* (1929), was set in his hometown of Asheville, North Carolina. The narrative follows Gant through his turbulent childhood and young adulthood, and its often negative depiction of the townspeople and the American South in general angered many residents.

- Wolfe's *Of Time and the River: A Legend of Man's Hunger in His Youth* (1935) continues the story of Eugene Gant, following him into adulthood and throughout Europe. Like its predecessor, the book was highly autobiographical and drew directly upon Wolfe's experiences in Europe, including his adventures with two contemporary writers, F. Scott Fitzgerald and Sinclair Lewis.

- At a writers' conference in 1935, Wolfe presented an essay describing the way that he wrote his books and his close editorial relationship with his editor at Scribner's, Maxwell Perkins. The essay was published in 1936 as *The Story of a Novel* and was reprinted with another essay in 1983 under the title *The Autobiography of an American Novelist*. Although both *The Story of a Novel* and *The Autobiography of an American Novelist* are currently out of print, they are available at many libraries.

- Voltaire's satirical prose work *Candide; or, All for the Best* was first published in both French and English in 1759. The story criticizes one of the optimistic philosophical theories of Voltaire's time, which stated that humans live in the best of all possible worlds, ruled by a benevolent God. Voltaire challenged this idealistic idea by placing a number of optimistic characters in realistic situations where they are forced to face war, dismemberment, and death, among other horrors.

This mood shift takes place at a very specific point in the story, directly after the engineer gets off his train and walks ''slowly through the station and out into the streets of the town.'' Everything up to this point is described in positive terms, while everything past it is negative. This is most apparent in Wolfe's use of imagery. When the story begins, the reader is exposed to part of the vision that the engineer has survived on for more than twenty years. The town is described as the place where the train ''halted for a breathing space'' on its journey between its two destination cities. This quaint description associates the town with restful images, making it sound like a comfortable, tranquil place. This idea is amplified by the initial description of the house that the engineer passes every day: ''a tidy little cottage of white boards, trimmed vividly with green blinds.'' The house also features ''a garden neatly patterned'' and ''three mighty oaks'' that provide shade. As the narrator notes, ''The whole place had an air of tidiness, thrift, and modest comfort.''

This positive image of the town and the cottage only increases when the engineer begins the waving ritual with the woman in the cottage, a routine that is prompted by the whistle of his train. ''Every day for more than twenty years . . . a woman had appeared on the back porch of the little house and waved to him.'' The simple image of a woman waving at him becomes fixed in his mind and helps flesh out his overall vision of the town, cottage, the woman, and her daughter. This idyllic image gets the engineer through tough times because he thinks his vision is ''something beautiful and enduring, something beyond all change and ruin.''

When he goes to meet the women and tell them how this positive image has profoundly affected his outlook on life, he expects that the whole experience will be positive, too, since that is how for years he has anticipated this day. However, when he walks into the town for the first time, the imagery does not match his mental picture: "Everything was as strange to him as if he had never seen this town before." This feeling grows in the time he takes to walk all the way through the town to the women's cottage. When he gets to the cottage, he is able to identify it by "the lordly oaks," "the garden and the arbor," and other familiar characteristics such as the house's proximity to the railway. However, these images do not have the same positive connotations that they did in the beginning. The town and cottage are no longer quaint and comfortable. Instead, "the town, the road, the earth, the very entrance to this place he loved" has turned unrecognizable, like "the landscape of some ugly dream." The ugliness of this imagery increases when he is finally let into the house and led into "an ugly little parlor."

The women also turn out to be contrary to what he expected. In the first half of the story, his unwavering belief in the goodness and beauty of the women—created by the image of their waving—leads him to believe that he knows "their lives completely, to every hour and moment of the day." Perhaps more importantly, he assumes that they will greet him as a welcome friend. However, in the second half of the story, this image is also shattered. When he meets the older woman face-to-face, he knows "at once that the woman who stood there looking at him with a mistrustful eye was the same woman who had waved to him so many thousand times." However, just as the correct identification of the house by its exterior brings him no joy, neither does the woman's appearance. Her face is "harsh and pinched and meager," and the flesh sags "wearily in sallow folds." Even more disappointing, she does not welcome the engineer but instead views him with "timid suspicion and uneasy doubt."

In addition to the stark contrast in physical imagery, Wolfe also chooses contrasting words to represent the distinctly positive and negative ideas and feelings of the story's two halves. In the beginning, Wolfe's narrator instills a sense of strength in the engineer's train. The train is "great," "powerful," and achieves "terrific speed," and its progress is "marked by heavy bellowing puffs of smoke." The engineer is also described in terms that emphasize his strength: "He had driven his great train, loaded with its weight of lives, across the land ten thousand times." The fact that the engineer has successfully completed so many journeys, safely delivering his human cargo, underscores the idea of strength and dependability. In addition, the engi-

"Unlike the first half of the story, when his age is described with terms like 'grandeur and wisdom,' old age by the end of the story is unpleasant. The shock of reality has withered him, and his heart is 'sick with doubt and horror.'"

neer has "the qualities of faith and courage and humbleness," and his old age is described in the best possible terms, with "grandeur and wisdom." He also feels "tenderness" for the two women, whose image is "carved so sharply in his heart." Even the tragedies he has seen on the railroad tracks have not affected his positive mood thanks to his idyllic vision of the two women.

However, when the engineer gets off the train and views the unfamiliar town, Wolfe starts to use words that seem uncharacteristic to the reader since they immediately follow the positive language of the first half. The engineer is no longer strong and sure, and neither is anything else. His "bewilderment and confusion" grow as he walks to the "straggling" outskirts of town, where "the street faded." Even the engineer's walk is described as a "plod" through "heat and dust." All of these words have negative connotations, which increasingly give the town and cottage a feeling of stagnation and impending death. These feelings intensify when he first sees the older woman and feels "a sense of bitter loss and grief."

Even sounds become negative, both the woman's "unfriendly tongue" and the engineer's own voice, which he is shocked to find sounds "unreal and ghastly." Like the descriptions of the town, the engineer's physical qualities, such as the strength of his voice, degrade in the second half of the story. After he spends his "brief agony of time" with the women, feeling "shameful" for coming, the man leaves, at which point he realizes that he is "an old man." Unlike the first half of the story, when his age is described with terms like "grandeur and wisdom,'' old age by the end of the story is unpleasant. The shock of reality has withered him, and his heart is ''sick with doubt and horror.'' The engineer is no longer part of the railroad company, and thus he can no longer identify with the train, which sustained his illusion. At this point, he is truly alone and without hope.

As Elizabeth Evans notes in her book, *Thomas Wolfe:* ''The engineer is left disappointed and lonely, since the reality of the unfriendly cottage inhabitants precludes his hopes of friendship with them and indeed ruins his memory.'' This painfully negative ending is a huge contrast to the extremely positive beginning. This distinct difference between the two halves of the story gives it more impact, since readers experience two emotional extremes within a very short period of time. Holman notes the effectiveness of stories like this one: ''On the level of dramatic scene, fully realized and impacted with immediacy, Wolfe could construct magnificently. Single episodes of his work, published separately as short stories, are powerful narrative units.'' In his article in *Thomas Wolfe: A Harvard Perspective,* James Boyer makes a similar observation about stories like this one, which were originally intended for Wolfe's novels. Says Boyer, they ''represent units complete in themselves which were to have functioned in the novel to illustrate various themes or facets of the national character.''

This idea may cause readers to question Wolfe's motives behind the story. What was he trying to say about the national character? When one examines the historical context in which the story was written and compares this context to the use of time in the story, a possible answer presents itself. In the story, the engineer staked his faith on an idyllic vision in the past, which has failed to come true in the present. In fact, the present reality is horrible for him, and it destroys his optimism and hope. This transition directly parallels the time in which the story was written. In the 1930s, when Wolfe wrote the story, the United States was caught in the grip of the Great Depression, a time when people's optimism from the past was shown to be unfounded. The previous decade, the 1920s, had been a very positive time, since the nation had a strong economy. Many people assumed that the economy, and life in general, would continue to improve, and so they staked their futures—and in some cases their fortunes—on this vision by investing heavily in the stock market. When this vision failed, many were overcome with despair and hopelessness, just like the engineer. In the end, images such as the woman's

''harsh and pinched and meager'' face—a sign of poverty and possibly hunger—may be Wolfe's way of indicating the tough times that his public was experiencing during the Great Depression, when reality intruded on many dreams, and optimism was often met with disappointment and sorrow.

Source: Ryan D. Poquette, Critical Essay on ''The Far and the Near,'' in *Short Stories for Students,* Gale, 2003.

Elizabeth Evans

In the following essay excerpt, Evans discusses and evaluates the writing of Wolfe's collections of short fiction From Death to Morning, The Hills Beyond, *and* The Short Stories of Thomas Wolfe.

Although Wolfe published many short stories, he admitted that he did not know what magazines wanted and declared he would ''like nothing better than to write something that was both very good and very popular: I should be enchanted if the editors of *Cosmopolitan* began to wave large fat checks under my nose, but I know of no ways of going about this deliberately and I am sure I'd fail miserably if I tried.'' Most often his short stories were segments of the larger manuscript he was always working on at the time, and he felt uncertain about excising a portion and shaping it as a short story. Once when he sent Elizabeth Nowell approximately seven typed pages out of a manuscript (a piece about two boys going to the circus) he wrote, ''The thing [''Circus at Dawn''] needs an introduction which I will try to write today, but otherwise it is complete enough, although, again, I am afraid it is not what most people consider a story.'' (''Circus at Dawn'' was published in *Modern Monthly* in 1935; it was also included in *From Death to Morning.*) Wolfe generally left such decisions and selections up to Nowell.

All fourteen stories that *From Death to Morning* (1935) comprises appeared in magazines or academic journals between July 1932, when *The Web of Earth* was published, and October 1935, when *''The Bums at Sunset''* appeared. Seven of these stories were published by *Scribner's Magazine,* two by *Modern Monthly,* and one each by *The New Yorker, Vanity Fair, Cosmopolitan, Harper's Bazaar,* and the *Virginia Quarterly Review*—a wide variety of publications. Letters in 1933 indicate that Wolfe was hard pressed for money; selling stories was therefore essential. He was down to $7, he said, when the sale of *No Door* to *Scribner's Magazine* brought him $200. Although he welcomed this sum,

Wolfe wrote George Wallace (a former member of Professor Baker's 47 Workshop at Harvard) that he was considering taking his stories to another agent, one who had indicated he could get higher prices than *Scribner's Magazine,* Wolfe's most frequent publisher, offered. Obviously Wolfe would indeed welcome ''large fat checks'' from *Cosmopolitan.* These stories earned him funds first as single sales and then in the collected volume *From Death to Morning.* This volume appeared eight months after *Of Time and the River* was published, making 1935 an important year of publication for Wolfe.

Wolfe attributed the unenthusiastic reviews of *From Death to Morning* to the criticism that continued to be made about *Of Time and the River:* excessive length. The favorable reviews stressed the lyrical prose, humor, realism, and engaging characters. Nevertheless, this neglected volume generally has been underrated, with just a few stories receiving serious attention; indeed, Richard Kennedy thinks that *From Death to Morning* is a book that discourages a second reading. While critics wisely avoid extravagant claims for this collection, they need not shy away from confidently praising Wolfe's variety of narrative forms, his range of subject matter, the large number of effectively drawn characters, the careful attention to place, and the emotional power. Indeed, emotional power is the significant feature, one that Wolfe conveys best through a pervasive feeling of loneliness in characters and through some extraordinarily violent scenes.

Narrative forms include the episodic, epistolary, stream-of-consciousness, as well as slice-of-life, the form that describes ''Only the Dead Know Brooklyn'' and ''The Bums at Sunset.'' Each of these stories concerns a problem, for which no solution is reached. Like most of the stories in this collection, these two implicitly explore the theme of loneliness that is prevalent even in *The Web of Earth,* a piece of writing whose main character, Wolfe says, ''is grander, richer and more tremendous'' than Joyce's Molly Bloom at the end of *Ulysses.* In both ''Only the Dead Know Brooklyn'' and ''The Bums at Sunset,'' the characters are flat, distinguished only by age and basic reactions. The bums are a chance collection of lonely men exiled for unknown reasons from families and productive work. Both stories center on the arrival of a stranger. In ''The Bums at Sunset,'' the appearance of the young, uninitiated bum threatens those who know the ropes and are suspicious of his lack of experience. ''What is dis anyway?'' one of them sneers,

> "The idyllic scene he saw for years now fades before her suspicious attitude, her harsh voice, and her unsmiling face. The engineer is left disappointed and lonely...."

''a——— noic'ry [nursery], or sump'n.'' In ''Only the Dead Know Brooklyn,'' the big guy who presumes to learn all of Brooklyn by asking directions and studying his map baffles the narrator, who declares, ''Dere's no guy livin' dat knows Brooklyn t'roo and t'roo.'' While the voice of the Brooklyn native narrates this story, an omniscient voice tells the story of ''The Bums at Sunset,'' and his diction contrasts with the bums ungrammatical speech and limited vocabulary in its use of figurative language; for example, the fading light of sunset looks, he says, ''like a delicate and ancient bronze.'' And in picturing these nondescript men, the narrator emphasizes that their inescapable loneliness tells ''a legend of pounding wheel and thrumming rod, of bloody brawl and brutal shambles, of the savage wilderness, the wild, cruel and lonely distances of America.''

''Gulliver,'' a brief character study of an excessively tall man, relates the discomfort of someone who never fits into chairs, beds, or Pullman car berths—of a giant in a world of normal-sized people. Furthermore, the central character is subjected to the same insults wherever he goes: ''Hey-y, Misteh! ... Is it rainin' up deh?'' His physical size dominates the story and causes the pain and incommunicable loneliness that mark his life. In ''The Far and the Near,'' a very short piece originally entitled ''The Cottage by the Tracks,'' Wolfe tells a sentimental story about a railroad engineer who finally discovers the reality of what he had thought to be an idyllic scene: a mother and a daughter who live in a country cottage near the tracks. For twenty years the engineer has waved to them as his train roared past, and now that he has retired, he comes to greet them in person. From the moment the older woman opens the door, he knows he should not have come. The idyllic scene he saw for years now fades before her suspicious attitude, her harsh voice, and her unsmiling face. The engineer is left disappointed and lonely, since the reality of the unfriendly cottage inhabitants precludes his hopes of friendship with them and indeed ruins his memory. If the engineer has any other life to go to, we are not told of it.

The subjects of loneliness and death coalesce in the story of the dying man in "Dark in the Forest, Strange as Time." Because he is ill, the man must go away alone for the winter to warmer climate; his wife promises that she will join him in the spring. Other people board the train, many of them talking and laughing as they leave. The dying man's wife settles him in the compartment, turns, and quickly leaves to join her young, robust lover who waits on the platform. This desertion is repeated in a lesser way with the American youth assigned to this same compartment. His good health and youth contrast sharply with the dying man's condition. And when the youth leaves the compartment for the conviviality of the dining car, the older man dies. He never fulfills his modest desire of knowing well just "vun field, vun hill, vun riffer."

As it appears in *From Death to Morning, No Door* is only the first segment of a much longer work of the same title, a short novel Max Perkins considered bringing out in a limited edition. He did not do so, however. In the original version, this first segment is subtitled "October 1931." Structurally, the brief version in *From Death to Morning* fails to develop a unified plot. The story begins in the luxurious apartment of the host, a rich man who has taken the requisite trip to Europe, collected a suitably impressive collection of sculpture and rare books, and lives among furnishings that are of "quiet but distinguished taste." His young mistress is at his side when his guest (a writer) relates painful glimpses of Brooklyn's low life. The host appears to listen, but he responds incongruously—"grand," "marvelous," "swell"—even though the young man tells of men who live in alleyways, beat their wives, and consider murder and robbery honest toil. In some detail the guest relates an episode about the loud demands of a lonely prostitute for her $3 payment. Her client refuses to pay her until, as he puts it, she will "staht actin' like a lady." Oblivious to the irony, the host continues to murmur "grand," and he envies the young man the rich experience of living among such people.

In the final pages Wolfe abandons the host, his mistress, the tinkling cocktail glasses, and the pent-

house balcony to recount the haunting story of a priest's death. One of Wolfe's finest vignettes, this episode stays in the narrator's mind "like the haunting refrain of some old song—as it was heard and lost in Brooklyn." At evening, a man and a woman appear in their respective apartment windows to talk, their voices issuing banalities such as "Wat's t' noos sinct I been gone?" Although Father Grogan has died while this speaker was away, the priest's death is little more than a piece of news to be reported by one nameless character to another. It is not a grief to be shared, as one can see by the response to the news: "Gee, dat's too bad . . . I musta been away. Oddehwise I woulda hoid." Although the narrator is fully aware of the tragic implications of the priest's death, he makes no overt judgments about the insensitive speakers. The scene ends with a simple line: "A window closed, and there was silence." The casual announcement of Father Grogan's death and the equally casual reaction lead the narrator to consider time, in whose relentless power fame is lost, names are forgotten, and energy is wasted. Indeed, Father Grogan and all mankind die in darkness; they are remembered only superficially, if at all.

Related as it is to loneliness and violence, the theme of human dejection is present throughout these stories. The host may be wealthy, but he is a man who has never really lived. Indeed, Wolfe says this man measures time not by actual deeds but "in dimensions of fathomless and immovable sensations." His young guest lives in a run-down section of Brooklyn, an environment in stark contrast to his host's penthouse. When the young man describes the abject conditions of his neighborhood, the host considers such tales colorful and alive, unlike his own rich but dead world. The diverse reactions of these two men cannot be reconciled. The unrelieved loneliness, the failure of communication, and the narrator's search for certitude and meaning are problems introduced but left unresolved. Solutions are hinted at through brief passages whose imagery expresses a momentary harmony—"all of the colors of the sun and harbor, flashing, blazing, shifting in swarming motes, in an iridescent web of light and color for an instant on the blazing side of a proud white ship." The color flashes and then is gone, however; what remains for the narrator is unspeakable loneliness. . . .

Source: Elizabeth Evans, "*From Death to Morning, The Hills Beyond,* and the Short Novels," in *Thomas Wolfe,* Frederick Ungar Publishing Co., 1984, pp. 95–133.

Sources

Boyer, James, "The Development of Form in Thomas Wolfe's Short Fiction," in *Thomas Wolfe: A Harvard Perspective,* edited by Richard S. Kennedy, Croissant & Co., 1983, pp. 31–42, originally a paper read at Harvard University, Cambridge, Massachusetts, on May 8, 1982.

DeVoto, Bernard, "Genius Is Not Enough," in *Thomas Wolfe: A Collection of Critical Essays,* edited by Louis D. Rubin Jr., Prentice-Hall, Inc., 1973, pp. 75, 77–78, originally published in *Saturday Review of Literature,* April 25, 1936, pp. 3–4, 13–14.

Evans, Elizabeth, "*From Death to Morning, The Hills Beyond* and the Short Novels," in *Thomas Wolfe,* Frederick Ungar Publishing Co., 1984, pp. 95–133.

Field, Leslie, "Thomas Wolfe," in *Dictionary of Literary Biography,* Vol. 9: *American Novelists, 1910–1945,* edited by James J. Martine, Gale Research, 1981, pp. 172–87.

Holman, C. Hugh, "Thomas Wolfe," in *American Writers,* Vol. 4, Charles Scribner's Sons, 1974, pp. 450–73.

McElderry, B. R., Jr., "Chapter 6: Wolfe's Shorter Fiction," in *Thomas Wolfe,* Twayne Publishers, Inc., 1964, p. 104.

Muller, Herbert J., *Thomas Wolfe,* New Directions, 1947, pp. 158–60.

Payne, Ladell, "Thomas Wolfe," in *Dictionary of Literary Biography,* Vol. 102: *American Short-Story Writers, 1910–1945, Second Series,* edited by Bobby Ellen Kimbel, Gale Research, 1991, pp. 366–70.

Roberts, Terry, "Resurrecting Thomas Wolfe," in the *Southern Literary Journal,* Vol. 33, No. 1, Fall 2000, pp. 27–41.

Wank, Martin, "Thomas Wolfe: Two More Decades of Criticism," in the *South Atlantic Quarterly,* Vol. 69, No. 2, Spring 1970, pp. 243–55.

Wolfe, Thomas, "The Far and the Near," in *The Complete Short Stories of Thomas Wolfe,* edited by Francis E. Skipp, Collier Books, 1989, pp. 271–73.

Further Reading

Bloom, Harold, ed., *Thomas Wolfe,* Modern Critical Views series, Chelsea House, 2000.

This collection of essays offers a representative selection of the current criticism on the author. Like other books in this series, this volume features an introductory essay by Bloom, a bibliography, and a chronology.

Griffin, John Chandler, *Memories of Thomas Wolfe: A Pictorial Companion to "Look Homeward, Angel,"* Summerhouse Press, 1996.

Wolfe was known for his use of autobiographical elements in his fiction, starting with *Look Homeward, Angel: A Story of the Buried Life.* In this book, Griffin collects extracts from Wolfe's novel, along with photographs from Wolfe's life, giving readers an insight into how Wolfe constructed the tale.

Holliday, Shawn, *Thomas Wolfe and the Politics of Modernism,* Peter Lang Publishing, 2001.

Holliday offers reasons why Wolfe, who was once held in the same esteem as writers like Hemingway and Faulkner, now holds an uncertain place in the literary canon. Holliday attributes this to many factors, including Wolfe's critics (who, according to Holliday, misunderstood Wolfe's modernistic writing style) and editors (who, according to Holliday, tampered excessively with Wolfe's drafts).

Nowell, Elizabeth, *Thomas Wolfe: A Biography,* Greenwood Publishing Group, 1973.

Drawing on her experiences as Wolfe's agent—particularly during the period in which he wrote much of his short fiction—Nowell gives an in-depth look at her famous client. This first full-length biography of Wolfe was originally published in 1960.

Thorne, Martha, ed., *Modern Trains and Splendid Stations: Architecture, Design, and Rail Travel for the Twenty-First Century,* Merrell Publishers, 2001.

Although the popularity of railroads reached their peak in the late nineteenth and early twentieth centuries in the United States, in Western Europe and Japan they are experiencing a renaissance. This book details the look and feel of the modern trains—many of which are high-speed vehicles—and their corresponding train stations.

The Half-Skinned Steer

E. Annie Proulx

1997

E. Annie Proulx's ''The Half-Skinned Steer'' was first published in the *Atlantic Monthly* in November 1997. It was originally written at the invitation of the Nature Conservancy, which asked Proulx to visit one of its preserves and then contribute a story, inspired by her visit, to *Off the Beaten Path* (1998), an anthology of short fiction. This assignment also inspired Proulx to write *Close Range: Wyoming Stories* (1999), in which the story was included. By the time it was published, Proulx was already famous for another collection of short stories and three novels, including *The Shipping News* (1993), which won both the Pulitzer Prize and the National Book Award. Like many of Proulx's works, ''The Half-Skinned Steer'' features gritty realism in a harsh, natural setting.

''The Half-Skinned Steer'' concerns Mero, an eighty-three-year-old man who left his family's ranch sixty years earlier and who must face his past when he is called back to attend his brother's funeral. The story examines human mortality, the power of memory to affect one's life, and the inevitability of fate.

The particularly graphic cattle-slaughter scenes in the story recall the brutality of Chicago's stockyards in Upton Sinclair's 1906 novel, *The Jungle*. Proulx's story was written in the mid- to late 1990s, when the prospect of diseased beef led to fear of the so-called mad cow disease in the United States, as well as to a lawsuit involving popular talk-show host Oprah Winfrey. The 1990s were also a decade

in which the government, nutritionists, and even individual consumers reexamined the long-held belief that meat is an essential part of one's diet. ''The Half-Skinned Steer'' was included in the *The Best American Short Stories 1998* and *The Best American Short Stories of the Century,* which were published by Houghton Mifflin in paperback in 1998 and 2000, respectively.

Author Biography

E. Annie Proulx was born on August 22, 1935, in Norwich, Connecticut, into a family of farmers, mill workers, inventors, and artists whose ancestors had lived there for three centuries. Proulx's mother, a painter and amateur naturalist, instilled in Proulx an appreciation for nature and the details of life. Because of her father's career in textiles, Proulx's family constantly moved, so she lived in several states, including North Carolina, Vermont, Maine, and Rhode Island. She earned a bachelor's degree in history from the University of Vermont in 1969 and then went on to graduate school at Sir George Williams University (now Concordia University) in Montreal. In 1973, she earned her master's degree in history, and in 1975, she passed her doctoral oral examinations. However, she did not finish her dissertation because there were few teaching jobs in history at the time. Instead, Proulx turned to freelance journalism. While living with a friend in a rural shack on the Canadian border in northern Vermont, Proulx wrote a variety of articles, book reviews, and on-assignment nonfiction books. She also founded and edited *Behind the Times,* a rural Vermont newspaper (1984–1986). Through all of this, she struggled to make enough money to support her three sons.

At the same time, she began to write fiction. She published several short stories in magazines, and in 1988, the stories were collected in *Heart Songs and Other Stories.* As they would continue to do, the critics praised Proulx's narrative gifts, harsh landscapes, and tough but compelling stories. In 1989, Proulx began writing fiction fulltime. In 1992, she published her first novel, *Postcards,* which won the PEN/Faulkner Award for Fiction in 1993. Proulx was the first woman to win this prestigious award. However, it was her next novel, 1993's *The Shipping News,* which made Proulx a household name. The book was a popular success, it won the National Book Award for fiction (1993) and the Pulitzer Prize for fiction (1994), and it was adapted into a feature film (2001). In 1999, she published *Close*

E. Annie Proulx

Range: Wyoming Stories, which includes ''The Half-Skinned Steer.'' This story was also included in *The Best American Short Stories 1998* and *The Best American Short Stories of the Century.* Proulx currently lives and works in Wyoming, a setting that allows her to pursue her many outside interests, which include hunting, fishing, canoeing, and bicycling. Her novel *That Old Ace in the Hole* was published in December 2002.

Plot Summary

''The Half-Skinned Steer'' begins with a short summary of Mero Corn's life, from the day he left his family's dilapidated Wyoming ranch to his life as a successful retiree in Massachusetts sixty years later. One morning, he gets a call from his nephew's wife, Louise, who tells Mero that his brother, Rollo, has been clawed to death by an emu. Despite Louise's misgivings, Mero says that he will drive from Massachusetts to the funeral in Wyoming. As Mero packs for the trip, the story reverts to one of the many flashbacks of Mero's life on the ranch. Mero remembers his father, his brother, and his father's girlfriend at the time. Mero imagines the girlfriend as a horse, given her characteristics, which he comments on throughout the story. In his memory, the girlfriend tells a gruesome story about Tin Head, a hapless rancher, and a half-skinned steer. The night following her storytelling, Mero has a disturbing dream, and he flees the ranch the next morning. Back in the present, Mero struggles with road construction and a speeding ticket. In the next flashback, Mero continues to examine his flight from the ranch and thinks that he left because of the love triangle between his father, his father's girlfriend, and Rollo.

Back in the present, Mero gets confused and causes an accident, wrecking his Cadillac in the process and using his wealth to buy a replacement. That night, he has a nightmare about his family's ranch. The next day, Mero reaches Wyoming. In another flashback, his father's girlfriend continues her story about Tin Head, who half-skins a steer that he presumes is dead. In the present, the bad weather and mountain altitude cause Mero to get fatigued while driving. He gets close to the ranch and starts looking for the entrance. In another flashback, the girlfriend continues her story about Tin Head, who goes out to finish skinning the steer. However, the steer is gone. Back in the present, Mero cannot find the entrance to his family's ranch and then gets stuck in the snow. He tries to free the car. In another flashback, the girlfriend finishes her story, explaining that the half-skinned steer escaped onto the open range and that as soon as Tin Head saw the mutilated animal's hate-filled gaze, he knew that he and his family were cursed. Back in the present, Mero breaks a window and kills the car's engine while trying to free the car. Half-frozen and feeling extremely weak, Mero realizes that he is doomed. He sees some cattle in the field next to him, and in his dying delusion, he thinks one of them is the half-skinned steer from the story and that the animal has come to get him.

Characters

Anthropologist

The anthropologist introduces a young Mero to sex by showing him Native-American stone drawings of female genitalia.

Louise Corn

Louise calls Mero to let him know about his brother's death. She expresses concern over Mero's

choice to drive from Massachusetts to Wyoming, instead of flying.

Mero Corn

Mero Corn is an old man haunted by his ranching past, which he must face when he drives to his brother's funeral—a journey that ultimately kills him. Sixty years before the story begins, at the age of twenty-three, Mero fled his family's Wyoming ranch and has never thought about going back until he hears that his brother is dead. Mero has tried many ways of escaping his past, including becoming a vegetarian, serving in World War II, and getting rich through investments. However, during the journey, he is plagued by painful memories that chip away at the calm, confidence, and mental awareness that he has built up since leaving the ranch. Most of these memories concern his father's girlfriend, a woman whom Mero describes as having horselike characteristics. In a nightmare, Mero associates horse breeding with the act of slaughtering cattle, a disturbing image that helps him decide to leave the ranch for good the next morning. He also leaves because he has witnessed Rollo's desire for the girlfriend, and Mero wants to have a woman of his own. The journey back to the funeral does not go as planned. Mero gets a traffic ticket, has his first car accident, and eats food that does not agree with him. By the time he reaches Wyoming, the long journey and the painful memories have left Mero weak, hungry, and confused. As a result, he is unable to find his family's ranch and ends up getting stuck in the snow when he makes a wrong turn. He mistakenly tries to get the car back on the main road, breaking the car's window and killing the engine in the process. At the end, frozen and delusional, Mero realizes that he is dying and envisions death as the half-skinned steer from one of the girlfriend's stories.

Rollo Corn

Rollo Corn is Mero's brother, who is killed by an emu on the family ranch, which has been turned into an Australian-themed attraction. The news of Rollo's death prompts Mero to take his cross-country road trip to attend his brother's funeral. This journey prompts bad memories of his ranch experiences, including Rollo's attraction to his father's girlfriend, and these memories make Mero weak and susceptible to his tragic fate.

Mero's Father

Mero's father is an old man who lets the family ranch deteriorate, while he gets a postal job and spends his free time in an alcoholic haze. Mero and his brother, Rollo, wish that their father, who is often referred to as the old man, would move in with his girlfriend so that Mero and Rollo could reclaim the ranch. Instead, the old man's girlfriend stays with the Corn men, where she openly flirts with Mero and Rollo. Mero's father does not notice or does not care, and this attitude helps inspire Mero to leave the ranch—and Wyoming—to find his own woman.

Mero's Father's Girlfriend

Mero's father's girlfriend, sometimes referred to in the story as simply the girlfriend, influences Mero's decision to leave the ranch at twenty-three. The woman, whom Mero describes in horse-like terms, creates tension among the Corn men, since she is officially Mero's father's girlfriend but flirts with Rollo and Mero, too. However, Rollo is the only one who expresses interest, since Mero wants a woman of his own. The girlfriend tells many stories about Tin Head, a poor rancher with a defective metal plate in his head, which affects his brain functions. One story in particular, the tale about the half-skinned steer, prompts Mero to have a nightmare, and he leaves the ranch the next morning.

Tin Head

Tin Head is a character in Mero's father's girlfriend's story; he believes that he is cursed when a half-skinned steer escapes and the mutilated animal fixes him with a hateful stare. Tin Head has a galvanized metal plate in his head, which affects his brain functions.

Themes

Memory

From the time that Mero leaves his family's ranch in 1936, he is determined to put the past behind him, and he chooses not to return "to see the old man and Rollo, bankrupt and ruined, because he knew they were." He makes many attempts to forget his past, beginning with his eating habits. In the train station on his way out of town in 1936, he cannot eat a steak. He cuts into it and sees "the blood spread across the white plate." He equates the bloody meat with "the beast, mouth agape in mute bawling," an image of the cattle he used to slaughter. As a result, he becomes a vegetarian. He also moves to Massachusetts, serves in World War II,

Media Adaptations

- *The Shipping News* was adapted as a feature film by Miramax Films and released in 2001. The film was directed by Lasse Hallström and featured an all-star cast, including Kevin Spacey, Julianne Moore, Judi Dench, Cate Blanchett, and Scott Glenn. It is available on VHS and DVD from Buena Vista Home Video.

- *The Shipping News* was also adapted as an abridged audiobook in 1995 and is available on four audiocassettes. The audiobook was re-released in 2001 in a special compact-disc format that coincided with the film's release. Both versions are produced by Simon & Schuster Audio and are read by Robert Joy.

gets married several times, makes many successful investments, and becomes a local politician. Ultimately, however, these attempts to bury the past do not succeed. When he begins driving west to his brother's funeral, the physical journey quickly becomes a psychological journey into Mero's insecure past. When he gets to Wyoming, the land looks exactly as he remembers it, a fact that disturbs him since he has worked so hard to change himself. "He felt himself slip back; the calm of eighty-three years sheeted off him like water." However, not everything is the way that he remembers it. He is surprised when he does not find the entrance to the ranch, since it is "so clear and sharp in his mind." After pulling into the wrong entrance and getting stuck, he realizes he has made a mistake. His faith in his memory starts to fade, and he starts to notice the harsh landscape: "The remembered gates collapsed, fences wavered, while the badland features swelled into massive prominence."

Mortality

Death is inevitable for all mortals, but those who think themselves invincible sometimes die earlier than they might have. This is the case with Mero, whose cockiness leads him into a fatal situa-

Topics for Further Study

- Research how many family-owned ranches there were in the United States in 1936 and how many family-owned ranches are in the United States today. Look up the geographic concentrations of these ranches in both time periods and plot them both on separate maps of the United States. Compare the two maps and discuss any related trends in ranching, the economy, or society that have affected the number of family-owned ranches.

- Research the methods used in modern cattle slaughter. Compare these methods to the method that Tin Head uses on the half-skinned steer in the story.

- Investigate the current research in the ongoing debate over whether meat is an essential part of a person's diet. Create a nutrition chart that compares the advantages and disadvantages of a meat-eater's diet, then do the same for a vegetarian's diet, using your research to support your claims.

- Research the psychology behind human memory. Create a diagram of the brain that indicates where memory functions reside and how they work.

- Find one other case from any point in history where a person died as a result of underestimating his or her susceptibility to death in a dangerous situation. Write a short biography of this person, including a description about the event that led to this person's death.

---

tion. Mero's overconfidence is a side effect of his attempts to bury the past. He has worked hard, lived a healthy life, and reached a point where he feels that his money and lifestyle have made him nearly invincible. When he first gets the call from Louise, he tells her he will drive from Massachusetts to Wyoming. She is concerned that Mero, at eighty-three, might not be able to make the trip. His response is confident: "Four days; he would be there by Saturday afternoon." However, on the trip, Mero begins to exhibit signs of his age. He gets confused in traffic and ends up causing a car accident. He is unconcerned and just buys a new car, relishing the thought that he is able to do whatever he wants: "He could do that if he liked, buy cars like packs of cigarettes and smoke them up." He cannot find the kind of food he likes to eat and goes hungry instead, thinking he is strong enough to handle it. When he is unable to find the entrance to the ranch, he briefly considers finding shelter then rules out this possibility, unwilling to give up. Mero looks for the entrance one more time and thinks that he has found it. "He turned in, feeling a little triumph." When he gets stuck, he realizes he was mistaken. He realizes that his old car, which he carelessly tossed away after the accident, contains all of his emergency road supplies like food, water, and car phone. Instead of staying in his new car all night and using its heater to keep himself warm, he tries to free the vehicle. In the process, he mistakenly thinks that he has locked himself out of the car and breaks one of the windows. This ruins his only shelter, bringing about a freezing death that might have been avoided if Mero had not forgotten his mortality.

Sexual Confusion

Although Mero successfully buries most aspects of his Wyoming life for sixty years, his past still haunts him in his love life. At one point, Mero is congratulating himself on all of the women he has had in his life: "How many women were out there! He had married three of them and sampled plenty." However, the truth is, Mero has a hard time sustaining a romantic relationship as a result of his confused sexual beliefs. His first exposure to sex came as a child, when his father told him to take an anthropologist to see some Native-American rock drawings. The anthropologist points out the stone carvings of female genitalia, an image that becomes fixed in his mind. From that point on, "no fleshly examples ever conquered his belief in the subterranean stony structure of female genitalia." The only woman he ever imagined differently was his father's girlfriend, whom he associates with a horse: "If you admired horses, you'd go for her with her arched neck and horsy buttocks, so high and haunchy you'd want to clap her on the rear." After the woman tells them the story of the half-skinned steer, Mero dreams "of horse breeding or hoarse breathing, whether the act of sex or bloody, cutthroat gasps he didn't know." Sex, horses, and his sense of revulsion over the cattle slaughtering that he has done in his life become fused in his mind with the image of this woman. He also notices the developing relationship between the woman and Rollo, which further encourages him to leave. Even this decision is described in animalistic terms. The narrator notes that Mero had "learned from television nature programs that it had been time for him to find his own territory and his own woman." Even when he is making the journey back to Wyoming, sixty years later, Mero wonders "if Rollo had got the girlfriend away from the old man, thrown a saddle on her, and ridden off into the sunset."

Style

Setting

"The Half-Skinned Steer" takes place in Wyoming, a setting that is crucial to the story's plot. Mero spends his life running away from his past, which he associates with Wyoming and the hardness of ranching life. However, Mero's physical journey from Massachusetts to Wyoming also prompts him to remember his past. As he gets closer to Wyoming and the ranch where he grew up, the setting affects him. He tries to beat the harsh weather and his lack of luck, using the calmness and confidence that he has built up during his sixty years away from Wyoming. However, he is unable to do so and dies in the process. As he is dying, the story about Tin Head and the half-skinned steer, told by his father's girlfriend, comes back to haunt him; he sees some cattle and hallucinates about one steer in particular: "It tossed its head, and in the howling, wintry light he saw he'd been wrong again, that the half-skinned steer's red eye had been watching for him all this time." Mero associates his troubled Wyoming past with the steer from the woman's

story. As a result, he imagines death as the half-skinned steer.

Imagery

Proulx is known for her striking imagery, and this story does not fail in this regard. The vivid images in this story come in many forms, and they collectively evoke a sense of harshness, decay, and violence. The Wyoming setting is depicted as an unforgiving land, where cattle die in many horrible ways and where "the wind packed enough sand to scour windshields opaque." When Mero takes the anthropologist to see the Native-American drawings, they travel along cliffs "ridged with ledges darkened by millennia of raptor feces." People are also depicted with gritty, unflattering imagery. Mero's father has a "gangstery face," with a "crushed rodeo nose and scar-crossed eyebrows" and a "stub ear." When Mero gets pulled over, the traffic officer is described as "a pimpled, mustached specimen with mismatched eyes." Finally, many events are described with expressive, often violent, imagery. When Louise tells Mero how his brother was clawed to death by an emu, she says that he "tried to fight it off with his cane, but it laid him open from belly to breakfast." This pathetic image of a feeble old man being ripped apart by a wild animal underscores the savage quality of the story. However, the most savage descriptions are those of cattle slaughter: "He ties up the back legs, hoists it up and sticks it, shoves the tub under to catch the blood. When it's bled out pretty good, he lets it down and starts skinning it." Proulx continues, going into excruciatingly vivid detail about how a steer is skinned. She maximizes the shock value of this image when she describes what the half-skinned steer looks like after it escapes: "It looks raw and it's got something bunchy and wet hanging down over its hindquarters."

Foreshadowing

Proulx includes several clues that foreshadow, or predict, the death of Mero. These clues often come in the form of events that go wrong. From the beginning, Mero is depicted as a strong, confident person who expects that everything will go his way and who feels that he can control any situation. However, events do not go as planned, and Mero steadily loses control over everything. Road construction affects his schedule, and he speeds to make up the time, getting a ticket in the process. The strain of his memories starts to affect him on the journey, making his mind feel "withered and punky." His lack of mental awareness causes him to get into an accident. This is a particularly significant clue for the reader that the story may have a tragic ending, since Mero told Louise in the beginning that he has "never had an accident in his life." His mental condition continues to deteriorate as he is unable to find the healthy food he usually eats. As a result of his famished and weary condition, he breaks one window in his car, his only shelter.

Proulx also foreshadows Mero's death with explicit references to death and misfortune. In the beginning, Mero gets the news that his brother has been clawed to death by an emu, a fate that Mero thinks he could avoid in similar circumstances: "He flexed his muscular arms, bent his knees, thought he could dodge an emu." Also, in the flashback to the story about the half-skinned steer, Mero's father's girlfriend explains that Tin Head is cursed for life after he botches the skinning of the steer. The placement of this particular flashback is important, since it happens right before Mero breaks the window of his car, thus sealing his tragic fate.

Historical Context

Nutritional Awareness in the 1990s

In 1990, the United States Congress passed the monumental Nutrition Labeling and Education Act, which required most foods to include a standardized information label. As a testament to the public interest in this issue, the United States Food and Drug Administration (FDA), one of two government organizations charged with implementing the act, received an unprecedented forty thousand comments from various individuals and groups. Still, nutritionists and many industry groups supported the new labels. By 1993, the regulations had been finalized, and over the next year, various manufacturers changed their labels. The new labels, entitled Nutrition Facts, listed a variety of information about a package of food, including standardized, realistic serving sizes and information on how the food fit into an overall daily diet. Raw meat and poultry products were one of the exceptions that did not require these packaging labels. In 1997, the Clinton administration acknowledged the success and consumer-friendliness of the food label by awarding it a Presidential Design Achievement Award.

In the 1990s, the government also revised the four food groups model of nutrition that it had used to educate the public for decades. While many nutritionists were in favor of the new model, it met with resistance from groups like the meat and dairy industries, which stood to lose business. In the four food groups model, emphasis was placed on the consumption of meat and dairy products. However, the new Food Guide Pyramid, which was eventually adopted in 1992 by the United States Department of Agriculture (USDA), diminished the importance of meats and dairy products in one's diet. In this new model, the original four food groups were expanded into six new categories, then arranged on a hierarchical pyramid. Meats and dairy products were located near the top, or least recommended, part of the pyramid.

The Fear of Diseased Beef

Besides the controversy over the nutritional value of meat, the meat industry and the general public had to deal with the serious prospect of diseased beef. In the 1980s in England, an epidemic of bovine spongiform encephalopathy (BSE), a brain disorder commonly known as mad cow disease, killed more than 140,000 cows. Little is known about this class of diseases, which includes Creutzfeldt-Jakob disease (CJD), a rare disorder that occurs in humans. However, enough was suspected about CJD and its link to BSE to cause a widespread panic in 1996. When several humans in England died of a new variant of CJD known as nvCJD, many people assumed that the disease was being transmitted through an English beef supply infected with BSE. As a result, the European Union banned the export of British beef from 1996 to 1999. Scientists proposed ideas about ways the bovine disease could get passed to humans, and one possibility became the dominant theory. The British cattle industry, like other countries, had long used a high-protein cattle feed made, in part, from the ground-up carcasses of other cows. If only one of these source animals had BSE, its disease could be transmitted to any cow that ate the feed.

The issue came to a head in the United States on April 16, 1996, when popular talk-show host Oprah Winfrey had invited Howard Lyman, an ex-rancher, onto her show. Lyman spoke about the possibility of a mad cow disease outbreak in U.S. cattle, since American ranchers were using similar protein feeds with their cattle. Winfrey was shocked to find out that naturally vegetarian animals like cows were being turned into meat-eaters and cannibals and said that she would never eat another hamburger. A year later, a group of Texas cattlemen claimed that Winfrey's remarks were responsible for a sharp drop in revenue following the 1996 broadcast and filed a multimillion-dollar defamation suit against the talk show host, the show's production and distribution companies, and Lyman. Jurors ruled in Winfrey's favor, saying that she did not maliciously hurt the beef industry with her comments. As a result of the increased exposure of this issue, however, the FDA issued new rules that banned most protein feeds made from ground-up animals. To this date, no case of mad cow disease or nvCJD has been reported in the United States.

Critical Overview

E. Annie Proulx's "The Half-Skinned Steer" and *Close Range: Wyoming Stories* have received mostly good reviews from critics. The reviewer for *Kirkus Reviews* notes that the story is one of two in the collection that particularly displays "Proulx's trademark whipsaw wit and raw, lusty language." Likewise, in his article for *Progressive,* Dean Bakopoulos calls the story "one of the highlights of this well-crafted collection" and says that the tale "sets up all the themes that dominate this volume: The struggle of hope against nature, mortality, and despair." In her book, *Understanding Annie Proulx,* Karen Rood notes that "Mero's trek evokes the traditional, mythic associations of the westward journey toward death, as he makes his solitary pilgrimage back in time as well as distance toward his boyhood home." Rood also notes that while this "powerful" story is "about an ending, it is also about returning to one's beginning, where, stripped bare of all defenses, one faces the harsh realities of life."

Not everybody gives the story or story collection total praise, however. In his essay for *Michigan Quarterly Review,* Michael Kowalewski says that, in the book, almost "all the men, young and old, seem capable of only a crude sexuality" and cites Mero's bestial sexual fantasies as an example. In a review for *Christian Science Monitor,* Merle Rubin says the story is not his favorite in the collection: "It's a bit portentous and heavy-handed in its symbolism, and parts drag, as Proulx piles on detail." Critics tend to either love or hate Proulx's attention to detail in the collection. The *Publishers Weekly* reviewer says that there is "stringent authority in

her meticulous descriptions." Likewise, Bakopoulos is surprised that Proulx is able "to give each story the plot, depth of character, sense of setting, and thematic weight of an entire novel." However, Bakopoulos also notes that Proulx's "talent is sometimes a flaw. On occasion, she packs in too much detail, particularly at the openings. . . . While impressive, this background information often slows the stories down."

The overwhelming majority of critics discuss Proulx's unique writing style. In his *English Journal* article, John Noell Moore says that he was not prepared for "the exquisite beauty of the language, the shaping of metaphor and symbol, the poetry in Proulx's pages." Likewise, in the *Georgia Review,* Erin McGraw cites Proulx's skill as a novelist but says that she is even more powerful in her short fiction, a form that "distills her strength of characterization and description." In fact, the effect of the tightly packed stories was powerful enough to make McGraw "have to close the book for a little while and recover from the shock." *Kirkus Reviews* gives the book a star, its designation for "books of unusual merit." In addition, the reviewer notes: "Nobody else writes like this, and Proulx has never written better." In fact, critics love Proulx's writing style so much that they are often inspired to create their own unique ways of describing it. In her *Booklist* review, Donna Seaman talks about Proulx's "booted and spurred sentences." McGraw says that "Proulx uses language like a glass-cutting tool to etch out her dark world."

Close Range: Wyoming Stories has also added to Proulx's enormous popular success. In fact, as Charlotte Glover notes in her *Library Journal* review, "Proulx's idiosyncratic writing style and offbeat characters are not for everyone, but her legions of fans will insure that this collection finds a home in every library."

Criticism

Ryan D. Poquette
Poquette has a bachelor's degree in English and specializes in writing about literature. In the

What Do I Read Next?

- In *Ranch of Dreams: The Heartwarming Story of America's Most Unusual Sanctuary* (1997), Cleveland Amory describes his many adventures for the Fund for Animals, which attempts to rescue endangered and abused animals. Many of these animals have been transferred to Amory's Black Beauty Ranch in East Texas. Amory has acquired a host of mistreated animals, including circus elephants, burros from the Grand Canyon, and even common farm animals like pigs.

- In *Breaking Clean* (2002), Judy Blunt recounts her experiences growing up as an independent tomboy on a Montana cattle ranch in the 1950s and 1960s. However, the gender roles for adult women were very narrow in this rural culture and did not allow her to be anything other than a wife and mother. For twelve years, Blunt suppressed her other desires, before breaking free from her past and leaving the ranch to pursue a new life.

- In *Heart Songs and Other Stories* (1988), Proulx's first collection of short stories, the author depicts the traditions and rituals of small-town life in her native New England.

- In her Pulitzer Prize–winning novel, *The Shipping News* (1993), Proulx depicts life in the harsh northern climate of Newfoundland, a maritime province of Canada. In the story, R. G. Quoyle, a journalist, returns to this land to start his life over after a failed marriage. In the process, Quoyle experiences a spiritual and psychological renewal.

- When Upton Sinclair's novel *The Jungle* was first published in 1906, it shocked readers with its graphic depictions of American capitalism, particularly life in Chicago's meat industry. In the story, Jurgis Rudkus, a Lithuanian immigrant, arrives in Chicago prepared to achieve the American Dream. Instead, he and his family are burdened by hardship and work under inhumane conditions in meatpacking plants, where they witness corruption such as the sale of spoiled or adulterated meat.

- In a collection of essays entitled *Where Rivers Change Direction* (1999), Mark Spragg recounts his life growing up on a ranch in rural Wyoming, a tough existence that forced him to become a man at age eleven. The author worked his family's land and escorted curious tourists—one of his few interactions with modern life—on camping trips into the Wyoming wilderness. As he grows up, Spragg realizes that he has a profound fear of death, which drives him to distraction.

---

following essay, Poquette discusses Proulx's use of bestial and violent images to underscore the inevitability of Mero's death.

Like most of Proulx's works, ''The Half-Skinned Steer'' draws readers into a tough world—in this case, the harsh ranching life and landscape of Wyoming. Mero tries to escape this world as a young man by moving far away. As he drives back to his family's ranch sixty years later for his brother's funeral, he immerses himself in this uncaring world once again, first through his memories, then in person. However, like before, he does not understand how to survive in this world, so all of his misguided attempts to get to the funeral ultimately lead to his tragic end. By examining Proulx's extensive use of bestial and violent images, one can see that Mero's death is inevitable.

Mero is haunted by his past life on the ranch, which he imagines and describes in animal terms. Most of this imagery is expressed in figurative language, which means using one or more figures of speech to embellish a description, as opposed to straight description without comparison. Writers use figurative language when they want to add meaning or create an effect. In this case, Proulx uses various types of figurative language, such as metaphors, to make life in Wyoming appear beastly and vicious. A metaphor is a comparison between dissimilar things in order to describe one of them in an unusual way. One obvious example of an animal metaphor in the story pertains to Mero's father's girlfriend. When Mero first introduces her, he describes her as if she were a horse: "If you admired horses, you'd go for her with her arched neck and horsy buttocks." A few sentences later, he talks about her "glossy eyes," another characteristic of horses. Mero also notes that she acts like a horse. She has the habit of biting her fingernails until they bleed, and Mero imagines her "nipping" her nails. At one point, after the woman has proven her ability to handle her liquor, Mero says that he "expected her to neigh."

The story includes figurative references to other animals, too. When Mero gets the call from his nephew's wife, Louise, Mero does not even know he has a nephew, much less one named "Tick," which makes Mero think of the insect: "He recalled the bloated gray insects pulled off the dogs. This tick probably thought he was going to get the whole damn ranch and bloat up on it." Once again, through the use of metaphor, Tick the human is compared to the insect in Mero's mind. When the young Mero observes the anthropologist pointing to various stone drawings, he uses a simile, another type of figurative language that differs slightly from a metaphor. Similes do not indicate that something is something else but that something is like something else. For this reason, similes are usually marked by the use of the word "like" or "as." Mero notes that the anthropologist is "pointing at an archery target, ramming his pencil into the air as though tapping gnats." In this simile, Mero compares the anthropologist's motion to the act of tapping gnats.

In addition to figurative language, the story has striking imagery. Imagery is description that draws images or verbal pictures with vivid, specific words. For example, the girlfriend vividly describes how Tin Head half-skinned a steer. But in this vicious world, animals also attack humans. Rollo is ripped apart by an emu. On the phone with Mero, Louise describes the emu's attack in slaughter terms: "it laid him open from belly to breakfast." This is the savage world of nature, especially in rural Wyoming.

The climate and landscape of this savage world are also expressed through animal imagery. When Mero drives through a Wyoming snowstorm, he notes the "snow snakes writhing across the asphalt." When he breaks the window of his car, he notes that the "snow roared through the broken

> " Mero is unable to live like an animal, and so he cannot just give in to his sexual desires like Rollo does, especially when they are linked in his mind with a revolting image of slaughter."

window," as if the snow were some wild beast. Shortly after this incident, when he is walking along the main road, he notices the beastly appearance of the harsh landscape. "Then the violent country showed itself, the cliffs rearing at the moon." A horse rears when it stands up on its hind legs, something that it does naturally when it is fighting. Since the cliffs are so high that they appear to be fighting with the moon, they provide a powerful image of nature's dominance on Earth. The same section of description also notes "the white flank of the ranch slashed with fence cuts." An animal's flank is its side, the meaty part between the ribs and the hip. By describing a ranch in terms of an animal flank that is being "slashed," and by placing this image in close proximity to the description of the towering cliffs, Proulx is evoking an image of human struggle with an overpowering nature.

As Erin McGraw notes in her *Georgia Review* article, "Proulx sees in the wild land a cosmic will to destroy. Her Wyoming, with its terrible summers and worse winters, grinds people down to their mean, bitter essentials." To survive in this raw world, people must be able to live raw, meeting their basic needs like animals do. In addition, they must not focus on anything that can take away from their ability to fulfill these needs or they will threaten their survival. However, Mero is unable to live in this way. Although he slaughters cattle, a necessary task for his survival, he feels guilty about it. After he flees the ranch, he orders a steak but is unable to eat it once he cuts into it and sees "the blood spread across the white plate." He envisions "the beast, mouth agape in mute bawling," an image of the cattle he has slaughtered.

The blood references in the story are a clear symbol for violence. A symbol is another type of figurative language. Symbols are physical objects, actions, or gestures that also represent an abstract concept, without losing their original identity. Blood is a literal, but blood has symbolical connotations as well, for example, of violence and savagery. Other references to blood in the story include the visual effect of Mero's taillights, which "lit the snow beneath the rear of the car like a fresh bloodstain." In addition, Proulx makes references to other fluids that evoke the image of blood in the way that they are depicted. After the car accident, Mero "watched his crumpled car, pouring dark fluids onto the highway, towed away behind a wrecker." Dark fluids in a car usually refer to oil and other lubricants, but in the context of this story, the image suggests that the car is dying, pouring its lifeblood onto the highway as it is towed away to its scrapyard grave.

Humans and animals have sexual drives. Proulx's descriptions of sexual matters are animalistic, especially when it comes to the horselike girlfriend, who inspires sexual desires in both Rollo and Mero. Rollo, who is as raw as the land in which he lives, welcomes these animal impulses. When he hears the story of Tin Head and the half-skinned steer, the brutality of the story only increases his passion for the girlfriend. On the other hand, Mero is attracted to the woman but not to her savage story. This contrast torments him, and subconsciously he links the two images: "Mero had thrashed all that ancient night, dreamed of horse breeding or hoarse breathing, whether the act of sex or bloody, cutthroat gasps he didn't know." This link does not go away. Says Karen Rood in her book *Understanding Annie Proulx,* "the alluring sexuality of his father's girlfriend and her gruesome story have become permanently linked in his mind, creating a simultaneous attraction and aversion to the opposite sex." Mero is unable to live like an animal, and so he cannot just give in to his sexual desires like Rollo does, especially when they are linked in his mind with a revolting image of slaughter.

Although Mero is not in touch with his animal side like the others in this story, he does not shun the animal world altogether. At one point, when trying to figure out the reasons why he left the ranch, Mero refers to the fact that he did not want to share his father's girlfriend. He had "learned from television nature programs that it had been time for him to find his own territory and his own woman." Watching nature programs, which Mero still does sixty years later, is as close to the animal world as Mero would like to get. Although he never realizes it, this is the essence of Mero's need to leave the ranch; he does

not belong in the raw, animalistic world of rural Wyoming. His subconscious knows this, so it produces Mero's dream, which makes him feel an urgent, unexplainable need to move several states away. Like a secondary male wolf in a pack, Mero seeks his own territory in which he can be dominant and claim his own female.

Sixty years later, Mero thinks that he left his Wyoming life because of the love triangle with his father's girlfriend. He does not understand that he really left as a young man because he was not cut out for Wyoming life; thus, his death is inevitable once he decides to go back as an old man. He feels he is up for the challenge of the physical and psychological journey because he has become fit and healthy through an active, vegetarian lifestyle and because he has attained wealth. In fact, he becomes overconfident and makes bad decisions that are based on this false sense of security. However, while these aspects serve him well in Massachusetts, they are useless in the raw, uncivilized world of rural Wyoming. As Rood notes, "he discovers that all his efforts to stave off death through a healthy vegetarian diet and vigorous exercise are of no avail against the powerful forces of nature." While he is making the trip to Wyoming, Mero's subconscious tries to warn him through another dream, in which the ranch house is blown apart by a violent war and Mero sees tubs full of "dark, coagulated fluid," or blood, beneath the floors. The fact that the dream ranch house is built on blood is an effective metaphor about the violence inherent in the ranching life and Wyoming. However, Mero does not heed this warning, as he did sixty years earlier when he left after his other dream, and continues on his journey. He also deliberately ignores advice from Wyoming locals like Louise, who are concerned that he might not make it in the winter weather.

This is a valid concern, as Mero does get stuck in the snow when he tries to get to the ranch. As he is freezing to death, Mero sees that a steer is keeping pace with him while he is walking: "It tossed its head, and in the howling, wintry light he saw he'd been wrong again, that the half-skinned steer's red eye had been watching for him all this time." Says Rood, the steer "clearly symbolizes the death he has worked so hard to avoid." For Mero, a civilized man born into a harsh world in which he could not survive and from which he could never quite escape, even his inevitable death appears in the image of an animal.

Source: Ryan D. Poquette, Critical Essay on "The Half-Skinned Steer," in *Short Stories for Students,* Gale, 2003.

Karen L. Rood

In the following excerpt from her book on Proulx, Rood provides an overview of "The Half-Skinned Steer" and comments on the meaning of the vulnerability of the story's characters.

In her acknowledgments Proulx writes that the idea for writing a collection of stories set in Wyoming came from an invitation by the Nature Conservancy to contribute a story inspired by a visit to one of its preserves to an anthology of short fiction titled *Off the Beaten Path* (1998). The result of Proulx's visit to the Ten Sleep Preserve on the south slope of the Big Horn Mountains in Wyoming was "The Half-Skinned Steer," first published in the November 1997 issue of the *Atlantic Monthly* and later selected by Garrison Keillor for inclusion in *The Best American Short Stories of 1998* and by John Updike for the best-selling *The Best American Short Stories of the Century* (1999). In his introduction to that anthology Updike describes Proulx's story as revisiting "the West that has seemed to this country the essence of itself." He adds, "I would have liked to finish this volume with a choice less dark, with an image less cruel and baleful than that of a half-skinned steer, but the American experience, story after story insisted, has been brutal and hard."

"The Half-Skinned Steer" follows the journey of Mero, a well-to-do man in his eighties, who makes an ill-advised cross-country journey from his home in Massachusetts to Wyoming for the funeral of his brother, Rollo, whom he has not seen in sixty years. He sets out to return to the family ranch he left in 1936. It is now a successful tourist attraction: Down Under Wyoming, where Rollo has been killed by the sharp claws of an emu, a nonindigenous bird brought there by the Australian co-owners of the park.

Mero's trek evokes the traditional, mythic associations of the westward journey toward death, as he makes his solitary pilgrimage back in time as well as distance toward his boyhood home. Overestimating his diminished capacities as a driver, he causes an accident near Des Moines, totaling his Cadillac. He buys another and drives resolutely onward, only to become lost and stuck during a snowstorm just miles from his destination, where he discovers that all his efforts to stave off death through a healthy vegetarian diet and vigorous exercise are of no avail against the powerful forces of nature.

> "Though 'The Half-Skinned Steer' is a story about an ending, it is also about returning to one's beginning, where, stripped bare of all defenses, one faces the harsh realities of life."

As he travels, Mero remembers the situation that precipitated his leaving home at twenty-three: the sexual longing aroused in him by his father's girlfriend and her telling of a grisly tall tale about a botched slaughter of a steer. In her story—which, according to Proulx is based on an Icelandic folktale called "Porgeir's Bull"—a hard-luck rancher, called Tin Head because of the metal plate in his head, sets out a butcher a steer, hitting it on the head with an axe and stunning instead of killing it. Thinking the animal dead, he hangs it up to bleed out for a while and then begins to skin it, starting with the head. Halfway through the job, he stops for dinner, after cutting out the steer's tongue so his wife can cook his favorite dish.

When he returns to finish the job, the half-skinned steer is gone. As he scans the horizon, "in the west on the side of the mountain he sees something moving stiff and slow" with "something bunchy and wet hanging down over its hindquarters." As the mute steer turns and looks back at him, Tin Head sees "the empty mouth without no tongue open wide and its red eyes glaring at him, pure teetotal hatred like arrows coming at him, and he knows he is done for and all of his kids is done for, and that his wife is done for"—and, the girlfriend explains, his intuition proves true.

This powerful story, with its pathetic and grotesque image of the death that comes for every living being, has turned Mero into a vegetarian, but it has also had another, greater impact on his life, as it has become associated with the sexual longings evoked in him by its teller. After hearing her tale, Mero "dreamed of horse breeding or hoarse breathing, whether the act of sex or bloody cut-throat gasps he didn't know." Years later he is still troubled by his dream, from which he awoke with the conviction that it was time to leave home. For a long time he believed that he had no "hard reason" for going off on his own, but at eighty-three he favors the straightforward explanation "that it had been time for him to find his own territory and his own woman," and he congratulates himself on having "married three or four of them and sampled plenty." Yet the alluring sexuality of his father's girlfriend and her gruesome story have become permanently linked in his mind, creating a simultaneous attraction and aversion to the opposite sex. As he travels into the country of his boyhood, he is still haunted by memories of the woman who "could make you smell the smoke from an unlit fire" and the image of the half-skinned steer, which clearly symbolizes the death he has worked so hard to avoid.

As he reaches the vicinity of the ranch at nightfall, falling snow and the absence of long-remembered landmarks confuse Mero. He turns on a narrow track that may or may not lead to the ranch, and his car becomes stuck in the snow. Ignoring his first impulse to wait in the car until morning, he exerts himself in an unsuccessful attempt to free the car. Then he begins walking through the snowstorm in the direction where he thinks he will find a neighboring ranch about ten miles away—if the house is still there and if he is correct in his intuition of his present location.

As he walks through "the violent country," feeling vulnerable in the wind and cold, he notices that one animal in a herd of cattle on the other side of a fence is walking with him. As he turns to look at it, he realizes that "he'd been wrong again, that the half-skinned steer's red eye had been watching him all this time." Coming face to face with his own mortality, Mero learns that neither money nor healthy living can insulate him from the traumas of his past or the inevitability of death. As he takes his final walk, "feeling as easy to tear as a man cut from paper," he has become like the half-skinned steer, robbed of all defenses against the forces of nature and stumbling mute and vulnerable toward death.

Though "The Half-Skinned Steer" is a story about an ending, it is also about returning to one's beginning, where, stripped bare of all defenses, one faces the harsh realities of life. As such, the story is a fitting introduction to a collection of short stories in which character after character faces an unforgiving environment, feeling as vulnerable as "a man cut from paper."

Source: Karen L. Rood, "*Close Range: Wyoming Stories,*" in *Understanding Annie Proulx,* University of South Carolina Press, 2001, pp. 153–91.

John Noell Moore

In the following review, Moore praises Proulx for her "complex plotting" and interweaving of the "two tales" in "The Half-Skinned Steer."

I discovered Annie Proulx's latest collection of short stories on the list of contenders for *The New Yorker* Book Award for best fiction of 1999. I resolved to read it because years ago I had purchased her Pulitzer Prize winning novel *The Shipping News*, and (need I say this?) I had never gotten around to reading it. The stories in *Close Range* grabbed me "like a claw in the gut," a simile I borrow from one of the stories: "This wild country—indigo jags of mountain, grassy plain everlasting, tumbled stones like fallen cities, the flaring roll of sky—provokes a spiritual shudder. It is like a deep note that cannot be heard but is felt, it is like a claw in the gut" ("People in Hell Just Want a Drink of Water"). I was not prepared for the "spiritual shudder" that came in the brutality of some of the trails, their terrifying imagery, their graphic sexual scenes. I was also not prepared for the exquisite beauty of the language, the shaping of metaphor and symbol, the poetry in Proulx's pages. Her title is literal and metaphoric. She startles us with her close-ups of life on the range; her characters move in landscapes that are unforgiving of their flaws, impervious to their tiny triumphs. Her vision is metaphoric: She studies her people and their land at close range, too, in detail that opens them up to our wonder and amazement, to our disgust, and, in some cases, to our admiration.

For the epigraph to these stories Proulx chooses a quotation from Jack Hitt's article "Where the Deer and the Zillionaire's Play" in the October 1997 edition of *Outside.* A retired Wyoming rancher explains, "Reality's never been of much use out here." In her acknowledgments, Proulx elaborates on his words and gives us a hint about how we might read her world: "The elements of unreality, the fantastic and improbable, color all of these stories as they color real life. In Wyoming not the least fantastic situation is the determination to make a living ranching in this tough and unforgiving place." The eleven stories in *Close Range* vary in length from the very short ones (2–7 pages) to a number of stories that are 35 or so pages long. Proulx juxtaposes tales about a story heard in youth that comes back to haunt a dying man ("The Half-Skinned

Steer''), a young bull rider following the rodeo circuit to avoid the pain of family life (''The Mud Below''), a mixture of fairy tale and romance (''The Bunchgrass Edge of the World''), and the deep and unspoken bond between two men (''Brokeback Mountain'').

Proulx's stories are about love and loss, about suffering and endurance. The last lines of ''The Bunchgrass Edge of the World'' speak a recurring theme: ''The main thing in life was staying power.'' In ''The Governors of Wyoming'' a rancher voices a similar world view: ''The main thing about ranchin,'' he says, is ''last as long as you can, make things come out so it's still your ranch when it's time to get buried. That's my take on it.'' Proulx explores the distance between where lives begin and end and the ways in which her characters negotiate the terrain in between. The last sentence of the last story makes a pronouncement on the way Proulx's characters read their world: ''There was some open space between what he knew and what he tried to believe, but nothing could be done about it, and if you can't fix it, you've got to stand it.'' Many of the stories are about just that: standing, enduring the way things work out.

''The Half-Skinned Steer,'' the first story in the collection, serves as a good introduction to this major theme of negotiating distance and to the complex plotting that we encounter in subsequent stories. It is a story about acts of storytelling, about fact and fantasy. in the first sentence we meet the aging Mero:

> In the long unfurling of his life, from tight-wound kid hustler in a wool suit riding the train out of Cheyenne to geriatric limper in this spooled-out year, Mero had kicked down thought of the place where he began, a so-called ranch on the strange ground at the south hinge of the Big Horns.

The story is about Mero's memory and his journey back to that beginning place.

The story opens as Mero learns of his brother Rollo's death and determines to drive the long distance to the funeral. Moving in and out of the past, Proulx weaves together his story and a fantastic tale he remembers from his youth. A map of these intertwined narrative threads illustrates her complex plotting:

Mero 1 Present: News of Rollo's death; the decision to travel

Storyteller 1 Past: Introduces Mero's father's girlfriend, a ''teller of tales of hard deeds and mayhem''

> **''...the way in which Proulx weaves together the two tales offers us that sense of having come to a moment in a story where what happens seems to be just right.''**

Tin Head 1 Past: The girlfriend's story about a man named Tin Head begins

Mero 2 Present: Mero's fitful sleep and bad dreams before the journey

Tin Head 2 Past: How ''things went wrong'' on Tin Head's ranch

Mero 3 Past: An anthropologist gives Mero a lesson in human sexuality.

Mero 4 Present. Travelling, near Des Moines, Mero wrecks the car, buys another. Approaches the ranch: ''Nothing had changed . . . the empty pale place and its rearing wind, the distant antelope as tiny as mice, landforms shaped true to the present.''

Tin Head 3 Girlfriend continues her story of a steer, half-skinned and left while Tin Head eats supper. ''She was a total liar,'' Mero thinks.

Mero 5 Traveling toward home

Mero 6 Memories of the past

Mero 7 Nearing the ranch, he senses ''an eerie dream quality'' about it. Mero runs ''on the unmarked road through great darkness.''

Tin Head 4 When Tin Head returns, the steer has disappeared.

Mero 8 Misses turnoff to the ranch, backs car into hole.

Tin Head 5 Tin Head finds steer, interprets it as a sign of fate.

Mero 9 No hope of getting the car out, Mero senses doom: ''It was almost a relief to have reached this point where the celestial fingernails were poised to nip his thread.''

Mero 10 The ending

I will not ruin the story by revealing how it ends, but I will say that the way in which Proulx weaves together the two tales offers us that sense of having come to a moment in a story where what happens seems to be just right.

In "People in Hell Just Want a Drink of Water." Proulx plots similarly, weaving together the stories of two families, the Dunmires and the Tinsleys. Their alternating stories pull us rapidly forward, but it all ends by challenging our belief in what we have just witnessed: "That was all sixty years ago . . . We are in a new millennium and such desperate things no longer happen." The final sentence teases us: "If you believe that you'll believe anything." Similarly, "The Governors of Wyoming" presents two sets of characters Who have opposite views about the value of cattle ranching. Wade Walls who "seemed to come from nowhere and belong to no one" believes that cows are "world-destroying," that the "domestication of livestock was the single most terrible act the human species ever perpetuated. It dooms everything living." He envisions a paradise where native grasses and wildflowers cover the earth, where antelope, elk, and bison roam: "If I ran the world, I'd . . . leave the winds and the grasses to the hands of the gods. Let it be the empty place." The story unfolds as Wade's determination to act against cattle ranchers escalates into a revenge plot with a surprising twist in its final scene.

"Job History," a tight little story told in the present tense, although it begins in 1947 with the birth of its central figure Leeland Lee, happens quickly and cuts through the imagination sharply. It is a perfect example of an idea about how a story happens, taken from *The God of Small Things:* "Little events, ordinary things, smashed and reconstituted. Imbued with new meaning. Suddenly they become the bleached bones of a story." "Job History" is seven pages long; its characters never speak. Their lives are stripped to the bone in Proulx's portrayal of the inexorable rush of time.

When I read "The Bunchgrass Edge of the World," the story of the Touheys—Old Red; his Vietnam veteran son, Aladdin, and his wife, Wauneta; and their three children Tyler, Shah, and Ottaline, "the family embarrassment," I found myself singing and remembering fairy tales. In a set of short stories filled with dashed hopes, violent and unrequited love, more miser' than we can take, this story offers a brief respite and even some humor. We follow the longings of Ottaline, the oldest daughter "distinguished by a physique approaching the size of a hundred-gallon propane tank." She despairs of ever escaping the ranch as her siblings have done, but she maintains a thread of hope: "Someone had to come for her." In the repetition of this idea in the story I found myself singing "Someday My Prince Will Come" from *Snow White and the Seven Dwarfs.*

Because she "craved to know something of the world" Ottaline listens to her scanner where she often only hears couples arguing.

Her story takes a wonderful turn when one of her father's discarded tractors strikes up a conversation with her one day as she walks though the family gravel pit: "'Hello, sweetheart. Come here, come here.' It was the 4030, Aladdin's old green tractor." Of course! This tractor is the frog prince of the fairy tale. Ottaline lives, after all, in a fantastic world; when your father's name is Aladdin, anything can happen. When she complains to the tractor that she is fat, it replies "What I like." The tractor explains that what tractors want is a human connection, and Ottaline sets out to repair the green machine. If you remember the fairy tale, you may be able to predict the ending of this story. Remember, though, this is a Wyoming story, and Proulx has made it clear that we live here in a fantastic unreality.

Each of these stories profoundly engages me as a reader. "A Lonely Coast" warns that "it's easier than you think to yield up to the dark impulse." The two shirts in "Brokeback Mountain" etch this tale of "the grieving plain" into my memory as they hang in the closet, a heartbreaking symbol of a love not tolerated at close range, "the pair like two skins, one inside the other, two in one." "The Mud Below" tells the sad story of Diamond Felt's hunger to know who his father is while he destroys his future and his body rodeoing. He learns that life "was all a hard, fast ride that ended in the mud." And I get the sense in "The Blood Bay" that, even though someone always has to pay the cost, some things do add up at close range: "The arithmetic stood comfortable." These are stories to savor, to read slowly, to read again.

Nowhere in *Close Range* does Proulx give me a better context for inviting you to read her stories than in the dosing scenes of "A Lonely Coast." We're driving toward the town of Casper, and our arrival becomes a metaphor for making meaning:

> You come down a grade and all at once the shining town lies below you, slung out like all western towns, and with the curved milk of mountains behind it. The lights trail away to the east in a brief and stubby duster of yellow that butts hard against the dark. And if you've ever been to the lonely coast you've seen how the shore rock drops off into the black water and how the light on the point is final.

At the shore, the narrator tells us, we see the "old rollers coming in for millions of years," and here, on the range at night, the wind rolls, reminding us that "the sea covered this place hundreds of millions of years ago, the slow evaporation, the mud turned to stone.'' Proulx wraps up the scene with an idea that seems to capture how I feel after reading this book: ''There's nothing calm in these thoughts. It isn't finished, it can still tear apart. Nothing is finished. You take your chances.''

I invite you to take your chances, to drive through Proulx's shining towns. Prepare to be deeply moved, angry, shocked. Keep driving, though. The journey is worth the effort.

Source: John Noell Moore, ''The Landscape of Fiction,'' in *English Journal,* Vol. 80, No. 1, September 2000, pp. 146–48.

Sources

Bakopoulos, Dean, ''Woes of the West,'' in *Progressive,* Vol. 63, No. 9, September 1999, p. 43.

Glover, Charlotte L., Review of *Close Range: Wyoming Stories,* in *Library Journal,* Vol. 124, No. 8, May 1, 1999, p. 115.

Kowalewski, Michael, ''Losing Our Place: A Review Essay,'' in *Michigan Quarterly Review,* Vol. 40, No. 1, Winter 2001, p. 242.

McGraw, Erin, ''Brute Force: Violent Stories,'' in *Georgia Review,* Vol. 54, No. 2, Summer 2000, p. 351.

Moore, John Noell, ''The Landscape of Fiction,'' in *English Journal,* Vol. 90, No. 1, September 2000, p. 146.

Proulx, Annie, ''The Half-Skinned Steer,'' in *The Best American Short Stories of the Century,* Houghton Mifflin Company, 2000, pp. 754–68.

Review of *Close Range: Wyoming Stories,* in *Kirkus Reviews,* March 1, 1999.

Review of *Close Range: Wyoming Stories,* in *Publishers Weekly,* Vol. 246, No. 13, March 29, 1999, p. 91.

Rood, Karen L., *Understanding Annie Proulx,* University of South Carolina Press, 2001, pp. 154–57.

Rubin, Merle, ''Cowboy Country,'' in *Christian Science Monitor,* June 3, 1999, p. 20.

Seaman, Donna, Review of *Close Range: Wyoming Stories,* in *Booklist,* Vol. 95, No. 14, March 15, 1999, p. 1261.

Further Reading

Barnard, Neal, *Food for Life: How the New Four Food Groups Can Save Your Life,* 1993, reprint, Crown, 1994.

In the story, Mero thinks that his vegetarian diet will help him postpone his death. Dr. Barnard also thinks that vegetarianism can increase life expectancy and advocates selecting foods from four food groups: grains, legumes, vegetables, and fruits. This system mimics the structure of the four food groups model endorsed by the United States Department of Agriculture (USDA) prior to 1992, but changes the actual groups (eliminating meat).

Carlson, Laurie Winn, *Cattle: An Informal Social History,* Ivan R. Dee, 2001.

This engaging and informative book examines the history of cattle in various eras and cultures, offering many anecdotes in the process. In addition to a study of the animal itself, Carlson also discusses the beef and dairy industries and the current controversies over safe methods of food production.

Lyman, Howard F., *Mad Cowboy: Plain Truth from the Cattle Rancher Who Won't Eat Meat,* Scribner, 1998.

Lyman's 1996 comments on *The Oprah Winfrey Show* about shocking, unsafe practices in the meat industry drew fire from a group of Texas cattlemen, resulting in a high-profile lawsuit. In his book, Lyman, a former cattle rancher, chronicles his journey from carnivore to vegetarian, gives an inside view of the meat and dairy industries, and discusses the potential for an epidemic of mad cow disease in American cattle.

Pflughoft, Fred, *Wyoming: Wild and Beautiful,* American World Geographic, 1999.

In her story, Proulx describes Wyoming's landscapes in striking detail. In his book, Fred Pflughoft, a western photographer, depicts the state's landscapes with more than 120 full-color images from all four seasons. Pflughoft's photos include a variety of famous and obscure locations, including national parks, deserts, rock formations, canyons, lakes, rivers, and streams.

"If I Forget Thee, O Earth ... "

Arthur C. Clarke

1951

"'If I Forget Thee, O Earth . . . ,'" by Arthur C. Clarke, was first published in *Future* magazine in 1951. However, it received its greatest exposure when it was collected in Clarke's *Expedition to Earth*, which was published in 1953. The story tapped into one of the great fears of the 1950s, the threat of atomic war. The U.S. decision to drop atomic bombs on Hiroshima and Nagasaki at the end of World War II ushered in the atomic age, and many writers, especially science fiction writers, wrote stories depicting an atomic apocalypse. In this story, Marvin, the ten-year-old main character who lives in a lunar colony, gets to see an earthrise for the first time. However, joy turns to despair as he sees the glowing, radioactive earth that has been destroyed by an atomic World War III. He realizes that he is in permanent exile and that only his descendants will be able to return home. Critics and popular readers alike appreciate the cautionary message in this story and note the quality of many of Clarke's short stories in general. However, it is Clarke's novels—most notably *Childhood's End*; the novelization of his screenplay for the movie, *2001: A Space Odyssey*; and *Rendezvous with Rama*—that have made him famous. "'If I Forget Thee, O Earth . . .'" can be found in Clarke's *Tales from Planet Earth*, published by ibooks, inc., in 2001.

Author Biography

Clarke was born on December 16, 1917, in Minehead, Somersetshire, England. Like many children in his generation, Clarke first discovered science fiction through *Amazing Stories,* one of the popular science fiction pulp magazines—so-called because they were printed on cheap, wood-pulp paper. Clarke moved on to reading books by H. G. Wells, Olaf Stapledon, and other British science fiction writers, and he wrote stories for a school magazine as a teenager. In 1936, he could no longer afford his education and dropped out to work as a government auditor. At the same time, he became involved with the British Interplanetary Society, an association formed by fans of science fiction and space science. Here, Clarke met many science fiction editors and writers, who helped him start selling some of his short stories.

In 1941, Clarke enlisted in the Royal Air Force. After teaching himself mathematics and electronics theory, he served as a radar instructor until the end of the war. In 1945, he published his famous article, ''Extraterrestrial Relays,'' in which he introduced the idea of communication satellites. After the war, he returned to school, earning degrees in physics and in pure and applied mathematics from King's College, University of London, in 1948. While working as an assistant editor for a technical journal, *Science Abstracts,* Clarke continued devoting time to both his science writing and his science fiction writing. In 1952, he published *The Exploration of Space*, widely regarded as the first nontechnical overview of space technology. The book was a hit with popular audiences and became the first science book chosen as a Book-of-the-Month Club selection. This success, coupled with the success of his novel *Childhood's End* (1953), gave Clarke the financial means to pursue his writing full time. In 1953, he also published *Expedition to Earth*, which collected many of his earlier magazine stories, including '''If I Forget Thee, O Earth . . .'''

A prolific writer, Clarke published many other science and science fiction books. In both, he earned a solid reputation for his understanding of science and for his ability to illuminate complex scientific concepts. This recognition led to Clarke's placement in several high-profile projects. Among these were the National Aeronautics and Space Adminis-

Arthur C. Clarke

tration's Apollo missions, for which Clarke served as a co-anchor with Walter Cronkite from 1968 to 1970. These included the historic Apollo 11 mission, in which Neil Armstrong and Buzz Aldrin became the first men to set foot on the moon on July 20, 1969. In the late 1960s, Clarke also worked with director Stanley Kubrick to write the script for and novelization of *2001: A Space Odyssey*. Both versions, released in 1968, were based on ''The Sentinel,'' one of Clarke's short stories.

Clarke's awards are as impressive as his writing output. He has won every major award given for science fiction works, including the Hugo Award for ''The Star'' (1956) and Hugo and Nebula awards for *Rendezvous with Rama* (1974) and *The Fountains of Paradise* (1980). In addition, in 1986, the Science Fiction Writers of America named Clarke a Grand Master. Clarke has also received countless awards for his nonfiction writing efforts, which have helped increase public understanding of science. However, perhaps the greatest honor came in 1997, when Clarke was knighted. Clarke continues to write from his home in Sri Lanka, where he has resided since the late 1960s. His other works include *3001: The Final Odyssey* (1997) and *The Trigger* (1999).

Plot Summary

"'If I Forget Thee, O Earth ... '" starts off by introducing Marvin, a ten-year-old boy. Marvin and his father walk quickly through a large building, which includes a greenhouse and an observatory, then enter an airlock chamber, where they get into a scout car and drive outside. Before now, Marvin has only seen the outside in photographs and on television. At this point, Clarke has not revealed where they are, but he starts to give clues that they are not on earth as soon as Marvin and his father leave the airlock. The sun is moving across a completely black sky, a sight not possible from earth due to earth's atmosphere. When the sky is black on earth, it is because the sun has set, in which case the moon comes out. Also, Marvin has read about the classic rhyme "Twinkle, twinkle, little star" in one of his father's books and is surprised to see that the stars do not twinkle. When stars are viewed by the unaided human eye from within earth's atmosphere, the turbulence in the higher ranges of the atmosphere causes the stars to look like they are twinkling, an effect known as scintillation. The absence of this effect is one more clue from Clarke that Marvin and his father are not on earth.

They drive at one hundred miles an hour in their car, which has balloon tires. This is different from most cars on earth, which have tires made of rubber. They pass a mine and drive down the steep edge of the plateau that contains their colony. They cross a shadow line, and the sun disappears, plunging them into darkness. Hours later, after driving through mountains and valleys, they pass the remains of a crashed rocket, another sign that they are not on earth. After many more hours, they reach the end of the mountain range and descend into a valley. Since the sun is hidden from the valley, Marvin is surprised to find the valley illuminated by a strange white light. Marvin and his father sit quietly for several minutes, as Marvin adjusts his eyesight to the glare of the planet that is giving off the bright white light.

At this point, the boy can discern through the hazy atmosphere the outlines of continents and the polar ice caps that identify the planet as earth. Marvin mourns the fact that he has never experienced the diverse climate of earth and wonders why this is, since earth looks so peaceful. However, as his eyes continue to adjust, he sees that the shadowed half of the earth, which should be totally dark, is gleaming with a radioactive glow—evidence of the atomic war that has taken place on earth. At this

point, Clarke reveals that Marvin and his father are watching from a quarter of a million miles away, which means that they—and their colony—are on the moon, something the reader might already suspect from the earlier clues.

Marvin's father tells Marvin the story of earth's destruction, which he has heard before, but which he has not understood until now. He also tells Marvin how the humans at this moon outpost, most likely the last remnant of human civilization, had to fight to survive. Without the regular supplies sent from earth, they had to adapt to the hostile environment of the moon, their new home in exile. This was not their biggest battle, however. As Marvin's father tells him, the biggest challenge to their survival is to maintain the will to survive, since none of them, including Marvin, will ever be able to return to earth. It will be centuries before earth has cleansed itself of the radioactivity, so only Marvin's distant descendants will be able to return to earth. Marvin realizes that, someday, he will bring his own child to this spot, as his father has done, to pass the tradition on and keep the dream alive of someday returning home. On the return trip, Marvin is sobered by the sight of the home that he will never see, and he does not look at earth again.

Characters

Marvin

Marvin is the main character, a boy in a moon colony, who sees the post-apocalypse earth for the first time during an earthrise when he is ten. The narrator tells the story through Marvin's eyes, revealing details as Marvin observes them; as a result, readers experience the shock of the ruined earth at the same time as Marvin does. Marvin is excited when he finds out his father is going to take him outside to the moon's surface. When they get into the scout car and start driving, Marvin is even more ecstatic. He has seen the surface of the moon in photographs and on television within the moon colony, but the surface is even more spectacular up close. The same is true for the stars, which Marvin and the others in the moon colony cannot see while they are inside the colony. However, when Marvin sees his first earthrise, his happiness turns to dread. Although the lighted half of earth looks perfectly normal, and Marvin imagines the lush forests and oceans that he has heard about, the half of earth that should be dark is glowing—a sign of the radioactive aftermath of atomic war. Marvin's father tells him how humanity destroyed itself, leaving only the small colony of humans on the moon. Now, they must wait hundreds of years until the radioactivity subsides, preserving the human race in the moon colony, before their descendants can make their way back to earth.

Marvin's Father

Marvin's father, one of the initial members of the colony on the moon, remains silent for most of the story. The narrator tells the story through the eyes of Marvin, who notices at one point during the journey to the dark side of the moon that his father is driving quickly and recklessly, as if he is trying to run from something. When they reach the spot where Marvin and his father observe the earthrise, Marvin sees the radioactive earth and understands why. Marvin's father has lived on earth, so he knows what he is missing by being forced to live in exile in the artificial environment of the moon colony. As they witness the earthrise, Marvin's father tells him the story of the atomic war that left his colony stranded on the moon and the struggle that they had to survive. More importantly, he impresses upon Marvin the importance of surviving and reproducing so that Marvin's descendants will someday be able to return to earth after it is no longer radioactive.

Media Adaptations

- Clarke's *Earthlight and Other Stories: The Collected Stories of Arthur C. Clarke* (1950–1951) features an audio adaptation of ''If I Forget Thee, O Earth . . . '' and other classic Clarke stories. This unabridged audio collection, which was produced by Audio Literature in 2001, uses a different reader for each story.

- Clarke's 1951 short story ''The Sentinel'' was adapted by Clarke and director Stanley Kubrick as the film and novelization *2001: A Space Odyssey* (1968). Clarke has a cameo role in the Academy Award–winning film, which was released in both VHS and DVD formats from Warner Home Video in 2001.

- *The Best Short Stories of Arthur C. Clarke: The Collected Stories of Arthur C. Clarke* includes an audio adaptation of ''If I Forget Thee, O Earth . . . '' as well as other classic and recent Clarke stories. This unabridged audio collection, which was produced by Audio Literature in 2001, is available on ten compact discs.

Themes

The Aftermath of Atomic War

When Clarke published his story in 1951, humankind had already witnessed the U.S. wartime detonation of two atomic bombs as well as several atomic tests. As people realized the destructive capabilities of atomic weapons, many science fiction writers envisioned the potential aftermath of atomic war in stories like this one. When Marvin views his first earthrise, he refers to the atomic quality of the destruction. As the narrator says, ''the glow of dying atoms was still visible, a perennial reminder of the ruinous past.'' Because radioactive atoms take a long time to die, they are visible from the moon even when their targets, the humans who fought in the atomic war, are long dead. Clarke was also familiar with the processes by which atomic radiation would eventually be cleansed from earth. Says the narrator, ''[t]he winds and the rains would scour the poisons from the burning lands and carry

them to the sea.'' It is in the vastness of the oceans that the radiation poisons will finally be diluted enough so that ''they could harm no living things.''

Exile

The characters in Clarke's story experience a planetary exile. Marvin has never even stepped foot on earth, having been born in the lunar colony. The narrator notes this fact when describing Marvin's first view of earth: ''There in that shining crescent were all the wonders that he had never known.'' Marvin has only read about earth in books, a thought that makes him feel even more ''the anguish of exile.'' This feeling gets worse as he sees the portion of earth that should be dark, ''gleaming faintly with an evil phosphorescence'' and remembers the stories of the atomic war that left his parents stranded on the moon. This lunar exile is different from anything that humanity has known thus far.

Topics for Further Study

- Research the countries that are currently believed to have nuclear weapons and create a detailed map that locates these countries. Use color coding or some other system to indicate approximately how many nuclear devices are in each of these countries.

- Choose two nuclear-capable nations that are currently in conflict with each other or that have experienced conflict with each other in the last two decades, including the allies of each country. Write a step-by-step scenario that describes what might happen in these countries and the rest of the world if nuclear weapons were used in such a conflict.

- Clarke is noted for the predictive quality in many of his stories. Review the current research being conducted into space travel and settlement of extraterrestrial environments. Discuss whether you think it will be possible for humans to live on the moon some day.

- Like many science fiction tales, this story is a cautionary one about humanity destroying itself. Discuss whether you think peace on earth is really possible, using research to back up your claims. If you believe that peace is ultimately impossible, find three battles from any time in human history that you feel illustrate humanity's tendency towards self-destruction.

- In the story, the lunar exiles must instill in their children the desire to go home, a rite of passage that will ensure the future survival of the human race. Pick any native society whose livelihood or cultural identity is dependent upon its own rites of passage. Discuss these customs and explore whether they are in danger of extinction due to technology, the encroachment of other civilizations, or other human factors.

People have often been exiled but sometimes have had the option of coming back. However, the residents of the moon colony do not have the option to return. In the final days of earth's destruction, they learn this fact and realize that "they were alone at last, as no men had ever been alone before, carrying in their hands the future of the race."

Survival

The current residents of the colony will never step foot on earth again. Says Marvin: "It would be centuries yet before that deadly glow died from the rocks and life could return again to fill that silent, empty world." However, following the destruction of earth, the colony members could not think too deeply about the implications of this situation; they were too busy fighting for their own immediate survival. Having grown accustomed to being dependent upon earth for their provisions, it came as a profound shock when "the colony had learned at last that never again would the supply ships come flaming down through the stars with gifts from home." For several years, the lunar exiles fight to make a sufficient home on the moon using the supplies that they already have, and, eventually, they prevail. As the narrator observes of the colony, "this little oasis of life was safe against the worst that Nature could do."

Once their short-term survival has been secured, the members of the moon colony realize that they must do more. They must transfer their cultural and scientific knowledge—as well as their desire to return to earth—to their children, who must in turn pass this goal to their own children. When his father takes him to view the ruined earth, Marvin understands that this rite of passage is crucial to the survival of the human race, even though he has to live with the fact that he will never get to see the earth himself. "He would never walk beside the rivers of that lost and legendary world. . . . Yet one day . . . his children's children would return to claim their heritage."

Style

Science Fiction

"'If I Forget Thee, O Earth ...'" takes place in the future, when humanity possesses technology that is greater than that in Clarke's time. Future scenarios are one of the hallmarks of many science fiction works. In some cases, as in this one, science fiction writers create their version of the future by extrapolating current technologies to a logical conclusion. For example, when the story was published in 1951, the United States and the [former] Soviet Union were just beginning to launch their space programs. And the moon, earth's closest neighbor, seemed a likely first target. The apocalyptic tone of the story is another common hallmark of many science fiction works. While some science fiction writers write stories that illustrate how science might make life better for humans in the future, others take a more negative view, offering tales that caution against the potential destructive power of science. As the narrator says of Marvin: "He was looking upon the funeral pyre of a world—upon the radioactive aftermath of Armageddon." The chilling picture that Clarke paints of the potential consequences of atomic war is a clear warning to humanity. When his father is describing the history of earth's atomic war, Marvin cannot understand "the forces that had destroyed it in the end, leaving the colony, preserved by its isolation, as the sole survivor." In the end, Clarke uses Marvin's innocence and horrible realizations in the story to underscore his own view that atomic war is ridiculous and incomprehensible.

Setting

Clarke's moon setting is necessary to achieve the full effect of his message. In order for the story to work, the characters must experience an exile beyond earth, where they can view the aftermath of earth's destruction at a safe distance. Since the moon is earth's closest neighbor, a mere "quarter of a million miles" away, it is the only planetary body from which a human could view the earth with the unaided eye. The moon is also an environment that is not naturally inhabitable, so this setting underscores for these viewers the danger of earth's destruction. Says the narrator of the time immediately following the colony members' exile: "Then had followed the years of despair, and the long-drawn battle for survival in this fierce and hostile world."

Point of View

Clarke uses a third-person narrator to tell his tale. In a third-person narrative, there is an outside narrator who refers to the characters. For example, the first sentence of the story says that Marvin's father took "him" through the colony. In addition, since the narrator tells the story through the eyes of Marvin alone, the third-person narration is also considered a limited point of view. This method is particularly effective in this story, since the reader only learns facts as Marvin does, so that neither finds out what is going on until the end of the story. The only difference between Marvin's and the reader's knowledge is that, in the beginning, Marvin knows he is on the moon, while the reader does not. Throughout much of the story, facts about the moon setting are revealed selectively to the reader, as Marvin views the outside surface of the moon for the first time. These clues include the description of the land "burning beneath the fierce sun that crawled so slowly across the jet-black sky," the presence of "a jumbled wasteland of craters, mountain ranges, and ravines," and "the skeleton of a crashed rocket." When Marvin and his father reach what should be a dark valley, he is surprised to find it "awash with a cold white radiance," which is soon discovered to be light from the damaged earth—a surprise for both Marvin and Clarke's readers.

Historical Context

The Dawn of the Atomic Age

In August 1945, in an effort to end World War II quickly and decisively, the United States dropped atomic bombs, also known as A-bombs, on the Japanese cities of Hiroshima and Nagasaki. The immediate explosive and long-term destructive forces were unlike anything that humanity had ever seen. These two events, which led to the rapid surrender of Japan and the end of World War II, also served to usher in the atomic age and the threat of further atomic war. During World War II, many countries had been working on their own atomic bombs. After the decimation at Hiroshima and Nagasaki, several countries rushed to complete these bombs. In 1946, the United States, the world's top superpower, again set an example when it began a series of peacetime atomic bomb tests at Bikini Atoll in the western chain of the Marshall Islands, in the central Pacific Ocean. In 1949, the Soviet Union, the other major superpower at the time, tested

Compare
&
Contrast

- **1950s:** The United States lives under the constant threat of nuclear warfare.

  Today: Following the terrorist attacks of September 11, 2001, in New York and Washington, D.C., the United States enters a new kind of war. The public lives with generalized fear of chemical and biological warfare.

- **1950s:** The United States government releases several propaganda films and newsreels that attempt to calm citizens' fears by saying that radiation from atomic bombs cannot harm them if they take proper precautions. These include building personal bomb shelters that are supposed to be able to withstand a nuclear blast, radiation, and fallout. Even respected media sources perpetuate these myths.

  Today: As more incidents of biological and chemical terrorism occur, both the United States

government and the media provide frequent updates on the possible destructive effects of these acts in an attempt to prepare citizens.

- **1950s:** The United States and the Soviet Union race to launch the first satellite and get the first spaceship to leave earth's atmosphere. Although space missions are initially based on political factors generated by the Cold War, when the National Aeronautics and Space Administration (NASA) is founded in the United States in 1958, the missions become more scientifically motivated.

  Today: The United States, Russia, and several other countries contribute components and staff for the International Space Station, which is currently operational and in orbit around earth. The station is set up for a variety of purposes, including scientific research.

---

its first atomic weapon, proving to the United States that it, too, had atomic capabilities. By this point, the Soviet Union and the United States, which were allies at the end of World War II, had already been on unstable terms for several years.

The Soviet–U.S. Rift

In February 1945, as Nazi Germany was getting ready to fall to the Allied powers, Franklin D. Roosevelt, Winston Churchill, and Joseph Stalin—the leaders, respectively, of the United States, Great Britain, and the Soviet Union—had an historic meeting at Yalta, a Russian city. Here, they discussed how Europe should be divided after the war. Stalin wanted to impose communist governments in Poland and Germany and wanted Germany, its biggest foe, disbanded as a nation. Churchill and Roosevelt feared the spread of communism, however, and wanted to maintain Germany's status as a nation. They negotiated a compromise, but Stalin did not abide by the agreement. Following the war, Stalin capitalized on the weakness of many Eastern

European countries, using the Soviet Union's military prowess to quickly place communist governments in much of Eastern Europe. On March 12, 1947, President Truman decided, in a declaration now known as the Truman Doctrine, to actively stop the spread of communism to other nations. He immediately petitioned Congress for funds to assist countries like Greece and Turkey, which were in danger of being overthrown by Soviet-backed militant groups. The decision to fight communism, which became part of U.S. foreign policy for decades, helped create a rift between the Soviet Union and the United States.

The Cold War Deepens

This rift grew in 1949 with the creation of the North Atlantic Treaty Organization (NATO), an alliance among the United States, Canada, and ten Western European nations. The Soviet Union responded with the Warsaw Pact, an alliance of Eastern European nations. These multiple conflicts—between the United States and the Soviet Union,

NATO and the Warsaw Pact, and democracy and communism—were labeled the Cold War, and for good reason. Although much of the period was technically spent in peacetime, the pervasive feeling of suspicion and paranoia that was generated by this clash of superpowers made many feel that they were living through a war. This feeling was underscored even further in 1948, when Congress approved the first peacetime draft into the military, reasoning that it was necessary to maintain a large standing army to combat communism. The United States had several opportunities to deploy this recently expanded military, including the Korean War—officially called a police action—in the early 1950s.

The Beginning of the Arms Race

During the Cold War, the two alliances, led by the United States and the Soviet Union, continued to try to convert the world to democracy and communism, respectively. At the same time, each side increased its supply of atomic bombs. However, in the early 1950s, these weapons of mass destruction were replaced by thermonuclear bombs, known as super bombs, which had an even greater explosive payload than atomic bombs. A-bombs relied on the energy released by the fission—or division—of atoms. On the other hand, thermonuclear bombs, also known as hydrogen bombs or H-bombs, harnessed an atomic explosion and used it as a trigger to ignite a thermonuclear fuel, resulting in the fusion, or combination, of atoms. Fusion, the same process used to power the sun, produces a vastly more destructive force than fission. The United States tested its first thermonuclear device, a behemoth weighing more than eighty tons, in 1952. From this point on, both the United States and the Soviet Union spent a massive amount of resources developing and producing lighter thermonuclear weapons that had greater payloads and that could be attached to missiles. The very existence of this increasing stockpile of nuclear weapons, which include any weapon using a fission or fusion device, was thought to be insurance. Each side knew that if one side launched a nuclear missile, the other side would have no choice but to retaliate by sending its own missiles, which would lead to nuclear war and most likely the end of the world. This insurance was known as mutually assured destruction, with the fitting acronym MAD.

The Public Prepares for World War III

In the United States, the public was well aware that one mistake on either side could inadvertently trigger World War III. As a result, the government formed the federal Civil Defense Administration (CDA) in 1951 to help calm the public. Schoolchildren were told—through their teachers and through movies and newsreels—that in the event of a nuclear attack, they would be safe if they ducked and covered their heads. The most destructive aspects of nuclear war were downplayed, and nuclear weapons were described in favorable terms in an effort to get people to support them. The government encouraged people to construct concrete bomb shelters in their basements or backyards, and even respectable media like *Life* magazine proclaimed the fiction that these bunkers would protect the majority of people.

The Beginning of Space Flight

While the United States and the Soviet Union were busy stockpiling nuclear weapons, the two superpowers were also engaged in another race: the space race. Each side wanted to demonstrate its prowess by being the first to get a man in space, and, ideally, on the moon. Although philosophers and scientists had studied the moon for thousands of years, only in the mid-twentieth century did humanity possess the technology to leave earth's atmosphere and try to reach it. In the early 1950s, all U.S. space research and missions were carried out through the Army and Air Force, as there was no specific space organization. This was appropriate, since the liquid-fuel propulsion systems used in spaceflight were initially developed for military applications such as missiles.

Critical Overview

"'If I Forget Thee, O Earth . . . '" was published in 1951, when most mainstream and literary critics thought science fiction had little literary value. This view persisted despite the fact that English authors from the late nineteenth and early twentieth centuries, such as H. G. Wells and Jules Verne, had written critically acclaimed science fiction works. Still, science fiction readers were hungry for short stories by their favorite authors, which they often read in science fiction magazines like *Future,* where "'If I Forget Thee, O Earth . . . '" was first published. In fact, science fiction's many pulp magazines helped give science fiction a negative image with critics, even while the cheap magazines attracted popular readers. When the story was collected in Clarke's *Expedition to Earth* in 1953, it did not receive much critical attention.

The use of atomic bombs during World War II introduced a common theme for science fiction writers in the early 1950s

However, in the second half of the twentieth century, as the science fiction publishing trend started to shift from magazines to books, critical focus shifted as well. This change was initially due to the literary quality of books by science fiction writers such as Clarke, Kurt Vonnegut, and Ray Bradbury. More critics started to review science fiction works, and more teachers started to use science fiction stories in their classrooms. Overall, Clarke has fared well with the critics since this shift, although it is his novels, such as *Childhood's End*, published in the same year as *Expedition to Earth*, which have earned the most critical acclaim.

The few critics who have commented specifically on "'If I Forget Thee, O Earth . . . '" have given the story high marks. In his entry on Clarke for the *Critical Survey of Short Fiction*, David N. Samuelson says that the story is one of Clarke's "best and best-known stories," noting "the haunting rite of passage of a young lunar exile getting his first glimpse of the unapproachably radioactive world of his ancestors." In his entry on Clarke for *Science Fiction Writers*, Samuelson adds that the story is "static," with "little or no plot complications," and "elegiac," meaning that it expresses

sadness for something in the past—in this case, the ruined earth. For Samuelson, the static quality is a positive, since it enhances the elegiac effect of the story. Likewise, in his essay "The Cosmic Loneliness of Arthur C. Clarke," Thomas D. Clareson calls Clarke's "'If I Forget Thee, O Earth . . . '" "one of his finest short stories" and notes that it falls into the category of stories that serve as a warning to society.

Clarke's short fiction in general was reviewed in 2001, upon the publication of *The Collected Stories of Arthur C. Clarke*. In her review of the book for *Library Journal*, Jackie Cassada says: "this collection of short fiction by Grandmaster Clarke serves as a definitive example of sf at its best." Cassada also notes that the book "displays the author's fertile imagination and irrepressible enthusiasm for both good storytelling and impeccable science." In his review of the collection for *Booklist*, Roland Green agrees. Says Green: "The stories demonstrate Clarke's dazzling and unique combination of command of the language, scientific and other kinds of erudition, and inimitable wit." Finally, the reviewer for *Kirkus Reviews* notes Clarke's "awesome inventiveness, sure grasp of scientific principle, readability, openness, and utter lack of viciousness or meanness." For these reasons, the critic is not surprised that Clarke is regarded as "the single most famous and influential non-American SF writer of the post-WW II period."

Criticism

Ryan D. Poquette

Poquette has a bachelor's degree in English and specializes in writing about literature. In the following essay, Poquette discusses the techniques that Clarke employs in "'If I Forget Thee, O Earth . . . '" to give his bleak message more impact.

In his entry on Clarke for *Science Fiction Writers*, David. N. Samuelson notes that "some of his early stories were essentially jokes" and that these stories were "whimsical." However, Samuelson notes in his entry that "Clarke could also write stories of a more somber, even melancholy tone—far-future tales in which man's science and technology seemed to lead to a dead end." "'If I Forget Thee, O Earth . . . '" is definitely one of the latter. In the story, Clarke sends a dark message to the world's inhabitants, urging them not to use atomic bombs. By

What Do I Read Next?

- Ray Bradbury's *The Martian Chronicles,* a short story collection first published in 1950, made the author famous and was one of the first critically acclaimed science fiction works. The stories concern humans' repeated efforts to colonize Mars and underscore Bradbury's opposition to having too much scientific and technological development at the expense of humanity.

- Clarke is best known for his novels, including *Childhood's End* (1953), one of his most popular and critically acclaimed novels. The novel details the appearance of the Overlords, aliens who help end war, poverty, hunger, and other social ills, convincing humanity to give up scientific research and space exploration in the process in order to maintain this utopia.

- Clarke's second nonfiction book, *The Explo-*

ration of Space (1952), was the first science book chosen as a Book-of-the-Month Club selection. This highly accessible book translated then current space technology accurately into language that a popular audience could understand. Although the book is out of print and some of the concepts are outdated, it is a good text for understanding the historical context of the 1950s space program.

- William Golding is best known for his first novel *Lord of the Flies* (1954), initially rejected by twenty-one publishers. This novel explores the dark side of humanity that can surface when people are separated from civilization. In the novel, a group of schoolboys is stranded on a deserted island. In the absence of civilization or adult supervision, the boys establish a war-like society and exhibit animal instincts.

---

depicting a post-holocaust scenario, in which a group of humans is stranded for centuries on the moon, he offers a vivid example of what could happen if an atomic World War III ever happens. In his essay ''The Cosmic Loneliness of Arthur C. Clarke,'' Thomas D. Clareson notes the cautionary message and calls Clarke's story ''one of his finest.'' However, Clarke does more than show an example. He amplifies the chilling impact of his antiwar message by using specific imagery, emphasizing the idea of silence, and choosing specific words to describe the radioactive aftermath.

The story begins, appropriately enough, with an image of life. Marvin, the ten-year-old main character who has grown up in the lunar colony, is drawn to the vegetation that he observes in the colony's farmlands. ''The smell of life was everywhere, awakening inexpressible longings in his heart: no longer was he breathing the dry, cool air of the residential levels.'' After this brief image of life, however, the rest of the story emphasizes death. During his trip to see the earthrise, Marvin sees only

hard, rocky landscapes; there is no vegetation: ''Ahead, as far as the eye could reach, was a jumbled wasteland of craters, mountain ranges, and ravines.'' After viewing the ruined earth, Marvin realizes that the vegetation of the farmlands is the only plant life that he will ever see. Worse, he realizes that he is missing much more by not being able to see the natural lands of earth. ''He would never walk beside the rivers of that lost and legendary world, or listen to the thunder raging above its softly rounded hills.''

The absence of life is made even worse by the pervasive darkness on the moon. As soon as Marvin leaves the confines of the colony, he sees many examples of darkness. Unlike earth's, the moon's thin atmosphere does not feature blue sky. Instead, the landscape burns ''beneath the fierce sun that crawled so slowly across the jet-black sky.'' Although the moon is lit by sunlight, the sky remains black. This blackness gets even worse when Marvin and his father drive through mountains that block out the sun. Says the narrator, ''Night fell with a shocking

> These obvious uses of silence in the story help illustrate a point. The human race has been largely silenced, diminished from billions on earth to only a handful of survivors on the moon."

abruptness as they crossed the shadow line and the sun dropped below the crest of the plateau.'' Even when the darkness is alleviated, the lighting has negative connotations. Marvin does not know at this point that they are going to view an earthrise, but he does realize that something is strange when they come out of the mountains: ''The sun was now low behind the hills on the right; the valley before them should be in total darkness.'' However, the valley is lit by the ''cold white radiance'' of the earth. At this point, Clarke has his narrator use imagery that suggests there is something wrong with earth. As the narrator notes, ''no warmth at all came from the silver crescent.'' Unlike the sun, a bright planetary body that does provide warmth, this bright world does not. As Marvin realizes that earth is dead, his initial assessment of its lack of warmth seems fitting.

Clarke also employs images of isolation to magnify the effect of despair in the story. Not long after they drive away from the airlock, Clarke reveals that Marvin and his father are alone. ''There was no sign of the colony: in the few minutes while he had been gazing at the stars, its domes and radio towers had fallen below the horizon.'' They do see another sign of civilization—''the curiously shaped structures clustering round the head of a mine''— after they have driven for about a mile. However, after this, they travel for a long time without seeing any other signs of humanity: ''For hours they drove through valleys and past the feet of mountains whose peaks seemed to comb the stars.'' In fact, the next sign of civilization is ''the skeleton of a crashed rocket.'' The image of a crashed rocket symbolizes the failure of science. In addition, by using the word, ''skeleton'' Clarke once again underscores

the idea of death. Clarke could have placed the colony anywhere on the moon, even right on the edge of the valley where Marvin views the earthrise. However, by placing it at a distance from the viewing point, he is able to emphasize the isolation of the colony members. He sends Marvin and his father on a long, lonely trip, during which the only sign of civilization outside the colony's plateau is the remains of a long-dead rocket. The ultimate isolation, however, comes when Marvin sees the earth and remembers hearing the stories of how the colony members learned of earth's destruction. As the narrator says, ''they were alone at last, as no men had ever been alone before, carrying in their hands the future of the race.''

In addition to imagery, Clarke's story is also marked by a conspicuous absence of sound. There is no dialogue in the story; discussions are only referred to. For the most part, the story is narrative description, as Marvin remembers his trip to see the earthrise. However, at one point in the story, the narrator indicates that Marvin's father has spoken, but the reader does not hear Marvin's father's words. Instead, they too, become part of the narration: ''And now Father began to speak, telling Marvin the story which until this moment had meant no more to him than the fairy tales he had heard in childhood.'' Even before this point, few sounds are described in detail. In the beginning, when they are inside the colony, the narrator observes that Marvin's father ''started the motor,'' the ''inner door of the lock slid open,'' and he listened to the ''roar of the great air-pumps fade slowly away.'' During the drive across the desolate landscape, however, the narrator does not describe the sounds that Marvin and his father might be hearing. In fact, the only other sound comes when Marvin's father stops the vehicle so they can view the earth, when Clarke draws attention to the silence: ''It was very quiet in the little cabin now that the motors had stopped.'' The only sounds are ''the faint whisper of the oxygen feed'' and the occasional noise of the metal walls of the vehicle as it ''radiated away their heat.'' These obvious uses of silence in the story help illustrate a point. The human race has been largely silenced, diminished from billions on earth to only a handful of survivors on the moon.

Samuelson, in the same entry mentioned above, notes these ''static'' qualities of the story, saying that it has ''little or no plot complications.'' Stories are often defined by the development of their plots. However, in this story, Clarke focuses on imagery and silence and relegates the main plot complications to the backstory—the events that have taken place before the story begins, in this case the destruction of earth's inhabitants and the subsequent stranding of the moon colony. As readers become aware of what is going on, they feel what Samuelson identifies as the ''elegiac'' effect of the story, and, like Marvin and his father, they are drawn in to mourn for the lost earth.

This tragedy is amplified by the word choice that Clarke uses, particularly when describing the radioactive aftermath. The atomic war that claims the earth's inhabitants and extends the colony exile is viewed as evil and unnecessary. When describing Marvin's first realization that the earth is contaminated, the narrator says that ''the portion of the disk that should have been in darkness was gleaming faintly with an evil phosphorescence.'' The use of the word ''evil'' is a direct commentary on the nature of atomic weapons. Clarke also chooses words that have destructive associations, such as fire. As Marvin continues to observe earth, he realizes that he is ''looking upon the funeral pyre of a world—upon the radioactive aftermath of Armageddon.'' Poison is another potent word that Clarke uses. Marvin realizes that the earth will eventually clean itself, that the ''winds and the rains would scour the poisons from the burning lands and carry them to the sea.'' It is here, in the oceans, that the radioactive poisons will ''waste their venom.'' Poisonous snakes are another negative image, so by associating the radioactive contamination with them, Clarke is implying in yet another way that atomic weapons are lethal.

In the end, Clarke is demonstrating that nothing is good for the people in this moon colony. Even the good aspects like the vegetation in the farmlands and the light from earth ultimately have negative connotations, since they illustrate what the colony is missing. Clarke also depicts life as a frail entity and saturates his story with references to the death, darkness, isolation, and silence of a post-holocaust world. By building his story with these techniques and by using words with evil connotations to describe the aftermath of atomic war, Clarke gives his antiwar message a greater impact. When the story was published in 1951, this message was particularly important. At the time, the United States government was trying to quell public fears with propaganda that downplayed the consequences of atomic weapons. Clarke, like other science fiction writers, was engaged in a battle of words, trying to appeal to the public to cry out against atomic bombs, even as the government was teaching people to accept and not fear them.

Source: Ryan D. Poquette, Critical Essay on '''If I Forget Thee, O Earth ...,''' in *Short Stories for Students,* Gale, 2003.

Douglas Dupler

Dupler has published numerous essays and has taught college English. In this essay, Dupler examines a prevalent theme of science fiction and its relationship to scientific knowledge.

A major theme of science fiction has been the destruction of earth. In addition, the manner in which science fiction writers have approached and developed this theme has evolved. Advances in space-related technology and in general knowledge have been factors leading to this change. Science fiction itself has done more than mirror these advances in technology and knowledge; imaginative stories in this field have helped to change people's perceptions and expectations about the world.

In this story, published in 1951, Clarke uses very few words and only two characters, a ten-year-old boy named Marvin and his unnamed father. The story has a vague and unearthly setting from the start. The setting is described as a ''jumbled wasteland of craters, mountain ranges, and ravines,'' and the night comes with ''shocking abruptness.'' As his father takes him on his first tour of the area ''outside'' the human dwellings, Marvin realizes ''that something very strange was happening in the land ahead.'' This sense of foreboding adds drama to the realizations that the characters, and the reader, will make later in the story, when it is revealed that earth and the human society upon it have been destroyed and that the characters are living in an isolated moon colony.

The story is permeated with a sense of longing and sadness, because the characters are misplaced and can only look into space at a planet that was their former home. Marvin and his father know that they will never ''walk beside the rivers of that lost and legendary world, or listen to the thunder raging above its softly rounded hills.'' Referring to the story of how they arrived there, the narrator states, ''they were alone at last, as no men had ever been alone before, carrying in their hands the future of the race.'' The story ends with Marvin and his father together in their lunar scout car, looking out upon the distant, unobtainable, and ruined earth. Marvin

> The story is permeated with a sense of longing and sadness, because the characters are misplaced and can only look into space at a planet that was their former home."

and his father know that it will be many hundreds of years before earth will be free of its deadly poisons. Together with the other survivors of the colony, they are all that remain of the human race. It is interesting to note that the narrator refers to the ''radioactive Armageddon'' that has destroyed earth. This science fiction story, taking place in the future, is still dependent upon the ancient biblical story of the apocalypse. However, in Clarke's apocalypse, human beings and their nuclear technology are responsible for the destruction.

Just as Clarke's main character, Marvin, is a child, it can be argued as well that in this story, humanity is still in a sort of childhood. Humans, stranded in an inhospitable place, have not moved farther out into space and are waiting for that future day when earth will be able to support human life again. Clarke's characters are looking backwards, down the gravity well to their past, to their womb, and are unable to move independently from their current place. Clarke's people are yearning only to walk once again upon earth, which they only know through stories and ''fairy tales.''

At the same time, Clarke's story contains glimmers of hope and hints of changes that may be germinating in people's ideas about space exploration. The adult in the story, Marvin's father, is full of a zest for pushing Marvin beyond his usual boundaries. When Marvin thinks that his father is behaving as though ''he were trying to escape from something,'' the narrator interjects that this is ''a strange thought to come into a child's mind.'' The adult in the story longs for change and freedom, while the child is apprehensive and passive about those changes. For the child, the tales in which he had once believed are now replaced with stark visions of reality.

Clarke was not the only author of his era to write about earth's destruction. *Caves of Steel* (1954) by Isaac Asimov, *The Green Hills of Earth* (1951) by Robert Heinlein, and *A Canticle for Leibovitz* (1959) by Walter M. Miller, Jr., all deal with the same theme of an innocent humankind being nearly overwhelmed by the partial or complete destruction of earth.

Later writers of science fiction have portrayed humankind as having already grown past its childhood and as being no longer dependent upon earth. It is not unusual or exceptional for later science fiction writers and their characters to view earth as a nest that has become used up and boring and a suitable home only for those too timid for the adventure of space. For example, in Charles Sheffield's well-received 1995 novel, *The Ganymede Club*, a woman says, ''if you ask me, the war [that destroyed much of earth] was a blessing in disguise. It moved the center of power of the solar system from earth out here to Jupiter, where it rightfully belongs.''

Some later science fiction writers, including Sheffield (often touted as the new Arthur Clarke), Spider and Jeanne Robinson, Greg Bear, and Larry Niven and Jerry Pournelle, among others, present characters who look outwards toward Mars and Venus, toward the asteroid belt, and to the outer planets with their many moons. For these writers, escaping from the gravity of earth for space, while there are still sufficient resources to do so, is the next adventure and collective goal for humankind and the next theme for science fiction.

Sheffield, in particular, shows how humankind could fill the entire solar system, using the various resources of the asteroid belt as well as those of both the inner and the outer planets. He shows how this would be much simpler and more economical than dragging resources up out of the gravity well of earth. When he recounts, in several of his novels, including *Cold As Ice, Dark As Day,* and *The Ganymede Club,* that much of earth has been destroyed by a war between the people of the asteroid belt and those of earth, the focus isn't upon the tragedy. Instead, the focus is upon the future of the human race, which is living freely and productively in space.

Thus, science fiction has developed different ways of relating to the theme of the destruction of earth. On the one hand, Clarke and other early writers saw it as a disaster for humanity. In Clarke's story, his characters have reached the moon, but with earth destroyed, they have let their "great ships" lie idle rather than use them to explore further. They have decided to save them for the possibility of an eventual return many hundreds of years later to their old home. On the other hand, later writers have shared a different vision of the human race, which is at home in space and living throughout the solar system and beyond. It is notable that Clarke further developed this theme of earth destruction and the resulting human travel into space. In his novel *Childhood's End*, Clarke again shows the destruction of earth. But this time aliens are involved and are helping humanity grow up and evolve to its next level of existence. When earth is finally destroyed, it is merely a by-product of this evolution.

Why were the early science fiction writers so pessimistic? Why did the characters in Clarke's story stay huddled beneath their domed and underground city and yearn always for earth? Why were they not out in their "great ships" exploring the rest of the solar system? Why, for Clarke, did the human race have to be helped by aliens to grow past its childhood? Why, on the other hand, are Sheffield, Robinson, and other later writers much more optimistic, with characters always looking outward toward the next frontier?

In Clarke's day, human beings had not yet reached space, let alone touched down upon the moon. Aircraft and computers were primitive compared to those of today. Perhaps that is why, in Clarke's story, the technological aspects are left completely vague. There is a moon colony, sheltered beneath a pressurized plastic dome. There are the lunar scout cars. There are the "great ships ... still waiting here on the silent, dusty plains." However, they are merely mentioned, never described, and are not essential to his story. What does figure prominently in Clarke's story is directly related to the technology of that time period: the nuclear bomb, which has made earth uninhabitable. For Clarke, scientific discovery has ruined the nest but has not yet given humankind the wings to fly to a new home.

Given the state of technology in the early new millennium, human beings are better prepared for venturing out into space than in Clarke's day. Since the late 1940s, there have been major advances in spaceship design and safety and in computers and guidance systems, for example. The space shuttles really work. An international space station is being built. There have been proposals to send humans to Mars. The Hubble telescope and other successful space probes have given new and exciting details of the universe. The moons of Jupiter have attracted interest as sources of water, and asteroids have been proposed as rich sources of water and minerals. Humanity has become more confident in its ability to leap into space. Science fiction has mirrored these changes in technology, creating new stories of space travel and adventures. At the same time, adventurous science fiction stories have spurred people to raise their sights on new possibilities. In the half century since Clarke wrote his wonderful and basic story, science fiction has attracted many writers with inspiring visions of humanity's future in space. These visions often have been coupled with understanding of biology, psychology, physics, astronomy, and other related disciplines.

When Marvin looks up at that "great silver crescent that floated low above the far horizon," he realizes that his father had shown him earth so that he would pass on this yearning for humankind's home to his own sons and daughters. Marvin knows that he will never reach earth himself, but he sees that "yet one day—how far ahead?—his children's children would return to claim their heritage." Marvin understands that unless this last remnant of humanity barely existing upon the moon had "a goal, a future towards which it could work, the Colony would lose the will to live."

Clarke's story ends as a starting place for other science fiction writers, declaring that it is human nature to have a goal and a vision of the future. Building upon Clarke's vision of the future and connecting that with the ever-increasing body of scientific knowledge, science fiction continues to tell new stories of great adventures into space.

Source: Douglas Dupler, Critical Essay on "'If I Forget Thee, O Earth ...,'" in *Short Stories for Students*, Gale, 2003.

Sources

Cassada, Jackie, Review of *The Collected Stories of Arthur C. Clarke*, in *Library Journal*, Vol. 126, No. 5, March 15, 2001, p. 110.

Clareson, Thomas D., "The Cosmic Loneliness of Arthur C. Clarke," in *Arthur C. Clarke*, edited by Joseph D. Olander and Martin Harry Greenberg, Taplinger Publishing Company, 1977, p. 54.

Green, Roland, Review of *The Collected Stories of Arthur C. Clarke*, in *Booklist*, January 1, 2001, p. 928.

Review of *The Collected Stories of Arthur C. Clarke,* in *Kirkus Reviews,* December 15, 2000.

Samuelson, David N., ''Arthur C. Clarke,'' in *Critical Survey of Short Fiction: Authors (A–Dah),* edited by Frank N. Magill, Salem Press, 1981, p. 1157.

———, ''Arthur C. Clarke,'' in *Science Fiction Writers,* 2d ed., Charles Scribner's Sons, 1999, pp. 203, 205.

Sheffield, Charles, *The Ganymede Club,* Tor, 1995, p.164.

Further Reading

Alling, Abigail, and Mark Nelson, *Life under Glass: The Inside Story of Biosphere 2,* Biosphere Press, 1993.
This book shows what it was like to live for two years inside Biosphere 2, the sealed-environment biodome located outside Tucson, Arizona. In 1991, eight men and women entered the dome, which was set up to be a complete ecosystem. Today, Biosphere 2 is part of a larger complex devoted to ecological research, education, and public outreach.

Beattie, Donald A., *Taking Science to the Moon: Lunar Experiments and the Apollo Program,* Johns Hopkins University Press, 2001.
The Apollo missions were originally intended only to win the space race to get the first man on the moon. However, there were many NASA scientists who fought to expand the scope of the missions by including lunar science activities. Beattie, an engineer who served as a NASA manager from 1963 to 1973, gives a thorough overview of the science activities during the Apollo missions.

Downing, Taylor, and Jeremy Isaacs, *Cold War: An Illustrated History, 1945–1991,* Little Brown & Company, 1998.
This book gives a thorough overview of the Cold War, beginning with its roots in the 1917 Russian Revolution. The book is illustrated with hundreds of photographs and includes special sections on spies, films, and literature.

McAleer, Neil, *Arthur C. Clarke: The Authorized Biography,* Contemporary Books, 1992.
Clarke is highly regarded as one of the greatest science fiction writers and visionaries of the twentieth century. While writing this comprehensive work, McAleer interviewed Clarke, his friends, and his family, as well as publishers, editors, writers, and others who had interacted with the author. The book covers Clarke's life until 1992 and includes in-depth discussion of all of Clarke's major novels and several of his short stories.

Reid, Robin Anne, ed., *Arthur C. Clarke: A Critical Companion,* Greenwood Publishing Group, Inc., 1997.
This collection of critical essays offers both conventional and alternative readings of eight of Clarke's most recent novels and discusses them within the context of Clarke's classic works.

Journey into a Dark Heart

Peter Høeg

1990

"Journey into a Dark Heart" was first published in Danish in 1990 in Peter Høeg's *Fortællinger om naten*, a collection of eight short stories about love that take place on the night of March 19, 1929. This collection, which was translated into English in 1998 as *Tales of the Night*, set the standard for contemporary Danish writers. Despite this fact, Høeg is mostly known for his novels. His most famous novel, translated into English in 1993, is *Smilla's Sense of Snow*. Høeg's short fiction displays the same blend of narrative skill and intellectual range that has made his novels so popular. "Journey into a Dark Heart" is saturated with historical references, including as characters two noted men from history: author Joseph Conrad (posing under his real name of Joseph Korzeniowski) and the German World War I veteran Paul von Lettow-Vorbeck. Conrad's novella *Heart of Darkness,* which is referred to several times in the story, draws on his knowledge of the horrors of colonialism, which he witnessed during a voyage up the Congo River. In a similar fashion, Høeg's "Journey into a Dark Heart" introduces the character David Rehn, a naïve young mathematician who is obsessed with truth. Through the many conversations with the other two men on their fateful train trip into the Congo, David's Western notions about colonial Africa are challenged. The story can be found in the paperback version of *Tales of the Night*, which was published by Penguin Books in 1999.

Author Biography

Peter Høeg was born in Copenhagen, Denmark, on May 17, 1957. He graduated from Frederiksberg Gymnasium in 1976 and then studied literary theory at the University of Copenhagen, earning his master's degree in 1984. While at school, Høeg began writing his first novel, *Forestilling om det tyvende arhundrede*, which he worked on for six years, endlessly revising as he gained greater skill in writing. When the book was published in 1988, Danish critics were quick to praise it. His next book, *Fortællinger om naten* (1990), also received positive criticism and established him as the premier contemporary Danish writer. However, it was his third book, the novel, *Frøken Smillas fornemmelse for sne* (1992), which established Høeg's international fame. The book, translated into English as *Smilla's Sense of Snow* in 1993, became a bestseller in the United States.

Following this success, Høeg's existing works began to be translated into English along with his new works, creating an odd situation in which English-speaking readers were exposed to both the author's newest and oldest works in the same time period. In 1994, Høeg's *De måske egnede* (1993) was translated into English as *Borderliners*. In 1995, Høeg's first novel was translated as *The History of Danish Dreams*. In 1996, his novel *Kvinden og aben* and its English translation, *The Woman and the Ape*, were released. Finally, Høeg's second book, the short-story collection *Fortællinger om naten*, which had originally been published in 1990, was not translated until 1998, when it was published in English as *Tales of the Night*. The collection, which includes the story "Journey into a Dark Heart," features a wide range of international settings and a diverse cast of characters. In 1997, *Smilla's Sense of Snow* was adapted into a film, which helped increase the author's exposure.

This fame is not something that Høeg wants, however. Høeg is famous for his aversion to publicity, and he rarely gives interviews. Unlike many other writers, he refuses to accept advances for his books, preferring to work at his own pace, without any pressure. He also does not discuss his books with anybody, including his family and friends. Even his publisher does not know when the next Høeg book will arrive or what it will be about.

Like the characters in his stories, Høeg has multiple interests. Before he began writing full-time, he worked as a classical ballet dancer, a sailor on pleasure boats, an actor, and a drama instructor. He has also competed as a professional fencer and has climbed mountains. Høeg is an extensive traveler, and much of his writing, including the story "Journey into a Dark Heart," has benefited from his firsthand experience in Third World regions like Africa, Cuba, and the Caribbean. Africa, in particular, is a frequent destination for the author and his wife, Akinyi, a native of Kenya. Høeg lives and works in Copenhagen.

Plot Summary

"Journey into a Dark Heart" begins by introducing David Rehn, a young Dane (citizen of Denmark), who is attending the 1929 dedication of a new railway line. The railway runs from the western coast of Africa in Cabinda through the Belgian Congo and deep into the heart of the continent. The dedication includes many representatives of royalty and international business, and the grand display reinforces David's view that European civilization is indeed great. David has come to this event as a fluke, having acquired a position with a global trading company after he gave up his lifelong pursuit of mathematics. David had always relied on the stability of mathematics to get him through any emotional crisis until one year earlier, when he met Kurt Gödel, a mathematician whose ideas were bound to shake up the world of mathematics. With his passion for mathematics threatened by these new ideas, David abandoned mathematics.

Despite his rejection of mathematics as a career, David is fascinated by the construction of the railway, which he sees in quantitative terms such as the number of workers and length of railroad track. During the dinner, everybody is in joyful spirits over the completion of the railway. This good mood intensifies when the Belgian king announces that, according to an English journalist who will be going on the train trip the next day, European forces have defeated the African rebel bands who have impeded the construction in the past. In addition, Lueni, the feared African leader, has been killed, and his body is to be shipped to Cabinda.

The next afternoon, the various delegates, including David, prepare to take the first train trip ever from Cabinda to Katanga. David ends up in a train car with three others: a distinguished soldier, a black servant girl, and the elderly white man whom she serves. The old man, who is the English journalist who told the Belgian king about the death of Lueni, introduces himself as Joseph Korzeniowski. This is the actual birth name of Joseph Conrad, an author famous for his stories about colonial regions like the Congo, which were largely based on his own travels. Joseph K. hints that he has made the journey into the Congo before, and, by virtue of this experience, declares himself the host of the train car, saying that they should make this trip an open and honest journey. David introduces himself as a mathematician, thus realizing that he has not given up on his passion totally. The German soldier, who is covered in medals indicating his military valor, introduces himself as General Paul von Lettow Voerbeck. This name is a slight variation from the real-life name of Paul von Lettow-Vorbeck, a German military official famous for his defense of German colonies in Africa during World War I.

Joseph K. refers to the books that the general has written, which have reinforced the European notion that Africa is dark and evil and that war and colonization are humane enterprises. Thus begins the first of many increasingly tense discussions between Joseph K. and the general. Joseph K. also says that he understands the dream of Africa better than anybody else. David challenges Joseph K., saying that the only African pictures that make their way to Europe are dark images of forests, which are accompanied by legends of murder by the natives. Joseph counters by saying that Africa is dark and opens the shades of the train car's window to prove it. It is pitch black outside. David suddenly blows out the oil lamps, and, after a moment, the formerly black landscape appears in the moonlight. David uses this as proof that Africa may not be as dark as outsiders think.

David says that he is only interested in the truth, but Joseph K. says that truth does not pay that well. He gives more information about his background, referring to his famous writing career and alluding to *Heart of Darkness*. He says that the public liked the fictional aspects of this colonial narrative but did not appreciate the truth, and so he has referred to his writing as fiction ever since. Joseph K. also rebukes the general for publishing his own lies as memoirs, an insult that causes the general to grab Joseph K. by the lapels. Joseph K. elaborates, saying that the general's published assertion that the African natives were happy to be conquered is a lie. The general agrees that some masks are necessary for politics. Joseph K. uses this moment as an opportu-

Peter Høeg

nity to expose the fact that the general is technically a prisoner of war, although he has been awarded diplomatic immunity for the occasion.

The discussion turns to the masks people wear, and David says that they are all wearing masks, except for the black servant girl, a representative of Africa. He says that Africa has nothing to hide, while Europe does. The general tries to leave the conversation, and the train car, but is stopped by the servant girl, who, to their surprise, speaks perfect English. She introduces herself as Lueni of Uganda, the supposedly male rebel leader who had been announced as dead the day before, and holds them at gunpoint. Lueni says that they are all going to die when the train goes over the next bridge because her people have removed most of the bridge supports. The conversation among the three men continues. David talks about his former passion for mathematics and the goal that he and other learned men had to reduce all life—including humanity—down to a set of equations. Joseph K. is quick to agree with this point, saying that he had suspected all along that this might be possible. However, David says that it is not possible because a fellow mathematician is working on proof that will show that complex systems, like humanity, include unpredictable variables like emotions.

David notes that all of them have left their homes behind, but Lueni seems to be in hers; she corrects him, saying that she is four thousand kilometers from home and that she was educated in England. She also challenges the positive European view of the railroad, saying that it was built mainly by African laborers, many of whom died while being forced to build it. At the next turn, the train slows down, and Lueni gets off. Joseph K. produces a gun of his own and says that he has sold Lueni some guns and that their lives are going to be spared; they will be jumping off the train at the next turn. In their last few minutes, Joseph K. tells a tale illustrating the ignorance and cockiness of Europeans when it comes to dealing with Africans. A German officer tried to buy an African mask that could not be bought. Even the mask warns him, saying that if the officer buys it, it will lead him into hell. The man ignores the advice, obsessed by the talking mask. The officer takes the mask with him everywhere, showing it off to everybody, but he can never get it to talk for him again. His obsession eventually kills him.

The train reaches the next turn, and Joseph K. forces them to jump. Once on the ground, the general thinks that Joseph K. is going to kill him, but Joseph K. says that he is a free man. The general begins the two-hundred-kilometer walk back to Cabinda. David talks briefly with the African woman, they shake hands, and she walks away. David buries his head in his hands, distraught over the fact that the foundations of his beliefs in mathematics, Africa, and even the sanctity of Europe, have been cracked.

Characters

Black Servant Girl
See Lueni

Joseph K.
See Joseph Korzeniowski

King of Belgium
The King of Belgium is overjoyed when he hears that the last group of African rebels has been defeated in the Belgian Congo. The rebels had been a constant threat during construction of the new railway.

Joseph Korzeniowski
Joseph Korzeniowski, the persona of the real-life, famous author Joseph Conrad, reveals himself to be an African sympathizer and arms supplier to the rebels. In 1929, Conrad was already five years dead, but Høeg resurrects him to play a part as one of the passengers on the first railway trip into the Congo. Conrad's African colonial narrative, *Heart of Darkness,* describes a similar journey up the Congo River in the late nineteenth century. Joseph K. mentions this work, although not by name, several times, the first being when he says that, since he has been this way before and he is very old, he has more experience than the other two passengers and so will be their host. He proves to be a subversive host, first of all indicating that they should all be honest with each other and then withholding pertinent information about himself until the end. In the meantime, he incites discussions that provoke both David and General Paul von Lettow Voerbeck. Joseph K. says that when he told the truth about the evils of colonialism in *Heart of Darkness,* the public did not like it. As a result, since then, even when he is writing the truth, he calls it fiction.

Joseph K. calls the general a liar, since the general has published his own views about Africa as truthful memoirs, claiming that the African natives appreciate being conquered, among other falsehoods. As the story progresses, Joseph K. criticizes the European colonization of Africa more explicitly. When Lueni, who is posing as Joseph K.'s servant girl, reveals herself to be the leader of the African rebels, Joseph K. acts like he did not know this. He and the general provide an example for David, who is afraid of dying, to be calm. After Lueni leaves the train, Joseph K. reveals that he is in league with Lueni, so their lives are going to be spared. At the urging of Joseph K. and his gun, the three white men jump off the train when it slows down to take a turn.

Lueni
Lueni, the black servant girl whose true identity is not revealed until the last part of the story, is the Ugandan leader of the African rebels, who plan to destroy the European train. The story never indicates whether Lueni is her first or last name, but what is certain is that none of the European delegates expects Lueni is a woman. Joseph K. brings news of Lueni's death to the Belgian king, which makes Lueni's appearance on the train even more surprising. Lueni tells the other passengers on the

train that she was educated in London, and the reader finds out at the end of the story that Joseph K. has sold her some rifles to use in the rebellion. Lueni offers stories from her African tribe that illustrate points she is trying to make.

David Rehn

David Rehn is a young, disillusioned Danish mathematician who goes to the railway dedication as part of a delegation from a Danish trading company. Up to the previous year he had followed his passion for mathematics, which he thought would always be a pure science founded on stability. However, after meeting Kurt Gödel, a mathematician who would prove that complex systems would always retain an element of unpredictability, David abandoned mathematics. On the train trip through the Congo, however, David surprises himself when he tells the others that he is a mathematician. His scientific desire for truth motivates much of the conversation in the train car, during which many assumptions about Africa and Europe are proven to be false. David has been under the impression that Europe is a great region and that Africa is a dark continent hiding many secrets.

At the end of the story, David realizes that the opposite is true. Europe's view of colonialism—and war—as a benevolent enterprise is shattered, and he sees the horrors of colonialism. This insight is similar to the revelation of Marlow, the main character in Joseph Conrad's novella *Heart of Darkness,* which Joseph K., the persona of the real-life Conrad, alludes to several times. David assumes that the black servant girl is obedient and cannot understand English, so he is very surprised when she reveals herself to be the London-educated leader of the African rebels. He also assumes the railroad is a great enterprise, until he finds out about the thousands of Africans who died at gunpoint while being forced to build the railway line. In the last scene, with all of his assumptions turned upside-down, David, who craves the order that he used to find in mathematics, is more disillusioned than ever.

General Paul von Lettow Voerbeck

In history, General Paul von Lettow Voerbeck (von Lettow-Vorbeck in real life) was a distinguished German military leader in World War I who successfully defended Germany's African colonies against much larger forces. During the story, it is revealed that this conquered military leader, who is technically a prisoner of war, has been granted diplomatic leave to make this symbolic train trip.

Media Adaptations

- Høeg's novel *Smilla's Sense of Snow* was adapted into a movie in 1997 and was released in the United States by Twentieth Century Fox. The film was directed by a Danish-born director, Bille August, and featured Julia Ormond as Smilla. It is available on VHS and DVD from Twentieth Century Fox.

This character serves as a symbol of successful colonization in Africa, an idea that helps reassure the railroad's stockholders. As the train trip progresses and all three men tell their stories, the general becomes increasingly antagonistic towards Joseph K., who says that the general's published observations about Africa are lies. The general is in favor of war, especially when it benefits his country. His comments allude to the impending rise of the Nazi Party in Germany and the beginning of World War II. When the general finally gets fed up with the antiwar comments from Joseph K. and David, he tries to leave, at which point Lueni, posing as the black servant girl, stops him, at gunpoint. After Joseph K. reveals himself to be associated with Lueni, the general assumes that Joseph K. will shoot him. However, Joseph K. lets him go, at which point the general begins the two-hundred-kilometer (roughly one hundred and twenty miles) walk back to Cabinda.

Themes

Love

In the introductory note to *Tales of the Night,* Høeg says: "These eight stories are linked by a date and a motif. All of them have to do with love. Love and its conditions on the night of March 19, 1929." Without this guiding motif, readers might have

Topics for Further Study

- Research the political policy of the Belgian government during the time of the story and discuss what kinds of actions it might have taken after finding out about the sabotage of the train. Write a synopsis for an extended ending to the story that includes the most likely actions of the Belgian government. In the synopsis, also indicate what you think would happen to David.

- Read several newspaper articles about Africa, circa March 1929. Pretend you are a news correspondent in the Congo, who has heard about the deadly sabotage of the train, and write an article about the incident. Write in the style of the times, making sure to preserve any bias or prevailing attitudes.

- Read Conrad's *Heart of Darkness* and compare David Rehn's revelatory colonial experience to the revelation of Marlow, Conrad's narrator.

- In the story, David Rehn assumes that Europe's story of Africa is true and is shocked to find out the truth of colonialism. Research any recent African issue that has made international headlines and discuss how Western nations responded to this issue. Pay particular attention to any cover-ups that have been brought to light.

- As the story indicates, during the construction of railroads in the Congo, thousands of Africans were forced into labor, and many of them died from disease. Research the types of diseases that claimed lives in this time and compare them to the current AIDS epidemic in Africa.

---

trouble picking out the theme of love in "Journey into a Dark Heart," since the story does not deal with love in the traditional, romantic sense. Instead, Høeg's exploration of love manifests itself in the characters' tales about their life passions. For David, this passion is mathematics, a vocation to which he is deeply devoted. As the narrator says, David "became a mathematician out of a deep, burning passion for that crystal-clear, purifying algebraic science from which all earthly uncertainty has been distilled." Joseph K.'s passion is for writing and exploration. He notes: "As a boy I used to look at maps, I was . . . obsessed with maps." This passion led him to go to sea, which in turn led him to write about his adventures. When referring to *Heart of Darkness,* he says, "I put my heart and soul into that book." Finally, the general is motivated by his love for "the spirit of Teutonic brotherhood" and as such spends most of his efforts on German military and political ventures.

Truth

When the three men board the train, Joseph K. suggests that they make the trip "an open and honest journey." This is the first invitation for the three men to give information about themselves, which continues as the trip progresses. Joseph K. is revealed to be first a journalist, then a famous author, and ultimately an accomplice to the African rebels. The general is revealed to have lied in his memoirs about World War I, and his presence on the train is only as a token of reassurance to stockholders nervous about the dark African colony. Technically, his active military role in World War I means that he needed to be granted amnesty before he could be allowed to make the journey.

As the men offer more truths about themselves, other truths about colonialism come to light. David notes: "You, Joseph K., have left your writing behind, the general his soldiers, and I mathematics. We seem to be on the wrong track." He then notes that Lueni appears to be in her place, since she is an African and they are in Africa. She dispels this myth that all of Africa is the same and says that she is several thousand kilometers from her home. Furthermore, she says that she was educated in England, thereby disproving the myth that Africans are an inferior race who cannot learn like Europeans. In fact, before she speaks, David naturally assumes that, even though it appears as if she is listening to them, Lueni "could have understood nothing." These and other truths about the horrors of colonialism come to light. The most powerful example is Lueni's debunking of the idea that there is no slavery in the African colonies. She talks about "the seven thousand slaves" who built the railway. The general reacts with the European belief, saying that slavery "has been abolished." Lueni counters this myth by illustrating the slave conditions to which African rail workers were subject: "They worked under armed guard, under the lash, and with steel rings around their necks so they would be easily recognizable should they run away."

The force of these horrible truths shatters David's idealism, which only adds to his feeling of instability about the world, driving him into despair at the end of the story. In the meantime, Joseph K. and the general go on with their lives; they have long since been hardened to the deceitful ways of the Western world.

War

The story is saturated with references to war. The general fought in World War I, a war that, Joseph K. notes, has sparked many "voices throughout Europe that rail against war." This war also served as a springboard for the general's published lies about African colonization. Joseph K. debunks these lies, which state that the Africans appreciate the civilizing effect of the Western world and that they willingly fought for the Germans in World War I. The truth, as Joseph K. notes, is that "they walked into that war on the point of a German bayonet, with their heads in a cloud of promises and religious hot air." Although David thinks that the general will kill Joseph K. for this accusation, the general admits that he lied, saying that "A military mask may be necessary . . . if one is to arrive at a deeper political truth." The general also feels that World War I, during which he successfully defended the German colonies of Africa against a much larger force, "proved the potential within our colonies for the founding of a new Germany." This statement foreshadows the new Germany of the Nazi regime, which would terrorize the world in World War II. War in a cultural sense is also addressed. Although the Western world has colonized Africa, peace has not been achieved. Rebel tribes, like those led by Lueni, attempt to avenge the deaths from their tribes by staging counterattacks like the sabotage of the Congo train bridge in the story.

Style

Fable

"Journey into a Dark Heart," like the other stories in the collection, is a fable. A fable is a narrative that is intended to convey a moral. However, unlike classical fables, this story does not include animals or inanimate objects as characters. The story does have some fantastic elements, however. To tell his tale, Høeg places actual historical figures in unrealistic situations. For example, Conrad died in 1924, but he is resurrected to play a part in this story about 1929. Conrad's role, as Joseph K., is extremely important to the fable. The moral of this story is that the Western view of colonialism in the early twentieth century was distorted, that true colonialism was much more evil than people realized. It is through Joseph K.'s background and prompting that the evils of colonialism are gradually revealed. In the beginning, he tells them that "no one has ever understood the dream of Africa as well as I." As the story progresses, he reveals his own experiences with the horrors of colonialism on his previous river trip through the Congo. In addition, he antagonizes the general until he disproves the general's—and the Western world's—assertions about the humanity of colonization.

Setting

The time in which this story takes place, March 1929, is extremely important to the story. This point in history precedes the Great Depression and the Holocaust. These two monumental events helped open people's eyes to many truths, including humanity's capacity for evil. The location, the Belgian Congo, is also important. It provides an unfamiliar and different setting—and because of that a wild one that is perceived as chaotic—in contrast to the supposed order and civility of Western cultures, a contrast that the supporters of colonialism take for granted as justification for what may essentially be imperialist invasion. With Joseph K.'s announcement of Lueni's death, the various governments at the dedication are not expecting an attack in the remote jungle.

Suspense

Høeg uses the technique of suspense to increase the anticipation of the reader throughout the story, placing David in what seem to be increasingly dangerous situations, where his sense of apprehension also increases. In the beginning, David sees everything in Africa in idealistic terms. The Belgian king gives a moving speech about the civilizing aspects of colonization, calling the railroad tracks "the pure lines of thought and commerce," an image that appeals to David. During the dedication dinner, news reaches the king that European forces have "defeated the native rebel bands that have posed the greatest problem to construction work in recent years." Everything seems to be going along even better than planned, and David is hopeful. However, the next day, "there arose a moment's doubt." A new car has to be added on to the train. While this is happening, David notices three "silent and strange" passengers. When David enters the train car, all of the inhabitants initially remain silent, creating "a narrow void of doubt and irresponsibility." Finally, Joseph K. breaks the silence, but David interprets the old man's offer to serve as their host as "a command."

In fact, at one point in their conversation, David challenges Joseph K.'s understanding of Africa, and the old man suddenly loses his good mood: "The smile left Joseph K.'s face, and when he answered his voice was quiet and cold." The story now starts to turn dark, and the reader wonders what is going to happen to David. This suspenseful mood increases as Joseph K. gives his dark vision of Africa, calling the Congo River "a mighty serpent, coiled up with its head in the sea and its body in a fever-ridden hell." As the antagonism between Joseph K. and the general increases, so does the suspenseful tension. At the same time, David starts to notice details that indicate something is not right. David is the only one who notices that a different African waiter comes to serve them "and that he wore a uniform that was far, far too small for him." He also notices that the waiter carries the wine bottle the wrong way. When Lueni identifies herself, the sound of her "dark and faultless English" comes as a shock to the characters and the reader. When Lueni draws her gun and tells them how they are going to die on the bridge, the story gets even more suspenseful. Lueni leaves, and the reader assumes that David and the others will die, but then Joseph K. draws his own gun and forces the two to jump with him. In the end, Joseph K. reveals that he is going to let David and the general live, and the suspense finally breaks, culminating in David's profound sense of despair at knowing the horrible truth about Europe and colonization.

Historical Context

The Congo in the Early 1990s

When Høeg was writing the story in the late 1980s, the situation in the Congo was deteriorating. After almost thirty years under a corrupt ruler, Mobutu Sese Seko (born as Joseph-Désiré Mobutu), the country, which had been known as Zaire since 1971, was nearly bankrupt. When the Cold War ended in the early 1990s, Mobutu lost financial support from Western nations, which had used the country's centralized location and Mobutu's resources to their advantage. As a result, he began to lose control of his regime.

The Escalation to World War II

The story takes place in 1929, another unstable time. The world was still recovering from World War I, while trying to prevent another world war. However, despite the Kellogg-Briand Pact, which outlawed war, attempts at world disarmament moved slowly. The more heavily armed states did not want to give up their military protection easily, while other states which had been forced to disarm after World War I wanted to rearm for their own protection. One of the biggest issues facing the Allies was the negotiation of final war reparations for Germany. As part of the Treaty of Versailles that ended World War I, the Allies included a war guilt clause, which stated that Germany caused the war and should therefore pay for the Allies's losses and damages. However, a specific figure was hard to assess. Under the 1924 Dawes Plan, the two sides agreed that, to start with, Germany would pay one million gold marks each year, rising to two-and-a-half million gold marks each year by 1928. By 1929, the plan was working so well that the British and French governments started renegotiations with Germany for their final reparations payments.

Germans, inspired by Adolf Hitler and frustrated over their rising unemployment, became increasingly hostile on the issue of war reparations payments. This issue helped Hitler and his Nazi Party gain in popularity, especially when the worldwide depression in the early 1930s affected Germany's ability to make its reparations payments. In addition to rebelling against making reparations, Hitler also spoke out against Jews, blaming the rising rate of German unemployment on Jewish businessmen. This charge was the beginning of an ethnic-cleansing policy that would eventually take the lives of millions of Jews. While Hitler enjoyed

Compare & Contrast

- **Late 1920s:** Adolf Hitler sets his ethnic-cleansing campaign into motion. His anti-Semitic propaganda helps gain the support of many Germans for his Nazi Party.

  Today: Following terrorist attacks on New York City and Washington, D.C., on September 11, 2001, the world experiences several other attempted terrorist attacks.

- **Late 1920s:** The stock market crash of 1929 marks the onset of the Great Depression. Although the causes of the crash are heavily debated, at least some blame goes to the massive amount of speculative trading in the 1920s, which was supported by the optimistic and naïve view that the good economy would continue to improve.

  Today: The crash of overinflated technology stocks, which many people had thought would continue to rise in value, helps initiate a recession in the United States. The economy gets worse as much evidence of rampant corporate corruption is brought to light through several lawsuits.

- **Late 1920s:** The violent regime of King Leopold II, in which millions of Africans were killed or forced into labor, has long since been replaced by a new Belgian government. However, Africans in the Congo are still abused and forced into labor, which leads to a revolt in 1928.

  Today: The effects of European colonization still plague Africa. While all regions have technically been decolonized, they retain their European-imposed boundaries that help create conflicts among the various ethnic groups in many countries. Africa experiences one of its most violent periods since the European conquest.

---

the support of many German veterans for his endorsement of their efforts in World War I, not all of them were swayed to support the Nazis. For example, Paul von Lettow-Vorbeck, a patriotic, conservative German, made an unsuccessful attempt to organize an opposition to Hitler and the Nazi Party.

Antiwar Sentiment

Most people were anxious to avoid another world war. The antiwar atmosphere manifested itself in many ways in the late 1920s, but one of the most prominent was in the publication of several literary works by veterans, all of whom indicted World War I. Siegfried Sassoon, an English poet who had been wounded while serving in the trenches in World War I, became famous during the war for his angry antiwar poems. In 1928, Sassoon published his autobiographical novel, *Memoirs of a Fox-Hunting Man.* After its success, he followed it with a 1930 sequel, *Memoirs of an Infantry Officer.* While he was injured during the war, Sassoon wrote a letter of protest to the war department, saying that he refused to fight any more. During this protest, he was supported by another English writer, Robert Graves. In 1929, Graves wrote his own antiwar novel, *Goodbye to All That,* which depicts in graphic detail his own experiences before, during, and after World War I. In *Farewell to Arms,* also published in 1929, Ernest Hemingway uses his own experiences to depict the fragile quality of love and relationships during wartime. However, the book that caused the largest stir was Erich Maria Remarque's 1929 novel, *All Quiet on the Western Front.* Remarque, a German Catholic, incurred the wrath of Adolf Hitler with the publication of his antiwar novel, which threatened Hitler's efforts to rally support for German military actions.

Scientific Theories

While the horrible realities of modern warfare were on many people's minds, others were caught up in more academic pursuits. In 1929, scientists were working on various theories that they hoped would either prove or disprove stability and uniform structure in the natural world. In "Journey into a Dark Heart," David notes Gödel's monumental conclusion, which was destined to shake the world of mathematics: "within any complex system there are certain elements that cannot be deduced from its basic characteristics." This evidence of unpredictability would be published in 1931 and would come to be known as Gödel's proof. Gödel's findings eliminated the possibility of standardizing the foundations of mathematics, something that mathematicians had been attempting to do for almost a century. In physics, however, scientists were still attempting to discover a unified field theory, a single theoretical structure that could encompass all fundamental physical forces. In 1929, Albert Einstein submitted a theory that supposedly united gravity and electromagnetism within one framework, a step that would have been a huge first step towards a unified field theory. Einstein's theory, however, was eventually proven wrong, as were the attempts of others.

Critical Overview

When *Fortællinger om naten* was first released in Denmark in 1990, the Danish press loved it. Says Thomas Satterlee, in his entry on Høeg for the *Dictionary of Literary Biography:* the book "confirmed for Danish critics what they had suspected from Høeg's first book: the author's talent was substantial, and the breadth of his knowledge was impressive." Satterlee also notes that Danish critics considered the book "a literary" work, especially with its similarities to the stories of Isak Dinesen. Satterlee also says that, with the publication of *Fortællinger om naten,* "Høeg's influence on contemporary Danish fiction increased," as critics started to "view his ambitious work as a standard by which other Danish writers might be judged."

The book was also received well when it was translated into English in 1998 as *Tales of the Night.* Katherine Dunn, in her 1998 review for *Washington Post Book World,* says that it is "an intriguing collection of short stories." Likewise, the 1998 reviewer for *Kirkus Reviews* calls the book "an accomplished and provocative debut collection from one of the world's least predictable writers." However, although most reviewers had at least one good comment about the book, several qualified their praise with negative criticism. For example, in the 1998 *Publishers Weekly* review, the reviewer says that there is "a certain stiffness in the prose."

Although, the reviewer says that this may be "the fault of the translation." In the end, the reviewer assesses the collection as "potent but problematic" and says that it "must make do without the dazzling lucidity of Høeg's more recent works." Bill Ott, in his 1998 *Booklist* review, says that, since this collection is one of Høeg's earlier works and does not show the skill of his later books, one can see in the stories a writer "struggling to come to terms with his craft." For this reason, Ott recommends the collection, but only to "anyone curious about the evolution of a great writer."

Several English-speaking critics also note the relation of Høeg's works to Dinesen's. Says Edward B. St. John in his 1998 review of the collection for *Library Journal:* "Høeg's use of a polished nineteenth-century prose style to examine twentieth-century issues strongly recalls the work of fellow Dane Isak Dinesen." Likewise, Dunn says that the stories reveal Høeg to be "an old-fashioned storyteller in fable forms reminiscent of Isak Dinesen and occasionally Joseph Conrad." The similarity of "Journey into a Dark Heart" to Conrad's *Heart of Darkness* is also commonly mentioned by critics. For example, Dunn calls the story "gleefully satiric" and says that it is a homage to *Heart of Darkness* that travels "by train rather than riverboat." In his 1998 review of the collection for the *New York Times Book Review,* Jay Parini says, "The main interest in the story lies with the narrative technique, borrowed from Conrad, of the tale told within tales."

The use of Conrad, who was dead at this point in history, has also attracted the attention of critics. Says Dunn: "Høeg inserts historical figures into several of these fictions, molding them for his own purposes." St. John thinks that this historical context in "Journey into a Dark Heart" helps make it "the strongest story in the collection." However, not all critics appreciate Høeg's use of many historical figures and other allusions. Says Parini: "Høeg is vastly learned, referring easily to a dizzying range of historic events, geographical places, figures from the past and scientific theories, but his learning often gets in the way." Parini finds this to be most apparent in "Journey into a Dark Heart." The blatant use of the 1929 date for Høeg's self-professed love stories is also a common topic of discussion for critics. Satterlee says that in this year "before Adolf Hitler's rise to power, Europeans had not yet suffered the disillusionment of the Holocaust, and simple romance was still possible." The *Kirkus Reviews* reviewer notes that, while the

"Journey into a Dark Heart" references the work of Kurt Gödel, shown here receiving the Albert Einstein Award for achievement in natural science

use of a "love motif" is "gimmicky," it does give Høeg the opportunity to place "these olden fancifully symbolic stories firmly within a context of political and economic ferment and approaching European war." Finally, the *Publishers Weekly* reviewer, referring to the famous 1929 stock market crash, links Høeg's choice of date with the moral quality of the stories, saying that the date is "a sort of universal Black Monday of the soul."

Criticism

Ryan D. Poquette

Poquette has a bachelor's degree in English and specializes in writing about literature. In the following essay, Poquette discusses Høeg's use of contrasting dark and light imagery in "Journey into a Dark Heart."

Høeg's moral message in "Journey into a Dark Heart" is clear. Western attitudes towards African colonialism in the early twentieth century were based on false assumptions or outright lies. However, while this idea comes through clearly with the dialogue, particularly that of Lueni and her accomplice, Joseph K., Høeg underscores this idea through the use of contrasting dark and light imagery and the meanings behind these images.

In the story, Høeg uses many contrasting images, such as the wealth of Europe compared to the poverty of Africa or the modern train with its European conveniences traveling through the primitive jungle. At one point in their conversation, David even introduces a number of opposites: "A great mathematician once said that when God created heaven and earth and separated light and dark and water from land and above from below, he showed himself to be a mathematician." However, the greatest contrast is between dark and light which is also the most prevalent contrast in the story.

Throughout the story, many items and people are described in terms of dark and light or black and white. "Black" servants wear "white" gloves or clothes, which helps emphasize the differences between the two races. Also, at one point, when describing David's adjustment to life in Africa, the narrator says that "David believed himself to be

What Do I Read Next?

- Edwin A. Abbott's classic *Flatland: A Romance of Many Dimensions* (1884) is a short, mathematical, fantasy novel featuring a flat, two-dimensional world inhabited by geometric shapes. When one resident, A. Square (which is also the pseudonym under which Abbott originally published the novel), discovers the third dimension, he is forced to change his assumptions about reality.

- Joseph Conrad's *Heart of Darkness,* originally published in 1899, details the journey of the narrator, Marlow, into the Belgian Congo. Marlow is sent to find a company agent who has gone mad and who has fallen out of touch with his European company while at the Inner Station. In the process, Marlow witnesses the horrors of European colonialism. The book inspired the famous 1979 movie *Apocalypse Now,* which set Conrad's story in Vietnam.

- Critics have noted that Høeg is one of the most popular and talented Danish authors since Karen Blixen, who wrote under the pseudonym of Isak Dinesen. Dinesen's *Out of Africa* (1937) is a novel based on her experiences in Kenya from 1914 to 1931, where she owned and operated a coffee plantation. The novel depicts life in colonial Africa during this time and is told from Dinesen's limited, and sometimes distorted, European perspective. The book was adapted into an Academy Award–winning film by the same name in 1986.

- Reviewers also note that Høeg's *Tales of the Night* owes a literary debt to Dinesen's *Seven Gothic Tales* (1934). Like Høeg's book, Dinesen's collection combines characteristics of the modern short story with the conventions of nineteenth-century Gothic tales and features many references to noted historical figures.

- Høeg's novel *Borderliners* (1994; originally published in Danish in 1993 as *De Maske Egnede*) depicts the life of three children at a Danish boarding school. The three children are social outcasts, and as they band together to survive in the hostile school environment, they realize that everything is not what it seems. The students, led by the narrator Peter, try to uncover the brutal social experiment that is being conducted by the school.

- Høeg's first novel published in the United States, *Smilla's Sense of Snow* (1993), was originally published a year earlier in Danish as *Frøken Smillas fornemmelse for sne.* The novel tells the story of Smilla, a half Inuit, half Danish glaciologist with a fascination for mathematics, whose extensive knowledge of the properties of snow and ice leads her to question the snow-related death of a neighbor boy. Smilla's investigation takes her on a geographical and scientific journey that ultimately leads her to uncover a crime—as well as Denmark's colonial exploitation of Greenland.

---

more or less accustomed to the sudden shifts between darkness and light,'' which had given him headaches when he first arrived.

Traditionally in literature, darkness and blackness have negative associations, such as death and evil. In fact, from the beginning, readers are led to believe that the "dark heart" of the title refers to the Congo, the region of the African interior through which the characters will pass by train. Africa is

viewed as a dark and evil place, which is demonstrated at the dedication dinner. When Joseph K. brings word to the Belgian king that the African rebel, Lueni, has been killed, everybody breathes a sigh of relief. As the narrator notes, Lueni—and the associated resistance movement—is a "name from the innermost chamber of Africa's dark hell."

By contrast, lightness and whiteness often have good associations in literature, such as life and goodness. This connection is also reinforced at the dedication dinner. During his speech, the Belgian king refers to the Europeans' African railroad rails as two "pure lines of thought and commerce that, as the arteries of civilization, shall carry clean, revitalized blood three thousand kilometers through the jungle, deep into the heart of the dark continent." This assumption that Europe is pure and civilized and Africa is dark and primitive reflects the prevailing prejudice of the time. David, a truthseeker, is nevertheless swayed by this powerful speech, which idealizes colonization by making it seem as though Europe's efforts to civilize the Africans are noble. This feeling of moral superiority is amplified when David goes outside into the garden. The narrator describes the setting in bright, idealistic terms: "With its white pillars the governor's palace looked for all the world like a floodlit Greek temple." The use of the color white is meant to indicate goodness and purity, and the allusion to a Greek temple symbolizes advanced learning and civilization. The picture is completed by the presence of "the constellation of Libra, that great celestial square." Libra is a European symbol of justice, and at this early point in the story, David thinks that Europe has been fair to the Africans. David takes comfort in these feelings and thinks that he is perhaps on the right track after all.

However, not all juxtapositions of the black and white imagery are flattering to the Europeans. There are also concrete images of the subordination of Africans by whites. As the narrator says when David is at the dedication dinner, "he mingled with black servants and white guests." Despite the fact that the Africans are supposedly being civilized, none of them is allowed to be a guest. Instead, they are all relegated to the subordinate position of servants. In fact, David even notes that the black servants will always symbolize Africa, and never Europe. The lavish dedication reminds him of home, but "the white tropical suits, the suntanned men, and the black servants in their livery and white gloves betrayed the fact that this was not Europe." Later in the story, after the general has introduced himself, the narrator gives background on the military leader, including his successful defense of Germany's African colonies with "white troops and black askaris." The fact that the black troops are referred to by a different name indicates the segregation. In fact, Joseph K. takes this a step further when he challenges the general's published assertion that the Africans volunteered to fight for the Germans. As Joseph K. notes, the truth is that

> **While Joseph K. has provided the majority of the debunking of Western notions about colonialism throughout the story, at the end, Lueni takes over and becomes the educator."**

"they walked into that war on the point of a German bayonet." This information reinforces the subordination of blacks by whites.

In fact, even David, an amiable, naive young man, is a product of his European background, which assumes that blacks are inferior to whites. When David first meets his traveling companions, he notices that Lueni, who at this point is posing as Joseph K.'s black female servant, "settled herself, unasked, on a stool in the corner." This language indicates the European expectation that blacks would ask their masters for permission before sitting down. David and the general also expect that Lueni cannot speak English, another side effect of the belief that the Africans are an inferior race. When David notices that she is watching him, he is surprised, because he believes that she "could have understood nothing." In fact, when Lueni does speak up, in "dark and faultless English," the general is so shocked that he just stares at her: "And he was looking at her still as he said, to no one in particular and without seeming to have heard a word of what she had said: 'She speaks English.'" The idea of an African girl speaking English is unfathomable to the general. He regains his composure and tries to enforce his white superiority on the servant: "Stand up when a white man is talking to you. Who are you?" However, as the general soon realizes when Lueni draws her gun, their roles have been reversed. Lueni is in control, and the white men are subordinate to her.

Besides the association of darkness with evil and subordination, the darkness of Africa also represents mystery in the minds of the Europeans. When David arrives on the continent, the "dark, inscrutable faces all around him . . . weigh on his mind." Furthermore, David is intrigued by the mysterious pictures of Africa that show up in Europe, which only "show the dark fringes of a forest, from which sudden death strikes in the form of a wild animal or a poisoned dart." At first, Joseph K. tries to support this idea that "Africa is dark" and attempts to prove it by opening the curtains to reveal "the tropical night, black and impenetrable." However, David challenges this notion by blowing out the lamp, which turns the dark landscape white from the moonlight. David says that "the light of learning" can blind people, making them think that their surroundings are "dark and unfathomable." Furthermore, he observes: "Anyone who travels through Africa in a brightly lit railway carriage is bound, on his return home, to tell everyone that Africa is a lowering forest fringe."

This is the turning point in the story. From this point on, Joseph K. and Lueni increasingly challenge European assumptions about colonialism, and even the general admits that he has lied about Africa for political gain. At one point, Joseph K. even reverses the traditional associations of black as mysterious, when he is discussing his passion for maps. Says Joseph K.:

> As a boy I used to look at maps, I was . . . obsessed with maps, the white areas most of all. They denote those places of which we know nothing, dark spots in the universe that exert a . . . savage attraction.

In this example, which closely echoes a passage in Joseph Conrad's *Heart of Darkness,* the color white suddenly represents the hidden, the unknown. This reversal is intentional in both texts. At this point in Høeg's story, enough hidden truths about Europe have been revealed, and its questionable practices in Africa are indeed starting to look "dark" and "savage."

If Europe is not to be trusted, where does one seek the truth? As Joseph K. and Lueni reveal, it is only through darkness that one may find the path to truth. Earlier in the story, Joseph K. has noted that "this expedition into the heart of darkness may also be a journey into the light." In the figurative sense, this is exactly what happens. In a 1997 article about Høeg's works for *Scandinavian Studies,* Hans Henrik Møller notes the following about this story: "The trip also assumes symbolic significance in its movement toward the characters' heightened comprehension: it is a journey into the mind, travel through the dark parts of a western civilization."

While Joseph K. has provided the majority of the debunking of Western notions about colonialism throughout the story, at the end, Lueni takes over and becomes the educator. In this way, the traditional roles of whites as the civilizing force on Africans is also reversed. During Lueni's speech, she educates the Europeans. Even after she has drawn her gun, Lueni remains quiet and calm. David notes that the three men are all away from their homes and assumes, based on Lueni's African status, that she is in her home. "You, Miss, on the other hand, appear to be . . . in your proper place." Lueni corrects him, noting that she is in fact several thousand kilometers from her African home.

She also notes that she was educated in London. Because of this, she is able to use the language of her oppressors to convey the massive destruction that Europeans have wrought in the Congo. "The European languages . . . are good for large numbers. In English, for example, the seven thousand slaves who built this railway are easily counted." Lueni continues, giving them detailed accounts of how Africans were forced into labor and killed in large numbers during the construction of the railroad and challenges the general's notion that there is no slavery in Africa. At the end, she notes the following: "In my tribe we say that the railroads across Africa run not over railway track but over African bones. What would you call slavery if not that, General?"

After David and his two companions jump safely from the train, he speaks briefly with Lueni, saying that "Europeans are experts when it comes to waging war." As the narrator says, David is "unaware that he spoke as though this were a class in which he no longer found himself a subset." David has become totally disillusioned at the end. All of his assumptions about the meanings of dark and light, Africa and Europe—like his previous assumptions about mathematics—have been challenged and debunked. As the *Publishers Weekly* reviewer notes of many stories in *Tales of the Night* "the deep despair and foreboding of well-intentioned Europeans victimized by the very culture that was supposed to educate them is often painfully credible."

When David sits down on the tracks and puts his head in his hands at the end, he is not sure what to do with himself or where to go. Meanwhile, as one final contrast, Høeg leaves his readers with the following image: "Libra crossed the zenith of the night sky and dropped toward the horizon. European justice descending over tropical Africa." However, the meaning of this image, like many of the contrasting images in the story, has changed. In the beginning, David, like most Europeans, viewed colonization efforts as a positive, civilizing force. It is only at the end, after David has been educated by Lueni, that this celestial image of justice becomes one more empty European symbol masking the terrible truth of the horrors of colonialism.

Source: Ryan D. Poquette, Critical Essay on ''Journey into a Dark Heart,'' in *Short Stories for Students,* Gale, 2003.

Kate Covintree

Covintree is currently pursuing a master of fine arts degree at Emerson College. In this essay, Covintree explores the way Høeg illustrates colonialism in his short story.

Almost one hundred years after Joseph Conrad wrote his acclaimed novella *Heart of Darkness,* Danish author Peter Høeg has written ''Journey into a Dark Heart.'' Like Conrad's, Høeg's story is set deep in the jungle of central Africa. Høeg follows many of Conrad's conventions, though this time, instead of a journey by boat, it is a journey by train. Høeg sets his story on March 19, 1929, five years after Conrad's death. Still, Høeg chooses to include a character on his journey that is a resurrected Conrad with the name Joseph K. (for Korzeniowski which was Conrad's real last name). He is one of three men in the train who are accompanied by one black female servant. The other male travelers are the German General Paul von Lettow Voerbeck, famous for his military skill during WWI, and a disillusioned Danish mathematician named David Rehn. The black female is assumed to be Joseph K.'s servant, but during the course of the tale is discovered to be a rebel leader. Parallels could be made between these characters and those in Conrad's story as well as between the two narrative styles, but Høeg's story is still unique, with new voices. As Hans Möller says in his article ''Peter Høeg or the Sense of Writing'' from *Scandinavian Studies,* Høeg uses his story ''to create [a] convincingly new and engaging fictional reality which is nonetheless a continuation of an older tradition.'' In following that older tradition, Høeg uses this story and its four main characters to look at Europe's colonization of Africa.

Like the Greeks before them, the Europeans of the late nineteenth and early twentieth centuries believe it is their duty to create empires outside of their own nations. By placing the story in 1929, Høeg examines a time in Africa when colonialism is still strong. In her essay ''The Other Woman and the Racial Politics of Gender: Isak Dinesen and Beryl

> **"** This is a completely different Africa, now revealed because it is not being 'blinded by the light source itself.' Invading colonists have manipulated the image of Africa and in doing so have manipulated their understanding of Africa."

Markham in Kenya,'' Sidonie Smith explores the various reasons for Europe's appeal in Africa. She observes that the African people were ''categorized as less civilized'' and ''located closer to nature.'' This immediate low status raised the status of all Europeans in Africa, because at least they weren't African. For Høeg's European characters, he shows that they have no desire to be African. As Smith explains, ''Africa represented a new kind of playground, 'a winter home for Aristocrats' as one Uganda Railroad poster advertised.'' In the opening scene, there is a large formal dinner set in the jungle. Even in the middle of this jungle, the colonialists engage in the habits of their home country. ''The dinner service was Crown Derby, the wine was Chambertin-Clos de Beze, and the saddle of venison tasted to David just like the red deer at home.'' During this elaborate dinner, the guests can imagine they are in Europe, because nothing of the African culture has been integrated into their experience.

When David enters his Pullman car to start the journey, he is again met with Europe inside Africa. He enters an elaborate car that is ''the most extreme and yet classic example of European comfort.'' David and his traveling companions can forget about their actual tropic location and settle themselves into the familiar. They are supplied with ''leather upholstered chairs,'' ''paintings of cool oak forests,'' and ''an open marble fireplace.'' None of these items have any logical use in the jungle. Though it could get cool at night in Africa, finding a fireplace and having it be of marble is highly unlikely. Such a thing is unnecessary in this environment. Leather chairs would be made from the hides of animals not traditionally found on the continent of Africa. In addition, having paintings of oak trees shows the vast contrast between the scenery in Europe and in the Congo. It also shows the aesthetic of the Europeans. They do not perceive Africa to contain beauty as Europe does. Africa only contains undiscovered resources.

These are the resources that propel the character of Joseph K. to come to Africa. Joseph K. confesses during their journey that as a boy he was "obsessed with maps, the white areas most of all. They denote those places of which we know nothing, dark spots in the universe that exert a . . . savage attraction." Since they are blank, foreign spaces to the Europeans, they believe they can claim them for their own. This idea of entitlement is strengthened by the fact that they color these unknown areas white. Though these parts of the maps are empty, the Europeans already connect this white space with their own skin color. Thus they see that land as already connected to them and want to impose their European identity on that space. Smith writes,

> the image of Africa constructed by Europeans both invited and justified colonization, on one hand the project of "civilizing" the native Africans, on the other the aggressive expression of the will to power, the desire to dominate, appropriate, and transform.

In their domination, the Europeans dismiss the culture and people of the land. In addition, they disregard the work they subject the natives to: "All the guests were filled with the sense of a tough job well done. Their limbs ached slightly, as though they personally had shoveled earth and sleepers into place." Not only have they appropriated the native land, they have also appropriated the feeling of satisfaction for doing exhaustive work. These noble Europeans did none of this work. Instead, they found a blank place on the map that intrigued them and used whatever means necessary to own that area. This railroad was not being built for the people of Africa but for the people who wanted to consume Africa.

Because the story is set in the jungle, however, most readers know these areas are not white, blank, or empty. The environment is lush with life and culture. To celebrate any existing culture would deny the discovery made by the Europeans. They want to make every part of the uncharted map their own. But this will never happen. The native people, who did not need a map to discover they exist already, occupy the white space Joseph K. and the other colonialists are interested in. For the Europe-

ans, these natives are a dark blemish on the vast, uncharted, white emptiness. These Europeans do their best to either ignore or control the darkness they perceive.

The darkness has several forms, most literally the night and the natives. The skin of the native people is dark and easily camouflaged at night. When Joseph K. pulls back a curtain in the train car, he shows "the tropical night, black and impenetrable." This darkness cannot be denied, but colonialists have generalized the continent based on these fixed circumstances. They have chosen to black out all African civilizations in order to create their own dream of the continent. As Joseph K. admits, "the dream . . . created by me, . . . and it is dark because Africa is dark." But when David turns out the lights in the train car, the jungle comes to life: "out of the gloom, the moonlit landscape outside emerged, glittering whitely, as if the treetops were covered with an endless carpet of snow." This is a completely different Africa, now revealed because it is not being "blinded by the light source itself." Invading colonists have manipulated the image of Africa and in doing so have manipulated their understanding of Africa.

In seeing themselves as governing the image of the dark land, they do not see what is possible in the people. In many ways, they do not see the people of Africa at all. Although von Lettow Voerbeck does not believe that the current railroad workers are slaves, when the facts are stated it becomes difficult to see it any other way:

> Belgian troops rounded up four thousand Africans from the Gold Coast and Angola. Some were drawn by the promise of what was a very low wage. . . . They worked under armed guard, under the lash, and with steel rings around their necks so they would be easily recognizable should they run away.

Clearly these workers are here because they have been forced. If they were free to leave, would rings around their necks be necessary? This is not equal or fair treatment and shows that the Europeans believed the natives to be less than human. They only see in the natives what they want to see.

When David turns out the lights, the outside moonlight can only reflect off the servant girl's dress. The servant girl's face disappears: "The light did not penetrate to her dark face." In the same way that the moonlight ignores her face, the three gentlemen also ignore her. Like the railway slaves, she is seen as an inconsequential member of the party. She goes unnoticed and remains a silent observer while the other three characters engage in a discourse as varied as math, religion, and colonialism. Though she listens to their opinions and ideas about Africa, she simply sits quietly. It is only when von Lettow Voerbeck tries to leave the car that she finally speaks.

Smith explains in her essay, "both woman and African remain the potential site of disruption—subjects waiting to speak," and to hear the black servant girl speak startles the men. Her words are simple, "the doors are locked," but the meaning is clear. She has understood their entire conversation and exposed them to their own vulnerability. By using her voice and speaking in their language, she has given Africa back some control of the European experience. She has disrupted the European balance. She can maintain this control even from a small stool. When ordered to stand, she simply makes herself more comfortable. She has subverted the notion of a passive Africa that will let anyone control her. She has, metaphorically speaking, turned out the lights again and forced them to look beyond their constructed image.

She further subverts their assumptions by being the leader of the rebel party. She is Lueni, the rebel leader whose name "constituted the essence of fear, it represented death" to the Europeans in Africa. At the beginning of the story, the Europeans assume that Lueni is a man, but she has shown otherwise. When she speaks her name, she is merely a girl, but a girl with immense power. When her role changes, the whole experience for the other characters is forced to shift dramatically. Their entire notion of power has been questioned, as has their destination.

Lueni becomes a symbol for the people affected by colonialism. The natives may appear silent and complicit, but they are observing their captors and will find ways to regain the power of their land and people. The three men are no longer heading for the African wilderness that will bring them uncharted riches, they are heading to an unknown they cannot have mastery over. With the destruction of the train, Høeg shows that colonialism will eventually crumble. Then, the Europeans will be forced to reexamine where they are. They are going to be consumed by Africa and will be forced to experience a truer version of Africa. This Africa will not have false European elegance, but African integrity.

Source: Kate Covintree, Critical Essay on "Journey into a Dark Heart," in *Short Stories for Students*, Gale, 2003.

Sources

Dunn, Katherine, "In the Gothic Mode," in *Washington Post Book World*, Vol. 28, No. 17, April 26, 1998, p. 4.

Høeg, Peter, Introductory Note, in *Tales of the Night*, translated by Barbara Haveland, Penguin Books, 1999.

———, "Journey into a Dark Heart," in *Tales of the Night*, translated by Barbara Haveland, Penguin Books, 1999, pp. 3–35.

Møller, Hans Henrik, "Peter Høeg, or The Sense of Writing," in *Scandinavian Studies*, Vol. 69, Winter 1997, pp. 29–51.

Ott, Bill, Review of *Tales of the Night*, in *Booklist*, Vol. 94, No. 9–10, January 1, 1998, p. 776.

Parini, Jay, "Mirrors within Mirrors," in the *New York Times Book Review*, March 1, 1998, p. 34.

Review of *Tales of the Night*, in *Kirkus Reviews*, December 1, 1997.

Review of *Tales of the Night*, in *Publishers Weekly*, Vol. 245, No. 1, January 5, 1998, p. 60.

Satterlee, Thomas, "Peter Høeg," in *Dictionary of Literary Biography*, Vol. 214: *Twentieth-Century Danish Writers*, edited by Marianne Stecher-Hansen, Gale, 1999, pp. 178–87.

Smith, Sidonie, "The Other Woman and the Racial Politics of Gender: Isak Dinesen and Beryl Markham in Kenya," in *De/Colonizing the Subject: The Politics of Gender in Women's Autobiography*, edited by Sidonie Smith and Julia Watson, University of Minnesota Press, 1992, pp. 410–35.

St. John, Edward B., Review of *Tales of the Night*, in *Library Journal*, Vol. 123, No. 2, February 1, 1998, pp. 114–15.

Further Reading

Césaire, Aimé, *Discourse on Colonialism*, translated by Joan Pinkham, New York University Press, 2000.

This classic work on colonialism, originally published in France in 1955, helped influence education and activism on colonial issues in Africa, Latin America, and the Caribbean. The author exposes the falsehoods of Western notions of colonial life and gives an accurate depiction of what life was really like in the colonies, for both the colonizer and the colonized.

Devlin, Keith J., *Mathematics: The Science of Patterns*, Scientific American Library, 1997.

Devlin goes beyond the assumption many people have made that mathematics deals only with numbers and places it within its cultural and historical context. The book, which features very little mathematical instruction, is nevertheless a great introduction for those interested in learning more about mathematical concepts.

Hochschild, Adam, *King Leopold's Ghost: A Story of Greed, Terror, and Heroism in Colonial Africa,* Houghton Mifflin Company, 1998.
> Hochschild's revealing history of King Leopold II's murderous regime in the Congo exposes the lengths to which he went to cover up his colonial crimes. Hochschild's many characters include Conrad, whose *Heart of Darkness* was based on the experiences he had in Leopold's Congo at the end of the nineteenth century.

Pakenham, Thomas, *The Scramble for Africa: White Man's Conquest of the Dark Continent from 1876 to 1912,* Avon Books, 1992.

In this book, Pakenham explores the colonization and division of Africa into European colonies. Also, while many of the horrific acts recounted in the book are condemned by modern readers, Pakenham explains the social attitudes of the time that led to these atrocities.

Reader, John, *Africa: A Biography of the Continent,* Vintage Books, 1999.
> Reader, a photojournalist, gives a sweeping history of Africa, from the formation of civilizations on the continent in ancient times to its circumstances in the present day. Along the way, he chronicles the continent's many historical, ecological, and geographical developments, providing a greater context for issues in modern Africa.

The Legend of the Christmas Rose

"The Legend of the Christmas Rose," by Selma Lagerlöf, was first published in 1908 in Swedish in a collection of stories, *En saga om en saga och andra sagor*, which was published in English as *The Girl from the Marsh Croft* (1910). The story is representative of most of Lagerlöf's tales, since it combines real-life details with legends and folklore. The story draws on the legend of the Christmas Rose, an actual flower—*Helleborus niger*—that blooms in winter conditions. The dominant legend of this flower's origin concerns the birth of Christ. However, as she does in other stories, Lagerlöf incorporates parts of this legend, but changes it to fit her own purpose and setting. Most of Lagerlöf's stories concerned Swedish legends and folklore. Because of this, "The Legend of the Christmas Rose" is unique. It takes place in Skåne, a modern-day Swedish province that was actually Danish during the twelfth century when the story takes place. The presence of Archbishop Absalon—the actual Catholic archbishop of Lund from 1177 to 1201—helps to pinpoint the story's time period. Through the seemingly simple tale of a miracle that is revealed every Christmas Eve to outlaws who live in exile in the forest, Lagerlöf explores some of the basic tenets of Christianity—including not judging people, the belief that anybody can be redeemed, and the rejection of materialism. More importantly, the story shows that any human, even a high-ranking member of the church, is susceptible to breaking these tenets. A current copy of the story can be found in *Girl from the*

Selma Lagerlöf

1908

Marsh Croft, which was published in 1996 by Penfield Press.

Author Biography

Lagerlöf was born on November 20, 1858, on her family's farm estate, Mårbacka, in the province of Värmland, Sweden. She was tutored at home, where she also heard many legends and folk tales from her family—most notably her paternal grandmother. An avid reader, Lagerlöf also composed her own poetry, which she read at community events. At a wedding in 1881, Eva Fryxell, a well-known feminist, heard one of Lagerlöf's verses and encouraged the young writer to dedicate her talent to women's causes. As a result, Lagerlöf attended the Royal Women's Superior Training College in Stockholm, Sweden, where she studied teaching. In 1885, her father died, leaving many debts, so Lagerlöf's beloved Mårbacka was sold. The same year, she began teaching secondary school for girls, devoting her free time to many social causes, while writing at night.

In 1891, Lagerlöf published her first novel, *Gösta Berlings Saga*. The book did not receive much attention until it was translated into Danish the following year, at which point an influential Danish critic helped to make it both a critical and popular success. To this day, it remains one of her most acclaimed works. In 1894, she published her first collection of short stories, *Osynliga Länkar*—translated into English as *Invisible Links* (1899). She received writing grants from both the Swedish royal family and the Swedish Academy and left teaching to become a full-time writer. During the next decade, Lagerlöf wrote several novels, childrens' books, and collections of short stories. The latter included *En saga om en saga och andra sagor* (1908), which was published in English as *The Girl from the Marsh Croft* (1910). This collection included the story, ''The Legend of the Christmas Rose.''

Sweden, and the world, recognized Lagerlöf's unique writing style, which was heavily influenced by the legends and folk tales she had heard as a child. Her imaginative, romantic tales directly contradicted the gritty realism that was in vogue at the turn of the century. In 1904, Lagerlöf was awarded a Gold Medal by the Swedish Academy. In 1907, her successful book sales gave her the money to buy back Mårbacka's house and garden. In 1909, Lagerlöf became the first woman, and the first Swede, to win the Nobel Prize for Literature. In 1910, with the money from her Nobel Prize, Lagerlöf was able to buy back the rest of the Mårbacka estate. In 1914, she received her country's highest honor when she became the first woman elected to the Swedish Academy.

During World War I and World War II, Lagerlöf contributed much of her time to helping others. During World War II, she participated in the Resistance movement against the Nazis and helped a number of German artists and intellectuals escape from Nazi Germany. She also donated her gold Nobel Prize medal to help Finland finance its fight against the Soviet Union. On March 16, 1940, Lagerlöf died of a stroke at Mårbacka.

Plot Summary

''The Legend of the Christmas Rose'' begins with a description of the Robber family, outlaws who live in exile in a forest cave, stealing from travelers to survive. In hard times, Robber Mother and her five children beg in the villages. On one trip, Robber Mother notices Abbot Hans's herb garden and is impressed, at first. She is interrupted by a lay brother, who orders her to leave the monastery. She ignores him, and the lay brother goes for reinforcements, but she and her children overpower them. Abbot Hans comes out and sees that Robber Mother is viewing his beloved garden. She says that it is a pretty garden, but it does not compare to the holy garden that blooms in the forest every Christmas Eve. The abbot has heard about this garden before but has never seen it. Robber Mother reluctantly agrees to take him to see it the next Christmas Eve.

The abbot tells the archbishop about the holy garden and asks the archbishop to pardon Robber Father's crimes. The archbishop does not believe in the legend, but nevertheless says that he will authorize the pardon if the abbot brings him a holy flower from the garden. On Christmas Eve, Abbot Hans and the lay brother go to the Robber family cave in the forest. While the abbot is excited, the lay brother is suspicious. They reach the bare cave, where Abbot Hans says that he is working on getting a pardon for Robber Father, but the Robber family does not believe it.

The appointed hour comes, and the forest goes through a rapid transformation from winter to spring. As each wave of heavenly light floods through the forest, trees bloom, forest animals appear, fruit begins to grow, and flowers appear. The abbot hears and sees the heavenly forms of angels, which come closer. However, the lay brother believes it is witchcraft and scares the miracle away with his violent reaction. The forest transforms back to its winter state, and Abbot Hans frantically searches through the reappearing snow for a flower to bring to Archbishop Absalon. In the process, the abbot, distraught over the angels' disappearance, has a fatal heart attack.

Abbot Hans's body is carried back to the cloister, where the monks pry a pair of root bulbs out of his tight grip. The lay brother plants the bulbs in the abbot's garden, where they lie dormant throughout spring, summer, and fall. The next Christmas Eve, the bulbs bloom into a large plant with beautiful flowers. The lay brother realizes that the miracle was real and takes flowers to Archbishop Absalon, who keeps his word and pardons Robber Father. The Robber family leaves the forest for good to live in the community once again, while the lay brother moves into their cave and lives alone, praying to be redeemed for his hard-heartedness. The forest never blooms again, but the single plant in the cloister does, as an annual reminder of the holy Christmas garden.

Selma Lagerlöf

Characters

Archbishop Absalon

Archbishop Absalon does not believe in the holy garden of Göinge at first but agrees to pardon Robber Father when the lay brother brings the archbishop some flowers as proof. Archbishop Absalon was an actual archbishop in the late twelfth century.

Abbot Hans

Abbot Hans feels blessed when he witnesses the blooming of the garden in the Göinge forest, but he has a fatal heart attack when the lay brother scares the miracle away. Abbot Hans is a peaceful man and does not judge others as quickly as the lay brother does. He loves his garden, which he has filled with many rare species of flowers. He is excited when Robber Mother tells him about the holy garden that blooms in the forest each Christmas Eve. Because he believes that God would not reveal such a miracle to evil people, he asks Archbishop Absalon to pardon Robber Father for his past crimes. The archbishop does not believe in the garden but does promise that if Abbot Hans can bring him a flower as proof, he will pardon Robber Father. Abbot Hans takes the lay brother with him to see the holy garden, and it is better than he expected. The forest is transformed from dark winter to a blooming spring of celestial light, from which angels steadily approach. The lay brother scares all of this away, and the abbot dies, heartbroken, but not before he is able to grab one of the roots from the holy garden. Back at the cloister, the monks find these roots in the abbot's hand, and the lay brother plants them. The resulting plant blooms every Christmas Eve in Abbot Hans's garden, although the holy garden in the Göinge forest never blooms again.

Lay Brother

The suspicious lay brother scares away the holy garden in the Göinge forest with his terrible outburst. The lay brother believes that Robber Mother and her family are evil. He tries in vain to kick her out of the garden, and is offended when she tells Abbot Hans that she knows of a garden better than his. The lay brother accompanies the abbot to the forest on Christmas Eve, where he expects that they will be ambushed. When the holy garden blooms,

Media Adaptations

- Lagerlöf's *Gösta Berling's Saga* was adapted into a feature film in 1924, the profits from which she donated to a fund for female authors. The silent film, entitled *The Story of Gösta Berling,* was directed by Mauritz Stiller and featured Greta Garbo in her first leading role. It is available on VHS from Timeless Video, Inc.

the lay brother mistakes the divine transformation for witchcraft. This delusion persists, even when he sees angels approaching. A small bird lands on his shoulder, and he thinks that it is an agent of the devil. He hits it, telling it to go back to hell. His outburst frightens the miracle away, and Abbot Hans dies, heartbroken at the loss of the miracle. The lay brother plants a pair of root bulbs that the abbot took from the holy forest, and when they bloom the following Christmas Eve, he takes some of the flowers to Archbishop Absalon, who gives the lay brother a letter of pardon for Robber Father. The lay brother delivers the letter to the Robber family, and when they move back into the community, he takes their place in their cave, living alone and praying for redemption for his hard-heartedness.

Robber Father

Robber Father is an outlaw who lives in a cave in the Göinge forest with Robber Mother and their five children. The ''Robber'' part of the family's name is a label that indicates the father is a thief. Robber Father survives mainly by stealing from travelers who pass through the forest. When Abbot Hans comes to see the holy garden, Robber Father is worried that the abbot is trying to get his wife and children to leave him and move back to the village. However, Abbot Hans says that he is trying to get a pardon for Robber Father, who says that, if this should happen, he will never steal again. When the forest fails to bloom the year following the lay brother's outburst, Robber Father is angry, but soon calms down when the lay brother brings a letter of pardon from the archbishop.

Robber Mother

Robber Mother is married to Robber Father, and begs in the villages when there are no travelers for her husband to rob. When she goes on such trips, she always gets what she wants, because the villagers are afraid to refuse her. When Robber Mother walks into the monks' cloister, she assumes she will be left alone to view the garden in peace, but the lay brother tries to force her out. Robber Mother and her children overpower him and two monks, but Abbot Hans welcomes her and asks her what she thinks of his garden. She tells him that she has seen better in the holy garden that blooms in Göinge forest every Christmas Eve. At first she refuses to take the abbot to see it, because she is afraid for her outlaw husband's safety. However, she wants to prove to the abbot that the holy garden is better, and agrees to take him and one of his followers.

The next Christmas Eve, Robber Mother sends one of her children to lead the abbot and the lay brother to her family's cave. The Robber family lives in absolute poverty, and their cave offers little comfort. Still, Robber Mother is a very strong woman, and bosses the abbot and the lay brother around as any comfortable peasant woman would. Abbot Hans tells Robber Mother that she may not have to live in such poverty, and describes the festivities that are going on in the village. Robber Mother is interested, but when the abbot tells her he is working on getting Robber Father a pardon, she does not believe it. However, when the lay brother brings the letter of pardon, Robber Mother says that her husband will never steal again, and the Robber family moves out of the forest and back into the community.

Themes

Judgment

Although Jesus Christ is never mentioned directly in the story, Lagerlöf's story embodies many of the beliefs of the Christian religion. These elements include the belief that one should not judge people by their outside appearances. In the story, the lay brother does this repeatedly. Even after Robber Mother has gained the approval of Abbot Hans to stay and view the monk's garden, the lay brother antagonizes her, because he does not think that she—or anything associated with her—can be good.

Topics for Further Study

- Research other legends surrounding *Helleborus niger,* the flower commonly known as the Christmas Rose. Compare Lagerlöf's version to these other versions.

- Archbishop Absalon was an actual archbishop in the twelfth century. Research his life and write a short biography about him. Compare his life and characteristics to the character in the story.

- In the story, Robber Father is formally forgiven by the Catholic Church through Archbishop Absalon's letter of ransom, or pardon, which frees him to live in society once again. Research the history of ransom letters during the Middle Ages. Write a sample ransom letter for another historical personage who was actually condemned by the church during this time period.

- Research the medieval feudal system. Imagine you are a feudal peasant during this time and write a sample journal entry that describes your typical day. Use your research to support your claims.

- Research the various positions in the Catholic Church hierarchy in twelfth-century Europe. Plot each of these positions on an organizational chart and include a short, modern-style "job description" for each position.

For example, after Robber Mother tells him about a garden that rivals Abbot Hans's garden, the lay brother is sarcastic to her. Says the lay brother: "It must be a pretty garden that you have made for yourself amongst the pines in Göinge forest!" Because of his inability to believe that the Robber family is anything but evil, he perceives the miracles in the forest as witchcraft. The lay brother thinks: "This cannot be a true miracle . . . since it is revealed to malefactors." This inability to look past his assumptions results in the lay brother's outburst, which scares the holy phenomenon away forever.

On the other hand, Abbot Hans does not judge people by their appearances and gives them the benefit of the doubt. When he first comes across Robber Mother in his garden, he is able to look past her reputation and the fact that she has just fought with some of his monks. "Wild and terrible as the old woman looked, he couldn't help liking that she had fought with three monks for the privilege of viewing the garden in peace." The abbot is also the only one who believes Robber Mother's story about the holy garden. In fact, the abbot uses this legend to lobby for the pardon of Robber Father. He tells Archbishop Absalon: "If these bandits are not so bad but that God's glories can be made manifest to them, surely we cannot be too wicked to experience the same blessing." Robber Mother also proves to be nonjudgmental. When she tells the abbot and the lay brother about a garden that rivals Abbot Hans's garden, she explains to the lay brother that she is being truthful, and that she does not "wish to make myself the judge of either him or you."

Redemption

The Christian idea of redemption is also expressed in the story. Abbot Hans believes that Robber Father can be redeemed. He speaks with Archbishop Absalon, "asking him for a letter of ransom for the man, that he might lead an honest life among respectable folk." However, the archbishop is not as forgiving and does not believe that the man can be redeemed. He tells Abbot Hans that he does not want "to let the robber loose among honest folk in the villages. It would be best for all that he remain in the forest." Nevertheless, the archbishop does tell Abbot Hans that he will pardon Robber Father if the abbot brings him a flower from the holy garden. The abbot is overjoyed that the archbishop is giving him a chance to help Robber Father and thinks that his superior is being sincere. However, the archbishop is only making to the promise so that he can satisfy Abbot Hans. The lay brother witnesses the conversation and realizes "that Bishop Absalon believed as little in this story of Robber Mother's as he himself.'' In the end, Robber Father is redeemed when Archbishop Absalon keeps his promise and writes the letter of pardon. The lay brother, on the other hand, trades places with Robber Father. He moves into the former outlaw's cave, where he spends his time ''in constant meditation and prayer that his hard-heartedness might be forgiven him.''

Materialism

Christians believe that too much attachment to material possessions or ideas separates one from the divine, whereas the poor are closer to God. This story offers a literal depiction of that idea. The outlaws in the forest, who live inside ''a poor mountain grotto with bare stone walls,'' are the ones to whom the divine miracle is first revealed. On the other hand, the people in the villages, who are attached to their material existence, do not see the miracle. They make extensive preparations for their Christmas celebrations, which are all based on material items, such as ''hunks of meat and bread.'' This image contrasts sharply with the ''wretchedness and poverty'' of the outlaws' cave, where ''nothing was being done to celebrate Christmas.'' The lay brother is also materialistic and would rather stay at home and join in the village celebration than go to see a miracle in which he does not believe. On the trip through the villages, ''the lay brother whined and fretted when he saw how they were preparing to celebrate Christmas in every humble cottage.'' The lay brother is also suspicious that the Robber family is going to trap them. This attachment to earthly attitudes affects the lay brother in the forest, where he is unable to let go of his materialism and see the truth of the heavenly miracle.

Abbot Hans, on the other hand, is one of few people outside the forest who is not ruled by an attraction to material possessions or attitudes. When the abbot passes through the villages, he notices the extensive Christmas preparations, but he is not impressed: ''He was thinking of the festivities that awaited him, which were greater than any the others would be privileged to enjoy.'' Even the abbot's beloved garden does not compare to his divine beliefs. ''Abbot Hans loved his herb garden as much as it was possible for him to love anything earthly and perishable.'' As a result, when the miracle is revealed to the abbot, he is gracious and humble, realizing that he is seeing something that far outweighs anything on Earth. ''He felt that earth could bring no greater happiness than that which welled up about him.''

Style

Setting

The story's medieval setting is very important. During the Middle Ages, the Christian faith was extremely strong, and many believed in the possibility of miracles. When Robber Mother tells the abbot and the lay brother about the annual miracle in Göinge forest, the abbot believes her: ''ever since his childhood, Abbot Hans had heard it said that on every Christmas Eve the forest was dressed in holiday glory.'' However, people in this time period also had particularly strong beliefs in evils like Satan. When the lay brother sees the miracle, he is blinded by his suspicion, and his mind makes him see witchcraft, which he thinks is sent by Satan. When a forest dove lands on his shoulder, ''it appeared to him as if sorcery were come right upon him to tempt and corrupt him.'' The fact that the story takes place several hundred years before Lagerlöf wrote it also helps to give the story a mythical feel. Lagerlöf draws attention to the legendary quality of the story by referring to the fact that the story takes place far in the past. For example, at the end of the story, the narrator says that ''Göinge forest never again celebrated the hour of our Saviour's birth.'' Finally, the remote location of Robbers' cave is also important. It is far enough away from the villages for the Robber family to live safely without fear of persecution. The cave's distance from civilization also helps to separate the divine miracle in the poor forest from the materialistic villages. When the abbot is traveling through the forest, the narrator notes that he journeys for a long time: ''He left the plain behind him and came up into desolate and wild forest regions.'' In fact, as they ride farther and higher, they reach ''snow-covered ground.'' The snow is important, because when the miracle takes place, those present can mark the beginning of the miracle by the disappearance of the snow.

Symbolism

A symbol is a physical object, action, or gesture that also represents an abstract concept, without losing its original identity. For example, in the story, the miracle takes place in a forest, which is physically just a group of trees. However, forests can also be symbolic, representing places of magical or spiritual occurrences, as the Göinge forest does in this story. Symbols appear in literature in one of two ways. They can be local symbols, meaning they are only relevant within a specific literary work. They can also be universal symbols, in which case their symbolism is based on traditional associations that are widely recognized, regardless of context. The story is saturated with universal symbols, such as the mystical forest. Other symbols include the two gardens, which traditionally represent paradise, as in the Garden of Eden. There are several animals in the story, which also symbolize other ideas. The dove that lands on the lay brother's shoulder is a traditional sign of peace, which the lay brother rejects by hitting it. The bear that comes into the forest is a sign of strength, which has no place in a holy garden. As a result, Robber Father strikes it on the nose and sends it away. Likewise, the owl, a night bird that is often associated with death or ill omens, also flees the holy miracle. Even the name, the Christmas Rose, is a symbol for something else. Technically, the real Christmas Rose flower, *Helleborus niger,* is an herb of the buttercup family, not a rose. However, out of all flowers, the rose is the most symbolic. Its many associations include purity and perfection, so it is appropriate that a holy flower would bear its name.

Irony

Irony is the unique sense of awareness that is produced when someone says something and means another, or when somebody does something, and the result is opposite of what was expected. In "The Legend of the Christmas Rose," the irony is the latter, situational irony. In the beginning, the abbot is the only one who believes that the Robber family can be redeemed. He believes it so strongly that he asks his archbishop to pardon Robber Father. However, the archbishop—and the lay brother—are unable to see the potential good in the Robber family. Since an abbot is far below an archbishop in the church hierarchy, the archbishop is depicted as the more believable character. This becomes especially clear when the narrator shows how the archbishop agrees to Abbot Hans's pardon request merely to appease the abbot, not because he believes in the miracle. In fact, even the narration is biased. The narrator says that "Robber Mother and her brood were worse than a pack of wolves, and many a man felt like running a spear through them." As a result, readers are led to believe that Robber Mother and her family are bad people and are encouraged to side with the archbishop and the lay brother.

However, in the story's ironic ending, the actual outcome contradicts these expectations. The abbot is proved right, but he dies in the process. Throughout the story, the lay brother was concerned that the Robber family would try to capture Abbot Hans and perhaps harm him. Yet, in the end, it is the lay brother's rash actions that "had killed Abbot Hans, because he had dashed from him the cup of happiness which he had been thirsting to drain to its last drop." In addition, the archbishop is forced to pardon Robber Father, an agreement that he made to appease Abbot Hans, but which he thought he would never have to honor. In the story's final, ironic twist, the lay brother delivers the letter of pardon to Robber Father and takes the family's place in exile. These ironic outcomes do more than just surprise the reader, they also illustrate Lagerlöf's moral. In the end, Lagerlöf shows that all of humanity is subject to error and lack of faith when they are too close to the material world, even an archbishop. Likewise, true to the Christian ideal, even society's outlaws can be redeemed.

Historical Context

Skåne

When Lagerlöf wrote the story in the early 1900s, Skåne, a province at the southern tip of modern-day Sweden, belonged to Sweden. However, the story takes place in the twelfth century—as evidenced by the real-life, twelfth-century character of Archbishop Absalon. In the twelfth century, Skåne was a Danish province. In fact, Lagerlöf's narrator refers to the Danish setting of the story when describing the audacity of Robber Mother. "It was obvious that she was as certain she would be left in peace as if she had announced that she was the Queen of Denmark."

Christianity in Medieval Scandinavia

It is important to understand Christianity at this time in order to grasp the historical context of the story. At this point in history, Christianity was the dominant religion in Europe, including Scandinavia. Sweden did not fully let go of its paganism until the twelfth century, while Denmark was Christianized in the mid-tenth century. As a result, Christian institutions were thoroughly entrenched in Denmark by the time the story takes place, which may be one reason why Lagerlöf chose Denmark instead of Sweden as the setting for her story. In the twelfth century, Christian meant Roman Catholic, which was the only accepted Christian denomination. Catholics then, as now, received their religious instruction from a pope, who was aided by a vast hierarchy of

Compare & Contrast

- **1100–1200:** Catholicism is the only approved Christian denomination in most of Europe, including Denmark. Sweden is also increasingly dominated by Christianity, and pagan religious practice comes to be suppressed.

  1900s: Following the Protestant Reformation in the sixteenth century, a Danish Lutheran Church and Swedish Lutheran Church form and quickly gain dominance over Catholicism, a trend that continues in the twentieth century.

  Today: More than 90 percent of both Danes and Swedes are Lutheran.

- **1100–1200:** Skåne is officially a province of Denmark. Danish control of the Baltic–North Sea waterway that separates Skåne from mainland Denmark helps to make Denmark a major maritime power.

  1900s: Following bitter struggles in the medieval and renaissance periods, Skåne is officially a province of Sweden.

  Today: Skåne is still a Swedish province, but ownership is no longer an issue, since Sweden and Denmark are both lesser powers that do not rely on maritime warfare.

- **1100–1200:** Pope Innocent III is the latest in a line of twelfth-century popes who increase the stature and influence of the Catholic papacy, which is increasingly involved in political matters.

  1900s: Pope Pius X works to repress Modernism, an intellectual movement that seeks to revise Catholic teaching so that it is more consistent with modern sensibilities and understandings. In 1907, he issues a decree that urges censorship of Modernist books.

  Today: Pope John Paul II is one of the most controversial and conservative popes, staunchly refusing to support many modern notions, including admitting women to the priesthood, allowing male priests to marry, and accepting abortion and homosexuality. In 1994, he releases *The Catechism of the Catholic Church* in English translation. This extensive document outlines the beliefs and moral tenets of the Catholic Church. The same year, he is named *Time*'s Man of the Year.

---

subordinates, including archbishops. These clergy differed from the monks and nuns who lived apart from the public in an attempt to achieve spiritual purity.

Life in a Medieval Abbey

In the story, Lagerlöf's narrator says that Abbot Hans lives in a cloister, a type of monastic establishment. The term cloister was generally used to refer to the square courtyard located at the center of most monasteries, or abbeys. A medieval abbey, as the name suggests, was an establishment where several monks lived and were ruled by an abbot, or in some cases an abbess—a female abbot. The monks in an abbey adhered to the Benedictine Rule, a strict, daily routine of prayer, manual labor, and study that they performed together in group rituals. The monks

were helped in their labors by a number of lay brothers, non-monks who lived at the monastery. Lay brothers performed various manual tasks, but generally did not take part in the holy rituals or scholastic activities.

Life in a Medieval Village

Although the Robber family is depicted as poor in the story, in the twelfth century, most peasants were poor, even those who lived in the villages. The majority of Europe, including Denmark, relied on the feudal system—an oppressive system of land ownership and employment that exploited peasant labor. On most days, peasant couples and their children worked from sunrise to sunset. Men would usually raise the crops, while the women cooked and cleaned, made clothes, and performed various other activities around the house. When the fields were frozen, peasants worked on indoor tasks, such as repairing tools for the next planting season. Christmas was one of the few reprieves from this schedule. As C. Warren Hollister notes in his book, *Medieval Europe: A Short History:* "The feast days of the Christian calendar—Christmas, Easter, and many lesser holy days (holidays)—provided joyous relief from an otherwise grinding routine."

Critical Overview

Not much has been written about Lagerlöf's "The Legend of the Christmas Rose." As Marguerite Yourcenar notes in a 1975 essay, the story's Christmas setting may be partly at fault. Yourcenar calls the story "an exquisite tale one might be tempted to overlook, so many stupid Christmas stories in illustrated magazines having disgusted us with that form of literature." Yourcenar is particularly interested in the forest miracle, which she calls a "profoundly satisfying notion of a biblical Eden." Likewise, in his 1931 book, *Selma Lagerlöf: Her Life and Work,* Walter A. Berendsohn calls the story "the most beautiful of the Värmland stories," and says that the story "is instinct with that blending of divine Love and human charity, of angel-vision and deep kindliness which lie at the very heart of Christianity."

In addition to the lack of critical attention paid to the story, the collection it was included in—*En saga om en saga och andra sagor*, published in English as *The Girl from the Marsh Croft*—is also rarely mentioned. In fact, it is sometimes conspicuously absent from lists of Lagerlöf's major works. This may be due to its short-story-collection status, since Lagerlöf's novels and other long narratives tend to receive more criticism. This absence might also be due to its publication date. When the Swedish edition was first published in 1908, Lagerlöf's reputation was very strong, due to the publication of her two-volume children's series, *Nils Holgerssons underbara resa* in 1906 and 1907. This series, which has since become one of her best-known works, has overshadowed many of Lagerlöf's other writings.

Some critics, like Hermann Hesse, feel that all of Lagerlöf's works share the same qualities, so by examining general commentary about Lagerlöf's works as a whole, one may be able to better understand the reception of individual works, like "The Legend of the Christmas Rose." In a 1908 essay that discusses Lagerlöf's *Gösta Berling's Saga*, Hesse notes that the work was perfect, and contained "all the essentials of the Lagerlöf gift; with it the author made her appearance as a finished, mature personality and since that time she has not changed in any characteristic." These characteristics include, most notably, the use of folk traditions in Lagerlöf's stories. Says Berendsohn, "the longing for her childhood's fairyland has always driven our author back to the folk-tale for her sources." Likewise, in her 1984 book, *Selma Lagerlöf,* Vivi Edström notes that the author's "interest in original narratives, in myths, folktales, fairy tales, and legends led her to delve into the depths of the folk culture." However, Edström, like other critics, also notes Lagerlöf's unique ability to blend folk traditions with other sources. Says Edström: "even though anonymous folk literature was one of her main sources, she often received inspiration from contemporary materials," such as newspaper articles. Lagerlöf's stories also incorporate contemporary narrative techniques, and thus transcend the traditional fairy tale. As Berendsohn notes: "Hers is not a realm of 'Once upon a time' and 'They lived happily ever after.'" Instead, as Edström says: "Her method is to turn a simple folk motif into a narrative with many different psychological dimensions."

In addition to their critical stature, Lagerlöf's works have always been well received by popular readers. As Berendsohn notes, her works share "a rich epic quality, common to the early narrative poetry of all nations, and this has made her works loved by readers throughout the world, wherever her books have been translated." Lagerlöf's books have been translated into an astonishing number of languages, another sign of her popular success. In his translator's note to Berendsohn's book, George F. Timpson says that "almost all Selma Lagerlöf's works have been translated into English, French, Russian, German, Danish, Norwegian, Finnish, Dutch, Polish and Japanese." In addition, Timpson notes that certain works have been translated into Spanish, Portuguese, Italian, Hungarian, Estonian, Lettish, Yiddish, Czech, Slovakian, Roumanian, Croatian, Serbian, Bulgarian, Modern Greek, Faroese, Icelandic, Greenlandic, Bengali, Armenian, Turkish, Arabic, Ido, Esperanto, and Braille.

This medieval cloister in Sweden sets a scene similar to that portrayed in ''The Legend of the Christmas Rose''

Criticism

Ryan D. Poquette

Poquette has a bachelor's degree in English and specializes in writing about literature. In the following essay, Poquette discusses the problem of categorization in Lagerlöf's works.

Lagerlöf's tales have been enjoyed by countless readers, but not many can say with conviction exactly what kind of stories they are reading. Since the publication of her first book, *Gösta Berling's Saga* (1891), Lagerlöf's unusual prose has defied conventional literary norms. In an age when Europeans were writing gritty, realistic stories, Lagerlöf's works were more idealistic and romantic. Readers would be mistaken, however, if they labeled her as merely a romantic writer. As Walter Berendsohn notes in his *Selma Lagerlöf: Her Life and Work:* "The critics have found it difficult to assign her a place in the course of Swedish literary development." Likewise, in her *Selma Lagerlöf,* Vivi Edström notes further that, with Lagerlöf's "unique mythical imagination and narrative talent," the author "cannot easily be placed into any literary-historical category. She is both a realist and a

romantic." It is this inability to be categorized that gives Lagerlöf's stories their universal appeal.

Many of Lagerlöf's stories exhibit characteristics of Romanticism, a literary movement that dominated much of Europe in the late eighteenth century. Romantic works feature idealistic settings and situations that depict life as one would wish it to be. For example, in "The Legend of the Christmas Rose," Robber Father is pardoned at the end of the story by Archbishop Absalon, because the archbishop is keeping a promise. "Abbot Hans has faithfully kept his word, and I shall also keep mine." However, in real life at this time, the Catholic Church did not always exhibit such compassion, and thieves were often punished by mutilation or death. Lagerlöf's idealism is rooted in her spirituality, which is another element that is commonly found in romantic fiction. Lagerlöf's strong belief in Christianity dominates many of her works, including "The Legend of the Christmas Rose," in which the tenets of Christianity provide the main themes. Throughout the story, characters of all backgrounds and stations refer to Christianity and "our Lord," as when Robber Mother explains how "on every Christmas Eve the great Göinge forest is transformed into a beautiful garden to commemorate the hour of our

What Do I Read Next?

- Danish writer Hans Christian Andersen became famous in the nineteenth century for his imaginative fairy tales, many of which have inspired twentieth-century books and films such as Disney's *The Little Mermaid. Hans Christian Andersen: The Complete Fairy Tales and Stories* (1974), translated by Erik Hougaard, presents Andersen's immortal tales as they appeared in the original Danish edition in the 1870s.

- One of the most famous saints of medieval Scandinavia was Bridget of Sweden. Bridget, also known as Birgit and Birgitta, became famous and earned respect for her religious visions. *Birgitta of Sweden: Life and Selected Revelations* (1990), edited by Marguerite T. Harris and translated by Albert Ryle Kezel, collects four of Birgitta's most renowned works, which were originally published in the fifteenth century.

- Lagerlöf's *Gösta Berling's Saga* (1891)—translated into English in 1898—was the author's first major published work, and is still one of her most popular books. The episodic story centers on the title character, a failed country pastor who falls in with a group of cavaliers intent on destroying the estate of the Lady of Ekeby.

- Many of Lagerlöf's works show the influence of her rural life at Mårbacka, a rural estate in the province of Värmland in southern Sweden. *Memories of Mårbacka* (1996) collects several of Lagerlöf's nostalgic, autobiographical writings about her childhood in this rural home.

Lord's birth." Natural settings like forests and gardens are also commonly found in romantic fiction, which elevates nature to the level of the sublime, or awe-inspiring.

However, Lagerlöf's works also exhibit characteristics of realism, another literary movement, which took place in the nineteenth century. Berendsohn notes that "the great wave of European Realism" reached Sweden in 1879, "and for twelve years dominated literature with its realistic descriptions of sordid scenes, its bitter criticism of society and its acrid discussion of social problems." Realism and its counterpart naturalism depict life as it really happens, stripping away any idealistic expectations and descriptions in the process. Realistic fiction generally relies on actual details of everyday life, incorporating believable characters in realistic situations. Critics such as Edström note that, while Lagerlöf's fiction is developed from myths and folklore, "she often received inspiration from contemporary materials. She was an avid newspaper reader, and the daily newspapers provided her with material for many a story." In this way, Lagerlöf's works blend romantic myth with realistic elements.

For example, while the story takes place in a quaint medieval setting, Lagerlöf does not let her readers escape totally into the fantasy of the fairy tale. In an idealistic way, the poor people in the villages receive "armfuls of bread and long candles" from the monasteries, and everybody prepares for a happy Christmas celebration. Abbot Hans gets a much different, more realistic depiction of the medieval poor when he goes to the Robber family cave. "Here were wretchedness and poverty, and nothing was being done to celebrate Christmas. Robber Mother had neither brewed nor baked; she had neither washed nor scoured." This stark description, which goes on to describe the "watery gruel" that the children are forced to eat, is a hallmark of realistic fiction, and it helps to balance the idealism of the story. Realistic fiction is often used as social commentary, and through the use of her ironic situations Lagerlöf also comments on social issues, specifically the hypocrisy and fallibility of the medieval Catholic Church.

As Gore W. Allen notes in his *Renaissance in the North,* "the religious opposition, as voiced by Kierkegaard in Denmark and Selma Lagerlöf in

> "Lagerlöf is criticizing the Catholic Church's hypocrisy, but she does not wage a crusade against Catholicism. Instead, she portrays its fallibility in a human way, so that even the lay brother inspires a reader's sympathy at the end of the story."

Sweden, repudiated the medieval Church no less vigorously than it was repudiated by the sixteenth-century Reformers.'' Yet, even in her criticisms, Lagerlöf was not as harsh as other social commentators. She did not work in absolutes, and even in her commentary, she incorporated her idealistic belief that nobody is totally bad. The church is not depicted in a completely negative fashion. While the lay brother is the one who causes all of the problems, and the archbishop is depicted as having little faith, the Catholic abbot is portrayed in extremely favorable terms. Unlike the lay brother and the two monks, the abbot does not try to physically throw Robber Mother out of the monastery. In fact, he chastises his brethren "for using force and forbade their calling for help." He does not judge Robber Mother as the others do; instead he gives her the benefit of the doubt. In addition, the abbot loves his garden, but only "as much as it was possible for him to love anything earthly and perishable." Finally, when he is witnessing the Christmas miracle, he is humble, bowing down to earth "in reverent greeting" to the angels. These qualities, along with many others that are given to him in the story, show that Abbot Hans is one Catholic who lives up to the Christian ideal. Lagerlöf is criticizing the Catholic Church's hypocrisy, but she does not wage a crusade against Catholicism. Instead, she portrays its fallibility in a human way, so that even the lay brother inspires a reader's sympathy at the end of the story.

In addition to the question of whether Lagerlöf's works belong to realism or romanticism, her writ-ings share characteristics with many other opposing categories. While her stories are often based in the legendary past and told in a fairy-tale style, they also incorporate modern narrative techniques, such as giving psychological depth to characters. In addition, Lagerlöf's works are hard to place as either popular or literary fiction. Her works were enormous popular successes, no matter what critics said about them. In fact, her works are often lumped in with other popular works, as is the case with "The Legend of the Christmas Rose." While Marguerite Yourcenar notes in her essay, "Selma Lagerlöf: Epic Storyteller," that the story is "an exquisite tale," she also says that people may overlook it, due to all of the bad, popular Christmas stories that have "disgusted us with that form of literature."

Lagerlöf considered herself a writer of the people, and was more concerned about everyday readers than critics. Her works themselves can be read on two levels. As Edström notes: "On the surface, the stories can appear artless and simple, but upon closer scrutiny they reveal a complicated structure." For example, "The Legend of the Christmas Rose" can be read as a simple idealistic fable, in which the moral of the story is to have faith and not let earthly attitudes cause one to judge people or situations by their appearances. On the other hand, when one digs beneath the surface and examines the story's realistic aspects, Lagerlöf's religious beliefs, and the influence of modern narrative techniques, the tale yields more complex interpretations. In this way, the story can be read as a literary work, as opposed to just a popular story.

In the end, it is Lagerlöf's ability to fit multiple categories in stories like this one that has allowed her works to be enjoyed by countless readers in many languages. Says Allen: "Selma Lagerlöf, through the untamed beauty of her rhythmic prose, had won the hearts of rich and poor, of countrymen, and secretly of urban intellectuals also." In 1909, when Lagerlöf was awarded the Nobel Prize for Literature, Claes Annerstedt—then-president of the Swedish Academy—summed up the universal quality of Lagerlöf's unique stories in his presentation address: "The greatness of her art consists precisely in her ability to use her heart as well as her genius to give to the original peculiar character and attitudes of the people a shape in which we recognize ourselves."

Source: Ryan D. Poquette, Critical Essay on "The Legend of the Christmas Rose," in *Short Stories for Students*, Gale, 2003.

Vivi Edström

In the following essay excerpt, Edström reviews Lagerlöf's many works.

Types of Short Stories

Throughout her literary career, Lagerlöf wrote many short narrative works, a number of which were commissioned for newspapers and journals. She especially had many requests to contribute stories to Christmas editions of newspapers, which explains why many of her short stories concern winter and the celebration of Christmas. Lagerlöf was extremely conscientious when it came to these occasional pieces, and some of her Christmas stories, such as ''The Peace of God'' and ''The Legend of the Christmas Roses'' (''Legenden om julrosorna''), have become minor classics in Sweden.

Lagerlöf's first collection of short stories, *Invisible Links* (1894), established her as a writer of short fiction. The collection came out in several editions, augmented in 1904 by additional short pieces that she wrote in the closing years of the 1890s, some of which are counted among her finest works. Lagerlöf's publisher, Bonniers, also decided to publish collections of her short stories, reminiscences, and speeches in the interludes between the publication of her longer novels. In 1908, *The Girl from the Marshcroft* (*En saga om en saga och andra sagor*) was published, followed by the first part of *Troll och människor* (*Trolls and Men*) in 1915 and the second part in 1921. An additional collection of short prose, *Höst* (*Harvest*) came out in 1933. The final collection was a two-volume posthumous edition, *Från skilda tider 1943–1945*, which contains many short stories from various periods in Lagerlöf's literary career.

Frequently, a short story reveals a more intimate picture of its author than does a long novel. This can be said of Lagerlöf's stories, which reflect the great range of her talent and present a variety of structures and styles. Her short stories are more experimental than her longer works, in which the plot often dominates the entire work in an explicit way.

For the most part, Lagerlöf's short stories are based on anecdotes or other clear and simple narratives. She works in a tradition in which the narrative concludes with a point, or a solution to the psychological problem that lies at the core of the story. Sometimes she strives to achieve a light style in the spirit of Maupassant, but these stories are not especially successful. On the other hand, she works

> "For the most part, Lagerlöf's short stories are based on anecdotes or other clear and simple narratives. She works in a tradition in which the narrative concludes with a point, or a solution to the psychological problem that lies at the core of the story."

extremely well within the model of the fairy tale and folktale, and she is also a master of the legend.

A line of development can be seen in her short prose works—from a narrative overloaded with symbols into a concentrated structure in which each word is carefully weighed. During an early period, she succumbed to a ''mania for description'' in the manner of the Danish symbolist Jens Peter Jacobsen, as can be seen in ''Stenkumlet'' (''The King's Grave'') in *Osynliga länker* (*Invisible Links*), a story with a number of visual elements, including the color red as a dominant symbol for the ruthless affirmation of life, as opposed to the acceptance of limits and responsibilities. A half-ruined cairn, the grave of a king, takes on the same fateful function as the famous millrace in Ibsen's *Rosmersholm;* Ibsen was, of course, an inevitable model for the symbolists of the 1890s.

Gradually, however, Lagerlöf's short fiction became oriented toward other models. The Icelandic saga and the works of Bjørnson and Jensen influenced her in developing a more concise form. Both the short stories and the fairy- and folk tales came to concentrate more directly on the action, with some of the later ones becoming almost expressionistic. Then, considerable tension arises from the discrepancy between the surface structure of a narrative and its deeper meaning.

Lagerlöf's short stories present a whole cavalcade of people: farmers and crofters, cavaliers and men of property, clergymen and beautiful girls, old people about to meet death, saints and murderers. She seems to understand them all and to be capable of interpreting their secrets, whether those secrets concern the sacrificial ardour of the saint or the hatefulness of the sadist.

In her short stories, Lagerlöf often depicts a person who has reached a turning point in life. Since guilt and responsibility are such essential problems in her writing, the moment is often one of enquiry or examination. The short story may be written in a lyrical vein, but at the same time it is dramatically effective in its focus on drastic change, the choice of path. The resolution usually takes the form of absolute happiness or tragic ruin.

Lagerlöf wrote contemporary short stories, historical narratives, and stories not bound to any particular time. While she often deals with contemporary social themes, it is clear that, like many other writers, she felt that she had greater freedom when writing from a historical perspective. She was particularly interested in the period of transition from paganism to Christianity in Sweden, and she included themes from this period in the stories "De fågelfria" ("The Outlaws"), "Stenkumlet" ("The King's Grave"), and "Reors saga" ("The Legend of Reor"), as well as in the stories in the collection *Drottningar i Kungahälla* (*The Queens of Kungahälla*). Her materials came from various literary sources, primarily Snorri's *Heimskringla*, which had been her favorite reading since childhood.

Set in various provinces of Sweden, Lagerlöf's short stories attest to her ability to create both historical and geographical authenticity. Several of the earlier stories are connected with Bohuslän, a western province she became familiar with when she visited her brother, a doctor in the small southern Bohuslän city of Kungälv. Another group of stories is set in the island of Gotland, Sweden's eastern outpost, which she visited during the 1890s, as did many other artists and writers of the period. Traces of her journeys abroad can also be seen in the stories set in Italy, the Near East, and other places. Of greatest importance, however, are the stories set in Värmland, with Lagerlöf's home district, often called Svartsjö, at the center. Several stories tell of what happens to the individual cavaliers from *Gösta Berling's Saga* after they leave the joyous life at Ekeby, while others, such as "Gravskriften" ("The Epitaph") and "Bröderna" ("The Brothers"), depict the problems of village folk, with the entire district as background.

In stories resembling folk tales or legends, the place names are especially important, for such tales are always rooted in a definite locale. Stories such as

En herrgårdssägen (*The Tale of a Manor*), "Tomten på Töreby" ("The Imp at Töreby"), and "Sankta Katarina av Siena" ("Saint Catherine of Siena") suggest by their very titles how important the setting is for the action. Lagerlöf belongs to those writers who with only a few details can create a memorable picture of a region, often integrating scenic depiction with psychological motifs. She often introduces a short story with a description of the setting that includes symbolic elements; the landscape thus foreshadows and accompanies the psychological problems of the story. This technique can be seen in "The Epitaph" and "En historia från Halstanäs" ("The Story of Halstanäs"), both of which appear in the collection *Invisible Links*.

Fairy-Tale Structure

In some of her short pieces that could be classified as fairy tales, Lagerlöf, in keeping with the demands of the fairy tales, avoids designating the exact geographical location of the action. Nor does she limit these stories with regard to time. She begins many of them with the fairy-tale formula, "Once upon a time" or, more often, with "There was," thereby allowing herself the maximum freedom in recreating a time and a place. This is the pattern she follows in stories such as "The Peace of God" and "The Sons of Ingmar," the narratives she incorporated into *Jerusalem*. They were not connected with either Dalecarlia or any specific time, which enables her to place the greatest emphasis on the moral problems her characters are involved in.

The fairy-tale genre arouses special expectations of excitement, suspense, and fantasy, all of which Lagerlöf's stories provide. But despite the fact that she is so often called a teller of fairy tales, she does not merely relate fantasy-filled stories; indeed, she very rarely writes what would be considered genuine fairy tales. She uses, rather, the method of the fairy tale as a basis for organizing a story. She is most successful when she strives to create the suspense and mystery characteristic of the fairy tale. She often builds her action according to the three-step rule and employs the matter-of-fact style typical of the fairy tale. This holds true even in situations such as fateful encounters between persons or between man and nature. She uses upheaval, surprise, and metamorphosis in a way that can be associated with the fairy tale. The successful solution to the problem that the fairy tale usually presents is also typical of many of her stories. Complete unity between man and nature, blurring the distinction between fantasy and reality—all this is characteristic of Lagerlöf's short tales. While these traits are also found in some of her other works, they often appear in a purer form in the short stories. The very title of one of her collections, *Trolls and Men*, illustrates this union of the real and the fantastic.

Lagerlöf uses the fairy-tale genre both freely and artfully. By adopting the method of the fairy tale, she achieves naive effects, but the psychology is far more complex. "Bortbytingen" ("The Changeling," 1908), published in *Trolls and Men*, is an excellent example of a story patterned after a folk legend but with a modern psychological meaning; it is actually an allegory of a marriage on the verge of breaking up because the mother is completely occupied with the child. The changeling motif in both fairy and folktales goes back to a popular fear that an infant would be exchanged for a troll child if its mother did not take special precautions, a notion that explains in folk superstition why some children are born deformed. Tales of changelings usually are concerned with how the kidnapped child lives among the trolls. Lagerlöf, however, reverses the motif, depicting instead a troll in the world of men. While traveling on horseback with her husband, a farmer's wife loses her infant child, who is stolen by an old troll woman. When the parents desperately look for the child, they find instead an ugly troll child, with claws and a tail. The wife takes it home with her and looks after it with the greatest care and attention. Her husband protests, but not even his threats to leave home keep his wife from fulfilling her difficult task of caring for the repulsive troll. In the end, the conflict is resolved in the harmonious manner typical of the fairy tale. When the situation appears to be hopeless, the husband and wife get their beautiful, fair-haired little boy back again. The woman's sacrifices not only helped the child to survive in the world of the trolls, but also brought about its release. The husband returns home with his son in his arms (where the troll child goes is not mentioned).

Folktale Structure

Lagerlöf's knowledge of folktales was of great importance for her short fiction, for she frequently employs its typical form, adhering to it stringently. In contrast to the fairy tale, which typically aims at a happy ending, the folktale usually has a tragic conclusion. The short stories of Lagerlöf most consistently based on folktale motifs deal most often with crime and punishment and sometimes evince a fascination for violence. "The Outlaws," "Tale Thott," and "The Story of Halstanäs" (all in *Invisible Links*), which are based on folktale motifs, are stories of criminals. And "The Imp at Töreby," "Vattnet i Kyrkviken" ("The Water in Kyrkviken"), and "Gammal fäbodsägen" ("The Tale of the Old Saeter")—all in *Trolls and Men*—end in horror. In all these stories, the idea of nemesis predominates, with human pride appearing to call forth, or contribute to, misfortune and unhappiness.

There are several different kinds of folktales. Among these is the ghost story, Lagerlöf's favorite type since the days when she experienced it, with all its terror-struck fascination, in the nursery at Mårbacka. As a teacher, she often told ghost stories to her pupils, something that was not always appreciated by school officials. Her first literary attempt at a ghost story was "Karln" ("The Man"), which was rejected for publication when she wrote it but published posthumously. She later took up the theme of "The Man" in one of her most clearly defined ghost stories. *Löwensköldska ringen* (*The Ring of Löwenskölds*), a short novel written in 1925.

Along with the gloomy narratives that show man at the mercy of the powers, there are also stories of a different kind, impressionistic sketches which point up the irony of life and love stories. Elements of both these genres are found in one of Lagerlöf's most beloved short stories, "Dunungen" ("Downie") in *Invisible Links*, a love story with a comic tone, narrated somewhat in the style of Hans Christian Andersen. Lagerlöf herself wrote a dramatization of the story, which was later filmed.

A frequent theme, especially in the early stories, is the struggle of the individual to find his way in a chaotic situation. In the narratives, as in *Gösta Berling's Saga*, passion is pitted against moral imperatives. The motif of sin and atonement is varied in connection with the problems that revolve around determinism and responsibility. The question of the extent of man's possibilities for mastering his own destiny occurs again and again in Lagerlöf's works.

The main character in a Lagerlöf short story is often a socially or psychologically disadvantaged person. In her earlier stories, man is often defeated in his struggle, but gradually the tone of her narratives becomes more optimistic, with the author presenting characters whose power and strength of will bring them to reconciliation. "The Wedding March" (in *The Girl from the Marshcroft*) exemplifies this optimism. The story deals with a poor violinist who does not enjoy public recognition, despite his indisputable genius. Ultimately it relates how fame comes to him and, above all, how his artistry influences those around him.

In some of the short stories, there are women who find their destiny through having been neglected. The Cinderella motif is, for example, the basic theme in "Downie," in which a tender, delicate young girl makes a courageous choice in the end, as well as in *The Girl from the Marshcroft*, in which a poor tenant farm girl marries a rich farmer. "The Epitaph" depicts a woman who is at first weak and submissive, but who finally asserts the right to her own feelings.

The Queens of Kungahälla

While their multiplicity of themes and forms make the collections of Lagerlöf's short stories fascinating, the author herself preferred to publish collections with a unified subject matter and a consistent theme. *Drottningar i Kungahälla* (*The Queens of Kungahälla*, 1899) is an example of such a collection. It tells of the Swedish queens of the Viking period who celebrated their weddings in the city of Kungahälla, the present-day Kungälv, near the border between Sweden and Norway. In this period of transition, there were frequent battles between the Nordic countries, and as Christianity began to drive out paganism, the religious and political complications increased. Lagerlöf, who found these conflicts fascinating, became well acquainted with the history and topography of Kungälv when she visited the city in the 1890s, just when an interesting archeological discovery had been made there. Her stories about the women who celebrated or wanted to celebrate their weddings in the city have a historical basis. *The Queens of Kungahälla* can be seen as a bold attempt to create a feminist counterpart to Snorri Sturluson's history of the kings of Norway, *Heimskringla*.

The purpose of this collection of short stories was also to describe different types of women, something in which Lagerlöf had already excelled in *Gösta Berling's Saga*. One encounters in these stories refined women and good women, dangerous women, and women with a zest for living. The longest story, entitled "Astrid," is one of mistaken identity, in which the title character, with craftiness and cunning, manages to get the husband she wants, Olaf, who was destined to become St. Olaf. Contrasting with Astrid is her half sister, the mild and saintly Ingegärd, who actually from the very beginning had been the one designated to marry Olaf.

Elements of the legend are strong in several of the short stories in *The Queens of Kungahälla*, as, for example, in the story in which Olaf Tryggvason rejects the pagan queen Sigrid Storråda. In a dream vision, he sees how his insult to the Swedish queen brings about his martyr's death. Margareta Fredkulla, in the story of the same title, is transformed by the pressure of circumstances into a saint. For the sake of peace and her impoverished people, she sacrifices herself, overcoming her aversion to the bellicose and faithless bridegroom who awaits her.

Legends

When *The Queens of Kungahälla* was published in 1899, the volume included a group of stories designated as legends and given the simple title *Legender* (*Legends*). In 1906, these legends appeared in a single volume. Two years earlier, in 1904, *Kristuslegender* (*Christ Legends*) was published, which together with *Legends* contain Lagerlöf's most important work in that genre.

Elements of the legend appear, however, as early as *Gösta Berling's Saga*, and they are common in the later novels, especially *The Miracles of Antichrist, Jerusalem II* (or *The Holy City*), and *The Emperor of Portugallia*. As early as 1892, the journal *Ord och bild* published "Legenden om fågelboet" ("The Legend of the Bird's Nest") in which a hardened, vengeful hermit is changed into a mild man resembling St. Francis of Assisi, who stands with upstretched arms to give the birds a haven in the wilderness. Lagerlöf's legends grew out of her strong interest in inner changes or conversions—transformations that frequently occur as miracles in her stories.

The legend is a genre difficult to define. Though it is close to the folktale and has its beginnings in pre-Christian times, it flourished especially during the late Middle Ages. At the end of the nineteenth century, the symbolists became interested in the legend form, seeing in it possibilities for describing religious experiences and elusive psychological phenomena. Around the turn of the century, the legend became Lagerlöf's most important medium for literary expression, evidenced by the fact that she wrote at least one legend a year between 1894 and 1906.

It was during her first journey to Italy, in 1895–96, that Lagerlöf developed her actual passion for the legend. She had, in a sense, entered into the world of the legend, and she eagerly collected material, especially popular anecdotes related to cloisters and churches in Catholic Europe. She also became acquainted with research being done on the legend, primarily with works on Sicilian folklore by the Italian scholar Giuseppe Pitré.

There are two main types of legends—stories of the lives of saints and stories related to the folktale. Lagerlöf wrote several saints' legends—"Saint Catherine of Siena," "Lucia," and "Ljuslågan" ("The Light of the Flame"), for example, but most of her legends are closer to the folktale. One of her plans was to write a series of legends linked with cities in Italy. Two that arose out of this project are "Fiskarringen" ("The Ring of the Fisherman"), set in Venice, and "Den heliga bilden i Lucca" ("The Legend of the Sacred Image"). The stress in these stories, however, is placed not on the local but on the psychological dynamics. In "The Legend of the Sacred Image," for example, Lagerlöf discusses the naive trust that provides the requisite basis for the miracle.

After the Italian legends, Lagerlöf, strongly inspired by her visit to the Near East in 1899–1900, approached the world of legends connected with the Holy Land. For *Christ Legends*, which she characterized alternately as a book for children and a popular book, she gathered material on the childhood of Jesus from the apocryphal Gospels, as well as from several other sources, including Giuseppe Pitré's work *Fiabe e leggende populari siciliane.* The *Christ Legends* have a more naive character than her earlier legends; the nucleus of each story is a miracle which is left unexplained, as is often the case in saints' legends proper.

Jesus is described as a normal child, full of life, whose unlimited trust and affection dominate the stories. In perfectly narrated episodes, the simple, concrete events of Jesus' childhood are told—his birth (the miracle of which is described from three different points of view), the impending danger from Herod, the flight to Egypt, and the visit to the temple when he was twelve years old. Last in the series is the complicated legend of St. Veronica's veil, which culminates in Jesus making his way to the cross.

Lagerlöf gradually became an expert on legends. She restored and adapted them, and she expanded them with additional levels of meaning. As the scholar Gunnel Weidel notes, "none of her legends bear the guise of the simple, objective narratives characteristic of medieval legends." Lagerlöf did, however, possess the ability to evoke a biblical or medieval atmosphere while at the same time creating characters whose problems appear real to the modern reader. Characteristic of the legend is its naive and almost idyllic atmosphere, in which the miraculous appears to occur naturally. In Lagerlöf's legends, the introduction of the miracle into the everyday world in a manner that is both shocking and, at the same time, quite natural is central to her narrative technique.

Several years ago in an interview, the Nobel Prize-winning Swedish writer Harry Martinson stated that he believed it was unfortunate that Lagerlöf devoted herself so intensely to the genre of the legend. Her contemporary critics, though, would scarcely have agreed. The critic Oscar Levertin advised her to remain in the forests of her fairy tales and the cities of her legends.

Later scholars have pointed out the contradiction between the skeptical Lagerlöf, well schooled in the natural sciences, and the author of the naive narrative stance. For Lagerlöf, the legend was an aesthetically fruitful form, not a religious statement. The legend was also a means of reaching many people. It was through that genre that she seriously gained the acceptance of an international public, especially in Catholic countries. According to one critic, it was with the legend that she "most strongly approached an international and universally human wave length," because "the themes she treats in her legends are no longer the exclusive heritage of her national homeland, but a common cultural heritage for peoples of all countries."

Source: Vivi Edström, "Short Fiction: The Short Stories, Legends, and Short Novels," in *Selma Lagerlöf,* Twayne Publishers, 1984, pp. 70–84.

Sources

Allen, Gore W., *Renaissance in the North,* Sheed & Ward, 1946, pp. 48, 106.

Annerstedt, Claes, "Presentation Address," in *Nobel Prize Library: Juan Ramón Jiménez, Erik Axel Karlfeldt, Pär Lagerkvist, Selma Lagerlöf,* Helvetica Press, Inc., 1971, p. 282, originally delivered in 1909 and originally published in English by Elsevier Publishing Company, 1969.

Berendsohn, Walter A., *Selma Lagerlöf: Her Life and Work,* translated by George F. Timpson, 1931, reprint, Kennikat Press, 1968, pp. 10, 57, 70, 91–93, 97.

Edström, Vivi, *Selma Lagerlöf,* translated by Barbara Lide, Twayne Publishers, 1984, pp. 121–34.

Hesse, Hermann, "Selma Lagerlöf," translated by Denver Lindley, in *My Belief: Essays on Life and Art,* edited by

Theodore Ziolkowski, translated by Denver Lindley and Ralph Manheim, Farrar, Straus and Giroux, 1974, pp. 317–23.

Hollister, C. Warren, *Medieval Europe: A Short History,* John Wiley & Sons, 1982, p. 174.

Lagerlöf, Selma, ''The Legend of the Christmas Rose,'' in *Girl from the Marsh Croft and Other Stories,* edited by Greta Anderson, Penfield Press, 1996, pp. 127–43, originally published in *The Girl from the Marsh Croft,* translated by Velma Swanston Howard, Little, Brown and Company, 1910.

Timpson, George F., ''Translator's Note,'' in *Selma Lagerlöf: Her Life and Work,* by Walter A. Berendsohn, translated by George F. Timpson, 1931, reprint, Kennikat Press, 1968, p. xi.

Yourcenar, Marguerite, ''Selma Lagerlöf: Epic Storyteller,'' in *The Dark Brain of Piranesi and Other Essays,* by Marguerite Yourcenar, translated by Richard Howard in collaboration with the author, Farrar, Straus and Giroux, 1984, pp. 129–53.

Further Reading

Ankarloo, Bengt, and Stuart Clark, eds., *Witchcraft and Magic in Europe: The Middle Ages,* University of Pennsylvania Press, 2002.

> In Lagerlöf's story, the lay brother mistakes the blooming forest for witchcraft and is so scared at this possibility, that he frightens the miracle away. In this collection of essays, noted experts examine the various views of witchcraft and magic in medieval Europe.

Nissenbaum, Stephen, *The Battle for Christmas,* Knopf, 1996.

> Nissenbaum explores the troubled history of Christmas celebrations, which, from the fourth until the nineteenth centuries, were characterized by wanton drinking, violence, and crime. It was only in the Victorian era that Christmas began to resemble the modern holiday, with its focus on family—and commercialism.

Sawyer, Birgit, and Peter Sawyer, *Medieval Scandinavia: From Conversion to Reformation, circa 800–1500,* University of Minnesota Press, 1993.

> This comprehensive study of medieval Scandinavia challenges long-held assumptions, which are largely based on nineteenth-century studies, including the differences between medieval Scandinavia and the rest of Europe. Topics include modern attitudes toward medieval history, medieval history writing, and the role of women in medieval Scandinavia.

Singman, Jeffrey L., *Daily Life in Medieval Europe,* Greenwood Press, 1999.

> Singman offers an in-depth discussion of what life was like on a daily basis in medieval Europe. In addition to four chapters on medieval society in general, he also gives overviews of what life was like in villages, castles, monasteries, and towns.

Mammon and the Archer

O. Henry

1906

"Mammon and the Archer," by William Sydney Porter—better known by the pseudonym of O. Henry—was first published in the *New York World* and later published in O. Henry's *The Four Million* in 1906. The title of the collection and the short stories themselves were a response to Ward McAllister's 1892 comment that there are only about four hundred people in New York City, referring only to those whom McAllister thought were of importance. O. Henry's collection, however, concerns the total population of New York City at the time, around four million, not just the aristocratic few. In fact, "Mammon and the Archer," which is considered to be one of O. Henry's best stories, depicts a rich entrepreneur, Anthony Rockwall, who does not belong to this aristocratic four hundred but whose son is trying to marry one of the aristocratic daughters. Anthony believes that money can buy everything and tries to prove it to himself by using his money to stage an elaborate event that helps his son win his bride.

Critics initially praised O. Henry for his stories, many of which featured surprise endings like the one in "Mammon and the Archer." O. Henry's New York stories introduced new character types that helped to shape the image and perceptions of America both at home and abroad. However, while O. Henry's acclaim with popular readers has remained consistent since his death in 1910, many critics have since found fault with O. Henry's techniques, including his formerly praised surprise

endings and plot constructions. To this day, O. Henry's literary reputation is in question, although his name still adorns one of the most prestigious short-story contests in the United States: the O. Henry Awards. A current copy of "Mammon and the Archer" can be found in *Tales of O. Henry: Sixty-Two Stories*, which was published by Barnes & Noble Books in 1993.

Author Biography

O. Henry was born as William Sidney (changed to Sydney in 1898) Porter on September 11, 1862, in Greensboro, North Carolina. After his mother died, Porter was raised by his paternal grandmother and his paternal aunt, who helped develop the young author's passion for reading and writing in her private school. Nevertheless, Porter dropped out of school in 1877 at the age of fifteen to work as a pharmacist's assistant. Porter became a licensed pharmacist at nineteen. In 1882, Porter moved to Denison, Texas, where he worked as a ranch hand. This was the first of many locations and experiences that Porter would draw upon later in his short fiction. In 1884, Porter moved to Austin, where he worked as a bookkeeper and draftsman (1884–1891) and as a teller at the First National Bank (1891–1894). In 1887, Porter eloped with Athol Estes.

While working as a teller, Porter began to submit his writing and illustrations to local publications, and in 1894 he began to publish his own weekly newspaper, called the *Rolling Stone*. What happened next is the source of much mystery. What is certain is that, at some point while working at the First National Bank, Porter began altering his accounts, leading to a discrepancy of more than five thousand dollars. Some critics and biographers say that Porter took the money as a temporary loan to support his fledgling newspaper. Others say that he was desperate for money and stole it outright. Porter claimed his innocence to his family and friends but would not speak about the incident in public. In any case, a federal bank examiner discovered the discrepancy during an audit and pursued the case, even though the bank eventually dropped the charges. Porter was arrested in 1896 on charges of embezzlement but fled—first to New Orleans and then to Honduras—before he was supposed to stand trial. He stayed in Central America until January 1897, when he got word that his wife was dying and returned to the United States to be with her.

Porter was convicted in 1898 and sent to the Ohio State Penitentiary, a fact that shamed him greatly. In prison, Porter continued to write and submit stories. With the publication of "Whistling Dick's Christmas Stocking" in *McClure's* in 1899, Porter adopted the now-famous pseudonym, O. Henry, which many believe Porter used to hide his status as a convict. In 1901, after being released from prison early for good behavior, Porter worked briefly in Pittsburgh and then moved to New York City, which he explored endlessly, translating his observations into stories. In 1903, Porter was hired by the *New York World* and soon began publishing one story each week for the newspaper. In 1904, Porter published *Cabbages and Kings*, a series of Central-American stories that he converted into a novel.

However, it was the publication of *The Four Million*—a collection of his New York stories that included "Mammon and the Archer" that secured Porter's fame. Over the next four years, until his death in New York City in 1910, Porter published seven more short-story collections, including *The Gentle Grafter* (1908); *Options* (1909); and *Strictly Business: More Stories of the Four Million* (1910), which was published shortly before his death. Porter had written many more short stories—about two hundred fifty in total—and many of these appeared in new collections in the years following his death.

Plot Summary

O. Henry's "Mammon and the Archer" begins with an example of Anthony Rockwall's unwillingness to accept the limitations of his position. As a self-made millionaire, Rockwall does not belong to the same aristocratic circle as his neighbors, who despise the fact that Anthony lives among them. When Anthony sees one of his neighbors turn his nose up at a renaissance sculpture in front of Anthony's home, Anthony tells himself that he will have his house painted red, white, and blue the following summer, to make his neighbors even more angry at him.

Anthony calls for his son, Richard, and proceeds to ask Richard how much he pays for soap and clothes. Anthony is satisfied with Richard's answers, which show that Richard does not pay as much as the other young, wealthy men in the city. Anthony tells Richard that, due to his money, Richard is a gentleman in one generation, whereas common wisdom has always stated that it takes three generations to make a gentleman. Despite Anthony's belief that money can buy everything, however, Richard says that he is distressed because his father's money cannot buy his way into the aristocracy. Anthony correctly guesses that it is a matter of love and encourages Richard to use his money and position to win the woman's hand in marriage. Richard informs his father that he has missed his chance, since Miss Lantry—the object of his affection—will be leaving the country in two days to live in Europe for two years. In addition, since she is part of the aristocratic social circle, she has a tight social schedule, which leaves no more than a few minutes for her and Richard to talk, while he accompanies her by coach to the theatre. Richard states that this is one situation in which his father's money cannot help him.

Anthony disagrees, however, and says that although money cannot buy enough time to make one live longer, it can be manipulated in certain situations. He is mysterious when he says this, giving no more details about his intentions. Later in the evening, Anthony's sister, Richard's Aunt Ellen, comes to see Anthony. Like Richard, Ellen believes that Anthony's money is useless in this case. The next evening, before Richard is going to leave to pick up Miss Lantry, Ellen gives her nephew a special gold ring. She tells him that the ring is supposed to bring good luck in love and that Richard's mother had entrusted it to her to give to Richard when he found the one he loved. The ring does not fit on any of Richard's fingers, so he puts it in his vest pocket.

Richard picks up Miss Lantry at the train station, as promised, and, following Miss Lantry's request, tells the driver to hurry to the theatre. However, along the way, Richard drops his mother's ring and tells the coachman to stop the cab so that he can get out and retrieve it. While Richard is reclaiming the ring, a sudden flood of traffic renders their cab motionless. Richard is apologetic to Miss Lantry, saying that if he had not dropped the ring, they would not be stuck, but Miss Lantry says she is not interested in the theatre anyway and asks to see the ring.

O. Henry

Later that night, Aunt Ellen comes to Anthony's study, telling him that Anthony and Miss Lantry are engaged and that it was the power of love—as symbolized by the ring that Richard dropped—that prevailed in the end, not Anthony's money. Anthony ignores this statement and implies that he and his money were involved in helping Richard. Ellen is confused, but Anthony sends her away, not explaining what he means so that he can go back to his story—an adventure story about a pirate whose money-laden ship is sinking.

The next day, a man who goes by the name of Kelly comes to collect money from Anthony. Through their conversation, it is revealed that Anthony hired Kelly to create the traffic jam by paying a number of wagons, cabs, trucks, two-horse teams, motormen, and even police to jam up the street that Richard and Miss Lantry were traveling on. Anthony writes out a check to Kelly and asks him if he happened to see a naked fat boy shooting arrows—a description of Cupid, the Roman god of love. Kelly thinks that Anthony is talking about a crazy person and says that if this boy was on the scene, the police probably arrested him before Kelly arrived. Anthony laughs, thinking that the absence of Cupid proves that money, not love, deserves sole credit for helping Richard to win the hand of Miss Lantry.

Characters

Brother Anthony

See Anthony Rockwall

Aunt Ellen

Aunt Ellen is Anthony Rockwall's sister and Richard Rockwall's aunt. Whereas Anthony believes that money can buy everything, Aunt Ellen does not believe it can buy love. Because of this, she gives Richard a special ring—which Richard's mother had entrusted to her—to help him to be lucky in love. When Richard accidentally drops the ring while he and Miss Lantry are in the coach, it sets the stage for Anthony's planned traffic jam. Since Aunt Ellen does not know about this deception, however, she thinks that the ring—and the love that it symbolizes—deserves all of the credit for giving Richard the time he needed to propose to Miss Lantry.

Kelly

Kelly is a man whom Anthony Rockwall hires to create an elaborate traffic jam so that Richard will get the time he needs to propose to Miss Lantry. Like Anthony, Kelly believes in the power of money, which he uses to pay for the traffic jam.

Miss Lantry

Miss Lantry is the young woman who is the object of Richard Rockwall's affections. Because she comes from an aristocratic family, her schedule—which is planned out very carefully by her family—is very tight, and Richard feels he does not have enough time to propose to her properly. However, when the traffic jam planned by Anthony Rockwall keeps Miss Lantry and Richard confined to their horse-drawn cab for two hours, Richard and Miss Lantry take advantage of the time and get to know each other better. As a result, when Richard proposes in the cab, Miss Lantry accepts.

Anthony Rockwall

Anthony Rockwall is a wealthy, retired soap manufacturer, who believes that money can buy everything; when a traffic jam orchestrated by him provides his son with the opportunity to propose to his love, Anthony takes this as proof of money's power. Because Anthony is one of the newer millionaires in New York, he is not accepted by others in the aristocracy, who have a heritage of wealth. Still, this does not stop Anthony from living his life the way that he chooses and from living like—and among—his aristocratic neighbors. He buys a lavish house in between the homes of two of his aristocratic rivals, an act that does not sit well with them. When his son, Richard, announces to Anthony that he is in love with Miss Lantry, another member of this aristocracy, Anthony encourages Richard to pursue her hand in marriage. Richard says that there is not enough time, explaining to Anthony that he only has a few minutes the next evening to talk to Miss Lantry as they are being driven to the theatre.

Nevertheless, Anthony is jovial when Richard leaves and also when his sister, Ellen, comes to talk to him. Ellen also tries to tell Anthony that money cannot help in this situation, but Anthony is stubborn. He says that money will prevail and, without Richard or Ellen's knowledge, pays a man who goes by the name of Kelly to help him out. Kelly hires a number of cabs, trucks, and even police to create the biggest traffic jam that New York has ever seen, which helps to give Richard the time he needs to successfully propose to Miss Lantry. In the final scene of the story, Anthony's role in the traffic jam is revealed when Kelly comes to collect his pay. Anthony believes that it was his money alone that helped create the circumstances in which Richard was able to propose. In fact, Anthony asks Kelly whether or not he saw Cupid, the mythical archer who shoots arrows of love, at the scene of the traffic jam. When Kelly says that he did not, Anthony takes this as fact that money has conquered over love.

Richard Rockwall

Richard Rockwall is Anthony Rockwall's son, who has just returned from college; Richard is desperately in love with Miss Lantry, a young woman who is a member of the aristocracy. Even though Richard has as much money as the aristocratic young men, he does not spend as much as they on clothes and soap. This humbleness and economy make his father happy. Anthony notes that Richard has seemed down lately. Richard explains that he has missed his opportunity to propose to Miss Lantry, since she is going to leave the country for two years and he has only a few minutes in a cab to talk to her. Anthony warns Richard not to overlook the power of money. Richard's Aunt Ellen, however, tells him to focus more on love and gives him a special ring—a symbol of luck in love—that Richard's deceased mother wished him to have. When Richard is riding in the cab with Miss Lantry the next evening, he accidentally drops the ring and has the cab stop so that he can pick it up. In this brief time, a massive traffic jam brings Richard and Miss Lantry's cab to a halt. This gives Richard the time he needs to successfully propose to Miss Lantry. Since Richard does not know that Anthony coordinated the traffic jam, he believes that it was his mother's ring that helped him win the hand of his love.

Themes

Money versus Love

"Mammon," the first word used in the title, is a synonym for wealth or money, so the reader is alerted right from the start that money will play a role in the plot. In fact, from the very beginning, Anthony Rockwall is shown as a man who believes that money can buy anything. Says Anthony to his son, Richard, "I'm for money against the field. Tell me something money won't buy." However, Richard, like his Aunt Ellen, believes that money cannot buy love. Specifically, Richard believes that money cannot buy him the time he needs to propose to Miss Lantry, who is leaving the country in a couple of days. Says Richard, "No, dad, this is one tangle that your money can't unravel." Ellen agrees with Richard and criticizes Anthony for believing solely in money. Says Ellen, "I wish you would not think so much of money. Wealth is nothing where a true affection is concerned. Love is all-powerful."

This contest of beliefs, the power of money versus the power of love, plays itself out over the course of the story. On the side of money, Anthony uses his wealth to buy a traffic jam so that Richard and Miss Lantry will be stuck long enough for Richard to propose. On the side of love, Aunt Ellen gives Richard a ring from his deceased mother. Says Ellen, "Good luck in love she said it brought. She asked me to give it to you when you had found the one you loved." During the trip in the coach, Richard drops this ring, forcing the driver to stop so that Richard can pick it up. During this time, however, Anthony's hired force of vehicles creates the traffic jam.

Media Adaptations

- *The Four Million,* a collection that includes the story "Mammon and the Archer," was adapted as an audiobook by Books on Tape in 1982. This unabridged adaptation consists of six audiocassettes. The stories themselves are narrated by various readers.

When Aunt Ellen reports to Anthony later that night that Richard and Miss Lantry are engaged, she attributes Richard's success to the ring that he dropped. "Money is dross compared with true love, Anthony," Ellen tells her brother. Meanwhile, Anthony believes that it was his traffic jam alone that led to the successful engagement. He asks his man, Kelly, whether or not he saw Cupid: "You didn't notice . . . anywhere in the tie-up, a kind of a fat boy without any clothes on shooting arrows around with a bow, did you?" Anthony is pleased to find that there was no sign of Cupid, a symbol of love and says, "I thought the little rascal wouldn't be on hand."

New Money versus Old Money

In addition to the power of money in general, O. Henry also explores the idea of new money versus old money. Anthony is a new millionaire, someone who has earned his fortune on his own, instead of having inherited it like the old millionaires of New York. Despite this fact, Anthony has chosen to live among the old rich in the city: "His neighbour to the right—the aristocratic clubman, B. Van Schuylight Suffolk-Jones—came out to his waiting motor-car, wrinkling a contumelious nostril, as usual, at the Italian renaissance sculpture of the soap palace's front elevation." Anthony is not welcome in this aristocratic neighborhood, but he ignores this social distinction, and uses his money to buy his place among the aristocrats. Although Anthony realizes that he may never be part of the aristocratic club, he has high hopes that Richard

Topics for Further Study

- Pick another writer from the twentieth century who writes or has written stories about New York. Read one of this author's stories, and compare the author's version of New York with O. Henry's interpretation of the city.

- Research what life was like for Miss Lantry and other wealthy young women in the early 1900s. Put yourself in her place, and write a journal entry that covers the day Richard proposes to her in the coach. Include as many details as you can from Miss Lantry's daily life—including any restrictions that might have been placed on her—using your research to support your ideas.

- In the story, Anthony Rockwall is one of the new rich, a self-made American man who has earned his money through industry. This fact does not sit well with his established neighbors, who have inherited their wealth. Research the current social designations for wealthy men and women in America, and compare these to the new rich and old rich categories of the early 1900s.

- In the story, Anthony Rockwall uses his money to literally buy a traffic jam in New York, inconveniencing all the other street traffic for two hours to give Richard the time he needs to propose to Miss Lantry. Compare this situation to one other real-life situation from both the early 1900s and the last ten years in which a wealthy person has been able to use his or her money to get special treatment that has inconvenienced other citizens. Discuss whether or not you feel money should give someone this much power.

- Research the actual volumes of traffic that New York experienced in the early 1900s, and compare this to the volume of traffic that New York experiences today. Also, research the various strategies that large cities have devised since the early 1900s to accommodate an increasing amount of traffic, and discuss whether or not these methods have been effective.

---

can. He tells Richard that, thanks to him, Richard is a gentleman: "They say it takes three generations to make one. They're off. Money'll do it as slick as soap grease." Anthony believes that his extreme wealth, which rivals the wealth of the old millionaires, can literally buy a place for Richard among them. In addition, the soap-manufacturing background that keeps Anthony out of the aristocratic club is not a problem for Richard. Says Anthony, "You've got the money and the looks, and you're a decent boy. Your hands are clean. You've got no Eureka soap on 'em."

Early Twentieth-Century Rules of Courtship

The dating rules in the early twentieth century were extremely different from the dating rituals of today. This was especially true among the aristoc-racy, which observed strict, formal dating rules. Since Anthony was not born into the aristocracy, he is not familiar with these rules, as Richard explains to him: "You don't know the social mill, dad. She's part of the stream that turns it. Every hour and minute of her time is arranged for days in advance." Miss Lantry is part of the social elite, so her time is managed very carefully. People, especially men interested in dating her, cannot just go over to her house to see her. They must receive permission beforehand. Richard notes this to Anthony when he talks about the time that he is scheduled to see Miss Lantry: "She's at Larchmont now at her aunt's. I can't go there. But I'm allowed to meet her with a cab at the Grand Central Station to-morrow evening at the 8:30 train." From the train station, Richard will accompany Miss Lantry in a coach to the theatre, so the only real time he has to talk with her is the few minutes during the coach ride from the train station to the theatre. Richard's Aunt Ellen is aware of the social rules and agrees with Richard that he has missed his opportunity to get on Miss Lantry's schedule to propose to her. Says Ellen to Anthony, "If he only had spoken earlier! She could not have refused our Richard. But now I fear it is too late. He will have no opportunity to address her."

Deception

Deception is another major theme in the story. Anthony deceives both Richard and Ellen, planning the traffic jam behind their backs, and he does not reveal that he was the one who orchestrated it. When Aunt Ellen comes to see him, telling him that love has provided the means for Richard to propose to Miss Lantry, Anthony ignores this and acts like he has helped in some way, saying only, "I'm glad the boy has got what he wanted. I told him I wouldn't spare any expense in the matter if—." Aunt Ellen is confused and cuts him off, asking how Anthony could possibly have helped, but Anthony sends her away, saying he wants to finish reading his story. In the end, only he, Kelly, and the drivers of the fleet of hired vehicles know that Anthony created the traffic jam.

Style

Setting

The setting is extremely important in the story, as it is in all of the stories in *The Four Million*. O. Henry placed all of the stories in this collection in New York to show the diversity of people and situations in the growing city. Specifically, the setting of "Mammon and the Archer" is important because its plot hinges on some distinctly New York situations. First of all, Richard is interested in one of the daughters of the New York aristocracy who make up "the exclusive circles of society," as Richard puts it. Richard's only chance to ask Miss Lantry to marry him is in the few minutes' drive from Grand Central Station to Wallack's, a famous New York theatre. Says Richard, "Do you think she would listen to a declaration from me during that six or eight minutes under those circumstances?" However, one final characteristic of New York ends up

working in Richard's favor—the legendary street traffic. When Anthony's orchestrated traffic jam blocks Richard and Miss Lantry in, they do not find it odd. As O. Henry's narrator says, "One of those street blockades had occurred that sometimes tie up commerce and movement quite suddenly in the big city." If the story took place in another, less-busy, city in the same time period, the traffic jam might look more suspicious.

Surprise Ending

O. Henry's trademark style in his short stories was to include a surprise ending, in which the reader was led to believe one thing at first but was then shown that the opposite was true. In this story, the surprise centers on the ring that Aunt Ellen gives to Richard and the traffic jam that Anthony creates. At first, the reader is led to believe, like Ellen, that it was the ring that led to the successful engagement. Says Ellen, "A little emblem of true love—a little ring that symbolized unending and unmercenary affection—was the cause of our Richard finding his happiness." However, at the very end of the story, O. Henry turns the tables on his readers. The day after the traffic jam, Kelly shows up to receive payment for something and tells Anthony that he will need to be paid more: "I had to go a little above the estimate. I got the express wagons and cabs mostly for $5, but the trucks and two-horse teams mostly raised me to $10." As Kelly goes into greater detail about what he is being paid for, the reader realizes that Anthony paid Kelly to create the traffic jam. Says Kelly, "It was two hours before a snake could get below Greeley's statue." With this surprise ending, O. Henry's readers have the sudden realization that Anthony did have a part to play in the success of Richard's engagement.

Narration

Although it may not appear so at first, "Mammon and the Archer" is ultimately a first-person narrative. The story begins in the third person, with the unnamed narrator giving details about Anthony Rockwall, his neighbor, and others. In third-person narratives, the narrator is not part of the story and is merely there to guide the reader through the characters' story. However, near the end of this story, right before the surprise ending, O. Henry talks directly to the audience, saying: "The story should end here. I wish it would as heartily as you who read it wish it did. But we must go to the bottom of the well for truth.'' With this statement, O. Henry draws attention to himself, and he becomes one of the characters.

Historical Context

''Mammon and the Archer,'' like other stories in O. Henry's *The Four Million*, touches on aspects of life in New York City at the turn of the century. During the Industrial Revolution of the late nineteenth and early twentieth centuries, many American cities experienced an unprecedented increase in immigration, much of which was handled through New York's Ellis Island. In its heyday, Ellis Island processed more than five thousand people per day, and on its busiest day it received almost twelve thousand arrivals. Of all the nation's major cities, New York experienced the greatest increase, more than tripling its population during the last four decades of the nineteenth century. This massive increase in people, coupled with the city planners' desire to surpass other American cities, culminated in 1898—with the consolidation of the city into five boroughs: Manhattan, the Bronx, Brooklyn, Queens, and Staten Island.

O. Henry was fascinated with New York and spent countless hours observing all aspects of the city. In many ways, New York in the early twentieth century was the city of the future because it either pioneered or adopted several new technologies and innovations. Many of these were introduced by necessity. This is most apparent in the area of transportation. As New York grew, it became imperative to find improved ways to move its residents from place to place. By 1901, streetcars and elevators in New York were being run by electricity; in 1904, the city completed construction on its subway system; and in 1907, the city replaced its Fifth Avenue horsecars with motorbuses. Still, New York had its share of disasters, such as in 1905 when an elevated train fell to the street, killing twelve.

Architecture was another area in which New York excelled. Inspired by such technological advances as steel-frame construction and the electric elevator, architects began to design more skyscrapers. The building revolution began in Chicago, following the 1871 Great Chicago fire, which de-

stroyed much of the downtown business district. Developers wanted to maximize the space of the small, expensive downtown lots when they rebuilt the city. This, in turn, inspired architects to find new ways to construct buildings. Chicago's Home Insurance Building, often considered the first true skyscraper, was designed by William Le Baron Jenney and was completed in 1883. New York followed suit five years later with its first skyscraper, the Tower Building. It was not long, however, before New York began to surpass Chicago in the height of its buildings. Skyscrapers were generally built by the corporations that owned them, so New York had an advantage—many corporations wishing to distinguish themselves had their headquarters there because New York was also the center of commerce.

In addition to all of the technological innovations, New York boasted the largest theatre scene, known as Broadway, named after the street that contained the theatres. One of the most influential theatres was the Wallack Theatre, named after Lester Wallack, an actor and playwright. In the story, Richard notes that he is supposed to drive Miss Lantry to this theatre. Richard says to his father: ''We drive down Broadway to Wallack's at a gallop, where her mother and a box party will be waiting for us in the lobby.'' O. Henry himself had some experience with Wallack's. Eugene Current-Garcia, in his entry on William Sydney Porter for the *Dictionary of Literary Biography* writes that O. Henry's story, ''"A Retrieved Reformation,' was dramatized with phenomenal success in 1910 at Wallack's Theatre in New York.''

Critical Overview

Perhaps no other American writer has gained and lost as much critical favor as quickly as O. Henry. Bruce Watson summed it up best in his 1997 *Smithsonian* article: ''When he died in 1910, O. Henry was in the pantheon of American writers. These days critics regard him as a clever hack.'' O. Henry received some of his strongest praise for his stories about New York, which include ''Mammon and the Archer.'' O. Henry published many of these stories under contract for the *New York World,* completing one story each week from 1903 to 1905.

Compare
&
Contrast

- **1900s:** By the end of the decade, America boasts more than forty thousand millionaires, many of whom earned their fortunes in industry.

  Today: America has countless millionaires and several billionaires. Industry, most notably information technology, is the major source of this income for some. However, an increasing number of sports stars, entertainers, writers, and other public figures—who often earn advances, sponsorship deals, and other supplemental income—join the ranks of the extremely wealthy.

- **1900s:** New York contains some of the tallest skyscrapers in the world, including the twenty-story, steel-frame Flatiron Building. Skyscrapers begin to include electric elevators.

  Today: On September 11, 2001, terrorists attack and destroy the twin towers of the World Trade Center in New York City. Each of the two 110-story buildings contained ninety-seven passenger elevators.

- **1900s:** New York is the hub of the theatre industry, represented by Broadway, and the early film industry, which is centered in Queens.

  Today: Broadway maintains its dominance of the theatre scene, although patrons also attend shows on the Off-Broadway and Off-Off-Broadway venues. Hollywood, California, is the generally acknowledged center of the modern film industry. However, New York's distinctive features—including its skyline and diverse city neighborhoods—make it an attractive choice for many on-location film and television shoots.

New Yorkers loved these stories, and O. Henry quickly became a legend in the city. O. Henry's reputation increased even more in the eyes of both critics and popular readers in 1906 with the publication of *The Four Million,* which collected several of his New York stories, including "Mammon and the Archer."

O. Henry's fame in 1906 extended well beyond New York. As Luther S. Luedtke and Keith Lawrence note in their entry on the author for the *Dictionary of Literary Biography,* the collection "sold phenomenally well and made Porter's pseudonym a household name across America." Critics and biographers cite many reasons for the passionate interest in O. Henry's short stories, but one factor stands out above the rest. In his 1916 biography of O. Henry, Alphonso Smith says, "Most of those who have commented upon O. Henry's work have singled out his technique, especially his unexpected endings, as his distinctive contribution to the American short story."

In 1916, the same year as Smith's biography, Katherine Fullerton Gerould, a noted short-story writer, became the first major critic to turn against O. Henry. Says Gerould in an infamous *New York Times Magazine* interview with Joyce Kilmer, "O. Henry did not write the short story. O. Henry wrote the expanded anecdote." This attack was answered two months later by a *Bookman* critic who suggests that Gerould might change her opinion if she read several of O. Henry's stories, including "Mammon and the Archer."

Despite the fierce defense of O. Henry by some critics, the attacks on O. Henry's works continued to build force in the 1920s. As Eugene Current-Garcia notes in his 1982 entry on the author for the *Dictionary of Literary Biography,* "critics such as F. L. Pattee and N. Bryllion Fagin denounced the superficiality and falseness in his stories and his failure, as they saw it, to take himself and his art seriously." And Luedtke and Lawrence note in their *Dictionary of Literary Biography* entry that "Critics of the 1920s satirized mercilessly the hundreds of would-be writers who emulated Porter's formulaic plot constructions." In 1943, this animosity reached a head, with the publication of the first edition of

The title The Four Million *is a response to a comment in 1892 by Ward McCallister (featured here) that there were only about four hundred people in New York City*

Understanding Fiction by Cleanth Brooks and Robert Penn Warren. In his 1974 entry on O. Henry for *American Writers,* Kent Bales notes that, in this book, O. Henry was "exhibited as a writer who did not understand fiction." This attitude persisted throughout the twentieth century, and few critics since have praised O. Henry's writings.

In addition, few critics have chosen to discuss O. Henry's specific stories in detail, even stories like "Mammon and the Archer," one of O. Henry's most popular and most anthologized stories. In his entry on O. Henry for *Twayne's United States Authors Series Online,* Current-Garcia calls Anthony Rockwall "the epitome of O. Henry's type of the self-made American business tycoon; he knows that money talks, even in affairs of the heart." However, Bales (writing in *American Writers*) offers a different interpretation of the story, saying that, although the story's surprise ending reveals that Anthony has orchestrated the traffic jam, "Kelly's report opens ample room for doubt." Bales notes that, since Kelly and his crew were exactly on time, "the traffic jam organized by Anthony's money would

have been several seconds late," if it had not been for Richard's dropping the ring—a distinct symbol of love. Says Bales, "it is left to the reader to see that the story is about Mammon *and* the Archer, not—as the apparent reversal in the ending suggests— Mammon *over* the Archer."

Despite O. Henry's fall with many of the critics, Luedtke and Lawrence cite many reasons why O. Henry has secured a place in American literature. These include the author's large body of work, his continued renown with popular readers, the many character types that he introduced, the perceptions of America that he created, and the credibility that he gave to the art form of the short story. Finally, Luedtke and Lawrence note that "The gap between public and critical opinion of Porter's work is tenuously, and ironically, bridged by one of America's most prestigious short-story awards, named in O. Henry's honor."

Criticism

Ryan D. Poquette

Poquette has a bachelor's degree in English and specializes in writing about literature. In the following essay, Poquette examines Henry's hidden meanings in "Mammon and the Archer."

Although Henry's literary reputation has declined since the early twentieth century, his works are starting to be interpreted by select critics. One of these critics, Kent Bales, notes in his *American Writers* entry that Henry, like Edgar Allan Poe, included hidden meanings in his fiction. However, Bales notes that "Henry keeps his suggested meanings well hidden," as Poe did, so that his message is not immediately apparent to the reader. In "Mammon and the Archer," these hidden meanings can be discovered by examining the story's ending, Henry's distinctive word choice, and his use of contradictions.

In the story, after it has been revealed that Anthony Rockwall has hired Kelly to create the traffic jam, he asks Kelly: "You didn't notice . . . anywhere in the tie-up, a kind of a fat boy without

What Do I Read Next?

- Although O. Henry's literary reputation is still in question today, his name has been attached to one of the most prestigious short-story contests in the United States: the O. Henry Awards. Each year, stories from this contest are published in a special volume of prize stories. The eighty-first edition of this series, *Prize Stories 2001: The O. Henry Awards,* was published in 2001 and contains works from established authors and newcomers alike.

- O. Henry's first book, *Cabbages and Kings* (1904), is referred to by some as a novel, by others as a collection of short stories. O. Henry created the book by combining a number of his previous short stories about Central America—along with some new stories—into one interlinked narrative. The main story concerns a president of a South American country, who flees the country after being deposed in a revolution.

- O. Henry's ''The Gift of the Magi'' is a Christmas story that was originally published in *The Four Million* in 1906. This classic story, one of O. Henry's best known, depicts the wonderful—and contradictory—sacrifices that a husband and wife make so that they can give each other special Christmas gifts.

- Although O. Henry is today remembered mainly for New York stories like ''Mammon and the Archer,'' he also wrote a number of western stories, many of which were based on his experiences in Texas and Latin America. He collected almost twenty of these tales in *Heart of the West,* which was first published in 1907.

- O. Henry also wrote a number of stories for young boys, the most famous of which is *The Ransom of Red Chief,* which was first published in 1907 and which was collected in *Whirligigs* in 1910. The story concerns two amateur crooks who kidnap a little boy in an attempt to get ransom money to fund their future crimes. However, in an ironic twist, the child proves to be more trouble than the crooks.

- In Steven W. Saylor's historical novel entitled *A Twist at the End: A Novel of O. Henry* (2000), O. Henry, as the real-life Will Porter from 1906, tries to solve an actual serial murder from 1885. Through a series of flashbacks, Saylor takes Will, and the reader, back through the past, relying on both fictional and historically accurate details to tell the tale.

- Samuel Langhorne Clemens, who wrote under the well-known pseudonym of Mark Twain, was a contemporary of O. Henry's. Known primarily as a humorist, Twain used his comedic talents in the social satire *The Gilded Age: A Tale of Today* (1873), a book that he cowrote with Charles Dudley Warner. The book detailed the corruption that was going on in America at the time, when Twain and Warner saw money as the biggest concern for most. The two writers mock many aspects of their society, including the aristocracy.

---

any clothes on shooting arrows around with a bow, did you?'' Anthony laughs when Kelly says he has not. Says Anthony, ''I thought the little rascal wouldn't be on hand.'' In Anthony's mind, money has triumphed over love, which he equates with Cupid, the Roman god of love. Likewise, since Ellen does not know that Anthony paid for the traffic jam, she believes that love—as symbolized by the ring—has prevailed. Both are correct. As

Bales notes, the story ''conceals in its ending a fact that brings that ending into doubt.'' Bales cites part of Kelly's report, in which the hired man says, ''The boys was on time to the fraction of a second.'' If this is literally true, says Bales, then both the ring (love) and Anthony's traffic jam (money) play a part in Richard's successful engagement. If Richard had not accidentally dropped the ring, the traffic jam would have arrived too late to block them in. And, if

"However, as tempting as it is to label the characters as distinctly good or evil, Henry himself discourages readers from doing this. Nothing is cut-and-dry, because Henry plants good qualities in Anthony and bad qualities in Ellen."

there had been no traffic jam, then Richard would have only gained the extra minute that it took him to recover his ring. In other words, neither wealth nor love prevails totally in the end. It takes a balance of both to pull off the engagement.

This tricky ending signals the reader that there may be other aspects of the story that require further exploration. Upon further scrutiny, readers may notice that Henry uses some very odd and distinct words when he is telling his tale. This starts with the very first word of the title, "Mammon," an uncommon word. "Mammon" is the word used to signify wealth in the New Testament of the Bible. The word is used in Jesus' famous sermon on the mount, in which he says that man cannot serve both God and mammon. In addition, in medieval times, scholars defined seven deadly sins, each of which was represented by a corresponding archdemon. For avarice, or greed, the archdemon was named Mammon. By using a word with such religious associations, Henry elevates the stage for the ideological battle between Mammon and the Archer—money and love.

Henry's use of religious references is consistent throughout the story. Early on, Anthony talks about the "Eden Musée," which he says will get his neighbor "if he don't watch out." *Musée* is the French word for "museum," and Eden is the garden in the Bible where Adam and Eve, the first created man and woman, dwelled until they were expelled for their sins. Although Anthony could just be talking about a real "Eden" museum, other religious references in the story suggest that he chose the word "Eden" to increase the religious quality of the story. For example, later on in the

story, Kelly tells Anthony of the traffic jam, "It was two hours before a snake could get below Greeley's statue." The use of the word, "snake," is particularly curious, since New York is a city. Cities, even in the early 1900s, did not often contain snakes, which are generally found in more rural areas. However, since Henry has already refer to Eden, it makes sense to include a reference to a snake—in the Bible, it is a snake that tempts Adam and Eve to sin.

Some of the divine references in the story are coupled directly with the idea of money. The most blatant examples occur when Anthony is trying to convince Richard that he should literally worship money. Says Anthony, "don't forget to burn a few punk sticks in the joss house to the great god Mazuma from time to time." "Mazuma" is Yiddish slang for money, but, in this instance, Anthony is making money a literal god. A "joss house" is a Chinese temple or shrine. Henry includes enough religious references to draw attention to them but seems to want to avoid subscribing to any one religion, and so he includes references from many. In addition to strictly religious references, Anthony includes Father Time, an imaginary personification of time that is often referred to as a god-like being. Says Anthony, in the same conversation to Richard, "I've seen Father Time get pretty bad stone bruises on his heels when he walked through the gold diggings." This comment, which is a response to Richard's statement that one cannot buy time, is an elaborate and heightened way of talking about the power of money to conquer.

This elaborate style of speech is also used when describing some of the characters. Anthony, in particular, is depicted as a god-like figure. In the beginning of the story, Anthony calls for his servant, Mike, "in the same voice that had once chipped off pieces of the welkin on the Kansas prairies." This confusing sentence makes a little more sense once it is deciphered. "Welkin" is another word for the vault of the sky, or heaven. If Anthony's voice is so loud that he has broken pieces off heaven, then he is a very powerful being indeed. As for the "Kansas prairies," Anthony most likely grew up in Kansas. That he has been able to leave the prairie and make his own fortune, and that he now lives among the aristocrats of New York, are further indications of his personal strength.

Anthony is also associated with a number of evils. When Ellen comes to see Anthony at the end of the story, Anthony is "in a red dressing gown, reading a book of piratical adventures.'' The choice of colors can be very significant in a story. In this case, red, a color often associated with the devil, makes Anthony appear devil-like, especially when he is reading a story about pirates—who are notorious for their crimes such as murder and theft. In fact, when Anthony talks about the pirate story to Ellen, he says, ''I've got my pirate in a devil of a scrape. His ship has just been scuttled, and he's too good a judge of the value of money to let drown.'' The use of the word ''devil'' is interesting, given Anthony's red gown. Also, normally, a reader does not refer to a character in a book as his own. The fact that Anthony takes ownership of the pirate seems to underscore his association with evil. Furthermore, the story itself is very telling, since the pirate loves money as much as Anthony does. The word ''evil'' is also used directly in the story in association with Anthony. When describing another one of Anthony's responses to Richard about money, Henry describes Anthony's remark in this way: ''thundered the champion of the root of evil.'' The thunder, like the earlier reference to Anthony's loud voice, is an indication of Anthony's god-like stature. The designation of money as ''the root of evil'' and of Anthony as its ''champion'' appears to be a clear labeling of his character.

Anthony is not the only character in the story with unsavory associations, however. Kelly is described as ''a person with red hands.'' Though the red in this case could be another reference to devil-like behavior, Henry could also be using the color in a literal sense, saying that Kelly is red-handed, as in somebody who gets caught red-handed—in other words, a thief. This is highly probable, since Henry says that the man ''called himself Kelly,'' which means that this is not his real name. Kelly does not use his real name in his deceptive dealings with Anthony and others, which is sometimes a sign that somebody is a crook. In addition to his questionable background, Kelly also says that he ''can lick the man that invented poverty.'' In most religions, poverty is considered a good thing, since the poor are less likely to succumb to vices like materialism and greed.

In addition to the evil references, there are references to the divine in the story, namely in the descriptions of Ellen and Richard. When Ellen comes to tell Anthony that love has triumphed, Henry says that she looked ''like a gray-haired angel that had been left on earth by mistake.'' To a lesser extent, Richard's purity is established. When Anthony is comparing Richard to himself, he tells

his son, ''you're a decent boy. Your hands are clean,'' implying that his own hands are not.

However, as tempting as it is to label the characters as distinctly good or evil, Henry himself discourages readers from doing this. Nothing is cut-and-dry, because Henry plants good qualities in Anthony and bad qualities in Ellen. At one point, Anthony is described as having a ''kindly grimace,'' while Ellen is described as ''gentle, sentimental, wrinkled, sighing, oppressed by wealth.'' If Anthony is truly supposed to be representative of a devil, he would not be ''kindly.'' And if Ellen is supposed to be a perfect angel, she would be poor, not ''oppressed by wealth.'' These opposites exist elsewhere in the story, further prompting the reader to be skeptical of any concrete labeling of characters or situations. For example, when Ellen gives Richard his mother's ring, she takes the ''quaint old gold ring from a moth-eaten case.'' Gold is a sign of wealth, as well as vanity when it is worn as an object. Conversely, a moth-eaten case suggests poverty and humility. The biggest contradiction in the story is in the idea of deception, which is normally considered bad. However, in this case, Anthony uses deceptive methods to do a good deed—secretly helping to buy time for his son to win over his love.

In the end, Henry's story, which on the surface appears to be a simple tale about the power of money, in reality is something much different. After reading through all of the clues that Henry imbeds in his tale, one can see that he is communicating two hidden messages to his readers. First, the forces of good and evil are equally matched and thus cannot succeed on their own. It is only when they work together, albeit unwittingly, that they achieve their goals. Says Bates, ''it is left to the reader to see that the story is about Mammon *and* the Archer, not—as the apparent reversal in the ending suggests—Mammon *over* the Archer.'' However, this is not the entire story. Henry is also telling his readers that the definition of evil is a tricky business, since neither Anthony nor Ellen, the two combatants in the ideological battle of money versus love, can be defined as purely evil or good. The idea of what makes a person bad was an important theme in both the writings and life of Henry—an ex-convict who, by most accounts, carried the shame of his prison experience with him for the rest of his life. It must have provided some comfort for him to be able to create characters that had some questionable associations or experiences, but which were not inherently bad, and to share these characters with a reading public who adored him.

Source: Ryan D. Poquette, Critical Essay on ''Mammon and the Archer,'' in *Short Stories for Students,* Gale, 2003.

David Partikian

Partikian is a freelance writer and English instructor. In this essay, Partikian explains that an epistemological approach to O. Henry's story is more helpful in understanding the story than merely analyzing the triumph of either love or wealth.

In a first reading, ''Mammon and the Archer'' is a straightforward tale that pits two contradictory characters and philosophies against one another. Anthony Rockwall is a self-made ''ex-Soap King'' who believes in the supremacy of money, even to the extent that money can buy love. Aunt Ellen, on the other hand, is sentimental and has a more idealistic notion concerning true love. By the end of the tale, both characters believe that their beliefs have been vindicated by the engagement of young Richard and Miss Lantry. However, neither Anthony Rockwall nor Aunt Ellen truly knows all the circumstances; each one has an opinion that is misinformed. The narrative contains lacunae—gaps in knowledge and an absence of adequate description of key events— that do not clarify or allow the reader to make an accurate assessment as to whether money or love triumphs in the end; for example, O. Henry completely neglects portraying what actually takes place in the carriage, the incident which leads to the engagement. The ending is ambiguous, particularly without the depiction of the crucial carriage scene. While the ending is neither an endorsement of the power of true love or money, it is an epistemological homage illustrating the bounds and limits of each character's and each reader's understanding of what has occurred.

Epistemology is the study of the nature and grounds of human knowledge. The theories place particular emphasis on the limits of knowledge and the degree that knowledge can be validated. For instance, an epistemological study of religion would involve exactly how human beings can or cannot prove the existence of God. What are the limitations to a logical attempt to prove God exists? Do these limitations, if sufficient enough, prove that God does not exist? O. Henry's story, with all its gaps and limitations on what is known to the two key characters and the reader, is an epistemological text. Any attempts at proving the superiority of either Mammon or the Archer must begin with a scrutiny of the limitations on knowledge inherent throughout.

Old Anthony Rockwall's entire outlook on life is defined by money. He is a self-made man whose position is validated by his fortune. The allusions to this within the text are so numerous that O. Henry could easily be accused of creating a character who is too one-dimensional. Old Rockwall talks of nothing but money. This obsession is parodied when Old Rockwall measures the ''worth'' of his son by how much Richard spends on soap: '''You're a gentleman,' said Anthony, decidedly. 'I've heard of young bloods spending $24 a dozen for soap, and going over the hundred mark for clothes.''' He even picks out vague references to money and profit while relaxing with a book: '''Sister,' said Anthony Rockwall. 'I've got my pirate in a devil of a scrape. His ship has just been scuttled, and he's too good a judge of the value of money to let drown. I wish you would let me go on with this chapter.''' This obsession with money limits Anthony's ability to evaluate a situation in any other terms. He knows that money has gained him access into the highest levels of New York society, although he admits that he is not readily accepted: ''I'm nearly as impolite and ill-mannered as these two old knickerbocker gents on each side of me that can't sleep of nights because I bought in between 'em.'' Anthony's status as a parvenu, a nouveau riche member of society, is further emphasized by the narrator snidely referring to him as the ''ex-Soap King'' and to his home as the ''soap palace.'' While an image of the King of England may command some respect, the image of a soap king living in a soap palace, presumably feverishly hoping that it never rains, invites mockery. Indeed, the descriptions of Anthony may be viewed as mocking in light of the fact that Anthony so clearly holds up wealth as a universal truth, almost a religion.

The very title of the tale includes a synonym for money with negative implications; the word mammon, as used by Matthew in the New Testament (6:24) refers to material wealth or possessions, especially in light of it having a debasing influence: ''You cannot serve God and mammon.'' Considering that Anthony invokes different religions and pagan cultural figures throughout the text in a derogatory way (''But don't forget to burn a few punk sticks in the joss house to the god Mazuma from time to time'' and ''You didn't notice . . . anywhere in the tie-up, a kind of a fat boy without any clothes on shooting arrows around with a bow, did you?''), O. Henry's use of a derogatory term for money in the title is ironic. Anthony's adamant nature, failing to allow for any other view but his own, is implied in his very name, Rockwall. He is indeed like a rock wall, intractable and unable to allow any concept into his world view except that of wealth. In terms of epistemology, Anthony's monomaniacal obsession with wealth limits his ability to see the truth.

Just as Anthony is obsessed with championing wealth, Aunt Ellen is adamant in her belief that love will triumph in the end. The narrator describes her as "sentimental" and "oppressed by wealth." Her belief that "Love is all-powerful" is partly wishful thinking and based on her ignorance of the mercenary ways of the world. She remains ignorant to the very end as to the cause of the fortuitous traffic jam, preferring her own romantic notion as to the power of a ring. O. Henry does not treat her with kid gloves in his choice of words. While Cupid, the Roman god of erotic love whom Anthony belittles, is usually viewed as a positive romantic figure, his depiction as an archer in the title brings to mind trivial and war-like connotations. Just as mammon is more negative than money, archer is more trite and commonplace than Cupid. The title of the story subtly questions the validity of the respective value systems of both Anthony and Ellen.

So where does the truth lie? If O. Henry is illustrating the limits to acknowledging the truth in the values of his two main characters, what is his solution to the question of money versus love? The question is, perhaps, impossible to answer because O. Henry has left gaps in the narrative and character development, which would have clued the reader into his sentiments and which are exactly what make the tale brilliantly ambiguous.

O. Henry is best remembered as a writer of a specific era and place—New York in the late nineteenth and early twentieth centuries. He is known for stories with a surprise ending that unexpectedly tie all the loose ends together. In this sense, he is the quintessential representative of an earlier pragmatic America where everything seemed black and white; there were no ambiguous shades of gray. Most of his body of work is made up of neat, tidy stories that have value as entertainment with neatly summed up conclusions rather than as serious literature with ambiguity that invites lingering questions.

However, in the case of "Mammon and the Archer," the ending is not so neat and tidy because O. Henry has held back information that would enable the reader to better comprehend and judge; the conversation and wooing that takes place in the carriage during the traffic jam is the crucial dialogue

> " O. Henry has left gaps in the narrative and character development, which would have clued the reader into his sentiments and which are exactly what make the tale brilliantly ambiguous."

of the whole tale. Without an accurate depiction of this scene, one cannot figure out which system triumphs. Yet, it is completely absent from the text. It is lacunae of this sort that often relegates O. Henry's fiction to the second rate but that works so well in this particular tale. An accurate depiction of this conversation would have involved subtle character development as well as hints of the differing classes of society that the two represent. Miss Lantry belongs to old money, long established in New York, while Richard is an upstart son of a parvenu. What did he say in the carriage that could have possibly convinced her of his sentiments towards her? There is nothing in the story to indicate that he is indeed worthy of Miss Lantry and even less of a hint that this busy society lady is worth chasing at all. The modern reader is left wishing that contemporaries of O. Henry, like Henry James and Edith Wharton who both portrayed social classes in New York with all their foibles, had described the carriage conversation between Miss Lantry and Robert with all the subtle ironic allusions to the pettiness and vacuity of New York high society. Instead, readers are left with O. Henry's depiction of the merest of situational factors, the dropping of a ring and the fabricated traffic jam, as the sole combatants that vie for superiority in the question of Love versus Wealth.

O. Henry's avoidance of complicated psychological motives is the reason for the great success he achieved during his lifetime as a short story writer. By keeping his characters one dimensional and his scenarios simple, he is able to manipulate a surprise ending that neatly ties together all the loose ends. Ironically, O. Henry's lack of critical acclaim today is a result of the same ability that made him a great success in his own lifetime. While the entrance of the shady character who "called himself Kelly" does introduce a twist to the end of the tale, the realization that Anthony has fabricated the traffic jam creates an ending not nearly as tidy as O. Henry's other tales. The lack of tidiness is exactly why "Mammon and the Archer" stands out in his body of work today.

"Mammon and the Archer" is an exception in O. Henry's body of work, in that the gaps in the narrative depictions and the inability of both Anthony and Ellen to acknowledge any factors outside their own narrow belief systems have led to a work with marvelously ambiguous epistemological implications. Can one ever really know whether wealth or love is triumphant in the end? The title's mocking allusion to the gods of both Anthony and Ellen leads the reader to believe that neither philosophy reigns supreme without help from the other. In this sense, neither mammon nor the archer is the key word in understanding the title. Rather, it is that largely overlooked conjunction "and." O. Henry was deliberate in titling the work. He did not choose "Mammon or the Archer." The two gods or philosophical systems are not mutually exclusive. They rely on one another to bring about a harmonious solution. Any attempt to define the world or seek truth in one at the exclusion of the other is doomed to a dismal failure.

Source: David Partikian, Critical Essay on "Mammon and the Archer," in *Short Stories for Students,* Gale, 2003.

Sources

Bales, Kent, "O. Henry," in *American Writers,* Supplement 2, Vol. 1, Charles Scribner's Sons, 1974, pp. 385–412.

Current-Garcia, Eugene, "O. Henry," in *Twayne's United States Authors Series Online,* G. K. Hall & Company, 1999.

———, "William Sydney Porter," in *Dictionary of Literary Biography,* Vol. 12: *American Realists and Naturalists,* edited by Donald Pizer, Gale Research, 1982, pp. 409–16.

Gerould, Katherine Fullerton, "An Interview with Joyce Kilmer," in *New York Times Magazine,* July 23, 1916, p. 12.

Henry, O., "Mammon and the Archer," in *Tales of O. Henry: Sixty-Two Stories,* Barnes & Noble Books, 1993, pp. 37–43.

Luedtke, Luther S., and Keith Lawrence, "William Sydney Porter," in *Dictionary of Literary Biography,* Vol. 78: *American Short-Story Writers, 1880–1910,* edited by Bobby Ellen Kimbel, Gale Research, 1989, pp. 288–307.

Smith, C. Alphonso, *O. Henry Biography,* Doubleday, Page & Company, 1916, p. 203.

"Strange Opinions," in *Bookman,* Vol. 44, No. 1, September 1916, pp. 31–33.

Watson, Bruce, "If His Life Were a Short Story, Who'd Ever Believe It?" in *Smithsonian,* Vol. 27, January 1997, pp. 92–102.

Further Reading

Blansfield, Karen Charmaine, *Cheap Rooms and Restless Hearts: A Study of Formula in the Urban Tales of William Sydney Porter,* Popular Press, 1988.
    This book explores the characters and plot patterns found in O. Henry's urban tales and offers a new evaluation of O. Henry's literary merit and contributions.

Bloom, Harold, ed., *O. Henry,* Bloom's Major Short Story Writers series, Chelsea House, 1999.
    Bloom, a noted literary critic, collects a variety of criticism on O. Henry from others. In addition, the book features a biography of O. Henry, themes and characters from selected O. Henry stories, a bibliography of O. Henry's writings, and notes and an introduction by Bloom.

Burrows, Edwin G., and Mike Wallace, *Gotham: A History of New York City to 1898,* Oxford University Press, 2000.
    This early history of New York is the most comprehensive study thus far. Burrows and Wallace combine both original and recent scholarship to provide a complete overview of the city, from the first discovery of the port city by Europeans to the 1898 formation of New York's five boroughs. This massive book also contains a bibliography as well as name and subject indices.

Langford, Gerald, *Alias O. Henry: A Biography of William Sidney Porter,* Greenwood Publishing, 1983.
    This definitive biography of O. Henry, originally published in 1957, offers a comprehensive, fact-filled overview of the author's life and career.

Wall, Diana Dizerega, and Anne-Marie E. Cantwell, *Unearthing Gotham: The Archaeology of New York City,* Yale University Press, 2001.
    Published on the eve of the September 11, 2001, terrorist attack on and destruction of the World Trade Center, this book serves as a timely reminder that New York's long heritage goes beyond its distinctive skyline. Using both historical and archaeological research, the authors explore New York's history, unearthing stories from all five boroughs.

Wuthnow, Robert, *God and Mammon in America,* Free Press, 1998.
    This book derives its title from the biblical instruction that humanity cannot serve both God and mammon, or wealth. Wuthnow poses the idea that modern-day religion does not always help people to be less materialistic and that it may, in fact, encourage people to be wealthy.

Mrs. Dutta Writes a Letter

Chitra Divakaruni's ''Mrs. Dutta Writes a Letter'' was first published in the *Atlantic Monthly* in 1998 and was included in Divakaruni's second short-story collection, *The Unknown Errors of Our Lives* (2001). Divakaruni is an Indian who immigrated to the United States, and ''Mrs. Dutta Writes a Letter'' is one of her many stories that explores the culture shock faced by Indian women who have made such immigrations. In this particular case, Mrs. Dutta, an Indian widow, bows to her sense of duty and pressure from her Calcutta relatives. She decides to come and live with her son and his family in the San Francisco Bay area—a setting that Divakaruni uses repeatedly in her fiction. Throughout the story, Mrs. Dutta tries to answer her Calcutta friend's question about whether or not she is happy in America, but she keeps putting her response letter aside. She is afraid to explore how she really feels, since this may conflict with her loyalty to her family. However, through a series of cultural conflicts, she finally gains the strength to be honest with herself about her unhappiness. When this story was published in 1998, India was highly visible in the international arena for the cultural conflict among its religious groups, its nuclear weapons tests, and its ongoing border dispute with Pakistan. A current copy of ''Mrs. Dutta Writes a Letter'' can be found in *The Best American Short Stories 1999,* which was published by the Houghton Mifflin Company in 1999.

Chitra Banerjee Divakaruni

1998

Author Biography

Divakaruni was born in Calcutta, India, on July 29, 1956, into a traditional, middle-class Indian family. She lived in several Indian cities while she was growing up and then attended the University of Calcutta, where she earned her bachelor's degree in English. Her family expected that she would get married after she finished her education and spend her time raising a family in India. However, in 1976, when she was nineteen, she immigrated to the United States. In 1978, she graduated with a master's degree in English from Wright State University in Dayton, Ohio. The next year, she married S. Murthy Divakaruni, although not in a traditional arranged marriage. In 1985, she graduated from the University of California at Berkeley with her doctorate in English. While she was a student at Berkeley, she volunteered at a women's center, where she worked with abused women. This experience would inspire her in many ways. After school, she taught creative writing at Diablo Valley College (1987–1989). She also began writing her own poems.

In 1989, Divakaruni began teaching creative writing at Foothill College. While teaching there, she published several works. In her poetry collection *Black Candle* (1991), the poems concern the various issues faced by women in India, Pakistan, and Bangladesh. The same year, she helped form Maitri, a nonprofit organization in the San Francisco Bay area that assists South Asian women facing domestic violence, emotional abuse, or family conflict. Maitri is a Sanskrit word that means friendship. Her volunteer work with other immigrant women at Maitri—where she also served as president for several years—inspired her to write *Arranged Marriage: Stories* (1995). This collection of short stories, which won the American Book Award in 1996, examined the experiences of immigrant Indian women who are torn between their Indian heritage and American culture. In 1997, she published two works, her first novel, *The Mistress of Spices*, and a poetry collection, *Leaving Yuba City: New and Selected Poems*. The latter was awarded the Allen Ginsberg Poetry Prize and the Pushcart Prize. In 2001, Divakaruni published her second collection of short stories, *The Unknown Errors of Our Lives* (2001), which includes the story ''Mrs. Dutta Writes a Letter.'' Her latest novel, *The Vine of Desire* (2002), is a sequel to her 1999 novel, *Sister of My Heart*. Divakaruni lives and works in the San Francisco Bay area.

Plot Summary

''Mrs. Dutta Writes a Letter'' follows two days in the life of Mrs. Dutta, an old, widowed Indian woman who had moved into her son's American home two months earlier. On the first morning, she gets up too early, prompting her son, Sagar, to tell her that she is waking up his wife, Shyamoli, and that Mrs. Dutta should get up later. In this way, Mrs. Dutta's habits, which she learned as an arranged wife in India, conflict with the American customs of her son's family. The next morning, Mrs. Dutta gets up later as ordered, but now she ends up being in the bathroom when her grandchildren need it, and they complain. Mrs. Dutta is surprised when Shyamoli does not punish the children for being disrespectful to Mrs. Dutta, their elder. As she does throughout the story, she compares this American behavior with the Indian customs that she has followed her whole life. She also thinks about the letter she received from her Calcutta friend, Mrs. Basu, who has asked if Mrs. Dutta is happy in America. Mrs. Dutta is struggling to be loyal to her son's family, although she feels uncomfortable about life in America, and so she has not sent a reply to her friend yet. She starts making alu dum, a traditional Indian meal. In her mind, she writes a response to Mrs. Basu, saying that she misses India and then rebukes herself for being nostalgic. She continues making her meal, noting that Shyamoli is worried that Mrs. Dutta's food has too much cholesterol and is making them gain weight.

Later in the day, Mrs. Dutta washes her clothes. She has insisted on doing her own laundry so that nobody else will have to touch her underclothes. However, she is terrified of the modern washing machine, so she secretly washes the clothes by hand. She hangs the clothes on the fence to dry, while crafting another mental response to Mrs. Basu—this time saying that she is fitting in very well in America. She remembers her departure from India, when she got rid of her house and gave away most of her possessions. When she is pulling the dry clothes off the fence, she notices the next-door neighbor and waves to her, but the neighbor ignores her. Sagar comes home early from work that day, and Mrs. Dutta is happy when he enjoys the story she tells him about his childhood. However, when Shyamoli arrives home, upset, Mrs. Dutta goes to her room to give them some privacy. She realizes that she left her unfinished response to Mrs. Basu on the kitchen table and goes to retrieve it. She overhears Shyamoli arguing with Sagar, saying that the next-door neighbor complained about Mrs. Dutta hanging her clothes over the fence. Although her sense of duty says that she should stay with her son's family, Mrs. Dutta realizes that she is an outsider and that she would be much happier back in India. She writes a response to Mrs. Basu, saying that she is coming back to India and asking Mrs. Basu to rent out her downstairs flat to Mrs. Dutta.

Characters

Mrs. Roma Basu

Mrs. Basu is Mrs. Dutta's longtime friend and neighbor in India. It is her letter that prompts Mrs. Dutta to examine whether or not she is really happy. At the end of the story, Mrs. Dutta writes to Mrs. Basu to ask if she can rent her friend's downstairs apartment, which has been recently vacated.

Mrinalini Dutta

Mrinalini is Mrs. Dutta's granddaughter, who is not interested in exploring her Indian heritage. Shyamoli calls Mrinalini ''Minnie''—a further sign of the family's assimilation into American culture.

Pradeep Dutta

Pradeep is Mrs. Dutta's grandson, who is not interested in exploring his Indian heritage. Shyamoli calls Pradeep ''Pat''—a further sign of the family's assimilation into American culture.

Mrs. Prameela Dutta

Mrs. Dutta is a dutiful Indian widow, who experiences cultural conflict while trying to live with her son's Americanized family. Mrs. Dutta wed Sagar's father in a traditional Indian marriage when she was seventeen. Throughout her life, she has been subservient to her husband and other family members, suppressing her own desires in order to fulfill their needs. When her husband dies, she lives as a widow in their home for three years, until she is stricken with pneumonia. Her son invites her to come and live with his family, and she feels that she is following her Indian duty by accepting his invitation. Despite the misgivings of her best friend, Mrs. Basu, Mrs. Dutta gives up her Calcutta home and gives away most of her possessions to friends. When Mrs. Dutta arrives at her son's home

Media Adaptations

- *The Best American Short Stories 1999,* which includes the story ''Mrs. Dutta Writes a Letter,'' was adapted as an audiobook in 1999. It is available on four audiocassettes from Mariner Books. ''Mrs. Dutta Writes a Letter'' is read by Divakaruni.

in California, she is shocked at the customs of American culture, which often clash with her traditional Indian upbringing. Throughout the story, she remembers what her life was like in India, as she compares it to her immigrant experience in America. Mrs. Basu writes Mrs. Dutta a letter, asking Mrs. Dutta if she is happy in America. Mrs. Dutta struggles to answer this letter in a positive manner but must keep putting it aside because she is not happy. However, Mrs. Dutta does not feel comfortable saying anything bad about her son and, at first, thinks that it would be shameful to return to India.

Although Mrs. Dutta tries to fit in at her son's household, there are some customs that she cannot understand. Shyamoli becomes frustrated when her mother-in-law throws out uneaten food, but saving leftover food is a practice that conflicts with Mrs. Dutta's Hindu belief about not saving contaminated food. Mrs. Dutta also does not condone her grandchildren's behavior toward their parents and is horrified when Shyamoli addresses Sagar by his first name and asks him to fold laundry—especially since the laundry includes Mrs. Dutta's underclothes. As a result, she volunteers to wash the laundry but is terrified of the washing machine and hand washes them instead. A neighbor sees her drying the clothes on her fence and tells Shyamoli, which leads to a fight between Sagar and his wife. Mrs. Dutta overhears this argument and realizes that she is not happy in America and that she should put her own needs ahead of her family duty. She writes to Mrs. Basu to let her know that she will be returning to India and that she wishes to rent Mrs. Basu's downstairs apartment.

Sagar Dutta

Sagar is Shyamoli's husband and Mrs. Dutta's son. He was born in India and was married to Shyamoli through a traditional, arranged marriage. Since moving to the United States, he has assimilated many aspects of American culture, although he still tries to be a dutiful Indian son. As a result, when Mrs. Dutta gets sick with pneumonia, he encourages her to move in with him and his family in California. When Mrs. Dutta arrives, Sagar tries to help her make a peaceful transition to American life. However, unlike Shyamoli, Sagar is still interested in various aspects of his Indian heritage. He likes his mother's cooking and appreciates hearing humorous stories from his childhood, which makes it harder for him to deny her. He does try to train his mother in various American customs—such as how to use a washing machine—but he is unsuccessful. However, he does not confront his mother on many issues that Shyamoli has with her, which leads to tension between Sagar and his wife. When Mrs. Dutta's Indian behavior draws negative attention from a neighbor, Shyamoli and Sagar have an argument. Although Shyamoli and Sagar resolve their conflict, he does not realize that Mrs. Dutta has overheard the argument and has decided to return to India.

Shyamoli Dutta

Shyamoli is Sagar's wife and Mrs. Dutta's daughter-in-law. She was born in India and was married to Sagar through a traditional arranged marriage when she was a young woman. However, when she moved to the United States, she totally assimilated American culture. Mrs. Dutta notes that, as a light-skinned Indian, Shyamoli—who is now a modern working mother—can almost pass for an American. Unlike Sagar, Shyamoli is not interested in revisiting her Indian heritage. In fact, she worries that Mrs. Dutta's Indian cooking is unhealthy for them. Shyamoli also kisses her husband in public, calls him by his first name, and asks him to do chores around the house—all nontraditional behavior that shocks Mrs. Dutta. Shyamoli, who goes by the Americanized name "Molli," is particularly anxious lest her neighbors perceive her family—the only Indian family in the neighborhood—as savages. This fear comes true when Mrs. Dutta dries clothes by hanging them over the fence into the next-door neighbor's yard. This incident causes an argument between Shyamoli and Sagar, which Mrs. Dutta overhears.

Minnie

See Mrinalini

Molli

See Shyamoli

Neighbor

Sagar's and Shyamoli's next-door neighbor complains to Shyamoli after Mrs. Dutta hangs clothes over the fence that divides the two properties. This incident leads to Shyamoli's argument with Sagar and makes Mrs. Dutta realize that she wants to return home to India.

Pat

See Pradeep

Themes

Cultural Conflict

The major theme in the story is the many differences between traditional Indians and modern Indians living in America and the conflict that this cultural divide can create. On one end of the spectrum is Mrs. Dutta, who has been raised to be a traditional Indian wife. In India, she was taught that her needs should be placed below the family's needs and is used to getting up earlier than everyone else to make breakfast. However, in America, her early morning activities are a problem, because they wake up Shyamoli. "But the habit, taught her by her mother-in-law when she was a bride of seventeen, *A good wife wakes before the rest of the household,* is one she finds impossible to break." This is the first of many cultural conflicts that Mrs. Dutta faces. On the other end of the spectrum are Shyamoli and Mrs. Dutta's two grandchildren, who have totally assimilated American culture. They do not like Mrs. Dutta's traditional Indian meals and would rather engage in American activities like reading the *Wall Street Journal* or playing video games than listen to Mrs. Dutta's stories. Finally, Sagar is trapped between the two cultures. He enjoys various aspects of American culture, such as watching television crime shows, but he also enjoys his mother's food and stories. Also, he wants to please his Indian-Ameri-

Topics for Further Study

- Research arranged marriages as they exist in India today, and compare these unions to the arranged marriages that take place among Indian families in the United States. Discuss how the respective women's movements in each country have affected the women in these marriages.

- Research what life is currently like for widows in Calcutta, and discuss some possibilities for what might happen to Mrs. Dutta when she returns to live with Mrs. Basu.

- In the story, Mrs. Dutta is an Indian living in America. Research what life is like for Americans living in India, and discuss the cultural conflicts that these men and women face. Choose one daily Indian ritual that seems alien to you,

and write a short report on the purpose of this ritual, how it got started, and how it has changed over the years.

- Research the varieties of traditional Indian food that are still enjoyed in India today. Create a sample Indian menu that includes several of these foods, and write a short description for each item. Try to come up with at least five items for each major meal course.

- Find another, non-Indian culture from any time in history, which believed women should be subordinate to men. Compare this culture to Indian culture. Find one woman from this other culture who defied this rule, and write a short biography about her.

can wife but feels compelled to be a dutiful son to his Indian mother. This creates the largest conflict of all, because he is unable to be totally supportive of either woman. At the end, Sagar bonds with his wife and family, and Mrs. Dutta realizes that her place is not with her family in America; it is with her friend, Mrs. Basu, in Calcutta.

Roles of Women

The story also explores the roles of Indian women in both India and America. Both Shyamoli and Mrs. Dutta have had arranged marriages, but their respective homes offer them very different environments. In India, women are expected to serve the family, to put their own needs last, and, above all, to be subservient to their husbands and other men. At one point, the narrator notes that ''Mrs. Dutta . . . had never, through the forty-two years of her marriage, addressed Sagar's father by name.'' Also, women are expected to live with a man, not on their own. Mrs. Dutta does live on her own for a few years after her husband's death, but her other relatives do not think this is appropriate and let her know that they are glad that Sagar asked her to come to America: ''Good thing that boy of

hers had come to his senses and called her to join him. Everyone knows a wife's place is with her husband, and a widow's is with her son.''

On the other hand, Indian women who live in the United States, like Shyamoli, often enjoy the freedoms that other American women have. Shyamoli is not subservient to Sagar. She argues with him when she is angry, such as when Mrs. Dutta's behavior attracts negative attention from their neighbor, and says, ''I know having her here is important to you. But I can't do it any longer. I just can't. Some days I feel like taking the kids and leaving.'' Shyamoli does not totally depend on Sagar, either. She has her own job outside of the home and expects Sagar to share the housework with her, a fact that mortifies Mrs. Dutta. Says Shyamoli, ''Here in America we don't believe in men's work and women's work. Don't I work outside all day, just like Sagar?''

Happiness

When Mrs. Dutta became a wife, her own needs were placed below the needs of her husband and family. As a result, her own happiness since then has been measured in terms of how much she is needed by others. When she displeases her son, she is sad, and when her son accepts her offer to make him a snack, ''it is as though merciful time has given her back her youth, that sweet, aching urgency of being needed again.'' When she receives the letter from Mrs. Basu that asks ''Are you happy in America?'' she is unable to answer it right away, because she has conflicting feelings: her duty tells her to serve her family, but her family does not want to be served. ''And so she has been putting off her reply, while in her heart family loyalty battles with insidious feelings of—.'' In this early part of the story, Mrs. Dutta is afraid to acknowledge that by following her duty she is not happy. However, as each attempt to adapt to American life and help her family fails, these feelings of unhappiness get stronger. When she overhears Sagar and Shyamoli talking about her, she realizes that she is unwanted and also that she does not want to be in America. It is only when she casts aside her expected duty that she is able to realize what will truly make her happy— returning to Calcutta.

Style

Setting

The setting is extremely important in this story. The differences between Indian life in India and Indian life in America are profound. Mrs. Dutta, Sagar, and Shyamoli were all born in India, but Sagar and Shyamoli have assimilated American culture, whereas Mrs. Dutta still follows traditional Indian customs. Mrs. Dutta notices this on many occasions. For example, unlike Indian women, Shyamoli expresses her frustrations often. ''Mrs. Dutta did not remember that the Indian Shyamoli, the docile bride . . . pursed her lips in quite this way to let out a breath at once patient and exasperated.'' Also, Shyamoli gives Mrs. Dutta instructions that contradict their mutual Hindu religion. For example, Shyamoli asks Mrs. Dutta to save food that has not been eaten: ''But surely Shyamoli, a girl from a good Hindu family, doesn't expect her to put contaminated *jutha* things with the rest of the food.'' However, Shyamoli, who has become as American as her surroundings, does expect Mrs. Dutta to go against her habits and religious beliefs. In the end, Mrs. Dutta cannot do this and chooses to return to India.

Flashback

The present action in the story consists of a number of events that take place during two days of Mrs. Dutta's stay with her son's family in America. However, this is only half of the story. The other half consists of flashbacks, each of which helps to give the reader more information about a specific aspect of Indian culture, while illustrating the conflict between Indian and American cultures. For example, while Mrs. Dutta is getting ready in the bathroom on the second morning, she hears Mrinalini complaining that Mrs. Dutta has been in the bathroom too long, which Mrs. Dutta thinks is disrespectful. She ''hopes that Shyamoli will not be too harsh with the girl'' and then remembers back to all of the times she had to punish Sagar. ''Whenever she lifted her hand to him, her heart was pierced through and through. Such is a mother's duty.'' When the narrator returns to the present, Shyamoli does not punish Mrinalini, further illustrating the difference between the two cultures.

In several cases, the flashbacks are more recent and take place after Mrs. Dutta has already arrived at her son's house. For example, when Mrs. Dutta is hand-washing her clothes in secret because she is afraid of the American washing machine, she remembers back to the day that she asked Sagar to hang up a clothesline for her so she could wash her own clothes. Shyamoli objected, saying that people do not do that in their neighborhood and told Mrs. Dutta to just store her dirty clothes in a hamper in her room until the end of the week when the family does their laundry. ''Mrs. Dutta agreed reluctantly. She knew she should not store unclean clothes in the same room where she kept the pictures of her gods. That would bring bad luck.''

Imagery

The story also juxtaposes many contrasting images that further help to underscore the conflict between Indian and American cultures. For example, in America, Mrs. Dutta uses ''her metal tongue cleaner'' but does not like ''the minty toothpaste'' that Sagar's family uses, since it ''does not leave her mouth feeling as clean as does the bittersweet neem stick she's been using all her life.'' Other contrasting images include food. When Mrs. Dutta prepares a traditional Indian meal, it is an involved process: ''With practiced fingers she throws an assortment of spices into the blender: coriander, cumin, cloves, black pepper, a few red chiles for vigor. No stale bottled curry powder for her.'' This exotic image contrasts sharply with the ''burritos from the freezer'' that Mrs. Dutta knows her grandchildren would rather eat. Also, when Mrs. Dutta looks out the window of her son's house, where one can stare ''for hours and not see one living soul,'' she offers some images of what life was like in India. She remembers ''vegetable vendors with enormous wicker baskets balanced on their heads,'' ''peasant women with colorful tattoos on their arms,'' and even animals, such as the ''cows that planted themselves majestically in the center of the road, ignoring honking drivers.''

Historical Context

The story was written and takes place in the late 1990s. As a result, the historical context of India in the story is very similar to its current context. In the story, Divakaruni demonstrates the various cultural conflicts faced by Indians who have immigrated to America. But Indians faced similar conflicts in their native land in the late 1990s, which they still face today. In area, India—which is one-third the size of the United States—is the seventh largest country in the world. In population, however, India is the second largest, with more than one billion people. This massive population occupies several distinct ethnic and religious groups. Despite efforts to find some common national identity under which all of these groups can exist in harmony, these groups sometimes clash with each other.

The greatest conflict involves religion. More than 80 percent of India's population is Hindu, and Muslims enjoy a significant percentage of the remaining minority. Hinduism, a religion that is not easily defined, is considered to be one of the oldest religions in the world, if not the oldest. Unlike most religions, it has no founder and has no set doctrine; several different, and sometimes contradictory, religious movements are considered to be part of Hinduism. However, what is known is that Hinduism provided the impetus for India's social caste system, which is thousands of years old and which most Indians conform to, regardless of religion. A caste is a rigid social class, by which people's rights and responsibilities are determined. People are born into their caste and generally are expected to marry within it.

The four traditional castes are the Brahmans (priests), Kshatriyas (warriors), Vaisyas (merchants),

and Shudras (serfs). These caste designations are based on the level of pollutants—such as blood, saliva, dirt, and leather—that people in each caste traditionally come into contact with. A fifth, unofficial, caste, known as the untouchables, is the lowest caste of all, because the members' poor lifestyles and occupations brought them into contact with a high level of pollutants. Although discrimination against members of a lower caste is technically banned, it does still occur today. At the end of the twentieth century, Hindu groups began a massive nationalist movement, placing pressure on non-Hindus to conform to Hinduism. This was confusing to many non-Hindus in India, given Hinduism's relatively indefinable nature. Also, many of the beliefs that are widely identified as belonging to Hinduism, such as the avoidance of contaminants, were already practiced by many non-Hindus. As part of the Hindu nationalist movement, pro-Hindu groups also tried to limit the rights of minorities like Muslims. These collective actions led to violent conflicts between Hindus and Muslims.

In the late 1990s, India also experienced conflict with its neighbors on the Indian subcontinent, most notably Pakistan, a former Indian land that became a new nation when the British sacrificed control of this land in 1947. India and Pakistan, the latter of which is predominantly Muslim, had a long-standing border dispute, dating back to the 1947 emancipation that gave both countries their independence. In 1998, this dispute erupted when India performed nuclear weapons tests, prompting a response from Pakistan, which conducted its own nuclear weapons tests.

Critical Overview

The Unknown Errors of Our Lives, the story collection in which Divakaruni included ''Mrs. Dutta Writes a Letter,'' has received mixed reviews since it was published in 2001. Some, like Frederick Luis Aldama, praise the collection in its entirety. In his review of the collection for *World Literature Today,* Aldama says that the stories ''lyrically describe and breathe life into the lives of South Asian characters.'' Aldama also notes that these characters ''struggle to discover freedom'' in a male-dominated world that seeks to oppress them. Likewise in her *Booklist* review, Donna Seaman says that Divakaruni has ''narrative elegance'' and notes that each story ''revolves around a reflective and strong-willed heroine.'' Seaman thinks that the ''hauntingly beautiful stories of epiphany and catharsis'' have universal appeal and places Divakaruni ''in the vanguard of fine literary writers.''

Not everybody liked the collection, however. ''Divakaruni's stories can verge on melodrama,'' says Sudip Bose, in the *New York Times Book Review*. Furthermore, Bose opines that ''the immigrant experience, at least in the terms Divakaruni considers it, has been mined almost bare in contemporary fiction.'' Because of this, Bose says that Divakaruni's ''reluctant immigrants, forever cursing their alienation, too often seem like characters we've met before.'' However, other reviewers find fault with some of the stories but praise the collection as a whole. The *Publishers Weekly* reviewer notes that it ''is a mixed collection.'' Still, the reviewer says that it is worth a reader's time, since many of the stories ''illuminate the difficult adjustments of women in whom memory and duty must coexist with a new, often painful and disorienting set of standards.'' This reviewer thinks that Divakaruni is ''at her best'' in tales like ''Mrs. Dutta Writes a Letter.'' The reviewer for *Kirkus Reviews* also feels that this story is ''the best piece'' in a collection that the reviewer calls ''solid if unexceptional.'' The reviewer says that ''Mrs. Dutta Writes a Letter'' is ''a touching and simply expressed account of feeling hopelessly lost in an unfamiliar country.''

Criticism

Ryan D. Poquette

Poquette has a bachelor's degree in English and specializes in writing about literature. In the following essay, Poquette discusses Divakaruni's use of letters as plot devices.

''Mrs. Dutta Writes a Letter'' is a relatively static story. Not much action takes place in the present, in which Mrs. Dutta spends a lot of time remembering her past. In the place of a lot of action, the tale relies instead on a plot device, which helps to drive the story forward. The plot device consists of two letters in the story—Mrs. Basu's letter and Mrs.

Dutta's response, the letter that is mentioned in the story's title. If it were not for these two letters, Mrs. Dutta probably would not have come to the same conclusions that she does at the end of the story. The letters become more than simple objects. They disrupt the normal pattern of Mrs. Dutta's life and ultimately force her to question and change her long-held beliefs.

Mrs. Basu's letter and Mrs. Dutta's many potential responses play an important role in the story. Although Mrs. Basu's letter is mostly harmless, ''filled with news from home,'' it also contains a short question: ''At the very bottom Mrs. Basu wrote, *Are you happy in America?*'' For Mrs. Dutta, the answer is not a simple yes or no, because she is in conflict. If she says she is happy, she will be lying to Mrs. Basu, her long-time friend, who will see through the lie. However, if she says she is unhappy, then she will sound as if she is complaining— something that, as a loyal Indian wife, she has been trained not to do. As a result, she has delayed her reply, ''while in her heart family loyalty battles with insidious feelings of—but she turns from them quickly and will not name them even to herself.''

Mrs. Dutta sets the letter aside, but it still preys on her thoughts. The pressure caused by Mrs. Basu's letter and Mrs. Dutta's attempted responses disrupts Mrs. Dutta's life. Mrs. Dutta is normally very religious and takes her Hindu rituals seriously. On the second morning in the story, she lies awake, waiting for the rest of the household to start getting up, which is her cue to start her day. Her first task is to repeat ''the 108 holy names of God.'' She starts doing this but notes that her mind is not totally focused on God this morning. Instead, ''underneath she is thinking of the bleached-blue aerogram from Mrs. Basu that has been waiting unanswered on her bedside table all week.'' Despite her best efforts to suppress her feelings of sadness, Mrs. Dutta is briefly overcome by them when she starts to craft her first mental response to the letter and thinks back to her life in India. ''In her mind she writes to Mrs. Basu: *Oh, Roma, I miss it all so much. Sometimes I feel that someone has reached in and torn out a handful of my chest.*'' However, Mrs. Dutta is still very much attached to her belief that she must not ''indulge in nostalgia,'' and so she ''shakes her head clear of images.''

She crafts her next mental response while she is washing her laundry. However, Mrs. Dutta does not think of telling Mrs. Basu that she is afraid of the

Park Circus in Calcutta, circa 1990

washing machine, which leads to her having to sneak around behind the backs of Sagar and Shyamoli to wash her laundry by hand. She also overlooks the "anxiety" produced from this need to be covert. Instead, she puts a positive spin on the situation: "In her mind she writes to Mrs. Basu: *I'm fitting in so well here, you'd never guess I came only two months back. I've found new ways of doing things, of solving problems creatively.*" Mrs. Dutta does not find anything wrong with her covert laundry behavior. "Ignorance, as Mrs. Dutta knows well from years of managing a household, is a great promoter of harmony." Mrs. Dutta is still focused mainly on following her duty and keeping everybody else happy while ignoring or suppressing her own feelings of anxiety.

This sense of duty is derived from her many years as a subservient wife in India, where she was constantly reminded of what she should and should not do. In fact, when Sagar invites his mother to come and stay with his family, Mrs. Dutta's relatives in India are relieved because they feel this is supposed to happen: "Everyone knows a wife's place is with her husband, and a widow's is with her son." Because of this deeply ingrained sense of duty to her son, Mrs. Dutta scolds herself once again when she starts to remember fondly her life in India.

She tries to make herself believe that she is lucky to be in America and that all of her Calcutta relatives envy her. She tells herself, "*After lunch you're going to write a nice letter to Roma telling her exactly how delighted you are to be here.*" Mrs. Dutta is in the process of doing this when Sagar comes home early that day.

Since Mrs. Dutta still bases her happiness on her ability to serve others, especially her son, she is overjoyed at Sagar's early arrival: "So it is with the delighted air of a child who has been offered an unexpected gift that she leaves her half-written letter to greet Sagar." However, her delight turns to anxiety as she waits to see if Sagar will accept her offer to make him a special Indian snack: "As she waits for his reply, she can feel, in the hollow of her throat, the rapid thud of her heart." When Sagar accepts, all is well, at least for the time being. This changes when Shyamoli comes home, obviously upset about something. Mrs. Dutta, still happy that Sagar was pleased with her act of servitude, looks upon Shyamoli's behavior in a negative manner. "In her mind-letter she writes, *Women need to be strong, not react to every little thing like this.*" As she continues crafting this latest mental response to Mrs. Basu, Mrs. Dutta regurgitates her decades of training, noting, "*we had far worse to cry about, but*

What Do I Read Next?

- Divakaruni's first short-story collection, *Arranged Marriage: Stories* (1995), tells many stories about Indian women who are in traditional, arranged marriages. The stories take place in either India or the United States, but in both cases these women face many challenges as they attempt to reconcile their Eastern heritage with Western ideas.

- Divakaruni was an established poet by the time she started writing short stories and novels. One of her volumes of poetry, *Black Candle* (1991), includes poems about the harsh treatment faced by many women in India, Pakistan, and Bangladesh.

- In Divakaruni's first novel, *The Mistress of Spices* (1997), Tilo is a young Indian woman who ends up on a remote island where she is taught the magical, curative properties of spices. She is sent to Oakland, California, as a spice mistress, destined to live alone while she heals others with her gift. However, when she meets an American man who sees through her old-woman disguise and falls in love with her, she must choose between love and duty.

- Some critics consider E. M. Forster's controversial *A Passage to India* (1924) to be one of the author's greatest novels. The book, which was published in the racially tense times when India was still under British control, examines whether or not it was possible for members of the two cultures to be friends.

- In *Pilgrimage: One Woman's Return to a Changing India* (2000), Pramila Jayapal, an Indian-born, Western-educated woman, describes what it was like for her to live in India for two years after living in the United States for twenty-five years. Her search for a cultural identity reveals an India in conflict, struggling to reconcile its traditional and modern aspects.

- Bharati Mukherjee's novel *Desirable Daughters* (2002) journeys to many locations, including Calcutta and San Francisco, to tell the story of Tara Bhattacharjee and her two sisters. Tara is an Indian woman—separated from her husband—who lives in the United States with her son and boyfriend. When a suspicious stranger shows up one day claiming he is related, Tara discovers secrets that force her to question her knowledge of her family.

---

we shed our tears invisibly. We were good wives and daughters-in-law, good mothers. Dutiful, uncomplaining. Never putting ourselves first.''

However, at this point, the tide starts to turn. Mrs. Dutta remembers a time when she burned a dessert and was punished by her strict mother-in-law. The young Mrs. Dutta had cried after everyone left the house and then ''washed her face carefully with cold water and applied *kajal* to her eyes'' so that her husband would not know she had been crying. She thinks about Shyamoli's own tearful face, and suddenly ''a thought hits her so sharply in the chest that she has to hold on to her bedroom wall to keep from falling.'' This thought, which is crafted as yet another response to Mrs. Basu, is the first real

defiant thought that Mrs. Dutta has had. She has felt sad before, but now she is angry and reflective, wondering if all of the punishment she received was worth it: ''*The more we bent, the more people pushed us, until one day we'd forgotten that we could stand up straight. Maybe Shyamoli's the one with the right idea after all . . .*'' This independent thought shocks Mrs. Dutta, and she tries to bury it and finish writing her letter to Mrs. Basu.

''Then she remembers that she has left the half-written aerogram on the kitchen table.'' This poses a dilemma for Mrs. Dutta. She wants to be respectful and give Sagar and Shyamoli space to talk about whatever is bothering her. But something new, ''a restlessness—or is it defiance?—has taken hold of her.'' She decides that she will retrieve her letter, even if it means interrupting her son's family. Mrs. Dutta is starting to defend her right to be an individual, making decisions that are based not on the family's needs but on her own. In her next mental response to Mrs. Basu, Mrs. Dutta criticizes the amount of television that the family watches and then quickly notes, ''Of course she will never put such blasphemy into a real letter.'' Her duty to herself is still struggling with the duty to her family, although the former is slowly starting to gain ground, because even though she cannot include this thought in a letter yet, ''it makes her feel better to be able to say it, if only to herself.'' This is a huge leap for a woman who felt guilty earlier in the day merely for entertaining the thought that she might be unhappy.

Mrs. Dutta's final leap happens when she overhears the argument that she has caused between Shyamoli and Sagar and sees their shadows reflected on the wall. At the end of the argument, their shadows, and the shadows of their children, ''shiver and merge into a single dark silhouette'' as the family resolves its issues in a group hug. She returns to her room and reads over the happy letter that she has started to write to Mrs. Basu, in which she puts a positive spin on her negative experiences. She starts to cry, and one of her tears falls on her unfinished letter. Bowing to her old habit of hiding her emotions from others, she carefully wipes up the tear. ''She blows on the damp spot until it is completely dry, so the pen will not leave a telltale smudge. Even though Roma would not tell a soul, she cannot risk it.'' Mrs. Dutta is still worried about what her relatives will think if they find out that she is not happy. Then, suddenly, she remembers the silhouette of her son's family and realizes that her duty to her son's family is useless; they are a separate unit that does not need, and does not appreciate, her help. With this newfound knowledge, she is finally able to break the chains of her past servitude, and she writes a new letter to Mrs. Basu, saying that she is coming home to India. ''Pausing to read over what she has written, Mrs. Dutta is surprised to discover this: now that she no longer cares whether tears blotch her letter, she feels no need to weep.''

In the story, Mrs. Dutta makes a rapid transformation over a period of two days. If Mrs. Basu had not written her letter, with its deceptively simple question about happiness, Mrs. Dutta might never have made this change. However, in her many attempts to write an honest response to her friend, Mrs. Dutta is forced to examine all of her long-held beliefs and to be honest with herself about their

> '' She decides that she will retrieve her letter, even if it means interrupting her son's family. Mrs. Dutta is starting to defend her right to be an individual, making decisions that are based not on the family's needs but on her own.''

flaws. In this way, the letters become a plot device. They give the story its narrative structure and provide the catalyst that drives Mrs. Dutta forward through her striking evolution—from a dutiful Indian widow to an independent thinker who puts her own needs first and does not care what others think.

Source: Ryan D. Poquette, Critical Essay on ''Mrs. Dutta Writes a Letter,'' in *Short Stories for Students*, Gale, 2003.

Candyce Norvell

Norvell is an independent educational writer who specializes in English and literature. In this essay, Norvell discusses the unexpected elements in Divakaruni's story that keep it from being entirely predictable.

In its opening pages, ''Mrs. Dutta Writes a Letter'' seems to be a well-written but predictable story of cultural and generational differences. An aging widow moves from her Calcutta home to live with her son and his family in California. Although Mrs. Dutta is already in the United States when the story opens, the early pages are liberally sprinkled with her recollections of life in India. Author Chitra Banerjee Divakaruni evokes Mrs. Dutta's life in India so beautifully and powerfully that even an American-born reader unfamiliar with the country does not merely understand Mrs. Dutta's homesickness but feels it. Mrs. Dutta stares out at her son's silent suburban neighborhood, emptied of humanity and activity on a weekday when everyone is at work or at school. In her mind, she compares the sterile scene to her Calcutta neighborhood, with its vegetable vendors and knife sharpeners (they are tradesmen, not appliances), its menagerie of dogs and goats and cows. There is so much to miss, and so little to take its place.

The pace of the story slows when the narrator begins to explain why Mrs. Dutta washes her clothes in the bathtub and hangs them over the back fence to dry even though her daughter-in-law, Shyamoli, has told her that this is not done in nice American neighborhoods. Divakaruni dwells on this in such detail that the reader knows that this is the conflict on which the story will turn.

And it does, so that right up until the last few pages, the story unfolds in a completely predictable manner. Just as one would expect, Mrs. Dutta's son, Sagar, is patient and solicitous toward her. Just as one would expect, his American-born children speak and behave in ways that she finds shockingly rude. Just as one would expect, his wife tries to be patient with Mrs. Dutta but lets the trying show, and, almost inevitably, it is finally the daughter-in-law who gives her husband an ultimatum about the mother-in-law.

It comes as no surprise that Mrs. Dutta overhears Shyamoli's tirade about her or that Mrs. Dutta then retreats to her room and cries. It is not a surprise, either, that she bravely joins the family at dinner and acts as if all is well, because Divakaruni has drawn her as a stoic woman. Besides, what alternative is there for an old woman who has sold her home and given away her possessions to move to America and be with her family? Her circumstances seem to allow her no choice, and her culture confirms what her circumstances suggest. ''Everyone knows a wife's place is with her husband, and a widow's place is with her son,'' she knew her relatives in India had thought when she told them of her planned move to America.

Of course, life is not that simple, and it is the complications—even familiar, predictable ones—that make a story. Though this particular story of conflict between two cultures and between a mother-in-law and daughter-in-law seems destined for a predictable ending, Divakaruni sneaks a couple of subtle but sweet surprises into her closing pages. These surprises are a delight for two reasons. First, they bring a happier ending for the brave and perceptive Mrs. Dutta than most readers will have dared to hope for. Second, because while they are unexpected, they are not at all artificial or incredible. Mrs. Dutta's surprising outcome illustrates one of the most admirable traits of the Indian character: the inspiring ability and the good-natured willingness to learn even from those who are hurtful or oppressive.

This is the story's first surprise: When Mrs. Dutta overhears her daughter-in-law's harsh words about her, her first reaction, which is to angrily think that Shyamoli should be more stoic, quickly gives way to an epiphany about the stoicism of Mrs. Dutta's generation of Indian women. She thinks:

> And what good did it do? The more we bent, the more people pushed us, until one day we'd forgotten that we could stand up straight. Maybe Shyamoli's the one with the right idea after all.

This is extraordinary. Not many people can, amid the storm of pain and anger that blows through the mind when one is wronged, conclude that perhaps the wrongdoer is right—not right to have caused pain, but right to think as she thinks and live as she lives. Even in the pain of the moment, Mrs. Dutta is able to acknowledge both that Shyamoli was wrong to say the hurtful things she said and that she was right to stand up for herself.

When someone has been hurt, the temptation is to see the person who caused the hurt as being wholly wrong and wholly bad. Mrs. Dutta does not succumb to this temptation. Further, she grasps immediately that she must learn from Shyamoli; she must now stand up for herself as she has seen Shyamoli do for herself. It does not occur to her that if she adopts this one trait of Shyamoli's she will be condoning the younger woman's outburst or the pain it caused. It also does not occur to Mrs. Dutta that if she accepts this one element of American culture she will be abandoning or betraying her own. Virtually all of American culture that she has experienced she judges to be far inferior to her own. She is not about to adopt it wholesale. But Mrs. Dutta is a pragmatist and a survivor. She will take from Shyamoli and from America the good she sees in them, and the rest she will distance herself from without bitterness. This bespeaks a rare kind of wisdom, insight, and maturity.

This mature, sophisticated response is characteristic of India and Indians. It has its roots in Hindu culture and religion, which acknowledge that all ways of life and all human beings are a mixture of good and bad, love and hate, wisdom and ignorance. Some, of course, are better than others, but neither a person nor a culture is to be condemned for imperfection or weakness. The wise course is to absorb the best of all cultures and leave the rest alone; to see the good in all people while protecting oneself from the bad. This is why, after more than three hundred years of unwanted and sometimes brutal British rule, the Indian people, on the whole, do not hate the British. Fifty-plus years ago, Indians won their independence from Great Britain through amazing courage, perseverance, determination, and stoicism—the same strengths that see Mrs. Dutta through her trial. The Indians celebrated the end of British rule, but many Britons remained in India, a land they had come to love and where they were, by and large, welcome to remain. India patterned its government after those of England and America. It made English one of its official languages, for the pragmatic reason that it served as something of a *lingua franca* (a widely understood language that serves as a medium of communication among groups with different native languages) in a nation with hundreds of indigenous languages. What could have been cast out as the language of the oppressor was adopted as a favored language of the new nation, because this served India. Similarly, India recognized the value of the infrastructure the British had built and made use of it to build their country. And today, the average Indian is at least as likely as the average Briton to stop everything at 4 p.m. sharp to enjoy a relaxing cup of tea. It is a British custom that Indians have made their own. All these reflections on India are inspired by old Mrs. Dutta, whose creator, Divakaruni, endowed her with the very best of Indian character and thus equipped her to rise above all the grief, disappointments, and rude awakenings that even mostly predictable lives and stories are all too likely to bring.

There is still one more factor in Mrs. Dutta's willingness to learn from Shyamoli that deserves mention. Mrs. Dutta's cultural background has prepared her to accept wisdom even from an adversary, but it has not prepared her to accept a much younger woman as her teacher. In Hindu families, the daughter-in-law occupies the lowest rank in her husband's extended family, and she is expected to be a humble student of her mother-in-law in all things. Divakaruni instructs American readers in this cultural reality by having Mrs. Dutta recall her relationship with her own mother-in-law. As a seventeen-year-old bride, Mrs. Dutta lived in the home of her husband's family. Her mother-in-law informed her that she was to get up before everyone else and make tea for all in the household. More than once in the course of the story, Mrs. Dutta recalls how her mother-in-law scolded her.

Divakaruni also reveals that the confident American businesswoman Shyamoli was once a shy Indian

> **"** It comes as a shock to Mrs. Dutta that her son's family is complete without her and that they do not need her. But, she absorbs the shock and very quickly figures out how to adjust her expectations and her course."

girl whom Mrs. Dutta prepared for marriage and sent off to her son, already in America. This strongly implies that the marriage was an arranged one, as is traditional in Hindu families. There was a time, then, when Mrs. Dutta held all the power. Back then, Shyamoli did not even have the power to choose the man with whom she would spend her life. Mrs. Dutta's expectation would have been that Shyamoli would live under her roof and under her supervision, as Mrs. Dutta had once lived with her mother-in-law. By tradition, it was Mrs. Dutta's turn to rule the roost.

This background gives non-Indian readers at least a hint of how upside-down Mrs. Dutta's life in California is. Instead of living in her own home and having authority over her daughter-in-law, Mrs. Dutta finds herself living in her daughter-in-law's home, once again in a position of powerlessness. As a young bride, she was forced to get out of bed each morning earlier than she wanted to. Now, as an old woman, she must stay in bed longer than she wants to so that she does not wake the others.

There is nothing in Mrs. Dutta's background that prepared her for this. She is forced to accept Shyamoli's authority in the home and, understandably and not surprisingly, she chafes at this. This makes it all the more remarkable that when crisis comes, Mrs. Dutta is able to acknowledge that, although Shyamoli's authority over her may be illegitimate in her eyes, the younger woman still has something to teach the older one. In addition to the wisdom that her traditions taught her, Mrs. Dutta shows a humility that requires her to reach beyond her traditions. Beyond being an exemplar of Indian wisdom, she is a remarkable individual.

This prepares the reader for Divakaruni's second surprise, which she saves for the very end of the story. Mrs. Dutta is not going to adopt Shyamoli's independent, outspoken spirit merely to carve out a place for herself in her son's house or in American culture. She is going to do what she truly wants to do, in spite of what her son and other relatives will surely think and in spite of having divested herself of her home and possessions. Mrs. Dutta, whose culture and religion have taught her to balance tradition and innovation, is going back to Calcutta to live out her days with her lifelong friend, whose ways are her ways and who both needs and nurtures her more than her closest relatives do. It comes as a shock to Mrs. Dutta that her son's family is complete without her and that they do not need her. But, she absorbs the shock and very quickly figures out how to adjust her expectations and her course.

Still willing to learn and adapt although she is old, Mrs. Dutta has learned what America had to teach her, and she is going home. To readers unfamiliar with Indian culture, this turn of events may seem not just surprising but incredible. Mrs. Dutta might be expected to be too old and frail, too tradition-bound, too weak to stand up to her family after a lifetime of acquiescence. But Mrs. Dutta is none of these things. The same traditions and beliefs that held her in her accepted role for most of her life also allow her to learn new lessons, adopt new ways, and seek happiness. Those traditions and beliefs, combined with her own courage and intelligence, allow her to triumph over all of life's trials, even one as difficult as a sojourn with her family in America.

Source: Candyce Norvell, Critical Essay on ''Mrs. Dutta Writes a Letter,'' in *Short Stories for Students,* Gale, 2003.

Sources

Aldama, Frederick Luis, Review of *The Unknown Errors of Our Lives,* in *World Literature Today,* Vol. 76, No. 1, Winter 2002, pp. 112–13.

Bose, Sudip, Review of *The Unknown Errors of Our Lives,* in *New York Times Book Review,* Vol. 106, No. 26, July 1, 2001, p. 16.

Divakaruni, Chitra, ''Mrs. Dutta Writes a Letter,'' in *The Best American Short Stories 1999,* Houghton Mifflin Company, 1999, pp. 29–47.

Review of *The Unknown Errors of Our Lives,* in *Kirkus Reviews,* February 15, 2001.

Review of *The Unknown Errors of Our Lives,* in *Publishers Weekly,* Vol. 248, No. 11, March 12, 2001, p. 61.

Seaman, Donna, Review of *The Unknown Errors of Our Lives,* in *Booklist,* Vol. 97, No. 13, March 1, 2001, p. 1187.

Further Reading

Arnett, Robert, *India Unveiled,* Atman Press, 1999.
Arnett, a non-Indian who is enamored with India, offers an in-depth discussion of India's geography, people, and culture. The book, which discusses India region by region, includes more than two hundred photographs and seven detailed maps.

Henderson, Carol E., *Culture and Customs of India,* Greenwood Press, 2002.
Henderson's book examines what life is like for the one billion residents of India, who represent hundreds of different social groups. The book includes sections on every major aspect of Indian life, including food and dress; women, marriage, and family; and religion.

Lakhani, Mrs., *Indian Recipes for a Healthy Heart: 140 Low-Fat, Low-Cholesterol, Low-Sodium Gourmet Dishes from India,* Fahil Publishing Company, 1992.
In Divakaruni's story, Shaymoli worries about the high-fat content of the traditional Indian dishes that Mrs. Dutta prepares for Sagar's family. In her cookbook, Mrs. Lakhani shows how the fat content can be cut out of many traditional Indian meals without sacrificing taste. The last section of the book includes information on spice usage and flavor; an explanation of proteins, fats, carbohydrates, and sodium; and the cholesterol differences between raw and cooked foods.

Moorhouse, Geoffrey, *Calcutta,* Harcourt Brace Jovanovich, 1971.
In one of few book-length profiles of Calcutta, Moorhouse discusses the social conditions, people, and politics of this massive city. Although this book is outdated, it does give an idea of what life was like in the city when Mrs. Dutta would have lived there with her husband and son.

The Rockpile

James Baldwin
1965

James Baldwin's "The Rockpile" was first published in 1965 in the author's first and only short-story collection, *Going to Meet the Man*. Critics believe that it may have been written much earlier, when Baldwin was working on his 1953 novel, *Go Tell It on the Mountain*. The short story draws on the same pool of characters from the novel, and the main incident in "The Rockpile" is similar to a scene from the novel. In "The Rockpile," which takes place in Depression-era Harlem, John, the illegitimate son of Elizabeth Grimes, is unable to stop his brother, Roy, from getting into a fight on a rockpile with some other African-American boys. Roy gets hurt, and John gets blamed by his stepfather, although Elizabeth faces her husband and sticks up for John. When the story was first published in the 1960s, America was in the midst of the Civil Rights Movement, in which Baldwin was an active participant. The story addresses the issue of violence between African-American men, the violence inherent in African-American families, and the power of religion in Depression-era Harlem. Most critics consider Baldwin's short stories inferior to his novels, which are in turn considered inferior to his essays. Baldwin's short stories contain many of the same themes he explores in other works and offer a portrait of the artist at various stages of his writing development. A current copy of the story can be found in the paperback version of *Going to Meet the Man*, which was published by Vintage Books in 1995.

Author Biography

James Baldwin, the illegitimate child of Berdis Emma Jones, was born in Harlem, New York, on August 2, 1924. Baldwin was the eldest of nine children and spent much of his time raising his younger brothers and sisters while his mother worked. This helped to shelter Baldwin from the harsh reality of Harlem street life during the Great Depression. Baldwin's stepfather, David Baldwin, was a religious man who ran a storefront church in addition to his day job. David forced his religious practices on all of his children, including the author, who tried unsuccessfully to please him. Failing to receive affection from his overworked mother and emotionally distant stepfather, Baldwin escaped into the world of literature, reading every book he could find. Throughout his public education, his own literary gifts were recognized and encouraged by influential people in his schools.

At fourteen, he underwent an intense religious conversion experience and formed his own ministry, which eventually rivaled his stepfather's church. Baldwin became disillusioned and left the church when he learned about the historical role of Christianity in the slavery of his ancestors. Baldwin moved to New Jersey, where he found work—and a vicious racism that he had not experienced in the mostly African-American community of Harlem. In 1943, Baldwin moved to New York's Greenwich Village, a poor artist community, where he started publishing in magazines and began work on a novel. He met his literary idol, Richard Wright, who helped Baldwin to secure a Eugene F. Saxton Memorial Trust Award, a gift that provides funds to help new writers finish their books. In 1948, Baldwin moved to Paris, where he remained for nearly a decade, only coming home for brief visits. In 1953, Baldwin published his first novel, *Go Tell It on the Mountain*, which drew heavily on the troubled relationship with his stepfather and his profound religious experience. The novel also provided the characters for ''The Rockpile,'' which was published in Baldwin's *Going to Meet the Man* (1965).

By the time Baldwin published this short story collection, the Civil Rights Movement was in full swing, and Baldwin had published a few collections of essays that discussed his own and others' experiences as an African American. These books included *The Fire Next Time* (1963), one of the books that helped Baldwin achieve celebrity status as a civil rights leader. In *Tell Me How Long the Train's Been Gone*, Baldwin addressed the difficulty inherent in trying to be both a celebrity and an artist. During the 1970s, Baldwin focused more on his art, publishing several books. These included a best-selling novel, *If Beale Street Could Talk* (1974). In 1985, Baldwin published *The Price of the Ticket: Collected Nonfiction 1948–1985*. Since the 1940s, Baldwin had lived off and on in France, where he found a greater acceptance of his homosexuality. He eventually settled in St. Paul de Vence, a French countryside town, where he died of stomach cancer on December 1 (some sources say November 30) in 1987.

Plot Summary

''The Rockpile'' begins with a description of the natural rock formation that gives the story its title. The rockpile is located across the street from the apartment of John Grimes and his African-American family. John's half-brother, Roy, plays there sometimes and watches as other African-American boys fight on the rockpile . Elizabeth, John's and Roy's mother, has forbidden them to go near the rockpile, which does not bother John, who is afraid of it. John and Roy have a habit of sitting on their fire escape every Saturday and watching the church-members, whom they consider redeemed, and the others, whom they consider sinners, walk along the street. The neighborhood in which they live is filled with dangers, including the Harlem River, where a boy drowned once.

One Saturday, John and Roy are sitting on the fire escape. John draws a picture while Roy is bored. Some of Roy's friends call for him, and Roy decides to go downstairs, which worries John, who thinks their mother will find out. Roy encourages John not to tell her and then sneaks outside. John becomes absorbed in his drawing and does not look up for a while. When he does, he sees a gang war on the rockpile and watches as Roy, who is at the top of the rockpile, is hit with a tin can—which cuts open his forehead and knocks him to the ground. John tells Elizabeth, and she and her church friend, Sister McCandless, bring Roy back to the apartment and dress his wound. The two women question John, and he tells them that Roy said he would be back in five minutes. This answer is not good enough for McCandless, who suspects that Gabriel, John's stepfather and Roy's father, will be angry with John. McCandless catches Gabriel on the stairs as he is coming home from work and warns him about Roy's injury.

Gabriel comes into the apartment, deeply concerned about Roy, who is his favorite. Roy is upset and begins to cry when he tries to tell Gabriel what happened. Elizabeth tries to explain for Roy, but Gabriel only gets angry with her and teases her about her physical features. He also criticizes her for not watching Roy, although she says that she cannot possibly do all of her chores and keep an eye on Roy, who has a mind of his own. Gabriel then tries to blame John, but Elizabeth sticks up for John and prevents him from getting beaten, telling Gabriel that Roy got his injury because Gabriel spoils him. Gabriel looks at Elizabeth with pure hatred, which scares her. She composes herself and leaves the room.

Characters

James Baldwin

Delilah Grimes

Delilah Grimes is John's half-sister and the second-youngest child of Elizabeth and Gabriel. Elizabeth uses Delilah as a shield to try to ward off Gabriel's aggression towards her.

Elizabeth Grimes

Elizabeth is Gabriel's wife and the mother of John, Roy, Delilah, and Paul. Elizabeth had John out of wedlock with another man and, as a result, Gabriel does not treat his stepson as well as he does his own son, Roy. Elizabeth, like the others, is constantly threatened by Gabriel's violent tendencies, and she nervously awaits her husband's arrival after Roy has been hurt. When Gabriel accuses her of neglecting Roy, she stands up for herself, saying that Roy is stubborn, just like Gabriel, and that she cannot control Roy. She also intervenes on John's behalf, saving him from a potential beating.

Reverend Gabriel Grimes

The Reverend Gabriel Grimes is Elizabeth's husband and the father of Roy, Delilah, and Paul. He is also the stepfather of John, whom he does not treat as well as his own son, Roy. Gabriel makes fun of his wife and John, whom he treats as separate from the other family members. Gabriel has a fiery temper and has instilled in his children an acute awareness of sin. However, he is unable to see that he has spoiled Roy, a fact that encourages Roy to get

into trouble. Gabriel has a violent temper and takes it out through beatings on his family. This fact becomes evident not through the actual beatings, although Elizabeth mentions them, but by the fear that Elizabeth, John, and Roy experience in Gabriel's presence—and in some cases even at the thought of his arrival.

John Grimes

John Grimes is Elizabeth's son, Gabriel's stepson, and the half-brother of Roy, Delilah, and Paul. John was born out of wedlock to Elizabeth when she was with another man. As a result, Gabriel does not treat him as well as he does his other children. John is subject to ridicule about his physical features and his intelligence. John is not as adventurous as Roy and is in fact afraid of Roy's friends and the rockpile on which they fight. John tries to stop Roy from sneaking out to the rockpile, but Roy, although he is younger, has a stronger will than John does. As a result, John is afraid to stop him. When Roy gets hurt, John calls his mother for help and eventually explains to her that he was not able to stop Roy from leaving. Whereas his mother sticks up for John's actions by telling Gabriel that John cannot stop Roy from getting into trouble, Gabriel blames John for letting Roy get hurt. In contrast to Roy's rebellious

Media Adaptations

- Baldwin's *Go Tell It on the Mountain* was adapted as a television movie in 1984 by Learning in Focus. The movie was directed by Stan Lathan and featured Paul Winfield, James Bond III, Alfre Woodard, Ving Rhames, and a cameo role by Baldwin. It is available on VHS from Monterey Home Video.

---

nature, John is the obedient son, doing whatever he is told.

Roy Grimes

Roy Grimes is John's half-brother and the son of Elizabeth and Gabriel. Roy is always looking for trouble and finds it in the rockpile located across the street from their apartment. Although John tries to talk him out of going, Roy sneaks down to go fight on the rockpile and gets cut by a tin can in the process. When Elizabeth and Sister McCandless get Roy back to the apartment, they clean the wound and see that it is a superficial cut but that Roy is close to losing an eye. Roy is frightened at what his father will say, but his father is sympathetic towards Roy—saving his anger for his wife and John.

Sister McCandless

Sister McCandless is Elizabeth's friend and a member of her church. McCandless prepares Gabriel, letting him know that Roy has been injured.

Themes

Violence in Harlem

"The Rockpile" addresses the issue of violence in Harlem. The story explores the issue in two ways. First, it examines violence among community members. In the beginning of the story, the narrator discusses the fights that take place on the rockpile during the afternoons and on Saturdays and Sundays: "They fought on the rockpile. Sure footed, dangerous, and reckless, they rushed each other and grappled on the heights." Later in the story, Roy becomes one of these boys, going over to the rockpile "with his friends." Roy's friends soon clash with another group of boys: "there was a gang fight on the rockpile. Dozens of boys fought each other." While this violence ends in Roy getting a cut above his eye, the damage is not as fierce as that caused by the emotional violence in the story. In the Grimes family, Gabriel rules with an iron fist.

Though his children and wife do receive beatings by his hand, the anticipation and threat of these beatings affects them even more. When Roy is lying on the couch waiting for his father to come in and see that he has been in a fight, Elizabeth notes that Roy is keeping his eyes closed. Yet, Elizabeth knows "that he was not sleeping; he wished to delay until the last possible moment any contact with his father." John is also terrified of Gabriel, his stepfather. "The child stared at the man in fascination and terror." Gabriel reserves his strongest intimidation for his wife. He stares at her, and "she found in his face not fury alone, which would not have surprised her; but hatred so deep as to become insupportable in its lack of personality." Reacting to this hate, Elizabeth, who is holding a child, moves the child as if it is a shield that will protect her from Gabriel.

Responsibility

In the aftermath of Roy's injury, Gabriel and Elizabeth offer different ideas about who is responsible. Gabriel first blames Elizabeth for not watching Roy close enough to prevent him from leaving the apartment. "Lord have mercy," he said, "you think you ever going to learn to do right? Where was you when all this happened? Who let him go downstairs?" Gabriel refuses to admit that Roy is responsible for himself. This is not the case with Elizabeth: "Ain't nobody let him go downstairs, he just went. He got a head just like his father, it got to be broken before it'll bow." Next, Gabriel tries to blame John, his stepson, for not stopping Roy from leaving or telling Elizabeth that Roy left. When John remains silent to Gabriel's questions, Gabriel threatens to whip him. It is at this point that Elizabeth sticks up for John and places the blame for Roy's accident squarely on Gabriel's shoulders. "Ain't a soul to blame for Roy's lying up there now but you—you

Topics for Further Study

- On a street map of New York, outline Harlem as it existed during the Great Depression. Using the geographic clues in the story, plot the Grimes house, the rockpile, the area where Richard's son drowned, and any other events or locations that you can identify from the story's descriptions.

- In the story, the Grimes family lives in a tenement apartment. Research how many African Americans lived in houses, apartments, and other types of housing developments in Harlem during the Great Depression and the Civil Rights Movement of the 1960s. Plot both sets of statistics on a chart or graph, and discuss the housing trends between the two time periods.

- Research the number of illegitimate African-American children in Harlem during the Great Depression, as compared to the number of illegitimate African-American children today. Write a profile of one famous illegitimate African American—other than James Baldwin.

- Research the psychology of violence, and map out the areas of the brain that cause it. Also, research any disorders or diseases that tend to increase violence in a person, and give a thorough description of each one. Finally, research the standard techniques used in a modern anger-management class, and give a short presentation about these techniques.

---

because you done spoiled him so that he thinks he can do just anything and get away with it.''

Religion

The story is saturated with religious references. Religion is not a comforting or joyful presence in the Grimes household or in the neighborhood in which they live. Instead, it is something to be feared and obeyed. Gabriel is a reverend, and he has raised his children to be God-fearing individuals. As a result, they see the world in extremes of people who are saved and people who are sinners. When John and Roy are sitting on the fire escape, they look down to the street, where ''below them, men and women, and boys and girls, sinners all, loitered.'' These people are contrasted with the churchgoers, ''the redeemed,'' who will sometimes wave to the sinners, unnerving them. ''Then, for the moment that they waved decorously back, they were intimidated.'' Religion is also used as a threat. When Elizabeth criticizes Gabriel for spoiling Roy, she warns her husband that he needs to seek God's help before it is too late: ''You don't pray to the Lord to help you do better than you been doing, you going to live to shed bitter tears that the Lord didn't take his soul today.''

Style

Setting

The setting is very important in the story. Since the early twentieth century until the time that Baldwin wrote the story, Harlem had one of the most concentrated areas of African Americans. Among these residents, violence was common, especially during the years of the Great Depression when this story takes place. In these lean times, tempers flared more easily among African-American males, even the boys who are depicted in the story. The physical setting is important for two other reasons. The Grimes's apartment building is located across the street from a large rockpile, which is essential for setting up Roy's injury. Since the rockpile is in sight of the Grimes's fire escape, Roy watches others fight there and yearns to go fight himself: ''Roy shifted impatiently, and continued to stare at the street, as though in this gazing he might somehow acquire wings.'' If the rockpile were not right in view of Roy, taunting him with its forbidden quality, he might not have been motivated to go fight. Finally, the story takes place near the Harlem River, in which an African-American boy drowned.

Imagery

The imagery in the story underscores the violence theme of the story. From the very beginning, the story offers several examples, real or imagined, of violent events. John's Aunt Florence, when explaining why the alien rockpile is still on the empty lot, concocts a violent story. She ''had once told them that the rock was there and could not be taken away because without it the subway cars underground would fly apart, killing all the people.'' When Roy and the other boys fight on the rockpile, their fight is depicted in the violent images of boys ''clambering up the rocks and battling hand to hand, scuffed shoes sliding on the slippery rock.'' The boys ''filled the air, too, with flying weapons: stones; sticks, tin cans, garbage, whatever could be picked up and thrown.'' When Gabriel tries to touch Roy's wound, Roy recoils, suddenly remembering the image of his fall—''the height, the sharp, sliding rock beneath his feet, the sun, the explosion of the sun, his plunge into darkness and his salty blood.'' In addition to the violent images, the story also offers one chilling image of a child's death, as if to emphasize the frailty of a child's life in Harlem. The image comes after a little boy has drowned in the river. The boy's father, Richard, carries his dead son through the neighborhood: ''Richard's father and Richard were wet, and Richard's body lay across his father's arms like a cotton baby.''

Symbolism

The story also contains several symbols. A symbol is a physical object, action, or gesture that also represents an abstract concept, without losing its original identity. Most of the symbols in the story are local, meaning that their abstract meaning is dependent upon the context of the story. For example, the rockpile is physically a rock formation. In the way that it is depicted in the story, the hard rocks and the fights that take place there become symbols for the hard struggles faced by African Americans in the Harlem ghetto. The rock is ''slippery,'' making it hard for the children to get a stable foothold, just as it is hard for them to get a stable foothold in their lives in the Harlem ghetto. It represents a challenge to the boys, something that needs to be conquered. Boys fight to reach the top, as Roy does, where they can declare themselves king of the mountain. This is similar to the social struggle that these African-American boys will face all of their adult lives, fighting with their brethren

for food, homes, and other resources needed for their survival. Although the boys fight there most days, the rockpile is never affected, and nobody ever wins the fights. Inevitably, one of the boys will get hurt, as Roy does with the tin can: ''Immediately, one side of Roy's face ran with blood, he fell and rolled on his face down the rocks.'' The boys then run away and keep their distance for a while, but they will soon come back to fight again. It is the pattern of their boyhood, and it will continue to be the pattern of their hard adult lives.

Other symbols in the story include Gabriel's hands and feet, which become potential weapons in the way that Elizabeth views them: ''John stood just before him, it seemed to her astonished vision just below him, beneath his fist, his heavy shoe.'' The description of the shoe as ''heavy,'' coupled with the image of Gabriel as an ''enormous'' man, makes the shoe seem dangerous, like it might be used to crush John. In fact, Baldwin elaborates on this symbol in the last sentence of the story: John bends to pick up his father's lunchbox, ''bending his dark head near the toe of his father's heavy shoe.'' Here, the symbol becomes more focused. When people kick something, they generally lead with their toe. John's head near Gabriel's toe sets up the apprehension in Elizabeth, and the reader, that Gabriel, who has illustrated his tendency towards violence, is entirely capable of kicking John in the head.

Historical Context

Harlem during the Great Depression

The Great Depression was one of the largest tragedies of the twentieth century, and it affected a wide range of people. When the stock market crashed in 1929, the mainly African-American population assumed that this was a white problem, since African Americans in the Harlem ghetto did not typically own stocks. As it turned out, the people of Harlem were the hardest hit in New York. During the Great Depression, many unskilled workers were laid off or had their wages cut. Because the majority of African-American workers were unskilled, they were seriously affected. In addition, before the depression, many African Americans had worked in low paid, working-class positions that white people did not want. Therefore, many African Americans had some degree of job security. As the unemployment rate increased during the 1930s, many of these traditionally African-American positions were given to whites. This was a sign of the racism and discrimination that was still inherent in the United States more than fifty years after the Civil War.

Buildings

Some of the discrimination in Harlem was in pricing. As more African Americans moved into Harlem, white building owners charged increasingly exorbitant rents. To pay the higher rents, many families moved in together or took in boarders to help shoulder the rent load. As a result, the population continued to swell, and the buildings became dilapidated from overuse and lack of repairs. While the people in Harlem got poorer, not too far away the rich were getting richer. Even during the depression, when most of the country was struggling to make ends meet, signs of enormous wealth were being erected south of Harlem, in the Manhattan business district. The proximity of the massive skyscrapers, including the new Chrysler and Empire State Buildings—completed in 1930 and 1931, respectively—were further evidence of the divide between the haves and the have-nots.

Riots

A combination of factors—discrimination, joblessness, high rents, overcrowding, and obvious signs of inequality—helped to enrage the Harlem residents, who often took out their aggressions on each other. On one notable occasion, March 19, 1935, the violence turned into a riot against whites. A Harlem boy was caught stealing a small knife from a white-owned store. The boy fought with the staff, hit a clerk, and ended up being taken away by the police, although he was later released. Bystanders spread wild rumors that the boy had been beaten or killed, and these rumors got worse when an ambulance arrived to help the injured clerk and when an unrelated hearse parked by the store. Harlem residents swarmed the streets, breaking windows, looting, and attacking city buses, while police tried to break up the disturbance. In the process, three African Americans were killed, two hundred were wounded, and millions of dollars' worth of property damage was done to the city. Following the riot, New York Mayor Fiorello La Guardia commissioned a biracial study of the causes of the riot. The study results underscored the economic and social problems in Harlem, and the mayor and others worked to build more housing and reduce the racism among police and others.

The Civil Rights Movement

Despite these efforts and advances, conditions in Harlem—and in other African-American communities—continued to deteriorate over the next few decades. It is unclear whether Baldwin completed "The Rockpile" in the 1950s when he wrote *Go Tell It on the Mountain* or finished it in the 1960s prior to its publication in *Going to Meet the Man*. In any case, over these two particular decades, civil rights became an increasingly important issue. Court cases and legislation reinforced the growing trend of desegregation and imposed bans on discrimination, and many African Americans in Harlem and elsewhere organized boycotts and nonviolent protests. Not all protests were peaceful, however. On July 16, 1964, a white police officer shot and killed a fifteen-year-old African-American boy. The combined New York chapters of the Congress of Racial Equality (CORE) sponsored a peaceful protest of the death, which resulted in violence between the protesters and police. The situation quickly turned into a riot, which spread to other parts of New York City.

Critical Overview

"The Rockpile" was first published in *Going to Meet the Man* (1965), a short-story collection that has received mixed reviews. In 1965, in the *Saturday Review,* Daniel Stern praised the collection, calling the short stories "closer in spirit, tone, and achievement to his best critical work than it is to his 'sensational' fiction. These are stories beautifully made to frame genuine experience in a lyrical language." On the other hand, in his 1965 *New Republic* review, Joseph Featherstone says that the collection is "problematic" and notes, "There are no resolutions here, no new departures." Likewise, in 1966, in *Partisan Review,* Stephen Donadio says that the stories "add nothing to Mr. Baldwin's stature, nor do they diminish it by much." However, a decade later, in 1975, in his review for *Studies in Short Fiction,* William Peden calls the book "the most important single short story collection" since the Harlem Renaissance, referring to the 1920s in Harlem, when there was an explosion of artistic output from African-American writers. In his 1978 entry on Baldwin for *Dictionary of Literary Biography,* Fred L. Standley gives the stories high praise, saying that they "indicate clearly the influence of Henry James." Standley also notes that

Compare
&
Contrast

- **1930s:** In 1935, Harlem erupts in a riot when an African-American mob falsely believes that an African-American boy has been beaten or killed by a white storeowner.

  1960s: In 1964, Harlem erupts in a riot when a black schoolboy is shot and killed by a white police officer in Yorkville, New York. The incident inspires riots in one other New York city and three New Jersey cities. More than two hundred other race-related riots break out from 1965 to 1968 in various cities around the United States, including Detroit and Los Angeles.

  Today: In 1992 in Los Angeles, a bystander catches an apparent act of police brutality on videotape, which he then sells to the press. In the resulting court case, a mainly white jury acquits the four white police officers of the beating of Rodney King, an African-American motorist. This verdict enrages many ethnic groups in South Central Los Angeles, including African Americans and Latin Americans, and they subsequently begin rioting in many areas of Los Angeles.

- **1930s:** Joe Louis, an African-American boxer, becomes a symbol of pride and inspiration to many Harlem residents, who cheer his long and successful career. While African Americans experience racism in many forms, even some white people are fans of Louis. When Louis is drafted into the military, he is given the same cold reception that other African Americans receive.

1960s: Following the enormous success in the 1940s of Jackie Robinson—professional baseball's first African-American player—other professional sports experiment with integration, including football, tennis, and basketball. Boxing continues to include African Americans, and one of the most celebrated boxers in the twentieth century, Muhammad Ali, fights during this decade.

Today: The majority of the athletes in certain sports, most notably professional basketball, are African Americans. For some inner-city youths, a basketball career becomes a way to transcend their class and get out of the ghetto.

- **1930s:** During the Great Depression, most African-American families in Harlem live a poor existence, barely making enough money to buy food and essentials, much less entertainment and other auxiliary expenses.

  1960s: Many poor African Americans in Harlem use credit plans to buy luxury items like radios, televisions, and cars. By committing most of their future wages to current luxuries, these residents commit themselves to a life of debt. This prevents them from acquiring enough capital to buy real estate and make other investments that could help them transcend their class or move to different communities.

  Today: Excessive credit debt is a problem among all races and classes in the United States.

"the stories reflect the range of Baldwin's early thematic interests and demonstrate a realistic sense of personal experiences." Finally, in his 1978 book, *James Baldwin,* Louis H. Pratt says, "These stories attempt to probe directly into the essence of the black experience in the United States and to expose the myths and the realities which lie at the root of that experience."

While the reviews of the collection are mixed, the discussion of "The Rockpile" is almost nonex-

istent. The critics who have talked about the story do so in comparison to Baldwin's first novel, *Go Tell It on the Mountain,* since the two works contain similar characters, themes, and events. In his 1979 entry on Baldwin for *American Writers,* Keneth Kinnamon notes, "'The Rockpile' and 'The Outing' clearly belong to the body of autobiographical material out of which *Go Tell It on the Mountain* comes." Standley says that the two stories "strongly resemble" the novel, whereas Donadio thinks that the entire collection represents ''the author's progress'' as a writer and considers ''The Rockpile'' and ''The Outing'' as ''halting first steps toward the first novel.'' In his 1977 essay for *James Baldwin: A Critical Evaluation,* Harry L. Jones is even more blunt. His essay examines the short stories in *Going to Meet the Man* but deliberately chooses not to discuss ''The Rockpile'' or ''The Outing.'' Jones feels they ''are obviously culls or unused remnants from *Go Tell It on the Mountain* and ought best to be considered in connection with that work. They will not, therefore, be discussed here.''

In fact, one of the only critics to discuss ''The Rockpile'' in detail is Carolyn Wedin Sylvander. In her 1980 book, *James Baldwin,* she too compares the short story to *Go Tell It on the Mountain.* However, Sylvander conducts an analysis of the differences between the two works and notes that the major event in ''The Rockpile''—Roy's injury— is similar to one of the scenes in the novel, where Roy also gets hurt. Beyond this similarity, Sylvander finds several ''significant'' differences between the two works. These include the fact that John is not present when Roy has his injury in the novel and so has no responsibility, whereas in the short story he is there when Roy gets injured. Sylvander also notes that in the novel, Roy fights white boys, but in the short story, he fights African-American boys.

Criticism

Ryan D. Poquette

Poquette has a bachelor's degree in English and specializes in writing about literature. In the following essay, Poquette compares Baldwin's story to his novel Go Tell It on the Mountain.

When Baldwin published his first and only short story collection in 1965, it included two stories— ''The Rockpile'' and ''The Outing.'' Most critics note that these two stories share similar aspects with the author's 1953 novel, *Go Tell It on the Mountain.* Some critics, like Harry L. Jones in his essay for *James Baldwin: A Critical Evaluation,* find these similarities to be proof that the stories should only be discussed in conjunction with the novel. Says Jones, they ''are obviously culls or unused remnants from *Go Tell It on the Mountain* and ought best to be considered in connection with that work.'' However, this is a misconception, especially in the case of ''The Rockpile.'' Despite the similarities

between this short story and its corresponding scene in the novel, the differences between the two works highlight the unique purpose of each one.

It certainly appears that Baldwin wrote ''The Rockpile,'' or at least its initial draft, during the process of writing *Go Tell It on the Mountain.* The story is more than just a ''halting first step'' in the process of writing this novel, as Stephen Donadio calls it in *Partisan Review.* If Baldwin considered the story to be a mistake, he most likely would not have included it twelve years later in a collection. The short story has its own merits, which become apparent when one reads ''The Rockpile'' and compares it to the corresponding scene depicting Roy's injury in the novel. As Carolyn Wedin Sylvander says in her book, *James Baldwin,* the differences between the two works ''are significant.'' Sylvander notes several, including the fact that Roy fights with other African Americans in the short story, whereas in the novel he fights with white boys; the fact that the fight takes place across the street in the short story and across town in the novel; and the fact that John has responsibility for Roy in the short story and is not responsible for Roy's action in the novel.

In addition to the differences pointed out by Sylvander, more differences are apparent when readers examine the two works in even greater detail. The short story draws attention to its immediate surroundings with the first sentence: ''Across the street from their house, in an empty lot between two houses, stood the rockpile. It was a strange place to find a mass of natural rock jutting out of the ground.'' As the story continues, this hard rockpile becomes symbolic of the violence that takes place there and of the harsh lives that the African-American boys face—and will face in the future. The entire story, with its limited setting, has a confining feel, which emphasizes the trapped quality of life in Harlem during the Great Depression. The novel scene, on the other hand, does not have a specific, isolated setting. Instead, it starts out with a more open feeling: ''As John approached his home again in the late afternoon, he saw little Sarah, her coat unbuttoned, come flying out of the house.'' John is coming home from another part of the city, which implies that he is not confined to the immediate area of his street.

Also, in the novel, John does not see Roy's fight. Sarah's actions tip John off to the fact that something is wrong, but he only finds out about the fight when Sarah says, ''Roy got stabbed with a

What Do I Read Next?

- Most critics believe that Baldwin's best works were his essays. In *The Fire Next Time* (1963), published during the Civil Rights movement, Baldwin wrote extensively about his own adolescence, which mirrored the experiences of John Grimes in "The Rockpile" and *Go Tell It on the Mountain*. The two essays in this book collectively discuss the racial relations between African Americans and whites and note that the two races are ultimately inseparable.

- Unlike his other works, including "The Rockpile," Baldwin's novel *Giovanni's Room* (1956) features all white characters. David, an engaged man and a homosexual, struggles to find his sexual identity and reconcile his troubled family past while living abroad in Paris.

- Ralph Ellison's classic novel about race, *Invisible Man* (1952), chronicles the experiences of a young, nameless African-American man. Through his travels north to New York City and several misguided attempts to find his identity, the man realizes that he will always be invisible to white people. He also realizes that African Americans are on a self-destructive path that they cannot see.

- In George M. Fredrickson's book *Racism: A Short History* (2002), the author gives a brief overview of modern racist attitudes, which he believes were developed from medieval anti-Semitism. Fredrickson also examines and compares various racial institutions, including American Jim Crow laws, Nazi Germany's persecution of the Jews, and South Africa's apartheid regime.

- *Their Eyes Were Watching God* (1937), by Zora Neale Hurston, drew criticism from other African-American writers like Richard Wright, who felt the book's thick dialect stereotyped African Americans. The novel concerns the life of an African-American woman who searches for her identity while living in the South. Modern-day readers credit Hurston's accurate portrayals of the lives of African Americans—especially women—in this time.

- Richard Wright's *Native Son* (1940), another classic novel about race, concerns the story of Bigger Thomas, a young African-American man in 1930s Chicago. The racism and poverty that he experiences lead to his unintentional murder of a white woman, and he finds that no one—even the liberal men and women who champion racial equality—is able to help him. Baldwin criticized this novel for its stereotypical portrayal of African Americans, an act that forever severed the friendship with Wright, his idol.

---

knife!'' In the short story, however, John is trapped at his house and has no choice but to see Roy's fight. As a result, the story offers an in-depth depiction of the fight from John's perspective: "Dozens of boys fought each other in the harsh sun. . . . filling the bright air with curses and jubilant cries.'' The story goes on to describe Roy's ascension to the top of the rockpile and his subsequent injury and fall. By doing this, the story places extra emphasis on the fight itself, underscoring the brutality of Harlem's African Americans towards each other. In the novel, the fight with the white boys takes place outside of the narration and is barely described. Violence between whites and African Americans had been going on for centuries, so nothing was special about a simple stabbing. As a result, Baldwin does not give the incident extra importance through heavy description. Aggression against one's own, however, was a disturbing trend that the pressures of Harlem ghetto life helped to increase. Since African Americans were packed into overcrowded, overpriced houses and were constantly subject to discrimination and persecution from the outside world, the isolation of a community like Harlem sometimes led to residents taking out their aggressions against each other.

Even the weapons used in the fight indicate a difference in focus on life outside Harlem as opposed to life inside. A knife is inherently a weapon, especially the kind of fighting knife that the white boys most likely used to cut Roy. As a result, the use of a knife to stab Roy in the novel does not come as a surprise to Baldwin's readers, many of whom were white. A tin can—the ''weapon'' that Roy gets cut with in the story—is not inherently a weapon at all. The fact that Roy is hurt by what is essentially a piece of garbage indicates the poverty faced by African-American people in the story. They cannot even afford weapons, and so must use ''stones, sticks, tin cans, garbage, whatever could be picked up and thrown.''

Although ''The Rockpile'' and its corresponding scene in *Go Tell It on the Mountain* share the same incident, some of the same characters, and similar themes, they are really two different stories. For this reason, it makes sense that Baldwin chose not to include ''The Rockpile'' version in his novel. The novel focuses on John's quest to find his identity and faith. As a result, the scene with Roy's stabbing is minimized, and more emphasis is placed on the relations between African Americans and whites—a consistent theme throughout the novel. In the short story, however, the main issue is one of violence, specifically among African Americans. This violence is largely due to the discriminatory treatment that African Americans have faced at the hands of whites, a fact that is not emphasized in the story.

So why would Baldwin decide not to publish this short story until the mid-1960s, when it was most likely written much earlier? By examining the historical context of the 1950s and 1960s, one can offer a potential reason. In the 1950s, at the beginning of the Civil Rights Movement, many African-American leaders spoke out against injustices and violence they faced at the hands of whites. With its offhand and minimal description of Roy's fight with the white boys, the novel underscores this feeling, making it seem like the incident is just one of many.

In the short story, on the other hand, African Americans take out their aggressions on each other, and Baldwin gives the incident a significant amount of description. Violence among African Americans was not a fact that Baldwin or others would have wanted to publicize to the white community during the early part of the Civil Rights Movement in the 1950s. To do so would have been to reinforce the stereotype of African Americans as savages and

> The fact that Roy is hurt by what is essentially a piece of garbage indicates the poverty faced by African-American people in the story."

would thus have undercut the ability of African Americans to be treated as equals with whites. Because of this realization, during the 1950s and early 1960s, African Americans focused primarily on nonviolent methods of protest. However, by the mid-1960s when Baldwin published ''The Rockpile,'' there had been a profound split in the ranks of African Americans. While some still pursued a nonviolent approach, an increasing number of African Americans did not think this was effective enough and began to favor other, more violent approaches. It could be that this story is a warning to other African Americans that violence is not the right answer and can only lead to harm in one's own community. By isolating the African Americans in the story, the author shows them to be ultimately responsible for their own actions—and their own destruction.

Source: Ryan D. Poquette, Critical Essay on ''The Rockpile,'' in *Short Stories for Students,* Gale, 2003.

Trudier Harris

In the following essay excerpt, Harris examines connections and differences in characterization between Baldwin's ''The Rockpile'' and Go Tell It on the Mountain.

''The Rockpile'' shares several parallels with *Go Tell It on the Mountain*, but it also deviates from the novel in its portrayal of the character of Elizabeth. The story recounts in concentrated detail the incident of Roy's fight and injury which, in the novel, takes place on the Saturday of John's birthday. Baldwin apparently found the story form too constricting in what it allowed him to accomplish in the development of Gabriel's character as well as Elizabeth's. They both have features similar to those they have in the novel, but the background information on how they came to be as they are cannot be handled very effectively within the story. For example, Gabriel is presented as an angry man, but we can only speculate on the causes of his anger. Elizabeth, obviously frightened of Gabriel, similarly lacks the extensive background that would make her interaction with him clearer. As the story is written, the lines of sympathy are drawn, but they are not as clear as they are in the novel. Because Gabriel is left fumbling at the end of the story, instead of performing a conclusive act such as the slapping in the novel, we are also left hanging. We have only been told that Gabriel is a villain; we have not seen any action in the story that would convince us of that. Therefore, there is no conclusive reaction to Gabriel as the authoritarian controller of his family that he is implied to be. The novel makes motivation clearer, sets up an uncluttered division of sympathies, and brings a conclusive resolution to the scene. The story is left at a level of frustration in which extraneous factors are allowed to obscure Gabriel's true personality.

We get two pieces of evidence that let us know that religion is prominent in the lives of the characters and that therefore allow us to judge what they do and say against what they profess to be. First of all, Sister McCandless is visiting the household when the injury to Roy occurs. The fact that she is ''Sister'' McCandless lets us know that she is connected to a church, and the fact that she is visiting Elizabeth lets us know that these are active members of the church. Second, after the injury but before Gabriel's arrival on the scene, Sister McCandless refers to him as ''the Reverend.'' We now know that this is the preacher's house the good sister is visiting and, from what our experiences have told us about preachers, we expect a tolerant if not an unqualifiedly good man (we already have indications from John's and Roy's reaction that Gabriel is strict); her tone, however, leaves enough ambivalence for us to perhaps anticipate revising our initial expectations.

In contrast to Elizabeth, who is presented as a concerned mother, though not a frightening one, Gabriel is presented as a frowner upon enjoyment who will come home early this Saturday and ''end'' the boys' freedom of sitting on the fire escape; he is a force of disapproval, from the boys' point of view, from the very first paragraphs of the story. No longer mired in the soapsuds washing image we last have of her before Roy's injury in *Go Tell It on the Mountain*, in the story Elizabeth leaves Roy and John on the fire escape to go into the kitchen ''to sip tea with Sister McCandless.'' Roy slips away to the rockpile across the street, where the fight will shortly occur.

Two differences in Elizabeth's portrayal are relevant here. First, the oppressive routine of work is momentarily lifted. No matter how well earned the break, that moment of seeming idleness could support, from Gabriel's point of view, the idea that Elizabeth is negligent of her children. She has gone to ''sip'' tea, which has sociability and lightheartedness as its connotations, not responsibility. Though she has warned her sons, especially Roy, of the dangers involved in playing on the rockpile, and has witnessed the dangerous play, she has left them in a tempting position while she tends her company. That is the kind of case Gabriel could make against her, because he disapproves of his sons sitting on the fire escape. Second, Elizabeth's realm of action in the incident is extended beyond the apartment; she and Sister McCandless run out to meet the man who picks up Roy after his injury. The action simultaneously increases her concern and heightens the guilt that Gabriel can use against her. She runs out in panic, with Sister McCandless behind her panting ''Don't fret, don't fret.'' Elizabeth is ''trembling'' when she tries to take Roy, so the ''bigger calmer'' Sister McCandless takes him instead. Though the man keeps emphasizing that Roy's injury is ''just a flesh wound,'' that it ''just broke the skin, that's all,'' Elizabeth is frantic. Her reaction borders on hysteria, in sharp contrast to the more stoic Elizabeth in *Go Tell It on the Mountain*.

The near hysteria has as its base an ever-present fear of Gabriel. Elizabeth is almost paralyzed into inactivity because of feelings of guilt probably induced by Gabriel's previous accusations and the anticipated resurgence of guilt once Gabriel arrives on the scene. Her fear combines with the comment that the boys see Gabriel as an end to their freedom to suggest that Gabriel is a terror who makes his entire family uncomfortable; he does so by evoking feelings in them which control certain parts of their behavior even in his absence. Although the scar is ''jagged,'' which would suggest an injury more serious than is the case, it is also ''superficial''; yet Elizabeth murmurs, ''Lord, have mercy . . . another inch and it would've been his eye.'' That line belongs to Gabriel later in ''The Rockpile'' and in *Go Tell It on Mountain*, where he exaggerates the wound in order to underscore Elizabeth's presumed negligence. Even as she makes the comment, she looks ''with apprehension'' toward the clock, knowing that Gabriel will be home shortly and that she will be held accountable no matter what her degree of responsibility.

Elizabeth's actions show that roles and expectations are more important to Gabriel than people. He values her primarily as the mother of his children, especially of Roy. She is expected to cook and clean for them, to protect them, and to know their whereabouts at all times. If she fails in her role, she must endure the consequences. Her nervous actions before Gabriel's arrival illustrate that she is perfectly aware and fearful of those consequences. She asks Sister McCandless "nervously" if Roy is going to keep the scar. The woman's response reveals a lot about Elizabeth and about Gabriel: "'Lord, no,' said Sister McCandless, 'ain't nothing but a scratch, I declare, Sister Grimes, you worse than a child. Another couple of weeks and you won't be able to *see* no scar. No, you go on about your housework, honey, and thank the Lord it weren't no worse.' She opened the door; they heard the sound of feet on the stairs. 'I expect that's the Reverend,' said Sister McCandless, placidly, 'I *bet* he going to raise cain.'"

The guilt that both Elizabeth and John feel causes them to realize that, blameworthy or not, they will both be implicated in Roy's injury. That realization comes out in John's declaration to Elizabeth that Roy's crossing the street to the rockpile was not "my fault" and his sense that Elizabeth's response that he "ain't got nothing to worry about" does not bring the comfort it should. It could be speculated, in fact, that John is somewhat taken aback by his mother's rather placid response; he looks at her in a direct, questioning way, but she turns to look out the window. From past experiences, both Elizabeth and John know that Roy is Gabriel's "heart" and that injury to him is a personal affront to Gabriel. They have both apparently been made to feel that they are intruders who are suffered but not loved, tolerated but not valued. And they have both been taught to know that the fault is within themselves, that they are somehow guilty and must suffer whatever befalls them. Elizabeth's guilt probably derives from John's illegitimacy, but John himself is unaware of that fact. From nuances of speech, however, and definitely from Gabriel's actions, John knows that he is not the favored child. In his own defense, therefore, he can only plead his case to Elizabeth, who can offer no appreciable comfort because she continually sees her own unworthiness and guilt reflected in John's actions and mannerisms, in his mere presence. John becomes inarticulate and visibly invisible in ways that are

> "It is easy to see why Baldwin rewrote the story. It lacks dramatization of Gabriel's fury, and it is inconsistent in the development of Elizabeth's character."

parallel to the anguish Elizabeth herself feels when confronting her husband.

The same tension between John and Gabriel exists here as in *Go Tell It on the Mountain*—or perhaps it is more visible here, since Gabriel literally frightens John into speechlessness—and Elizabeth understands in both instances, but Gabriel refuses to in either. Without Florence's presence, however, the scene with Gabriel is anti-climactic. Standing up to Gabriel and forcing him to place responsibility where it belongs, Elizabeth changes character and becomes much more assertive than her trembling nerves suggested earlier. Her interruptions of Gabriel's questions to Roy and her continuing refusal to be quiet show an Elizabeth who contrasts too directly with the character we have seen earlier in the story:

"How you feel, son? Tell your Daddy what happened?"

Roy opened his mouth to speak and then, relapsing into panic, began to cry. His father held him by the shoulder.

"You don't want to cry. You's Daddy's little man. Tell your Daddy what happened."

"He went downstairs," said Elizabeth, "where he didn't have no business to be, and got to fighting with them bad boys playing on that rockpile. That's what happened and it's a mercy it weren't nothing worse."

He looked up at her. "Can't you let this boy answer for hisself?"

Ignoring this, she went on, more gently: "He got cut on the forehead, but it ain't nothing to worry about?"

"You call a doctor? How you know it ain't nothing to worry about?"

"Is you got money to be throwing away on doctors? No, I ain't called no doctor. Ain't nothing wrong with my eyes that I can't tell whether he's hurt bad or not.

He got a fright more'n anything else, and you ought to pray God it teaches him a lesson.''

''You got a lot to say *now*,'' he said, ''but I'll have *me* something to say in a minute. I'll be wanting to know when all this happened, what you was doing with your eyes *then*.''

Tensions underlying this relatively controlled conversation have their basis far beyond the incident itself. Gabriel, who has been presented as a destroyer of freedom and a creator of nervous tension in his wife, is all of a sudden a caressing, considerate father who desperately tries to soothe his injured son. The posture is not inconsistent because we know, through Elizabeth, that John is illegitimate and that Roy is Gabriel's oldest son. Gabriel, who wants to show love at this point, is unaccustomed to doing so; he therefore sounds gruff and inadequate, and his efforts at soothing only increase Roy's crying panic. It is only with Elizabeth's assistance that he is able to take the bandage from Roy's face and look at the wound. John, also witnessing the scene, can see that Gabriel's gruff tenderness will never be directed toward him. Elizabeth can see that Gabriel's overindulgence of Roy will forever cause problems for this favored son of his, and she can see, too, that John, who will never give Gabriel any trouble, will always be outside the realm of concern he shows toward Roy. Ironically, though it is not clear if he is aware of it, Gabriel must depend upon Elizabeth if he is to attend Roy properly. The fight may have caused conflict among the family members, but it forces them to work together—John holds the baby while Elizabeth and Gabriel tend to Roy's wound. It is not togetherness that Gabriel wishes to dwell upon, however, for as soon as he is satisfied that the wound is not major, he resumes his accusatory stance toward Elizabeth and John.

Gabriel's anger is undramatized throughout the scene of examining the wound; it is like a volcano waiting to explode. Wondering when Elizabeth will learn to ''do right,'' Gabriel tries to reclaim his authoritarian superiority, but Elizabeth stands firm in maintaining that no one has ''let'' Roy go downstairs: ''He just went. He got a head just like his father, it got to be broken before it'll bow. I was in the kitchen.'' Elizabeth's retorts force Gabriel to turn on John, who lapses into a silence that Gabriel threatens to break with a strap. ''No, you ain't,'' Elizabeth says. ''You ain't going to take no strap to this boy, not today you ain't. Ain't a soul to blame for Roy's lying up there now but you—you because you done spoiled him so that he thinks he can do just

anything and get away with it. I'm here to tell you that ain't no way to raise no child. You don't pray to the Lord to help you do better than you been doing, you going to live to shed bitter tears that the Lord didn't take his soul today.'' Such spunkiness is again too drastic a change in personality from the apprehensive Elizabeth we have seen earlier in the story.

Elizabeth's comment on Gabriel's hard head and her admonition that he should do better than he has been doing neutralize Gabriel's active anger, but the silent intensity of it remains; she sees fury and hatred in his eyes, which ''were struck alive, unmoving, blind with malevolence.'' The summary of Gabriel's anger, no matter how poignant, still has less force than that of a dramatization. Gabriel has no further speech in the story; he stands in silent fury as Elizabeth, leaving the room, directs John to pick up his father's lunchbox. The silence is problematic because what we know of Gabriel would suggest that it is impossible for him to be calmed into passivity. John scrambles to pick up the box, ''bending his dark head near the toe of his father's heavy shoe,'' the final clause in the story and the final indication of how Gabriel would like to resolve his angry dissatisfaction.

It is easy to see why Baldwin rewrote the story. It lacks dramatization of Gabriel's fury, and it is inconsistent in the development of Elizabeth's character. It is not clear what kind of prior knowledge she would have had of Gabriel's hard head, nor is her suggestive comment that he had better pray to the Lord for improvement ultimately a forceful one. In the novel, Florence is the medium for providing information on Gabriel's background and his own sins: if Elizabeth is to have such knowledge, and present it convincingly, then that knowledge should serve as more of an equalizer in her position in relation to Gabriel; she should not be so panicky, nervous and trembling. In its delineation of character, therefore, as well as its development of motive and action, the novel is much more forceful in presenting the rockpile incident than the story is.

Elizabeth, in standing up to Gabriel, *seems* to win the argument against him. It can be argued, however, that her changed action does not suggest a substantially changed personality from *Go Tell It on the Mountain*. As a black woman who has mothered an illegitimate son and found a haven in a hardworking churchman, Elizabeth is sensitive to that haven and to her own tainted position. Her actions indicate that she does not wish to allow anything to anger

Gabriel because that anger would be turned against her and toward the fact that, to Gabriel, she and John are still interlopers in a paradise that should be forbidden to them. Then, too, it is Elizabeth who leaves the room, not Gabriel. It is she who sees in his eyes his desire "to witness her perdition," not he who is overcome by her spoken fury. In the contest of wills and of self-imposed guilt, it is Elizabeth who finally retreats, not Gabriel. Her retreat would be all the more vivid if Gabriel had slapped her as he did in *Go Tell It on the Mountain*. For without Florence, and without Roy, who has turned into a screaming child instead of the perceptive father-hater he is in *Go Tell It on the Mountain*, Elizabeth has no other support for her position than the momentary shock of surprising Gabriel with her outburst. Her triumph, therefore, is a pyrrhic victory at best, a slinking away from the battlefield at worst.

Elizabeth has almost unconsciously used one of the children as her defense against Gabriel's retaliation for her outspokenness. After her outburst at Gabriel, she takes Delilah from John and stands looking at Gabriel as if to say, "Trust me; I have mothered your children. How can you assume that I would not want the best for them?" Delilah is her tangible shield against Gabriel's fury, and the child's presence conveniently prevents Gabriel from striking her mother. It is because of the child that the hate and anger Gabriel shows in his eyes finally changes: Elizabeth "moved the child in her arms. And at this his eyes changed, he looked at Elizabeth, the mother of his children, the helpmeet given by the Lord." Elizabeth must symbolically stand in wait for the change in Gabriel even as she starts to leave the room.

As in *Go Tell It on the Mountain*, then, Elizabeth and her children must live in an environment permeated with tension and potential disapproval. Gabriel's pompous shadow falls on them all, unapprovingly, whether he is present or not. Consequently, Elizabeth has as much personality, in a way, as Gabriel allows, and as much as he is willing to recognize in her role as mother of his children. By her actions and the tone of fear she conveys to us, she almost succeeds in suggesting that Gabriel is somehow correct in his evaluation of her guilt. Her ultimate self-realization depends upon being at peace with Gabriel, who is unquestionably the master of his house and family, but at the end of the story that peace is not even a promise. . . .

Source: Trudier Harris, "To Be Washed Whiter than Snow: *Going to Meet the Man*," in *Black Women in the Fiction of James Baldwin*, University of Tennessee Press, 1985, pp. 60–95.

Sources

Baldwin, James, *Go Tell It on the Mountain*, in *James Baldwin: Early Novels and Stories*, The Library of America, 1998, pp. 38–47.

———, "The Rockpile," in *Going to Meet the Man*, Laurel, 1965, pp. 9–19.

Donadio, Stephen, "Looking for the Man," in *Partisan Review*, Vol. 33, No. 1, Winter 1966, pp. 136–38.

Featherstone, Joseph, "Blues for Mister Baldwin," in *Critical Essays on James Baldwin*, edited by Fred L. Standley and Nancy V. Burt, G. K. Hall & Company, 1988, p. 154, originally published in the *New Republic*, Vol. 153, 1965, pp. 34–36.

Jones, Harry L., "Style, Form, and Content in the Short Fiction of James Baldwin," in *James Baldwin: A Critical Evaluation*, edited by Therman B. O'Daniel, Howard University Press, 1977, p. 143.

Kinnamon, Keneth, "James Baldwin," in *American Writers*, Supplement 1, Charles Scribner's Sons, 1979, pp. 47–71.

Peden, William, Review of *Going to Meet the Man*, in *Studies in Short Fiction*, Summer 1975.

Pratt, Louis H., *James Baldwin*, Twayne, 1978, p. 31.

Standley, Fred L., "James Baldwin," in *Dictionary of Literary Biography*, Vol. 2: *American Novelists Since World War II, First Series*, edited by Jeffrey Helterman, Gale Research, 1978, pp. 15–22.

Stern, Daniel, "A Special Corner on Truth," in *Saturday Review*, Vol. 48, No. 45, November 6, 1965, p. 32.

Sylvander, Carolyn Wedin, *James Baldwin*, Frederick Ungar Publishing Company, 1980, pp. 110–11.

Further Reading

Anderson, Jervis, *This Was Harlem: A Cultural Portrait, 1900–1950*, Farrar Straus Giroux, 1982.
    Anderson's book offers an in-depth discussion of what life was like in Harlem in the first half of the twentieth century. This cultural study is organized into six parts, which reflect the major movements and historical trends in the city, including the conversion of Harlem into an African-American city, the Harlem Renaissance, and the Great Depression.

Balfour, Katherine Lawrence, *The Evidence of Things Not Said: James Baldwin and the Promise of American Democracy*, Cornell University Press, 2001.
    In this book, Balfour discusses Baldwin's works published in the 1960s, within the context of the author's views about democracy. Balfour also examines the conflicts that these works created among various groups in the Civil Rights movement, compares Baldwin's works to contemporary works that discuss racial conflict, and discusses what role Baldwin's ideas can play in current racial debates.

Greenberg, Cheryl Lynn, *"Or Does It Explode?": Black Harlem in the Great Depression,* Oxford University Press, 1991.

This book offers a comprehensive look at African-American life in Harlem during the Great Depression. Greenberg draws on an extensive amount of statistical data—much of which is included in the book's appendices—and offers several anecdotes from the major struggles faced by African Americans in the 1930s. The title is derived from a famous poem by Langston Hughes, a poet from the Harlem Renaissance.

Leeming, David Adams, *James Baldwin: A Biography,* Knopf, 1994.

Leeming offers an intimate portrayal of the author, who was one of his personal friends. This authorized biography discusses Baldwin's struggles, including the racial injustice he witnessed, his attempts to come to terms with his homosexuality, and his religious experiences. Leeming also offers insights into Baldwin's works.

Miller, D. Quentin, ed., *Re-Viewing James Baldwin: Things Not Seen,* Temple University Press, 2000.

Throughout his career, most of Baldwin's critics praised only a handful of the author's works, and they either criticized or ignored the others. In this new collection of essays, several critics discuss these other works and collectively offer a new assessment of Baldwin, whose popularity with many critics has diminished since his death.

Three Thanksgivings

Charlotte
Perkins Gilman

1909

"Three Thanksgivings," by Charlotte Perkins Gilman, was first published in Gilman's magazine, *Forerunner*, in 1909. The story and many of the other works published in the magazine have received very little critical attention, since most critics have tended to focus on Gilman's novella, *The Yellow Wallpaper*. Nevertheless, "Three Thanksgivings" contains themes that are common to many of Gilman's stories, including women's struggle for economic independence despite social pressures and the possibility of women being forced to enter into undesirable marriages. The protagonist, Mrs. Delia Morrison, is a widow who wishes to remain in the house that her father built and where she has lived most of her life. However, in two years, Mrs. Morrison owes a small mortgage to Mr. Peter Butts, a persistent man who hopes to marry her. If she cannot pay the mortgage and interest, she will have to sell the house and live with one of her children or marry Mr. Butts and live with him in her house as his servant. In addition to sharing the traits of many of her other stories, Gilman's "Three Thanksgivings" gives a portrait of the times, accurately reflecting the attitudes toward women that were prevalent in the early twentieth century—when women were fighting for many rights, including economic independence and the right to vote. A copy of the story can be found in *The Yellow Wallpaper and Other Writings*, which was published by The Modern Library in 2000.

Author Biography

Charlotte Perkins Gilman was born as Charlotte Anna Perkins on July 3, 1860, in Hartford, Connecticut. Gilman's father, Frederick Perkins—a librarian and editor—deserted the family when the author was an infant. As a result, Gilman, her siblings, and her mother lived with relatives, including the famous abolitionist author Harriet Beecher Stowe. Under the instruction of Stowe and her two sisters, Isabella Beecher Hooker and Catharine Beecher, two feminist activists, the young Gilman developed her independent spirit and desire for equality.

Despite her doubts about the institution of marriage, Gilman married Charles Walter Stetson in 1884, at the age of twenty-four. The union was disastrous. Within a year, Gilman had given birth to a daughter, Katherine, and had entered into a state of deep depression. Under the advice of a noted neurologist, Gilman tried a cure of bedrest and seclusion. The cure only made Gilman's condition worse. However, it did provide Gilman with the background for her first published novella, *The Yellow Wallpaper*—first published in the *New England Magazine* in 1890; published on its own in 1899—which depicts such a treatment failing miserably. Although Gilman later admitted that the work was merely an attempt to get back at the neurologist who suggested her rest cure, it is generally considered her finest work and a key feminist work. During the 1890s, Gilman produced two other works that displayed her feminist activism: *In This Our World* (1893), a mainly satiric collection of poetry, and *Women and Economics* (1898), an indictment of a male-dominated society that suppressed women.

Gilman's second marriage in 1900—to her cousin, George Houghton Gilman—was more successful. Her second husband was sympathetic to Gilman's feminist activism and encouraged her in her efforts. One of Gilman's most notable endeavors was *Forerunner*, a self-published journal that Gilman wrote, edited, and produced for seven years, from 1909 to 1916. Each issue included a wide range of writings, including short stories that addressed women's issues. One of the first short stories published in *Forerunner* was "Three Thanksgivings" (1909). In addition to shorter fiction, Gilman also used *Forerunner* to publish novels in serial form. The most famous of these is *Herland* (1915), a utopian fantasy in which three men from the United States discover a fabled country that is ruled entirely by women.

After *Forerunner*, Gilman published only two more books, *His Religion and Hers: A Study of the Faith of Our Fathers and the Work of Our Mothers* (1923) and *The Living of Charlotte Perkins Gilman: An Autobiography* (1935). The latter appeared post-humously, since Gilman had committed suicide the same year, after being diagnosed with an inoperable form of breast cancer.

Plot Summary

When "Three Thanksgivings" begins, Mrs. Delia Morrison, a fifty-year-old widow, has just finished reading two letters—one from Andrew and one from Jean, her two children. Both have sent travel money to Mrs. Morrison, asking her to come and stay with them for Thanksgiving. In addition, they have both requested that she sell her house. Andrew is most interested in Mrs. Morrison's safety, whereas Jean's husband, Joe, mainly wants to invest her money in his own business.

Mrs. Morrison ponders her financial situation. She has stopped taking in boarders at the Welcome House, a spacious manor built by her deceased father. She hates having boarders and decides that it is useless anyway, since the money is only enough to pay the interest—but not the principal—on her small mortgage. After dinner, Mr. Peter Butts, a friend and lifelong suitor of Mrs. Morrison, pays her a visit. Mr. Butts holds the mortgage on the Welcome House and tries to use this fact to pressure Mrs. Morrison into marriage. He says that if she cannot pay her loan when it is due in two years, she will either have to sell the house or marry him anyway. He also believes that she will not be able to raise the money on her own. Nevertheless, Mrs. Morrison says that she will find a way and politely declines Mr. Butts's offer.

Mrs. Morrison decides to go to Andrew's house for Thanksgiving. Although Andrew and his wife, Annie, are gracious, Mrs. Morrison is not happy. She is used to her spacious home, so the room they give her feels very small. Although Mrs. Morrison is a skilled manager—from her many years as a minister's wife—there is no place for her to help out; Annie, Andrew's wife, is more than capable enough to help Andrew in his own ministry. In addition, Andrew, Annie, and their neighbors insist on treating Mrs. Morrison as if she is old. She only stays a week before returning to the Welcome House, determined to save her home.

Mrs. Morrison makes a thorough inventory of her assets, finding that her father's political meetings and her husband's religious events have helped to increase the stock of supplies in the house. She finds hundreds of extra chairs and a large stock of bedding, towels, and table linens, but she rules out the idea of opening a hotel because the other hotel in Haddleton is never full. She finds a large stock of china and cups, but she rules out the idea of a girls' school, which would take time and money to establish. As she starts to think of all of the women she knows in the community, she has a brainstorm and gets to work.

Shortly thereafter, word spreads that Mrs. Morrison is going to entertain all of the country women at the Welcome House. Hundreds show up to hear Mrs. Isabelle Carter Blake—a noted social activist and family woman—and her friend, a European countess, talk about the rapid growth of women's clubs in the United States and Europe. Over the next few days, Mrs. Blake goes to many church meetings, encouraging the farm women to start their own dues-based clubhouse in Haddleton, which they could use on Saturdays when they are in town doing their shopping. The women think it would be too expensive to find a facility and hire a manager, but Mrs. Morrison offers to convert the Welcome House into a women's club and to manage the organization for a mere ten cents a week from each woman. By the time Mrs. Blake leaves, the Haddleton Rest and Improvement Club has been established at the Welcome House. Hundreds of women join immediately, and the small weekly due paid by each woman adds up quickly.

The next Thanksgiving, Mrs. Morrison goes to Jean's house. The room that Jean gives her is small, like the one in Andrew's house. However, instead of being coddled, Mrs. Morrison gets put to work helping out with Jean's four children, ruining her silk clothes in the process. At the same time, Joe urges her to sell the house and come and stay with them, because he could use the capital for his business. As at Andrew's house, Mrs. Morrison stays only one week before leaving.

Mrs. Morrison pays her yearly interest to Mr. Butts and renews her efforts at growing the club and paying off her loan. Using management skills and a refined personality that she has honed as both a senator's daughter and a minister's wife, Mrs. Morrison expands the range of the organization. She rents out rooms for all sorts of club meetings, including boys' clubs, and invites speakers and

Charlotte Perkins Gilman

other entertainment. Mrs. Morrison makes a nice profit the first season, and the second season is even better.

By the next Thanksgiving, Mrs. Morrison has made enough profit to pay back her interest and principal on the loan, as well as a little extra money. She sends part of this money to Andrew and Jean, inviting them and their families to come and stay with her for Thanksgiving. After dinner, Mr. Butts shows up, thinking he will be taking either the house or Mrs. Morrison—or preferably both. He is therefore very surprised when she hands him a check for his interest and principal and says that she could not possibly have made all that money from her club and that she must have had help from her family. Nevertheless, he takes the check and leaves.

Characters

Andrew

Andrew, a minister, is Mrs. Morrison's son, who is concerned about his mother's welfare. Andrew encourages his mother to come and live with them, saying that she can sell her house and he will invest the money for her. Andrew is worried that Mrs.

Morrison cannot take care of herself, and he is overjoyed when she comes to stay with him and his wife, Annie, the first Thanksgiving. However, Andrew's house is small compared to his mother's, and Mrs. Morrison is not comfortable there. Andrew is somewhat angry when his mother leaves after a week to return to the Welcome House. For the third Thanksgiving, Mrs. Morrison makes enough from her women's club to send travel money so that Andrew and Annie can come stay with her.

Annie

Annie, Andrew's wife, is very efficient in helping her husband with his ministry. Because of this, there is nothing for Mrs. Morrison to do when she stays at their house. Also, Annie insists on treating Mrs. Morrison like an old woman and needlessly coddles her.

Mrs. Isabelle Carter Blake

Mrs. Isabelle Carter Blake, a noted social activist, is one of Mrs. Morrison's childhood friends. Mrs. Morrison invites her to speak at the Welcome House, where Mrs. Blake encourages the Haddleton women to organize their own rest and improvement club. Mrs. Blake also speaks to individual churches in Haddleton, where she suggests that the Haddleton women rely on Mrs. Morrison and the Welcome House for their club needs. Mrs. Blake is a very influential woman because she has done wonderful work with children, has successfully raised her own six children, and has just written a novel.

Mr. Peter Butts

Mr. Peter Butts is a persistent suitor of Mrs. Morrison, and he also holds the small mortgage on her house. Mr. Butts, a wealthy entrepreneur, has pursued Mrs. Morrison's hand in marriage since they were both young, when he was poor and she was rich. Although he is not unkind, he is tactless and takes great, visible pride in the fact that their financial situations have reversed. Mr. Butts was friends with Mrs. Morrison's husband and is Mrs. Morrison's friend, although she does not wish to marry him. Still, Mr. Butts continues to encourage the now-widowed Mrs. Morrison to marry him. The greatest pressure comes from the loan that Mrs. Morrison has taken from him. He hoped, when loaning her the money for her small mortgage, that Mrs. Morrison would not be able to pay the money in the end. He thinks that this situation would cause Mrs. Morrison to marry him so that she can keep her house, which he knows she loves and refuses to sell.

In addition to his desire for Mrs. Morrison, Mr. Butts also desires to own her house, the Welcome House, and thinks that he will get both in the end. He is confident that Mrs. Morrison will not be able to pay the loan, since she is a single woman and, he thinks, a single woman cannot make much money in two years. Therefore, he is very surprised when Mrs. Morrison's women's club pays off her debt, and he believes that Mrs. Morrison's family has helped her pay the loan. At the end of the story, they go their separate ways.

The Countess

The Countess is an American-born, Italian woman, who uses inspirational stories of European women's clubs to help convince the women of Haddleton to form their own rest and improvement club. The Countess is a friend of Mrs. Isabelle Carter Blake.

Jean

Jean, who also goes by Jeannie, is Mrs. Morrison's daughter. Jean encourages his mother to come to live with them and says that her husband will sell her house and invest the money in his own business and then pay her interest. Jean and Joe are overjoyed when Mrs. Morrison comes to stay with them the second Thanksgiving. Unlike Annie, who needs no help, Jean depends heavily on her mother to help take care of Jean's four children. Jean also babbles constantly about her problems. As a result, Mrs. Morrison is not comfortable at Jean's house either, and she leaves after a week. For the third Thanksgiving, Mrs. Morrison makes enough from her women's club to send travel money so that Jean's family can come stay with her.

Jeannie

See Jean

Joe

Joe is Jean's husband, who focuses on getting Mrs. Morrison to sell her house and invest the money in his business. Joe says he will pay her good interest, but Mrs. Morrison does not want to sell her house. Nevertheless, when Mrs. Morrison visits, he asks her many questions about the Welcome House.

Mrs. Delia Morrison

Mrs. Delia Morrison is a strong, independent woman who uses her many social and management skills to achieve financial self-sufficiency—by forming a local women's club. In the beginning of the story, Mrs. Morrison, the daughter of a senator and the widow of a minister, is faced with a dilemma. She is having a hard time paying off the mortgage on her house, which is due in two years. Mrs. Morrison loves her house, which was built by Senator Welcome, her father. However, Mrs. Morrison does not want to take in boarders at the Welcome House, something that she has done in the past to support her family. Both of her children, Andrew and Jean, encourage her to come and live with their respective families, but Mrs. Morrison tries each home for a week and is not comfortable at either one. Nor does she relish her third option, to marry Mr. Peter Butts—a friend who holds the mortgage on the Welcome House—since Mrs. Morrison still loves her deceased husband. The mortgage is due in two years, on Thanksgiving, and Mr. Butts is hoping that Mrs. Morrison will marry him in a desperate attempt to avoid having to sell the Welcome House. Although her family and Mr. Butts think that Mrs. Morrison will eventually have to choose to live with one of them, she refuses to give up hope that she can keep her house without sacrificing her independence or integrity.

In an effort to explore her options, Mrs. Morrison inventories all of her assets in the Welcome House and realizes that she could turn the house into a hotel or a girls' boarding school. She dismisses these ideas as financial liabilities and ultimately seizes on the idea of using the Welcome House as the site for a women's club. Using one of her girlhood connections, Mrs. Morrison invites Mrs. Isabelle Carter Blake—a noted social activist, mother, and author—to speak to all of the women who live in and around Haddleton. Mrs. Blake encourages the Haddleton women to form a club at the Welcome House, and it becomes wildly successful under Mrs. Morrison's skilful management. By the third Thanksgiving, Mrs. Morrison has made enough profit to pay off the loan from Mr. Butts and even has enough left over to bring her children and their families to the Welcome House for Thanksgiving.

Sally

Sally is Mrs. Morrison's longtime housekeeper. She is a black woman who collects the weekly membership dues from the women in the Haddleton Rest and Improvement Club.

Delia Welcome

See Mrs. Delia Morrison

Themes

Self-Sufficiency

Mrs. Morrison's goal in the story is to reach self-sufficiency so that she can keep her beloved house without having to marry Mr. Butts. For a widowed woman with little money in the early twentieth century, this was a difficult task. Men had a better chance for economic survival, even if they started out poor like Mr. Butts. In addition, most men assumed that a woman, especially a fifty-year-old woman like Mrs. Morrison, would have a hard time surviving on her own. Says Mr. Butts, "But you can't, I tell you. I'd like to know what a woman of your age can do with a house like this—and no money?" Mrs. Morrison's situation is complicated by the fact that she has to pay off a small mortgage on her house. Although the two thousand dollars that she owes to Mr. Butts is not a large sum for a mortgage, Mr. Butts notes the prevailing attitude at the time, saying that it "is considerable money for a single woman to raise in two years—*and* interest." Despite this opposition, which Mrs. Morrison also experiences from other men like her son-in-law, Joe, she is able to make "all expenses ... her interest ... a little extra cash, clearly her own, all over and above" the two thousand dollars she owes. By paying off the loan and having money left over, Mrs. Morrison is now debt-free and self-sufficient and so can choose to do whatever she wishes from this point on. However, Mr. Butts still refuses to believe that Mrs. Morrison did it on her own and says, "I believe some of these great friends of yours have lent it to you."

The Expected Roles of Women

During the early twentieth century, most women were expected to get married and raise children, as Mrs. Morrison did. However, if a woman became a widow and did not have enough money to support herself, she was generally expected to depend upon someone else. In the story, Mrs. Morrison's options for whom to depend upon are representative of the few options most women had. She can marry Mr. Butts or live with one of her children. Above all, Mrs. Morrison does not want to remarry. Mr. Butts, however, does not care about Mrs. Morrison's feelings and says to her in regard to the desire to marry: "You've made that clear. You don't, but I do. You've had your way and married the minister. He was a good man, but he's dead. Now you might as well marry me." Men's needs were often put ahead of women's needs, and in this case Mr. Butts is

Topics for Further Study

- Research the early 1900s, and find one woman who became a successful entrepreneur in this time period. Compare this person's real-life story with the life of Mrs. Morrison, focusing on the challenges that both women faced in becoming self-sufficient.

- A longtime topic of debate is the inequality of pay between men and women for comparable work. Research the history of this debate; then explore the current situation. Plot out a timeline that depicts the major events in this debate, and write a one-page summary that describes how and where this issue started and where it stands today.

- In the story, Mrs. Morrison is a widow who refuses to remarry, a fact that puts her at an economic disadvantage. Compare Mrs. Morrison's situation to the situation of a modern-day widow, and discuss the different obstacles that women from each era have faced. Use

economic facts from both the early 1900s and today to back up your assertions.

- Research the state of women's organizations today, and compare them to the Rest and Improvement Club that is depicted in the story. Discuss the economic, political, and social factors that have influenced the structure of both the Rest and Improvement Club and modern-day women's organizations.

- Review several news articles from the first decade of the 1900s, paying particular attention to any articles that discuss the expected roles of women. Pretend that you are a male reporter in 1900s Haddleton, who learns of the success of Mrs. Morrison's Rest and Improvement Club. Write an article about Mrs. Morrison and her club that is written in the style of an early-1900s article, preserving any attitudes or biases that one might expect to find in an article like this.

---

saying that he is a man, he wants to marry her, and he intends to keep pushing her to accept his proposal, despite her protests. Mrs. Morrison refuses to marry Mr. Butts, however, because she still loves her husband. As she notes to herself, "Some day she meant to see him again—God willing—and she did not wish to have to tell him that at fifty she had been driven into marrying Peter Butts."

If she does not marry Mr. Butts, her only other option, at first, appears to be living with one of her children. She gives each of her children's respective homes a one-week trial run, but is not comfortable at either place. With Andrew and his wife, Annie, Mrs. Morrison is treated like a relic. Andrew and Annie cannot see Mrs. Morrison as anything but old, so when she stays with them and is "set down among the old ladies and gentlemen—she had never realized so keenly that she was no longer young." At Jean's house, Mrs. Morrison is not coddled; she is put to work. Jean expects that her mother will pitch

in and take some of the burden off Jean. As a result, Jean is very dependent upon her mother: "By the hour she babbled of their cares and hopes, while Mrs. Morrison, tall and elegant, in her well-kept old black silk, sat holding the baby or trying to hold the twins."

In addition to the roles women were expected to play—wife, mother, old person, babysitter—there were roles that women were expected not to have. Chief among these was businesswoman. This does not stop Mrs. Morrison from trying, however, and when she realizes that she does not like the idea of marrying Mr. Butts or living with her children, she puts her brain to the task of creating a business. "Two years were before her in which she must find some way to keep herself and Sally, and to pay two thousand dollars and the interest to Peter Butts." Most people expect that she will fail in her undertakings, but she surprises them all by starting and running a very successful women's club: "The financial basis of the undertaking was very simple, but it would never have worked so well under less skilful management." Still, some people, most notably Mr. Butts, are not used to the idea of a woman running her own financial affairs. When Mrs. Morrison hands Mr. Butts the check to pay off her loan, he is shocked: "'I didn't know you had a bank account,' he protested, somewhat dubiously."

Mrs. Morrison is only one of the women in the story who demonstrates to the Haddleton women—and Gilman's readers—that women can surpass the expectations put upon them. Mrs. Blake is known internationally for "her splendid work for children. . . . Yet she was known also to have lovingly and wisely reared six children of her own—and made her husband happy in his home." Mrs. Blake is a well-rounded woman, not confined by society's expectations of her. As a result, she is able to fulfill some of the traditional roles of women—wife and mother—while still making a name for herself through her social activism.

The Power of Organization

One of the key messages that Gilman gets across in the story is that, on their own, women cannot effect a huge change in society, but there is strength in numbers. When Mrs. Blake speaks to the various churches in Haddleton, she talks about "the women's club houses, going up in city after city, where many associations meet and help one another." Mrs. Blake fires up the crowds by telling them that they will have control over the club, for a small price: "All you have to do is organize, pay some small regular due, and provide yourselves with what you want." The women are excited to form their own club, especially since the fee seems so small: "Five dollars a year these country women could not have faced, but ten cents a week was possible to the poorest." Five dollars a year *is* roughly ten cents per week, but since the women only have to pay a small portion of it each week, they do not even think about the money.

However, while the fee "was very little money, taken separately . . . it added up with silent speed." This is the power of organization. One person or one small payment on its own cannot create much change. However, when the women band together, they are able to help Mrs. Morrison pay back her loan and retain her self-sufficiency. In the process, the Haddleton women collectively strike a victory for feminism, since they will get to keep their club and Mrs. Morrison will keep her independence—a good thing for all women. The countess notes the

positive power of women's organization, which was going on in many places at the beginning of the twentieth century. The countess addresses the women of Haddleton, saying that she expects if she returns to the town, "it would have joined the great sisterhood of women, whose hands were touching around the world for the common good."

Style

Setting

"Three Thanksgivings" takes place mainly at the Welcome House, which quickly becomes the focal point of the story. Mrs. Morrison loves her home, a fact that is made clear at the beginning of the story: "Even after living with her father at Washington and abroad, after visiting hall, castle and palace, she still found the Welcome House beautiful and impressive." It is because of the house that Mrs. Morrison is forced to look at her options. She does not have enough money to pay the mortgage, and at first it looks as if she will not be able to do anything to raise enough money. As a result, she feels that she may have to choose between selling her house or marrying Mr. Butts. However, as she makes clear to her persistent suitor, "I should prefer to keep the house without you, Mr. Butts." This becomes the goal that motivates Mrs. Morrison throughout the story.

Characterization

Mrs. Morrison is well suited for this challenge, because Gilman gives her a number of winning characteristics. When the reader first meets Mrs. Morrison, she is described as "a tall woman, commanding of aspect, yet of a winningly attractive manner, erect and light-footed, still imposingly handsome." Physically, she is a very striking presence, something that Gilman emphasizes elsewhere in the story, by talking about Mrs. Morrison's "full graceful height" and describing her as "tall and elegant." However, Mrs. Morrison's positive characteristics do not end with her looks. She is also very refined and gracious, and as a result she has built up a great reputation with the women of Haddleton. The narrator remarks that Mrs. Morrison "had no enemies, but no one had ever blamed her for her unlimited friendliness.'' Mrs. Morrison's regal manner is illustrated repeatedly throughout the story. For example, when she gets the brainstorm to start the women's club, the narrator describes it as follows: ''Suddenly she stopped short in the middle of the great high-ceiled room, and drew her head up proudly like a victorious queen.'' The women of Haddleton also notice Mrs. Morrison's queenly grace: ''Some were moved to note that Mrs. Morrison looked the easy peer of these eminent ladies, and treated the foreign nobility precisely as she did her other friends.'' This graciousness and elegance helps to sell the Haddleton women on the idea of the club.

Once the club has been established, Mrs. Morrison proves herself again with her good management skills. In the past, these skills have allowed her to be successful in business, even when it meant enduring unpleasant situations. For example, Mrs. Morrison has never liked taking in boarders, something she was forced to do to provide for her children when they lived with her. However, ''her youthful experience in diplomatic circles, and the years of practical management in church affairs, enabled her to bear it with patience and success.'' When she manages the women's club, these skills are put to good use. Says the narrator, ''There was a good deal of work, a good deal of care, and room for the whole supply of Mrs. Morrison's diplomatic talent and experience.''

Description

Throughout the story, Gilman describes certain sections in more detail than in others. These highly detailed sections are generally either negative sections about what Mrs. Morrison's life will be like if she does not pay off the loan or positive sections about Mrs. Morrison's efforts to come up with the loan money. Examples of the first category occur when Mrs. Morrison goes to visit her children on successive Thanksgivings. Gilman's description of the ''affectionately offered'' guest room in Andrew's house is extensive. Gilman describes the exact size dimensions and then goes on to explain the bleak views from each of the room's two windows, ''one looking at some pale gray clapboards within reach of a broom, the other giving a view of several small fenced yards occupied by cats, clothes and children.'' Following this, Gilman gives a description of a certain flower that Mrs. Morrison does not like,

the unwanted hot-water bag that Annie forces on Mrs. Morrison each night, and the tiny dining room. All in all, the detailed description serves as an effective counterpart, showing the readers the type of misery that Mrs. Morrison will have to live in if she loses her beloved house. This type of description is repeated when Mrs. Morrison stays with Jean and Joe, except this time the misery takes the form of a house ''full of babies'' who ruin her ''well-kept old black silk'' by the end of her one-week stay. Gilman uses these and other descriptions to show the reader the potential bleak futures that could await Mrs. Morrison. In turn, these nightmare scenarios help to give her character the motivation to shape her own future.

By contrast, the overly descriptive sections that depict Mrs. Morrison's efforts to pay off the loan are very positive. For example, when she first attacks the problem, Mrs. Morrison explores her assets in full: ''She went over the place from garret to cellar, from front gate to backyard fence.'' Gilman could have left the description of this brief, with perhaps a paragraph about the types of items that Mrs. Morrison finds. Instead, Gilman writes several paragraphs of description, recording in detail, as Mrs. Morrison does, aspects of the garden and the amounts and condition of furniture, linens, china, and other assets. As she does so, the reader can start to sense that something positive will come from all of this stock, even if the reader does not know exactly what that is. These positive sections also demonstrate Mrs. Morrison's capability for thinking as a businesswoman. This talent is demonstrated, in part by additional descriptions, later on in the story, when Gilman displays in detail how Mrs. Morrison is successful in managing her club.

Historical Context

First-Wave Feminism

Although women had been fighting for equal rights in various areas since the late eighteenth century, around the time that Mary Wollstonecraft wrote her seminal *A Vindication of the Rights of Woman* (1792), most historians consider modern feminism to fall into two time periods. The first

Compare & Contrast

- **1900s:** More women join the fight for women's suffrage, or the right to vote. Suffragettes begin to campaign in areas like New York City.

  Today: Women have the right to vote, and an increasing number of women hold some of the nation's most prestigious government positions. Sandra Day O'Connor and Ruth Bader Ginsberg occupy two of the nine seats on the United States Supreme Court, while in the 107th Congress, 13 percent of the members of the Senate and roughly 14 percent of the members of the House of Representatives are women. In addition, in 1996, President Bill Clinton appoints Madeleine Albright as the first woman Secretary of State, a nomination that is unanimously approved by the Senate the following year.

- **1900s:** In addition to the fight for voting privileges, some women—including Charlotte Perkins Gilman—speak out about other inequalities between the sexes, particularly the economic disadvantage faced by most women. When women are allowed to work in the same fields as men, they generally earn much less.

  Today: Thanks to legislation from the last half of the twentieth century, many inequalities between men and women in the workforce have been eliminated, although in some areas, women still fight for equal pay. As more equality issues are resolved, the new issue for many women becomes the struggle to strike a balance between their careers and their families. For some women, it becomes a choice between the two, since mothers who take time off to raise children often find it hard to reenter the workforce.

- **1900s:** Women are thought of by many as physically inferior to men. This assumption is supported by the prevention of female competition in certain sports. In the 1900 Olympics, women are limited to two events—tennis and golf.

  Today: Women compete professionally in basketball and other contact sports, as well as in most of the Olympic categories as their male counterparts. The first female cadets enter into traditionally male military institutes. Movies like *G.I. Jane* and television shows like *Alias* and *Buffy the Vampire Slayer* feature tough women who are more than a match for their antagonists, many of whom are tough men.

---

period, known as first-wave feminism, consists of the efforts of women—primarily in Europe and the United States—in the nineteenth and early twentieth centuries to gain more rights, mainly legal rights such as voting, or suffrage. Second-wave feminism, a movement that reached its height in the 1960s and 1970s, had a larger focus and strove for equality between the sexes in every category. Second-wave feminism is commonly known as the women's movement.

During the first-wave feminism period, in the first decade of the twentieth century when Gilman wrote "Three Thanksgivings," women's rights were a hot issue. Says J. M. Roberts, in his *Twentieth Century: The History of the World, 1901 to 2000:* "Virtually nowhere could women be said to enjoy as much freedom or so high a legal status as men." This situation differed little from the situation that women had faced for much of recorded history. However, following the American Civil War, when blacks—but not women—were given the right to vote, more women began to organize and demand the right to vote, and women's issues became a hot topic. Says Roberts, "By 1901, the words 'feminism' and 'feminist' had come (from France) to be well-established in English in association with the promotion of women's rights."

Women's Suffrage

By far, the biggest issue that women fought for in the beginning of the twentieth century was suffrage. The issue was complicated by the fact that there were two major women's suffrage organizations, with opposing viewpoints, which fought each other. The National Woman Suffrage Association (NWSA), which was founded in 1869, was the more radical of the two, as it did not accept male members, and it denounced the Fifteenth Amendment for not including women. Formed later that same year, the American Woman Suffrage Association (AWSA) was a more conservative organization, and it praised the Fifteenth Amendment as a necessary first step. The organization, which was founded by both men and women, also accepted men as members. In 1890, these two organizations joined forces to become the National American Woman Suffrage Association (NAWSA).

By the turn of the century, several American states and territories in the West had given women the right to vote. Although women's suffrage is not one of the major issues in "Three Thanksgivings," Mrs. Morrison does mention it briefly to Mr. Butts when discussing how much higher the interest is in Colorado: "Do you know the average interest they charge in Colorado? The women vote there, you know." However, in the eastern United States, there was a greater battle for women to win the right to vote, and women spoke out on many occasions. The formal, opening rally of the American suffragettes took place in 1907 in New York City, when a group of women spoke to a group of hundreds, mainly men, many of whom supported their suffrage efforts.

Women in the Workforce

While suffrage was the main issue during first-wave feminism, some women wanted to pursue equality in other areas. Says Paul Johnson, in his book, *A History of the American People:* "They had to secure, for instance, equality of pay and equality of opportunity in job selection and promotion, and over a whole range of other matters." The situation for American women in the workforce in the last two decades of the nineteenth century was bleak. The three fields commonly open to most women were domestic service, nursing, and teaching. This situation began to change somewhat by the turn of the century. Says Johnson, "By 1890 there were 4 million employed women, rising to 5.1 million in 1900 and 7.8 million in 1910, and by this date educational facilities for women were available in

all the arts and sciences." Despite these advances, however, inequalities still existed between men and women in the workforce.

Fighting Misconceptions

Part of the problem that women faced in their struggle for equality was the misconceptions that society had about women's abilities. In 1871, Charles Darwin had published *The Descent of Man,* in which he claimed that men were more evolved than women. Gilman herself was one of the most outspoken about the issue of male superiority. In her controversial *Women and Economics* (1898), her best-known nonfiction work, she posed the theory that women are the losers in social evolution, which favors males. Gilman stated that women, like Mrs. Morrison in "Three Thanksgivings," are just as capable as men but that due to their cultural suppression, they are at an economic disadvantage to men in human society. As a result, women are usually forced to depend on men. Says Gilman, "We are the only animal species in which the female depends on the male for food, the only animal species in which the sex-relation is also an economic relation." However, others continued to disseminate information that suggested women were inferior to men. In 1906, Dr. Dudley Sargent, the physical director at Harvard University, focused on the physical weakness of women, saying that women should not play any contact sports and should instead focus on more graceful, lady-like forms of athletics. In addition, in 1907, W. I. Thomas, a University of Chicago professor, published *Sex and Society,* a book that, among other assertions, stated that women were intellectual savages.

Critical Overview

Gilman's story "Three Thanksgivings" has received very little critical attention. It was first published in 1909 in Gilman's journal, *Forerunner,* which may have been part of the problem. Gilman had attracted the attention of critics before. In her entry on Gilman for the *Dictionary of Literary Biography,* Robin Miskolcze notes that Gilman's first published poem, "Similar Cases," received "a letter of praise from William Dean Howells, a respected writer and editor of the *Atlantic Monthly*." However, though Gilman's earlier writings attracted critics, *Forerunner* was largely ignored by reviewers. As Gary Scharnhorst notes in his 1985 book, *Charlotte Perkins Gilman,* "Unfortunately, few critics, not even Howells—though Gilman twice sent him bound volumes—deigned to notice the magazine."

Part of this neglect was due to some early critics' assertion that most of the writings in *Forerunner* were too heavy-handed in their feminist approach. In his 1991 *Charlotte Perkins Gilman: A Nonfiction Reader,* editor Larry Ceplair notes of Gilman's magazine that "Charlotte's commentaries ranged over a wide range of topics, but the central theme never varied." Ceplair further says that this "sameness of tone" was most prevalent when Gilman "used a sermonizing form, as she increasingly did."

Following Gilman's death in 1935, scholarship concerning the writer dried up. In her introduction in 1992's *Herland and Selected Stories by Charlotte Perkins Gilman*, editor Barbara H. Solomon notes this phenomenon: "Descriptions of her life and contributions simply disappeared." Solomon cites an example from 1962, *The Reader's Encyclopedia of American Literature,* which includes three other Gilmans, but not Charlotte. However, as Solomon explains, in the mid-1960s "a burgeoning interest in feminist issues led historians, social critics, teachers, and students to search for the best sources about the conditions of women." Gilman's works began to be reprinted, including a reprint of all seven years of *Forerunner*, in 1968.

Even after the *Forerunner* stories resurfaced, however, they were not given as much critical attention as Gilman's *The Yellow Wallpaper* (1899), her first published work of fiction. Scharnhorst divides the *Forerunner* stories into two categories: "fantasies with a feminist message" and "illustrations of women's economic independence." While Scharnhorst says that the former are usually "whimsical," he considers the latter to be "contrived and repetitive" and says that they are "more heavy-handed, formulaic, and predictable than her feminist fantasies." "Three Thanksgivings" falls into this second of Scharnhorst's categories, and, based on the lack of critical attention given to the story, it would appear that many critics agree with his negative assessment. For example, in a book devoted

entirely to Gilman's short stories, 1997's *Charlotte Perkins Gilman: A Study of the Short Fiction,* Denise D. Knight offers only a small comment on the story, saying that it underscores "the theme of economic independence," like several of Gilman's stories.

One of the most in-depth studies of the story was by Solomon, in her introduction to *Herland and Selected Stories by Charlotte Perkins Gilman*. Solomon notes that Mrs. Morrison is representative of many of the women characters that Gilman wrote about in her stories: "Sensible and intelligent, she is at an economic disadvantage as a woman in a society with low expectations for women." Solomon notes additional aspects of "Three Thanksgivings" that are representative of Gilman's other works. For example, "Like Delia Morrison, numerous Gilman heroines find that in addressing their own desire to do meaningful work, they can aid other women, bringing about significant and much-needed social change." One of the other recurring topics that Solomon notes is "the evaluation of possible or existing marriages from the perspective of whether they are desirable for the woman." Finally, Solomon notes that the positive conclusion of "Three Thanksgivings," like the ending of many Gilman stories, is "neither a forced nor a tacked-on ending. It develops from the characters' traits and the events and has an emotional as well as a logical rightness."

Criticism

Ryan D. Poquette

Poquette has a bachelor's degree in English and specializes in writing about literature. In the following essay, Poquette explores Gilman's use of characterization to underscore her feminist message in "Three Thanksgivings."

It is no surprise that Gilman's works resurfaced in the 1960s and 1970s when the women's movement began. As Barbara H. Solomon notes in her 1992 introduction to *Herland and Selected Stories by Charlotte Perkins Gilman,* "a burgeoning interest in feminist issues led historians, social critics, teach-

Volume 18   *2 1 5*

This early twentieth century women's club sets a scene similar to Mrs. Morrison's organization in ''Three Thanksgivings''

ers, and students to search for the best sources about the conditions of women. And their search inevitably led to Charlotte Perkins Gilman.'' The majority of Gilman's works, both fiction and nonfiction, address women's issues in some way. For example, although she claimed in her autobiography that the real purpose of her novella, *The Yellow Wallpaper*, ''was to reach Dr. S. Weir Mitchell, and convince him of the error of his ways''—as a response to the disastrous rest-cure treatment he prescribed for her— the work has had a much broader effect. Many, like Carol Fairley Kessler in her entry on Gilman for *Modern American Women Writers,* have called it Gilman's ''masterpiece'' and hold it up as a key work of feminism for its social message—which encouraged women to rebel against the male-dominated society and its rules. Likewise, Gilman's short story ''Three Thanksgivings'' uses specific characterization techniques to underscore her message: women must not compromise their feminine values and morals in the process of becoming economically self-sufficient like men.

In the story, Mrs. Morrison's character is set up as the moral center of the tale. She is a woman of integrity, who is always true to her values. She also has many other equally desirable qualities. She is

willing to make sacrifices for others, even when it means discomfort or potential ruin for herself. For example, in years past, after her husband died, she took on boarders to raise enough money to support her family: ''This had been the one possible and necessary thing while the children were there, though it was a business she hated.'' Another key example of Mrs. Morrison's thoughtfulness is demonstrated when she is considering her assets to determine how she can survive and pay off her loan to Mr. Butts. She initially considers growing crops in her garden. Says Mrs. Morrison, ''This garden . . . with the hens, will feed us two women and sell enough to pay Sally.'' The economical choice would be to fire Sally and clean the house herself, since Mrs. Morrison is capable of doing so. However, she watches out for Sally, who is older and who might have difficulty finding work elsewhere in town because of her age. In fact, Sally might even be willing to work for her board instead of working for payment, but Mrs. Morrison does not even think about taking advantage of Sally in this way.

In addition, Mrs. Morrison has a strong faith that good will prevail. Even after an unpleasant visit from Mr. Butts in which he reminds her that the mortgage is due in two years, Mrs. Morrison is able

What Do I Read Next?

- Betty Friedan's controversial *The Feminine Mystique* (1963) helped to launch the modern women's movement. The book shatters the myth that post–World War II housewives were happy taking care of their husbands and children. Friedan labeled this misconception the feminine mystique and used her book to reveal the pain and frustration that many women faced when their needs were placed below the needs of their families.

- Gilman originally published ''Three Thanksgivings'' in *Forerunner,* a magazine that she published for seven years, from November 1909 to December 1916. Each issue of *Forerunner* contained a wide range of short fiction, serialized novels, poetry, articles, and other works, all written by Gilman. All seven volumes were reprinted in 1968, and although they are currently out of print, they are still available at some libraries. In addition, the first volume was reprinted in a different edition in 2002 and is widely available.

- One of Gilman's best-known novels, *Herland* (1915), describes a witty, feminist utopia. In the idealistic world that Gilman creates, women rule their own country, where they do not need men to reproduce. Three male explorers from the United States find the isolated country, which they name Herland. The men are surprised to find that the women are equal to them and are shocked when the women do not respond to the same types of charms that work on women in the United States.

- Many critics consider Gilman's novella *The Yellow Wallpaper* (1899), which is based on events in her own life, to be her finest literary work. The story consists of ten diary entries by Jane, a wife who is under the care of her husband, a physician, for what he thinks is a mild case of depression. While they are staying at a summerhouse, Jane's husband locks her in a third-floor room, thinking that the seclusion will help her get well. As the story progresses, Jane increasingly relates with a trapped woman whom she envisions living inside the room's yellow wallpaper.

- In Edith Wharton's *House of Mirth* (1905), Lily Bart is an aristocratic woman with no income who rebels against the conventions of her social class, including refusing to marry a suitor to maintain her economic stability.

- In Virginia Woolf's essay *A Room of One's Own* (1929), the writer argues that, in order for women to achieve the same greatness that male writers have, women need an income and privacy. In addition, Woolf discusses the fact that the idealistic and powerful portrayals of women in fiction have historically differed from the slave-like situations that many women faced in real life.

---

to watch Mr. Butts ''go with a keen light in her fine eyes, a more definite line to that steady, pleasant smile.'' She has strong convictions and knows that she will find some way to pay the mortgage and thus avoid having to compromise her integrity by marrying Mr. Butts.

Finally, Mrs. Morrison is happiest when she is able to do good work, not just make money. She enjoyed working with people in her husband's church, even though ''she was not strong on doctrine.'' And when she considers her options for businesses to

form, she initially seizes on the idea of a girls' school: ''A boarding school! There was money to be made at that, and fine work done.''

Taken alone, Mrs. Morrison's commitment to integrity and her moral characteristics are impressive. However, her character becomes even more powerful when compared with the weak men in the story. The three males—Andrew, Joe, and Mr. Butts—all have serious character flaws that cause them to be foils to Mrs. Morrison. A foil is a character that contrasts strongly with another char-

> "Gilman's moral message is clear to her turn-of-the-century audience: if women want to get ahead in a man's world, they will have the most success if they maintain their integrity and charity and do not adopt self-serving attitudes."

acter, in order to make the first character seem more prominent in a specific way. In this case, all of the male characters are deliberately given negative or inadequate characteristics to make Mrs. Morrison appear stronger. The foils get increasingly more negative—and therefore more effective—as the story progresses. When Mrs. Morrison reads the letter from Andrew, it is immediately apparent that Andrew is overprotective of his mother, which is not inherently a bad quality. However, he is also narrow-minded, thinking that she cannot take care of herself. In his letter Andrew writes, "It is not right that you should live alone there. Sally is old and liable to accident. I am anxious about you. Come on for Thanksgiving—and come to stay."

Mrs. Morrison notes to herself that Andrew's statement is false, because Sally is a woman "of changeless aspect and incessant activity," meaning that, although Sally may be advanced in years, she is still very youthful and energetic. However, Andrew is unable to look past his own impressions and so continues to view both Mrs. Morrison and Sally as old and feeble. Also, if one examines Andrew's letter closely, it appears that Andrew's intentions are not so charitable. Though he is certainly concerned about his mother's welfare, he is also feeling inadequate. At the beginning of his letter, he writes: "You belong with me. . . . It is not right that Jean's husband should support my mother. I can do it easily now." Andrew feels insecure about the fact that Joe has been helping to support Mrs. Morrison and wants to prove to himself, and possibly others, that he is capable of taking care of his own mother.

Though Andrew is narrow-minded, at least he is selfless when it comes to selling Mrs. Morrison's house. Andrew encourages his mother to sell the house but says that he will invest it for her and that she will keep all of the profits. The same is not true for Jean's husband, Joe. He wants Mrs. Morrison to sell her house and put the money into his business, although he offers to pay her interest on the investment. When she comes to stay with Jean and Joe, he tries to press Mrs. Morrison into selling her house by telling her "how much he needed capital, urging her to come and stay with them; it was such a help to Jeannie; asking questions about the house."

The biggest foil in the story is Mr. Butts, because he wants to own Mrs. Morrison and her house, giving her nothing in return. He is obviously attracted to her but is more attracted to the domestic skills she can offer him. Says Mr. Butts, "You aren't so young as you were, to be sure; I'm not, either. But you are as good a housekeeper as ever—better—you've had more experience." In addition to his blatant disregard for Mrs. Morrison's feelings, Mr. Butts has no dignity. When Mrs. Morrison tells him that she cannot remarry, he tells her, "It wouldn't look well if you did—at any rate, if you showed it." Mr. Butts does not want to marry Mrs. Morrison out of love. She is an object to him and one that he is willing to hide from society, as long as he gets his housekeeper. Because Mr. Butts is obviously lacking in dignity, it makes Mrs. Morrison's displays of dignity that much more effective. In fact, throughout the story, Mrs. Morrison is so dignified that even when she is dining alone with Sally, she goes to the table "with as much dignity as if twenty titled guests were before her."

All three men have motives for wanting Mrs. Morrison to give up her independence, and they are willing to sacrifice her happiness to get what they want. In the end, however, all three men fail in their goals to have Mrs. Morrison, her house, or her money. Mrs. Morrison, on the other hand, does not put anybody in a bad situation when pursuing her economic self-sufficiency. As a result, she is rewarded. In some cases, the rewards stem from her past good acts. For example, in the past she has gone out of her way to help the Haddleton farm-women. When her husband was alive, it was one of Mrs. Morrison's joys "to bring together these women—to teach and entertain them." This fact, coupled with the fact that "the whole town knew and admired" Mrs. Morrison, has given her a solid reputation in the community. As a result, Mrs. Morrison's announcement attracts "hundreds upon hundreds" of women, all of whom eventually join Mrs. Morrison's club.

Even in the management of the club, Mrs. Morrison's past good deeds come back to help her: "The town was full of Mrs. Morrison's ex-Sunday-school boys, who furnished her with the best they had—at cost." In other words, Mrs. Morrison's good reputation has extended to the young boys that she mentored in her husband's church. Now that the boys have grown up and are in a position to repay Mrs. Morrison's kindness, they do so willingly.

Though she certainly reaps rewards for her past good works in the community, the club would not be as much of a success as it is if Mrs. Morrison did not continue to demonstrate her good characteristics. First and foremost, unlike the men in the story, Mrs. Morrison is open-minded. Instead of excluding men, like men often excluded women, she rents out rooms in the Welcome House to an increasing number of people, male and female:

> Circle within circle, and group within group, she set small classes and departments at work, having a boys' club by and by in the big room over the woodshed, girls' clubs, reading clubs, study clubs, little meetings of every sort that were not held in churches, and some that were—previously.

Of course, if Mrs. Morrison were like Joe, concerning herself only with money, she could just take the admission fees and keep most of the profits. However, she keeps only a portion of the money, using the rest to invest back into the club, stocking "the library with many magazines for fifty dollars a year," feeding "her multitude with the plain viands agreed upon," and providing many other "collateral entertainments." In other words, she goes the extra mile to make sure that anybody who pays her dime admission fee has a comfortable and fulfilling experience. As a result, the club gets a great reputation, the membership grows, and Mrs. Morrison achieves her ultimate goal of financial self-sufficiency. However, her reward is even sweeter, because she achieves it by helping others—in this case, the Haddleton women. As Solomon notes, this is a common theme in many of Gilman's works: "Like Delia Morrison, numerous Gilman heroines find that in addressing their own desire to do meaningful work, they can aid other women, bringing about significant and much-needed social change."

In the end, the strong moral characterization of Mrs. Morrison, the portrayal of weakness in the three men in the story, and the successful completion of Mrs. Morrison's goal through honest, charitable work all underscore the point of the story. Gilman's moral message is clear to her turn-of-the-century audience: if women want to get ahead in a man's world, they will have the most success if they maintain their integrity and charity and do not adopt self-serving attitudes. In the race for equality with men, women should not be so foolish as to think they must become like men to achieve their goals.

Source: Ryan D. Poquette, Critical Essay on "Three Thanksgivings," in *Short Stories for Students,* Gale, 2003.

Charlotte Mayhew

Mayhew is a freelance writer. In this essay, Mayhew examines the way Gilman slowly draws the reader into her short story.

In the short story "Three Thanksgivings," Gilman carefully sets up the story so that the reader is slowly introduced to the idea that a woman can thrive without the standard husband-wife-child model of domestic bliss. At the time this story was written, Gilman's ideas on what woman's role in the world should be were radical. If she had used a less subtle approach in writing her story, she might have alienated her contemporary readers immediately. Instead, Gilman very cleverly enlists the reader's sympathy and draws the reader in slowly to her way of thinking. Rather than focusing on lengthy passages introducing each character, she painstakingly exposes her characters to the reader through their actions and words.

The main character, Mrs. Delia Morrison, is a widow. To make ends meet after her husband dies, she runs a boarding-house. Though she detests the intrusion and constant care boarders require, she never lets it show. Mrs. Morrison lives by herself and continues to take in boarders sporadically after her children have grown and started their own lives. When finances become too tight, she agrees to mortgage her beloved house to one Mr. Butts, a friend who wishes to marry her. She pays him interest on a yearly basis. The story opens just before Thanksgiving, two years before the $2,000 mortgage will come due.

What is shown at the beginning of the story gives the reader a limited, and conventional, impression of the characters. Running a boarding-house was one of the few respectable options open to women at that time. The plot appears to be setting up the classic you-must-pay-the-rent-I-can't-pay-the-rent scenario, but this theme is turned on its head when it is Mrs. Morrison who saves herself from the

> By the time the story draws to its close, it seems only logical that Mrs. Morrison should continue to live her life on her own terms, which is a radical notion indeed for the average nineteenth-century woman."

story's mild villain, Mr. Butts. She does this by starting a successful small business.

At the beginning of the story, Mrs. Morrison reads two letters from her children. Both children write asking her to come visit for Thanksgiving and to consider moving in with each of them respectively. Both children insist that their spouses would love to have Mrs. Morrison live with them. And both offer her her own small room to live in. Both children have suggestions on what to do with the money from the rental or sale of her large, empty house—her son would invest it and she could have the income from the investments, and her son-in-law would like to use it for capital for his business (he would pay interest, of course).

Her son Andrew writes that "it is not right that you should live alone there." He also says "it is not right" that his sister's husband should support Mrs. Morrison. He suggests that, instead, she come to live with him and his bride. Her daughter, Jean, on the other hand, suggests that her mother should come live with them because she could be "pretty comfortable" there, and her presence would "be such a comfort to me, and such a help with the babies." Both children wish their mother would do the accepted thing for a widow of her advanced years—either re-marry or move in with one of her children.

The first Thanksgiving is spent with her son, Andrew, and his wife, Annie, in their small parsonage. It is clear to Mrs. Morrison that she would mostly be in the way. They treat her with a great deal of deference on account of her age, which she hardly pays notice to at home. She feels smothered by the tiny house and is relieved to go home after a week.

Upon arriving home, she sets her "clear and daring mind" to work on the problem of what she can do with the house and all its contents to earn the money to pay off the mortgage interest and its principal in the two years she has left. Selling items would not raise enough ready cash, though there are many items in the house and its large attic. Mr. Butts says, "I'd like to know what a woman of your age can do with a house like this—and no money?" Mrs. Morrison sets out to figure out what she can do to earn money; she is sure there must be some way she can stay in the house and avoid marrying Mr. Butts.

She starts by taking a full inventory of the house and all its contents—from front to back, side to side, inside and out. This inventory is several pages into the story, and the reader is now firmly on Mrs. Morrison's side. Gilman has waited this long to show readers that Mrs. Morrison, though a woman and under such duress, is capable of clear thought and careful planning. Mrs. Morrison considers several possible options—continuing to take in boarders, turning her home into a hotel or a school for girls—and rejects each of these ideas. She then lights upon the idea of using her house as the meeting place for a women's club. She enlists the help of two old friends, who are both strong reform-minded women in their own right.

Mrs. Morrison invites her two friends, Mrs. Isabelle Carter Blake, of Chicago, and an Italian Countess, to visit and give a lecture at her house for the many women who live in the town and surrounding area. Between the persuasive efforts of Mrs. Morrison and her friends, they sell the idea of a women's club to the hundreds of local women who come to attend this lecture. The women's club will provide light refreshments and open rooms for meeting or resting once a week for a nominal fee. This club is a success almost immediately and the money starts rolling in. Thus passes an extremely busy year for Mrs. Morrison.

The second Thanksgiving finds Mrs. Morrison visiting her daughter, Jean, and her husband, Joe. They have three young children who keep their mother constantly looking out for them and leave her little time to socialize or even to leave the house. The room Mrs. Morrison is given is again very small, and she longs for her own house. She is glad to see the week end. She returns home to immerse herself in her fledgling business. By now, it does not seem odd that Mrs. Morrison is running the women's club, nor does it seem odd that she wishes to stay in her own house. The reader has seen the other options and they are clearly inferior to Mrs. Morrison staying in her own home.

To the reader, it is at first unclear why Delia Morrison will "not, at any price, marry Peter Butts." At the beginning of the story, Mr. Butts does not seem to be that bad, really. Gilman describes him thus:

> Mr. Peter Butts . . . had been a poor boy when she was a rich girl; and it gratified him much to realize—and to call upon her to realize—that their positions had changed. He meant no unkindness, his pride was honest and unveiled. Tact he had none.

At the beginning, Mr. Butts appears to be a benevolent, if not particularly attractive, figure who has been in love with Delia Morrison for many years and who wishes to help her. He sees their potential marriage as mutually beneficial—he will get her house and her status, and she will regain her purpose in life. Though Mrs. Morrison repeatedly refuses to marry Mr. Butts, he continues to ask, apparently believing that it is only a matter of time before she realizes that this is the way things should be. When she says, "I do not wish to marry again, Mr. Butts; neither you nor anyone," he responds: "Very proper, very proper, Delia. . . . It wouldn't look well if you did—at any rate, if you showed it. But why shouldn't you?"

Indeed, why should she not marry again though she does not wish it? Surely it is improper for a woman to live alone in a large house, even though that is where she has always lived. What could she possibly do with herself? Surely being alone, with no one to care for, would not make her happy. At least, not according to the feminine ideal at the time the story was written. But Mrs. Morrison is not a normal nineteenth-century heroine. She has her own ideas about how she should spend the rest of her life.

Barbara H. Solomon, writing in the Introduction to *Herland and Selected Short Stories of Charlotte Perkins Gilman,* states that Gilman

> was reared in a world which considered her being female as the foremost fact about her. Thus, she was raised to take her place in the domestic sphere in which it was assumed all normal women would find happiness and fulfillment. . . . she attempted to live in the sphere assigned to women, with the goals which were described in her era as 'the cult of true womanhood.'

Gilman has, in Mrs. Delia Morrison, shown readers a heroine who smilingly disproves many commonly-held nineteenth-century beliefs about women. Gilman leads the reader so slowly to this point that the reader is hoping for the success of Mrs. Morrison's endeavors without even realizing just how far from the norm those endeavors are. Mrs. Morrison clearly states her desire to continue to live, unmarried, in the house she loves. Mrs. Morrison's opinion is dismissed as unimportant by her children and by Mr. Butts. It is simply too unbelievable in that day and age. The nineteenth-century notion of true womanhood was one that limited woman's path to happiness to pursuits inside the home. Without a family to care for, Mrs. Morrison is useless indeed—and should be unhappy. That is not, however, the case. In fact, as Gilman writes, "Mrs. Morrison was alone, and while living in the Welcome House she was never unhappy."

Gilman sets up Mrs. Delia Morrison as a quiet and gracious rebel. Mrs. Morrison's usual response to disagreement is to smile in some way, state her case clearly, and then continue on her chosen path. Gilman uses Mrs. Morrison's actions and words to impress upon the reader how important living in her home is to her. Mrs. Morrison is unmoved by the pressure brought to bear from her children and Mr. Butts to change her life to suit them better. When Mr. Butts leaves after the first conversation in the story, "Mrs. Morrison saw him go with a keen light in her fine eyes, a more definite line to that steady, pleasant smile." This is just a hint of her determination to carve out a new life for herself that is free from her indebtedness to him.

Mr. Butts' visit after the second Thanksgiving is a bit different from the first. Mr. Butts is somewhat astonished that Mrs. Morrison has earned enough to pay the interest. He says, "'How on earth'd you get it, Delia?' he demanded. 'Screwed it out o' those club-women?'" This little glimpse into the workings of Mr. Butts' brain does him no favors in the reader's eyes. By the third visit, it is clear that Mr. Butts wants Mrs. Morrison and her house more as a social prize to increase his standing in the community than for any caring for her or respect for her numerous capabilities. He says, "'I'd like to know how you got this money. You *can't* a' skinned it out o' that club of yours.'" It is simply impossible for him to believe that she has earned enough money to pay back the $2,000 mortgage, with interest, in 10-cent increments over two years' time. Mr. Butts is incapable of believing a woman capable of that kind of meticulous planning and foresight. He is hardly unusual for his era.

Indeed, the average nineteenth-century reader of ''Three Thanksgivings'' would normally agree and identify with Mr. Butts. It is Gilman's careful treatment of the subject matter as a story, that draws the reader into sympathetic agreement with her. The idea of Mrs. Morrison keeping her house and her independence becomes the most obvious solution. In this way, Gilman turns the usual nineteenth-century belief that women are less capable than men on its head very slowly so that it draws the reader into a sort of complicity with the author. It is subtle enough that the reader does not notice the shift in perception.

The story ends at the third Thanksgiving, when Mrs. Morrison gathers her family to her and tells them of her future plans: to stay where she is and continue to run the women's club out of her home. By the time the story draws to its close, it seems only logical that Mrs. Morrison should continue to live her life on her own terms, which is a radical notion indeed for the average nineteenth-century woman.

Source: Charlotte Mayhew, Critical Essay on ''Three Thanksgivings,'' in *Short Stories for Students,* Gale, 2003.

Sources

Ceplair, Larry, ed., *Charlotte Perkins Gilman: A Nonfiction Reader,* Columbia University Press, 1991, p. 189.

Gilman, Charlotte Perkins, *The Living of Charlotte Perkins Gilman: An Autobiography,* University of Wisconsin Press, 1990, p. 121.

———, ''Selections from *Women and Economics:* A Study of the Economic Relation between Men and Women,'' in *The Yellow Wall-paper and Other Writings,* Modern Library, 2000, p. 235.

———, ''Three Thanksgivings,'' in *The Yellow Wall-paper and Other Writings,* Modern Library, 2000, pp. 31–46.

Johnson, Paul, *A History of the American People,* HarperCollins, 1998, pp. 656, 659.

Kessler, Carol Fairley, ''Charlotte Perkins Gilman,'' in *Modern American Women Writers,* Charles Scribner's Sons, 1991, pp. 155–70.

Knight, Denise D., *Charlotte Perkins Gilman: A Study of the Short Fiction,* Twayne Publishers, 1997, p. 68.

Miskolcze, Robin, ''Charlotte Perkins Gilman,'' in *Dictionary of Literary Biography,* Vol. 221: *American Women Prose Writers, 1870–1920,* edited by Sharon M. Harris, Gale, 2000, pp. 148–58.

Roberts, J. M., *Twentieth Century: The History of the World, 1901 to 2000,* Penguin Books, 2000, pp. 26–27.

Scharnhorst, Gary, *Charlotte Perkins Gilman,* Twayne Publishers, 1985, pp. 85, 96–97.

Solomon, Barbara H., ''Introduction,'' in *Herland and Selected Stories,* by Charlotte Perkins Gilman, edited by Barbara H. Solomon, Signet Classic, 1992, pp. xii, xvii, xx–xxii, xxiv.

Further Reading

Baker, Jean H., ed., *Votes for Women: The Struggle for Suffrage Revisited,* Viewpoints on American Culture series, Oxford University Press, 2002.

This book includes eleven essays, which collectively give an overview of the American women's suffrage movement in the nineteenth and twentieth centuries. The discussion includes key figures such as Susan B. Anthony and Sojourner Truth and key events such as the 1848 gathering at Seneca Falls, New York. In addition, the book features an introductory essay by Baker that gives the suffrage movement context within other events of the times.

Crittenden, Ann, *The Price of Motherhood: Why the Most Important Job in the World Is Still the Least Valued,* Owl Books, 2002.

In this book, Crittenden, a noted economic journalist, asserts that mothers are penalized for their childbearing role. Whether mothers stay at home, work, are single or married, Crittenden uses studies and financial facts to show that they are all at an economic disadvantage to others in society. However, Crittenden does not just define the problem; she also offers solutions based on working models found in such diverse areas as Sweden and the United States military.

Freedman, Estelle B., *No Turning Back: The History of Feminism and the Future of Women,* Ballantine Books, 2002.

In this engaging, narrative history of feminism, Freedman explores a wide range of associated issues, including race, politics, economics, and health, while providing her own critical interpretations of these topics.

Gilbert, Sandra M., and Susan Gubar, *The Madwoman in the Attic: The Woman Writer and the Nineteenth-Century Imagination,* Yale University Press, 2000.

Sandra M. Gilbert and Susan Gubar originally published this groundbreaking volume of feminist literary criticism in 1979. The book offered revolutionary concepts in literary criticism about women and gave critical studies of the works of major nineteenth-century women authors, such as Jane Austen, Mary Shelley, and Charlotte Brontë. This latest edition includes a new introduction from the two authors.

Helgesen, Sally, *The Female Advantage: Women's Ways of Leadership,* Currency/Doubleday, 1995.

Helgesen explores the difference between how women's management style differs from their male counterparts. The author says that women—who tend to lead via a relationship web—are better suited for the modern business environment than men—who tend to lead via old-fashioned hierarchies. The book also provides in-depth profiles of four women executives who became successful as a result of their female qualities of leadership.

Karpinski, Joanne B., ed., *Critical Essays on Charlotte Perkins Gilman,* G. K. Hall & Company, 1992.
This book includes a short biography by Karpinski, reprints of original reviews of Gilman's works, and several essays from modern critics. Collectively, the book offers a biographical and critical overview of Gilman's life and work.

Schneir, Miriam, ed., *Feminism: The Essential Historical Writings,* Vintage Books, 1994.
In this book, Schneir compiles an impressive anthology of the writings that helped to define the feminist

movement. The volume includes essays, fiction, memoirs, and letters by Mary Wollstonecraft, Virginia Woolf, Emma Goldman, John Stuart Mill, and many other feminist writers. Schneir also provides commentary on the writings.

————, ed., *Feminism in Our Time: The Essential Writings, World War II to the Present,* Vintage Books, 1994.
This book completes the history that Schneir started with *Feminism: The Essential Historical Writings.* The anthology focuses on contemporary writings from the second half of the twentieth century and features fifty selections, including many excerpts from longer works. As in her first collection, Schneir provides commentary on the writings.

The Toxic Donut

Terry Bisson

1993

"The Toxic Donut," by Terry Bisson, was first published in the June 1993 issue of *Science Fiction Age* magazine. It was included later that year in the short story collection *Bears Discover Fire and Other Stories*. The story, which takes place in the future, consists of one long monologue, in which a television production assistant walks a guest through the rehearsal for an awards show later that night. However, unlike the recipients at other awards shows, who receive a gift of some sort, the special guest on this show must sacrifice her life by consuming all of humanity's toxic waste from the previous year—which has been condensed into a single, edible donut. Like many of his other works, "The Toxic Donut" combines both humor and social commentary. In this case, Bisson uses his strange depiction of a fictional future to comment on the environmental destruction of earth. The story was very timely, as it was written during the escalation of the environmental movement in the early 1990s, when many organizations and news media raised public awareness of the environment. A copy of the short story can be found in *Bears Discover Fire and Other Stories*, which was published by Tor Books in a paperback reprint edition in 1995.

Author Biography

Terry Bisson was born on February 12, 1942, in Hopkins County, Kentucky. After graduating from the University of Louisville with his bachelor's degree in 1964, Bisson worked for nine years as a magazine comic writer. Following this, he worked as an auto mechanic (1972–1977) and as an editor and copywriter with Berkley Books (1976–1985). In 1980, Bisson published his first novel, *Wyrldmaker*. Over the next decade, Bisson wrote three more novels: *Talking Man* (1986), *Fire on the Mountain* (1988), and *Voyage to the Red Planet* (1990). Although these initial novels earned Bisson some good reviews, it was not until Bisson started publishing his quirky short stories in science fiction magazines that he began to win awards and earn widespread critical acclaim. His short story "Bears Discover Fire" (1991) won both a Hugo and a Nebula award, science fiction's two highest honors, as well as a number of other awards. In 1993, Bisson collected this story and several other magazine stories, including "The Toxic Donut," in *Bears Discover Fire and Other Stories*.

Bisson is a versatile writer who has pursued science fiction across a number of media. He has adapted several of his stories into stage or audio dramas, and he has adapted several science fiction films by others into novelizations, including *Johnny Mnemonic: A Novel* (1995), *Alien Resurrection* (1997), and *Galaxy Quest* (1999). However, one of Bisson's biggest science fiction writing challenges came in the mid-1990s when he was contracted by Walter M. Miller, Jr. to complete the long-awaited sequel to the author's classic 1960 science fiction novel, *A Canticle for Leibowitz*. Miller had become ill and could not finish the novel. Working from Miller's notes and outline, Bisson wrote the final sixty pages of the work. The sequel, entitled *St. Leibowitz and the Wild Horse Woman*, was published posthumously in 1997, with no cover credit to Bisson's involvement.

In addition to his adult science fiction works, Bisson has also written or cowritten several young adult novels and nonfiction books. These include a biography, *Nat Turner* (1987); a nonfiction book, *Car Talk with Click and Clack, the Tappet Brothers* (1991), with National Public Radio's call-in mechanics, Tom and Ray Magliozzi; the science fiction novel *Boba Fett: The Fight to Survive* (2002); and two science fiction novels with Stephanie Spinner—*Be First in the Universe* (2000) and *Expiration Date: Never* (2001). Finally, Bisson has adapted several works into comics or graphic novels. These have included selections by science fiction and fantasy authors such as Greg Bear and

Anne McCaffrey and classics by William Shakespeare and Jane Austen.

Bisson's science fiction books include his second collection of short stories, *In the Upper Room and Other Likely Stories* (2000), and his sixth novel, *The Pickup Artist* (2001). Bisson lives and works in New York City.

Plot Summary

At the beginning of the futuristic story "The Toxic Donut," two characters, Ron and Kim, are on an awards show stage, where Ron, the administrative assistant for the annual show, is conducting a rehearsal. As Ron explains to Kim, the guest, how the live show will work, he establishes the pattern that the rest of the story follows. The story consists entirely of Ron's instructions to Kim. Ron gives a little information about the show, and then Kim responds with a question or statement, although the reader never hears what Kim says. As a result, the reader must derive what Kim is saying from Ron's responses to her questions and statements.

Ron starts by introducing himself and then congratulates Kim, who finds this odd. Ron explains that Kim has been chosen to represent all of humanity and nature for one half-hour that night and then asks questions about her family, whom Ron is sure will be watching the show—since it has higher ratings than the Academy Awards. Ron takes Kim over to another area of the stage and starts to walk her through the half-hour program. In the first ten minutes, Ron tells Kim that she will wait off to the side and that she is the first woman in two years to be on the show. Kim asks that, if this is the case, why men are not going to lead her out onstage instead of the women assistants, and Ron assumes she is making a joke. Kim asks why the annual guests on the show are called Consumers, and when she offers another name, Ron assumes she is joking again. Kim asks if she can meet the host, Mr. Crystal, but Ron stalls, saying that the host is very busy— although he will see what he can do.

At the ten-minute mark, the Presidents of the world's five regions will come out and praise Kim for her courage, and then the host will explain to the audience how the Lottery works. The Lottery— which is involuntary this year for the first time—is how Kim was chosen for this show. Kim was obviously chosen for the show against her will—but Ron dismisses this concern. The Presidents will give Kim a plaque, which is to be given to her parents after the show. They will watch a presentation from a group of Native People, who will praise the fact that science is no longer humanity's enemy. Kim will walk out to the center of the stage with the host.

At the twenty-minute mark, the President of the International Institute will bring out the Donut in a paper sack. He will present a sad video—showing the pollution problems and environmental consequences that people faced in the past—followed by the glad video, which praises science and explains how they are able to contain all of the year's toxic wastes and pollutants into one super-concentrated donut. The President will hand the bag with the donut to Kim and then go backstage again. Ron tells Kim that, at the end of the show, she will need to pull the donut out of the bag. Kim asks what she does with it then, and Ron thinks she is joking. Very seriously, he tells her that she is supposed to eat the donut. Kim does not realize until the end that she has been chosen, against her will, to sacrifice herself and save the environmental health of the world by eating the toxic donut.

Characters

Kim

Kim is a Consumer, the one human sacrifice who has been chosen by a worldwide lottery to eat the toxic donut—a super-concentrated pastry made from all of humanity's toxic pollution and waste from the previous year. This sacrificial act is going to take place at an annual awards show, which will be televised live that evening. In the story, Ron, the administrative assistant for the show, walks Kim through the rehearsal. As Ron explains how the show works, the reader finds out that, unlike previous years, this year's lottery was involuntary. Throughout the story, Bisson does not reveal why Kim is on the show. This ambiguity is magnified by the fact that only Ron's part of the dialogue is revealed—Kim is not heard.

However, although the reader never hears exactly what Kim is saying, her part of the dialogue can be reconstructed through Ron—who repeats many of her statements and questions and who gives distinctive responses that indicate the nature of what Kim might be saying. By examining Ron's responses to Kim, the reader can get a better picture of Kim's background and experience. Ron is surprised to find out that Kim speaks English, given the country that she is from—which is never stated. However, since he says that the country used to be British, Kim is most likely from some region that was colonized by England or the United States. Kim has been chosen for the lottery against her will, because somebody bought a ticket for her. Throughout the story, Kim has some doubts about being on the show, but the reader does not find out why until the end of the rehearsal—which is also the end of the story. At this point, both the reader and Kim realize that she is supposed to sacrifice her life by eating the toxic donut.

Ron

Ron is the Chief Administrative Assistant of Mr. Crystal, the host of the annual television show where Kim, a Consumer, is going to sacrifice her life and save the environment by eating the toxic donut. Ron is the only one who speaks in the story, although his responses to Kim indicate the types of things that she is saying. In the story, Ron walks Kim—and the reader—through the rehearsal for the half-hour television show. From the beginning, Ron is all business, giving Kim a minute-by-minute rundown and rushing her through each part of the rehearsal. Ron is interested only in getting the rehearsal over with, to the point that he quickly dismisses Kim's questions and concerns—which he often mistakes as jokes. Because of this, and because he thinks that everybody knows about the show, Ron attribute's Kim's ignorance of the sacrifice to her sense of humor.

Ron sees the show itself as more important than Kim's sacrifice—so much so that he is not even able to promise that Kim will be able to meet Mr. Crystal before the show. To Ron, everything is about maintaining the show's schedule and image, so Ron does not even really pay attention to the content of the annual telecast. As a result, when he is walking Kim through the rehearsal, he is unable to give her specific details about many parts of the show, such as how the lighting is going to work or how scientists are able to compress all of the world's wastes into one small donut. This uncaring attitude extends to the treatment of Kim, and Ron is very cold and emotionally detached, glossing over potentially pain-

Media Adaptations

- "The Toxic Donut" was adapted by Bisson as a stage play and produced at West Bank Theatre in New York from 1992 to 1993, along with five other stories from *Bears Discover Fire and Other Stories*—"Two Guys from the Future," "They're Made out of Meat," "Next," "Are There Any Questions?" and "Partial People." The script for "The Toxic Donut," which can be found on the World Wide Web at http://www.terrybisson.com/donutplay.html (last accessed January 2003), features both characters, as the story does. However, in the stage play, Bisson has Kim mouth her words silently, to achieve the same monologue effect as the story.

- "The Toxic Donut" was also adapted by Bisson as an online audio drama for the Sci-Fi Channel's Seeing Ear Theatre. The play was directed by Brian Smith and features Peter Coyote as Ron and Rebecca Nice as a character named Bound N' Gagged. The downloadable audio file of the play, which is available for free at http://www.scifi.com/set/playhouse/meat/ (last accessed January 2003), also includes two other audio dramas by Bisson—"They're Made out of Meat" and "Next." Like "The Toxic Donut, "both of these plays are based on stories from *Bears Discover Fire and Other Stories.* The three audio dramas are also available under the title "Three Odd Comedies" on an abridged audiocassette entitled *Seeing Ear Theatre: A Sci-Fi Channel Presentation,* which was released by Dove Books Audio in 1998.

---

ful topics, such as the fact that at the end of the show, Kim is expected to sacrifice herself.

Themes

Environmentalism

The main theme of "The Toxic Donut" is concern for the destruction of earth's environment. While the story takes place in the future, after humanity has devised a solution for environmental destruction, Ron, the administrative assistant, talks about humanity's past—in other words, the time in which Bisson and his readers live: "I mean it all really happened! Dead rivers, dead birds, dioxins." In Ron's time, environmentalism is a worldwide concern, so much so that there is an "International Institute of Environmental Sciences." As Ron notes, Kim represents "everybody in the world who cares about the environment, and these days that includes everybody." However, instead of trying to mini-mize pollution, as today's environmentalists advocate, the futuristic human society in the story is free to produce as much toxic waste as it wants, since at the end of the year, it can be compressed into one donut with one human sacrifice designated to eat it.

Science and Technology

Like many science fiction stories, "The Toxic Donut" includes several references to science and technology, the most overt of which is the nanotechnology that is used to compress all of the world's toxic wastes into a single donut. As Ron says, the president of the International Institute of Environmental Sciences will give "the Wonders of Science rap, where he explains how they have managed to collect and contain all the year's toxic wastes, pollutants, etc., and keep them out of the environment—." However, while science is viewed positively on the television show, the depiction in the story is a negative one, as human values and the importance of individual human lives are both sacrificed for the greater good of technology. Toxic waste and pollution is generally a by-product of

Topics for Further Study

- Imagine that you are a television producer in the year 2050. Research projected forecasts from sociologists, economists, environmentalists, and others to get a picture of what life might be like in this era. Develop an idea for a new television show that captures the spirit of this future time, using your research to support your ideas.

- When Bisson wrote his story, environmentalism was a key public issue, and many regular citizens became activists by conserving resources, reusing items whenever possible, and recycling items when done with them. Research the state of environmentalism today, and discuss how these community efforts have or have not made a difference in helping to heal and protect the Earth's damaged environment. If they have not made much of a difference, give some reasons why.

- On the southeast side of Chicago, there is a public housing project called Altgeld Gardens, but the locals have dubbed it the "Toxic Donut," since there are a number of landfills, sewage treatment plants, steel mills, and toxic chemical factories that surround it. Research the history behind this region, and discuss whether or not you think the title of Bisson's story had an effect on the nickname, or vice versa, using your research to support your claims.

- Pick one environmental issue, other than toxic pollution, that is a cause for concern today. Research the details behind this issue, and plot the major events in this issue's history—such as disasters, court rulings, and public-awareness campaigns—on a time line.

- Research the current legislation that regulates the dumping of toxic wastes. What kinds of restrictions are imposed on companies that dump toxic materials, and what kinds of penalties do companies have to pay when they violate these restrictions? Discuss whether you think these restrictions should be more or less strict and why you feel this way.

---

technological production. In the story, Bisson singles out the large manufacturing corporations that create much of this waste, although he does it in a subtle way. In response to one of Kim's unheard questions, Ron says, "No, the corporations themselves don't make a presentation. They want to keep a very low profile." The companies in Bisson's story do not want to be linked to their pollution or to the sanctioned murder that is necessary to make up for it.

Entertainment

In Ron's futuristic society, watching a human sacrifice himself or herself on live television is considered entertainment. As Ron notes, "everybody watches it anyway. More than watch the Academy Awards. Eight to ten points more. A point is about thirteen million people these days, did you know that?" Ron is concerned only with the entertainment value of Kim's death and with the success of the television show that will broadcast it live. Kim's death itself is given little importance outside of the show. For example, in one of Kim's unheard questions, she asks whether or not she can meet the host. Ron responds, "Well—of course—maybe—tonight right before the show, if time allows. But you have to understand, Mr. Crystal's a very busy man, Kim." The host's schedule is ranked a higher priority than Kim's life, even though it is Kim who is saving humanity by making her sacrifice. Kim's lack of importance is emphasized even more by the fact that, for part of the half-hour television show, she will be waiting on the side of the stage. In addition, when she is officially honored, it is short. Says Ron, "There's a brief statement; nothing elaborate. 'Your great courage, protecting our way of life' sort of thing."

Style

Satire

Satire is a form of humor that comments on a social situation by portraying it in an unflattering or absurd manner. Using satire to comment on a situation is often more effective than merely discussing the issue directly, since satire tends to leave lasting, humorous images in a reader's mind. It is ludicrous to imagine that a society could condense the sum total of a year's toxic waste and pollution to the size of a donut. However, Bisson makes this laughable idea a reality in a future society so that he can point out some real issues, such as the problem of consumption, which is closely linked to pollution. Currently, humans in industrialized countries are consuming many of earth's natural resources faster than these resources can be replenished. Some of these resources are used by corporations to manufacture products, and the by-products of this manufacturing are the source of much toxic pollution. These products are in turn sold to the public, who are often referred to as consumers because of their financial value to corporations. In other words, many of the corporations that are polluting earth exist only to feed the growing human consumption of various products. Because of this, it makes sense that Bisson chooses to have the television show refer to Kim—and the other annual human sacrifices—as "Consumers."

Monologue

The entire story consists of one long section of monologue from Ron. It becomes clear in the beginning of the story that Ron is the only one whom the reader will hear speak. In the first paragraph, Ron says, "Let me begin, at the risk of seeming weird, by saying congratulations." However, in the beginning of the next paragraph, Ron says, "Of course I know. I've been doing this show every year for six years; how could I not know?" The reader may be confused at first by gaps like this, which occur throughout the story. Ron is responding to questions and statements from Kim, which Bisson has not included, as an author would in a normal, two-sided conversation, or dialogue. The use of this type of conversational monologue affects the exposition—the method by which a writer informs the reader of what is going on in the story. Kim's half of the dialogue must be reconstructed or inferred from Ron's responses, which, in turn, encourages the reader to look more closely at the story.

Foreshadowing

Bisson does not reveal until the very end of the story that Kim is supposed to kill herself on the television show by consuming the donut. Says Ron, "Okay. We all know what happens next . . . You eat it." However, even though this fact is not revealed to both Kim and Bisson's readers until the end, the author foreshadows Kim's death several times in the story. Foreshadowing is a technique that an author uses to give clues as to what might happen later in the story. In "The Toxic Donut," Ron does this many times. Says Ron, "Did you, I mean do you have a family?" His speaking about Kim in the past tense alerts the reader that there might be some reason Kim will not be around at the end of the story. On a similar note, Ron tells Kim that, during the show, the presidents will "have a plaque that goes to your family after." Since the plaque will not be going to Kim, there is more reason to suspect that something bad is going to happen to her.

Historical Context

In the late 1980s and early 1990s, environmentalism was on the rise. Although the Environmental Protection Agency and the first Earth Day were both in 1970 and there were miscellaneous environmental disasters and planning initiatives in the 1970s and early 1980s, it was not until the mid-1980s that things really started to heat up—both literally and figuratively. In 1985, the *Rainbow Warrior,* the flagship of the nonviolent, environmental pressure group Greenpeace, was bombed and sunk by French government agents in Auckland Harbor, New Zealand. Greenpeace had been trying to protest French nuclear testing in the South Pacific. Fernando Pereira, a Dutch photographer, was killed in the aftermath of the explosion. The same year, British meteorologists confirmed their earlier suspicion that there was a hole in earth's ozone layer over Antarctica. The hole was created from chemicals like chlorofluorocarbons, which at the time were being widely used in commercial products such as aerosol spray cans. In 1986, a nuclear power plant at Chernobyl in the Ukraine had a full-scale meltdown, leaking toxic radiation into the surrounding area. The same year, a chemical warehouse in Basel, Switzerland, had a massive fire, which caused more than one thousand tons of toxic chemicals to be dumped into the Rhine River. The accident killed much of the river's wildlife and contaminated drinking water supplies. These and other incidents helped to ignite the public's passion and gave some bargaining power to environmental activists.

However, it was not until 1989 that the public really started to get involved. On March 24, 1989, the oil tanker *Exxon Valdez* crashed into an underwater reef, dumping more than ten million gallons of oil into the pristine waters of Alaska's Prince William Sound. This oil spill spread quickly, killing wildlife and causing years of ecological damage. Environmentalists were starting to gain a greater foothold before this disaster, but the incident ignited a public outcry and led to massive media coverage of all environmental issues. These included pollution, deforestation, acid rain, the widespread use of landfills and incinerators, overpopulation, and wildlife extinction. One of the biggest issues that concerned both environmentalists and the general public in the late 1980s was the greenhouse effect—also known as global warming. The greenhouse effect is the gradual warming of earth's atmosphere, which is caused when an increasing amount of the sun's heat reaches earth's surface. Normally, earth's atmosphere radiates much of the sun's heat back into space. However, when certain gases—most notably, carbon dioxide—build up in the atmosphere, the gases reflect the sun's extra heat back onto earth's surface. Environmentalists warned that if the rate of deforestation in developing areas like South America and the worldwide consumption of natural resources continued to rise, so would earth's temperature.

Global warming was one of the key topics discussed at the 1992 U.N. Conference on Environment and Development, a meeting in Brazil that brought together delegates from more than 170 nations. Although this massive environmental forum, known as the Earth Summit, opened up international discussion on many environmental issues, some prominent leaders like former president George Bush proclaimed that there was not enough scientific evidence to justify restrictions on the use of natural resources. As a result, no binding treaties came out of the conference.

Critical Overview

Although Bisson's first science fiction novel was written in 1980, he did not receive widespread critical acclaim until the early 1990s, when he began to publish science fiction short stories in magazines. In 1993, he collected a number of these stories into *Bears Discover Fire and Other Stories.* In a 1993 review of the collection for *Kirkus Reviews,* the reviewer notes of Bisson that "at his best, he combines a splendidly loopy inventiveness with real poignancy, a hard-edged sense of wonder and a grasp of the genuinely alien." Other 1993 reviews of the collection are equally favorable. A critic from *Publishers Weekly* notes "the astonishing range of Bisson's talent" and calls Bisson "one of science fiction's most promising short story practitioners."

Within the collection, most reviewers single out the award-winning title story, "Bears Discover Fire," as worthy of the highest praise. Says Martha Soukup in her 1993 *Washington Post Book World* review, the collection "is worth it for the title story alone." Soukup includes this tale in the category of "Bisson's homier tales of people living on in a world that can change itself more than it can change them." Nevertheless, critics still enjoy "The Toxic Donut," a story that falls into Soukup's category of "very brief japes," which she says can be read "as transcripts of sketch comedy." The story is one of the collection's three environmental stories. The *Publishers Weekly* critic notes of this trio of stories that they "address environmental concerns with a black humor that enhances rather than mitigates their impact." Likewise, the reviewer from *Kirkus* labels it as one of the many "agreeably batty commentaries" in the collection. In fact, reviewers have often noted the humorous aspects of Bisson's writing, to the point that in his entry on Bisson in the *St. James Guide to Science Fiction Writers,* Paul Kincaid labels Bisson as "a humorist." In addition to Bisson's critical success, he has also enjoyed favor with popular audiences, who appreciate his brand of humorous science fiction.

Criticism

Ryan D. Poquette

Poquette has a bachelor's degree in English and specializes in writing about literature. In the following essay, Poquette discusses the relative unimportance of Kim's involuntary sacrifice in Bisson's story, while exploring the sinister implications of the act.

Kim is expected to sacrifice herself for the benefit of the entire world, something that Ron alludes to in the beginning of the story when he says, "You have been chosen to represent all humanity for one evening.'' However, Kim's sacrifice is involuntary; she has not chosen to die. In one of her unheard statements, Kim notes this. Ron responds, saying, ''I'm sorry you feel that way. I'm sure voluntary would be better. But somebody must have bought you a ticket; that's the way it works.''

Although Ron and the producers of the television show go to great lengths to conceal it, Kim's sacrifice is relatively unimportant, a fact that readers can see when they dig beneath the surface of the story. Bisson encourages his readers to do just this, through the use of several cues. First of all, there is the nature of the sacrifice itself. The idea of a person sacrificing himself or herself to save humanity is present in many cultures throughout history, one notable example being the Christian religion—Jesus Christ's willing death on the cross. In this case, however, the producers of the toxic donut show—and indeed the human world who supports this sacrifice—are making a mockery of the act. Kim's forced sacrifice is neither divine, since it is not done to save humanity's souls, nor eternal, since it only saves humanity for one year. Despite this fact, everybody involved with the show gives the act an increased importance. Says Ron at the beginning of the rehearsal, ''You are, for one half hour tonight, the representative of all life on the planet. Hell, all life in the Universe, as far as we know.''

Yet, even in this statement, Bisson is having Ron undercut the importance of Kim's death. Kim is supposedly the representative of everybody and everything—but only for ''one half hour.'' In fact, the half-hour format of the show, which also provides the structure for the rehearsal, helps lead a reader to understanding the real importance of Kim's sacrifice. Since Ron is all business and cares most about the show's success, he speeds through the rehearsal, giving a minute-by-minute breakdown of how the show will play out. For Ron, there is no time for small talk. At one point, in one of her unheard responses, Kim tries to remind Ron that they have already established what Mr. Crystal, the Host, should call her on the show. Ron is briefly apologetic and then goes back to his itinerary: ''Okay. Anyway. A little ad-lib and it's 9:10. I have it all here on my clipboard, see? To the minute.''

Ron is also unresponsive to many of Kim's concerns, such as the fact that she has been chosen against her will. Ron thinks that Kim is joking when she brings up such issues. For example, at one point, Kim asks why she and the other annual guests on the show are called ''Consumers.'' Ron responds, ask-

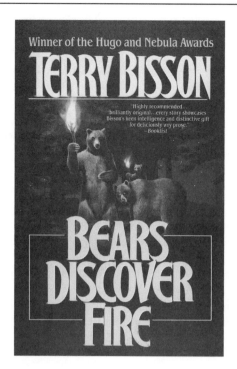

Cover for the short story collection featuring ''The Toxic Donut''

ing, ''What would you want us to call you?'' Kim's response causes Ron to think that she is just being funny. Although it is impossible to guess exactly what Kim might have said, given the context of Ron's responses, one assumes that it is a derogatory name. Kim is obviously not happy. But Ron's only concern—and the main concern of the producers—is to maintain the good image of the show, which, as he tells her, everybody watches. Says Ron, ''More than watch the Academy Awards. Eight to ten points more. A point is about thirteen million people these days, did you know that?''

Bisson helps to underscore the importance of this image campaign by giving capitalized titles to many people and items on the show. To begin with, almost everybody in the story has a capitalized title that denotes his or her position. Mr. Crystal is ''the Host,'' Ron is ''the Host's Chief Administrative Assistant,'' there is going to be a presentation by the ''Native People,'' and there is going to be a brief statement by the five ''Presidents of the Common Market.'' Even Kim has a title—''Consumer.'' In addition to these actual titles or designations; however, there are some people and items that are capitalized, which normally would not be. For example, the women who lead people on and off the

What Do I Read Next?

- Douglas Adams is widely considered to be one of the funniest science fiction writers ever, and his *The Hitchhiker's Guide to the Galaxy* (1979), the first in a multivolume series, is a classic satirical science fiction work. The story centers around the interstellar mishaps and adventures of Arthur Dent, a human who is transported off earth right before its destruction by an interplanetary construction crew—which plans to build an interstellar freeway. Dent's companions include an alien, Ford Prefect; a chronically depressed robot, Marvin; and a computer travel guide.

- Like the successful *Bears Discover Fire and Other Stories,* Bisson's second short story collection, *In the Upper Room and Other Likely Stories* (2000), addresses a wide range of topics, including the danger of technology, virtual reality, and cloning. The collection also includes his award-winning short story, "macs," which takes the idea of victim's rights to a chilling extreme.

- In the satirical novel *Voyage to the Red Planet* (1990), Bisson creates a futuristic world where, thanks to a massive economic depression, government services have been sold to private corporations. A movie producer named Markson leaves on a long voyage to Mars to shoot a film, but when the corporation in charge of mission control runs short on money and turns their attention elsewhere, Markson's ship goes off-course, and he and his crew get stranded.

- The end of the world, by man-made or natural disasters, has been a favorite topic of science fiction writers for the last century. In *Bangs and Whimpers: Stories about the End of the World* (1999), editor James Frenkel collects nineteen apocalypse tales by noted authors, including Isaac Asimov, Arthur C. Clarke, Connie Willis, and Robert Heinlein.

- Stephen King first published his novel *The Running Man* in 1982, under the pseudonym of Richard Bachman. The book depicts a futuristic society, in which television entertainment has become very deadly. In the story, Ben Richards, a desperate father who cannot afford medicine for his sick infant, enters himself in a battery of life-or-death contests, which yield big cash prizes for survivors. Richards is assigned to *The Running Man* game, in which he must run to survive, while being hunted down by bounty hunters.

- *Pollution: Opposing Viewpoints* (2000), edited by Tamara L. Roleff, collects contradictory arguments on various aspects of pollution. The thirty-one essays in the book fall into five question categories, which ask the contributors whether pollution is a serious problem, whether chemical pollutants pose a health risk, whether recycling is an effective response to pollution, how air pollution can be reduced, and how pollution should be managed.

- Duff Wilson, an investigative journalist for the *Seattle Times,* was nominated for a Pulitzer Prize for his hard-hitting series on hazardous wastes. In *Fateful Harvest: The True Story of a Small Town, a Global Industry, and a Toxic Secret* (2001), Wilson draws on this series of articles, as well as real-life case studies from a small town in Washington State, to show how some companies are disposing of toxic wastes by including them in fertilizer.

stage are called "the Girls," and the toxic pastry that Kim is expected to eat is called "the Donut." The effect of all of this capitalization is to give an added importance to the whole production. However, this importance is fake, just as all of the glitz and glamour of the show is fake. The trumped-up titles are merely an aspect of the television show's image, and—like Kim's death—hold no importance outside of the live production.

However, Kim cannot say much about her unimportance, because Bisson removes her dialogue. Bisson's use of a monologue, which he uses in other stories in the *Bears Discover Fire and Other Stories* collection, is particularly effective here. As the story progresses, Kim's silence helps to underscore the urgency of the story, since the reader does not have to bounce back and forth between Ron and Kim's dialogue. As a result, Bisson pulls his readers quickly through the story. However, Kim's obvious problem over her involuntary selection and the excessive use of capitalization, among other clues, tip readers off, letting them know that they might want to go back and read between the lines. If readers do this, the real importance of the television show is revealed.

Bisson is making a statement with Kim's silence. She is already dead. She stands for the silent masses of people who are being killed, and who will be killed in the future if something is not done to address the toxic pollution problem. In the story, however, Kim's death is buried, just as the involvement of the businesses that ultimately kill her is buried. Says Ron, "No, the corporations themselves don't make a presentation. They want to keep a very low profile."

On the surface of the story, just as on the surface of this futuristic society, it appears that the environment is a top priority to everybody. Says Ron, ". . . everybody in the world who cares about the environment, and these days that includes everybody." However, once one examines the nature of Kim's sacrifice—and the glitzy television production that showcases it—it is apparent that businesses rule this world. The show tries to distract its viewers from this fact by including several traditional icons of environmentalism, such as colors, and by including aspects that are guaranteed to get an emotional response. The producers of the television show feature the rainbow, one of the symbols used in modern-day society to denote environmentalism. Ron tells Kim that "there will be one song from the International Children's Rainbow Chorus," an ob-

> " [Kim] stands for the silent masses of people who are being killed, and who will be killed in the future if something is not done to address the toxic pollution problem."

vious ploy by the producers to use both children and the environment to tug at viewers' heartstrings. Even more apparent than the rainbow, however, is the color green, which is synonymous with environmentalism. In the television show, the girls who help lead people on and off stage will be wearing "little green outfits." Also, there are "green marks" on the stage designating where "the President of the International Institute of Environmental Science"— whom Ron and the others call "the Green Meany"— will stand.

This widespread use of an established environmental color is recognizable to most readers. What may not be as apparent at first is the fact that green is also the color of money, at least in the United States. Once again, by reading in between the lines, the reader can see that in the case of this story, green stands for both. The environment has become big money for corporations. Many of the wastes that comprise the toxic donut are from technological corporations. When Kim eats the donut, she may be saving humanity and the environment for a year, but she is really preserving the corporations' ability to continue to serve the human desire for consumption— the by-products of which become toxic wastes. With Kim's sacrificial murder, the companies will now have free license to produce as much toxic waste over the next year as they need to make big money in their manufacturing operations. The whole television production is ruled by this very money-centric idea, as evidenced by Ron's explanation about the year's worth of wastes that Kim is going to eat. Says Ron, "The fiscal year, by the way. That's why the Ceremony is tonight and not New Year's Eve." In fact, the story seems to imply that the corporations, who want to keep "a very low profile," are probably sponsoring the show. This is a small price to pay to avoid the types of expensive, image-damaging battles and economic sanctions that some corporations in Bisson's time had to contend with to continue dumping their hazardous wastes.

In the end, Bisson's message is simple. Many people are at fault for the current state of the environment, but unless everybody works to solve the problem, technology may come up with its own solution—one that involves sacrificing the individual consumer to save production.

Source: Ryan D. Poquette, Critical Essay on "The Toxic Donut," in *Short Stories for Students,* Gale, 2003.

Curt Guyette

Guyette is a longtime journalist who received a bachelor's degree in English writing from the University of Pittsburgh. In this essay, Guyette discusses Bisson's use of satire as a literary device employed to draw attention to serious issues.

In his short story "The Toxic Donut," science fiction writer Terry Bisson effectively draws attention to a variety of important issues by employing the literary device of satire, which can be defined as using humor to ridicule vices, stupidities, or abuses. With remarkably spare prose, the author's sharp wit and pointed barbs are directed at the shallow nature of popular culture, secretive corporate control, the primitive bloodlust that shadows even the most technologically advanced societies, and, most significantly, a lifestyle of consumerism and waste that threatens the future of the entire planet.

"The Toxic Donut" is a deceptively simply story that must be read more than once if it is to be fully appreciated. Although amusing from the outset, the tale takes on a whole new level of poignancy, or significance, when the true fate of the character Kim is revealed in the story's final line. Once the reader learns that this woman must eat that toxic donut, is there any doubt she is the subject of a very public execution? The author foreshadows her predicament within the first two lines as the administrative assistant Ron suffers a slip of the tongue and refers to her in the past tense when he queries, "Did you, I mean do you have a family?" It is not until the concluding sentence, however, that the lethal purpose of her appearance on the show is made certain. The fact that the character Kim is doomed makes the black humor pervading this story even darker. Almost every line contains a satiric jab of some sort. For example, in the first reading, the

fact that an International Rainbow Chorus provides the equivalent of a musical happy face by singing a lilting, optimistic tune by the Beatles titled "Here Comes the Sun" does not seem all that remarkable. But when seen as the prelude to a televised execution, the morbid irony of music that upbeat being played as a sort of processional to the gallows is overwhelming. Examples of this kind of satire permeate the story.

There is, however, more to this tale than dark comedy. When one looks at it closely, the story reveals itself to be a masterful work of art. Although it is impressive that Bisson can achieve so much in a piece so sparse, what elevates this accomplishment to an even higher level is that it serves as an ironic antithesis, or counterpoint, to what appears to be his main theme. In a story that warns mankind that it is at risk of killing itself with the excessive toxic waste it produces, Bisson does not waste a single word. Taking brevity to the extreme, he creates a story featuring just two characters, and only one of those is ever heard actually speaking. He achieves this in large part by merely outlining the subjects of his satire without filling in the details. Think of the targets found at shooting ranges that are simply the black silhouette of a human form. That's the way Bisson handles this story. He does not dwell on the subjects being stung by his jibes; instead, he merely alludes to them, letting the reader fill in all the implications. Take, for example, this passage in the story where Ron tells Kim:

> You're the first woman in two years, by the way; the last two consumers were men. I don't know why, consumers is just what we call them; I mean, call you. What would you want us to call you?

Those few lines accomplish so much. For one thing, the brief passage reveals how little value is being placed on human life in this world Bisson depicts. Kim is no longer seen as a person; she is simply a consumer. The description can be interpreted in a strictly literal sense: she will actually consume that toxic donut as the climax of the game-like show upon which she appears. But the idea of her as a consumer can also be viewed in a much broader way as a metaphor that implies deeper meaning. After all, as the author tells readers at the outset of the story, Kim represents all of mankind. In that context, consumerism dovetails perfectly with this story's overarching concern with the issue of pollution and its lethal potential. In a throwaway society, consumption and waste are inevitably bound together. Evidence of this is everywhere, from fuel-inefficient cars that create poisonous carbon monoxide when gasoline is "consumed," to the prevalence of items like disposable razors, which are used a few times then discarded, ending up in municipal trash incinerators that spew from their smokestacks pollutants such as the dioxin Bisson mentions. But the author does not bog down his story exploring these sorts of tangents. The same is true when it comes to pollution and the role corporations play in the problem. Bisson does not launch into a diatribe attacking companies that wield so much power over the direction society takes, and play such a large role in creating the pollution that poses such a threat. Instead, he refers to them only once, in an almost offhand manner, introducing the subject with an unheard question from Kim and Ron's response: "What? No, the corporations themselves don't make a presentation. They want to keep a very low profile." And that is it. The issue raised, Bisson is content to let the cryptic reference end there, with all its implications of string-pulling corporations left hanging, hovering like a shadow. It is almost like a game of tag. Bisson quickly hits on one theme, then moves on to the next.

There are certain issues, however, that emerge throughout the story. It is as if Bisson is using satire as a microscope that allows us to examine society in ways we don't usually see it. Although this takes place in the future, it is not at all distant. Published in 1993, this story was written at a time when newscasts were already providing frightening predictions from many scientists warning about the potential threat of global warming being caused by polluting greenhouse gases. And as far back as the 1950s, writers such as Rachel Carson were raising alarm over the threat which pesticides and other toxic chemicals posed to both human beings and nature as a whole. So the problems the author focuses on are not at all remote. Compounding the problem is what Bisson apparently sees as a lack of urgency on the part of society at large to understand and deal with the issue. This attitude is reflected in the way Ron describes the part of the program portraying the "evils of science." A video depicting poisoned rivers and dead animals accompanies the presentation. But for Ron, it is all just part of the show. That attitude is made perfectly clear when he tells Kim: "You don't have to watch if you don't want to. Just look concerned, alarmed, whatever." And when he is asked by Kim how it is that science is able to condense a years worth of toxic waste into one donut, Ron replies, "I don't know exactly. I never listen to the technical part. Some kind of sub molecular-nano-mini-mumbo-jumbo."

> "It is almost like a game of tag. Bisson quickly hits on one theme, then moves on to the next."

Ron and the show he works for are the epitome of a shallow culture. Almost everything about it is slick and fabricated and false. Presidents are scheduled to present Kim with a plaque honoring her for her courage, but she is warned not to touch it. Native-American performers will give her a bark scroll, but she is cautioned not to try and unroll it. Obviously, it is fake. And while this is happening, a wind machine will be providing the illusion of nature. However, despite all the phoniness, the main feature of the show could not be more real, and the resulting popularity is quite telling. Despite living in a society so technologically advanced it can compress uncounted tons of toxic waste from across the planet into a single pastry, the people inhabiting this world still have not evolved. What could be more primitive than a ritual human sacrifice? As Ron tells her, for this one night Kim represents all humanity, all life on the planet, perhaps the entire universe for all he knows. Like some sacrificial lamb being led to the slaughter, Kim will eat this donut and, in a way that is both symbolic and quite literal, suffer the consequences that would otherwise be shared by all the inhabitants of this world. And what is the public's response to this? Morbid fascination on a global scale. Viewers tune in by the millions to watch the spectacle of it all. The big moment arrives with the fanfare of a drum roll. Even someone as crass as Ron cannot helped but be moved by the moment, with the camera pulling slowly in on the subject, standing there alone, clutching a white, grease-stained bag holding all the world's poison.

Bisson ends the story with a punch line that hits hard. It is really a message to every reader who, like Kim, continues moving inevitably toward a lethal end, cracking jokes all the way up to the last moment. As with all good satire, the underlying message being conveyed is completely serious. In fact, the moral of this story can rightfully be said to be of life and death importance. Continue on this course, Bisson seems to be saying, and the world will present to each of us a life filled with toxic donuts, and there will be no choice but to follow the instructions Ron gives Kim: "You eat it."

Source: Curt Guyette, Critical Essay on "The Toxic Donut," in *Short Stories for Students,* Gale, 2003.

Sources

Bisson, Terry, "The Toxic Donut," in *Bears Discover Fire and Other Stories,* Tor, 1993, pp. 142–46.

Kincaid, Paul, "Bisson, Terry," in *St. James Guide to Science Fiction Writers,* 4th ed., St. James Press, 1996, pp. 75–76.

Review of *Bears Discover Fire and Other Stories,* in *Kirkus Reviews,* September 1, 1993.

Review of *Bears Discover Fire and Other Stories,* in *Publishers Weekly,* November 1, 1993, p. 70.

Soukup, Martha, Review of *Bears Discover Fire and Other Stories,* in *Washington Post Book World,* November 28, 1993.

Further Reading

American Association for the Advancement of Science, *AAAS Atlas of Population and Environment,* University of California Press, 2001.

This in-depth guide depicts the relationships between human population and the environment. The book employs a number of maps, diagrams, and other visual aids to explore the links between population and natural resources, land use, atmosphere, waste and chemicals, ecosystems, and biodiversity.

Brown, Michael, and John May, *The Greenpeace Story,* Dorling Kindersley, 1991.

This book gives a comprehensive overview of Greenpeace, the nonviolent environmental pressure

group that was founded in the 1970s. Illustrations and photographs accompany each section of the book, which covers the organization's history, its major initiatives, and the various retaliations it has experienced from international governments and industry.

Rischard, J. F., *High Noon: Twenty Global Problems, Twenty Years to Solve Them,* Basic Books, 2002.

Rischard, the World Bank's vice-president for Europe and a noted economist, defines what he sees as the twenty most pressing environmental issues. He proposes a system of global networks—which can monitor illegal environmental activity—to address these concerns.

Santos, Miguel A., *The Environmental Crisis,* Greenwood Press, 1999.

This highly informative book offers a good, one-volume introduction to the history of the environmental crisis, as well as the efforts made in the twentieth century to address this crisis. The book explains the science behind key environmental issues, such as global warming and pollution, and provides an in-depth chronological time line of major environmental events.

Wolf, Michael J., *The Entertainment Economy: How the Mega-Media Forces Are Transforming Our Lives,* Times Books, 1999.

Wolf, a top strategist in the media industry, states that all businesses, regardless of type, will need to entertain their customers in the future—since the public is obsessed with entertainment. Wolf cites many examples, such as CNBC network and Tommy Hilfiger, to show how certain businesses have learned this lesson and thrived. He also gives many inside stories about the media industry.

Worldwatch Institute, ed., *State of the World 2002,* W. W. Norton & Co., 2002.

The latest edition of this annual report gives the most up-to-date research statistics concerning the state of the earth and its environment. Topics covered include global governance, agriculture, resource conflicts, toxic wastes, population, and global warming, among others. This is an indispensable source book for all environmental studies.

The Way It Felt to Be Falling

"The Way It Felt to Be Falling," by Kim Edwards, was first published in the *Threepenny Review,* although it received greater exposure when it was reprinted in the author's first and only book—*The Secrets of a Fire King*—in 1997. Edwards wrote the story as part of her first fiction workshop that she took in college, but revised it several times over the next decade as she honed her writing skills through creative writing programs and personal experience. Like many of Edwards's stories, "The Way It Felt to Be Falling" features a strong female protagonist. Kate is a nineteen-year-old woman who is working to save up money for college, and who hangs out drinking and shooting pool with her unstable boyfriend, Stephen, in her off time. Kate gets talked into going skydiving, an event that helps her overcome her fears of going mad like her father. In order to accurately reflect the skydiving sequences in the story, Edwards took skydiving lessons at a local airstrip, which helped give the story a greater sense of realism. The story also addresses many realistic issues, including mental degradation, the burden of responsibility, and suicide. A copy of the story can be found in the paperback version of *The Secrets of a Fire King*, which was published by Picador USA in 1998.

Kim Edwards

1997

Author Biography

Edwards was born on May 4, 1958, in Killeen, Texas. When she was only two months old, her parents moved the family back to upstate New York, where Edwards grew up. Although she was interested in writing since she was a little girl, it was in her college years that the wheels were set in motion for her writing career. After transferring from Auburn Community College (now Cayuga Community College) to Colgate University in 1979, she signed up for a fiction workshop. Here, Edwards wrote her first story, ''Cords,'' which eventually became ''The Way It Felt to Be Falling.'' Edwards's instructor told her that she should do research to get her facts right in her fiction. As a result, the author took skydiving lessons at the local airstrip.

After graduating from Colgate University in 1981 with her bachelor's degree, Edwards earned her master of fine arts degree in the writing of fiction from the University of Iowa's internationally renowned Writer's Workshop. After graduating in 1983, Edwards began teaching composition classes, and in one class she had a number of international students. This experience, along with her desire to travel, encouraged her to pursue teaching English as a second language. To this end, she earned a second master of arts degree in linguistics, also from the University of Iowa, in 1987. The same year, Edwards married Thomas Clayton, who was also interested in teaching English as a second language. The couple spent five years living and teaching in Malaysia, Japan, and Cambodia.

Edwards's short stories reflect these diverse experiences. Several of the stories in her first collection, *The Secrets of a Fire King* (1997), depict life and situations in Asia. The collection also includes ''The Way It Felt to Be Falling,'' which received a Pushcart Prize; ''Sky Juice,'' which received the 1990 Nelson Algren Award for short fiction; and ''Gold,'' which was included in the *Best American Short Stories of 1993*. In addition, Edwards has received grants from the National Endowment for the Arts, the Pennsylvania Council on the Arts, the Seaside Institute, the Kentucky Arts Council, and the Kentucky Foundation for Women. Her fiction and essays have appeared in the *Paris Review, Redbook, Ploughshares,* The *North American Review, Iowa Woman, River City, Michigan Quarterly Review,* the *Threepenny Review, Story, American Short Fiction,* and the *Chicago Tribune.*

Edwards, who is currently at work on her first novel, lives in Lexington, Kentucky, with her husband and two daughters.

Plot Summary

''The Way It Felt to Be Falling'' starts out with Kate, the narrator, describing the summer she turned nineteen. In the midst of a recession, her father's consulting business has failed, an event that causes him to retreat into madness. Kate and her mother visit him in the hospital, but he does not notice them. Kate's mother works as a secretary during the day and decorates cakes as a side job, in order to support the family. Kate recalls one day where the bottom layer of a finished wedding cake collapsed, and her mother, normally a calm person, broke down crying. Kate talks about her boyfriend that summer, Stephen, the unstable older brother of her friend, Emmy—who has left town with a number of others to follow the Grateful Dead on tour. Kate wanted to go, but is working in a convenience store to save money, and also does not want to leave her mother. Instead, Kate stays in her small town and watches the planes and skydivers. Kate also monitors herself in the mirror, searching for signs of the madness that has claimed her father.

That summer, Kate and Stephen, who is known for his violent and suicidal episodes, usually met at Mickey's tavern to play pool. Kate did not like Stephen at first, because she was afraid of his scarred wrists and his massive consumption of Valium. After Emmy leaves town, Stephen starts to call Kate more often, and they begin to see each other. Stephen describes his suicide attempt to Kate, and Kate tries some of his Valium, liking the way that the drug blurs the lines of reality. The day that the wedding cake collapses, Kate arrives at Mickey's tavern, and Stephen is worried about something. Kate finds out that he has lost a bet during a pool tournament and that he must go skydiving. Stephen says he will go alone, but when Ted, the winner, says he wants to be there to witness it, Stephen refuses, and asks Kate to serve instead. He also asks Kate to jump with him. Kate agrees, then leaves to go to work. When she gets home that night, Kate's mother expresses concern about Kate's relationship with Stephen, and is even more frustrated when Kate says she cannot see her father the next day because she has plans with Stephen.

The next day, Stephen and Kate drive to the airplane hangar, where they meet their instructor, Howard. Even though they are not pulling their own ripcords, Howard has them practice all of the movements, including emergency maneuvers. Stephen's form is perfect, but he is still nervous. They break for lunch, and Kate says that they do not have to go through with this, but Stephen says his personal integrity is at stake. Kate jumps first, and immediately forgets all of her training, getting lost in the motionless feeling of falling. She feels her parachute open, and finally remembers her training, landing in a cornfield and twisting her ankle in the process. Stephen comes up to her, and she is surprised that he arrived first. He says he landed on target, but when Kate goes to collect her certificate from Howard, she finds out that Stephen did not jump.

Stephen takes Kate to the hospital to get her sprained ankle X-rayed, and halfway home, Kate tells Stephen she knows that he did not jump. Stephen says that he saw Kate falling, and was afraid of jumping. Kate tells Stephen that it felt like floating, not falling. She refuses to lie to Ted about Stephen backing out of the jump, and Stephen destroys the film in Ted's camera, then physically threatens Kate into lying for him. When they get to Kate's house, Stephen tries to make up, but Kate tells him she never wants to see him again, and says that if he bothers her, she will tell the whole town that he did not jump.

When Kate gets inside her house, her mom is waiting up for her. Kate considers lying, but then tells her mother about her skydiving experience. Her mother is furious, and is concerned how Kate is going to work that week. Her mother calms down and uses the ruined wedding cake as a peace offering. They both laugh at their situation, and Kate's mother confesses that she is unsure what to do about anything, especially with Kate's father in the hospital. Kate tells her she is doing fine, and feels angry at her father for doing this to them. She realizes that she is no longer worried about going mad, and remembers what it was like to be falling, floating, in the air.

Characters

Emmy

Emmy is Kate's best friend and Stephen's younger sister, who leaves during the summer to go

Media Adaptations

- On January 20, 1999, the book club of Kentucky Educational Television (KET), an affiliate of the Public Broadcasting System, interviewed Edwards in her home about *Secrets of a Fire King*. KET's book club Web page—located online at http://www.ket.org/content/bookclub/books/1999_feb (last accessed January 2003)—hosts a copy of the interview transcript. This page also links to other information about Edwards, including a transcript of a talk she gave to her alma mater, Colgate University, right before *Secrets of a Fire King* was published. This transcript, which can be accessed directly at http://www.colgate.edu/scene/may1997/edwards.html (last accessed January 2003), also features specific discussion about ''The Way It Felt to Be Falling.''

follow the Grateful Dead tour. Emmy's leaving brings Kate and Stephen closer together.

Howard

Howard is the instructor who teaches Kate and Stephen how to skydive. Howard is surprised when Stephen does not jump, since Stephen was the best in his class.

Kate

Kate is the narrator of the story, whose father has gone mad, and whose boyfriend, Stephen, is unstable. In the story, Kate recalls the summer that she was nineteen, when she was afraid of going mad like her father, who slipped away after his consulting business failed. She looks in the mirror, searching for a sign of the madness in her face, and spends her off hours drinking, playing pool, and gambling with a rough group of friends. Stephen is the most unstable of this bunch, and Kate finds herself drawn to his dangerous personality. She also believes that he can help her make sense of the world between sanity and madness, where her father is, and where

Kate assumes she will end up. In addition to drinking, Kate has tried Stephen's Valium, and likes the way that the pills make reality seem fuzzy. Kate has to constantly defend her relationship with Stephen, whom her mother does not like.

One day at Mickey's Tavern, the local hangout where Stephen and Kate meet each day, Kate finds out that Stephen has lost a bet, and must go skydiving as a result. Stephen asks Kate to jump with him, to serve as a witness for Ted, the winner of the bet. Kate agrees, although she gets nervous during their skydiving class, and considers backing out. However, she decides to go through with it, and ends up being the first one to jump. Kate loses her sense of time and forgets the training from her class, marveling at the floating sensation of freefall. Her parachute opens, and Kate is entranced by the scenery, although she snaps out of it in time to land in a cornfield, spraining her ankle in the process. Stephen meets Kate at her touchdown point, and says that he landed on target, although Kate finds out from Howard that Stephen did not jump. Kate confronts Stephen on the way home, and refuses to lie for him, until he physically threatens her. This severs the relationship between them. Kate tells her mother about the skydiving incident, and her mother is upset at first, although they soon reconcile. Kate realizes that with this onset of anger over Stephen and her father, she is no longer afraid of going mad. In a private moment, she remembers the peaceful feeling she had while falling.

Kate's Father

Kate's father loses his consulting business during the recession, which causes him to retreat into madness. This situation puts increased financial strain on Kate's mother, and influences Kate, who worries that she will go mad like her father.

Kate's Mother

Kate's mother is a secretary who also works a side job as a cake decorator, supporting her family completely while her husband is in the hospital. The day that one of Kate's mother's wedding cakes collapses, Kate notices that it is the first time her mother has cried since Kate's father went into the hospital. Her mother is worried about Kate's relationship with Stephen, and is frustrated when Kate says she will not accompany her mother to the hospital one day, since she has plans with Stephen. When Kate returns home with a sprained ankle after skydiving, her mother is furious, but they soon reconcile over a piece of the ruined wedding cake.

Kate's mother also breaks down and tells Kate that she is not handling the situation with Kate's father very well, although Kate reassures her that she is.

Stephen

Stephen is Kate's boyfriend and the older brother of Emmy, Kate's best friend. Stephen is twenty-seven and still lives at home with his parents. Stephen has a reputation for being crazy and dangerous, because he is a thief, he has smashed out an ex-lover's window, and he has tried to kill himself. Stephen is on a high dose of Valium, which he takes every few hours to calm himself. When Emmy leaves town for the summer, Stephen starts to call Kate every day, and they begin to hang out more. They meet every day at Mickey's Tavern, where they drink, play pool, and gamble with a rough group of other young people. One day, Stephen loses a bet, which states that the loser has to go skydiving. Since he needs a witness to document his skydiving experience, Stephen chooses Kate, who agrees. During the skydiving class, Howard, the instructor, notes that Stephen has perfect technique. Stephen fails to jump, however, and his lie does not work on Kate, who finds out the truth from Howard. Kate confronts Stephen about his failed jump on the way home, and says she will not lie for him. This enrages Stephen, who drives out to a deserted country road, destroys the film, and threatens Kate, who then agrees not to tell. Stephen tries to apologize, but it is too late. Kate is angry at his threats and tells him she never wants to see him again.

Ted

Ted is one of the regulars at Mickey's Tavern, who beats Stephen in a pool tournament, forcing Stephen to go skydiving. Ted does not trust Stephen to go alone, but agrees to let Kate serve as witness. He gives Kate his camera, to document Stephen's jump.

Themes

Fear

Near the end of the story, after Stephen has threatened Kate, he asks her if she thinks he is crazy. She tells him, ''No. . . . I think you're afraid, just like everybody else.'' Throughout the story, the characters exhibit many kinds of fear. Kate is afraid of going mad like her father, and carefully monitors herself. Says Kate: ''I'd find myself standing in

Topics for Further Study

- In "The Way It Felt to Be Falling," Kate's father succumbs to a form of madness when he loses his consulting business during a recession. Using the clues in the story, research the specific condition that Kate's father most likely has, then put yourself in his place. Write a one-page description of what a typical day is like living with this mental condition, using your research to support your ideas.

- Research the Grateful Dead phenomenon that swept through the United States in the late twentieth century. Imagine that you are making a contribution to a time capsule, in which you record what it was like to be a "Deadhead"—a devoted fan who followed the Grateful Dead on their concert tours. Use a combination of words,

photos, illustrations, or other printed media in your description.

- Investigate and discuss the current psychological theories behind what drives certain people to be thrill-seekers. Choose another extreme sport besides skydiving, and write a one-page fact sheet on the sport, including information on its history, equipment, rules, competitions, and demographic statistics on people who participate in it.

- In the story, Kate works to save money for college, while many of her friends prefer to spend time having fun. Research the current statistics that show how most students paid for college in the 1980s as well as how most students pay for college today. Plot your findings on a chart or graph, and discuss the similarities and differences between the two time periods.

---

front of mirrors with my heart pounding, searching my eyes for a glimmer of madness." Stephen is also afraid, even though he says at one point that he does not worry about anything. He is afraid of being shamed in front of his friends, so much so that he believes he cannot back out of the jump. As he tells Kate: "For me it's my personal integrity at stake, remember?" Kate reassures him, saying that Stephen has the best technique of anybody in the class, so he should have no problems.

However, Stephen's fear of death outweighs his fear of shame and makes him discount his perfect skydiving technique, and he does ultimately back out of his jump. Says Stephen: "I don't know what happened, Kate. I stood right in that doorway, and the only thing I could imagine was my chute in a streamer." However, after the fear of death has passed, Stephen's fear of shame returns, and manifests itself when he threatens Kate. Other characters are afraid, too. Kate's mom is afraid that she is not doing a good enough job in the absence of her husband, and even her clients exhibit fear over their wedding cakes not being perfect or on time: "That

summer, brides and their mothers called us on a regular basis, their voices laced with panic." However, Kate is one character who realizes that fear can be overcome. Her skydiving experience has changed her. Says Kate: "Whatever had plunged my father into silence, and Stephen into violence, wouldn't find me. I had a bandaged ankle, but the rest of me was whole and strong."

Responsibility

From the beginning, the story illustrates two types of people, those who are not responsible and those who are. Kate's father neglects his responsibility when he allows his stress to close him off from his family and the world. Says Kate: "My father had left too, but in a more subtle and insidious way. . . . he had simply retreated into some silent and inaccessible world." Likewise, Stephen retreats into his own world by ignoring responsibilities like work and by constantly consuming tranquilizers to escape from reality. "He collected a welfare check every month, took Valium every few hours, and lived in a state of precarious calm." Even Kate's friend, Emmy, abandons any responsibilities she has, taking off for the whole summer to follow the Grateful Dead on tour. She tries to get Kate to go with her, but Kate has responsibilities she feels she cannot ignore. ''Come with us, she had urged, but I was working in a convenience store, saving my money for school, and it didn't seem like a good time to leave my mother.'' Kate's mother is also very responsible, working long hours to support herself and Kate in the absence of Kate's father: ''My mother had a job as a secretary and decorated cakes on the side.'' At the end of the story, as Kate realizes that she has conquered her fear of going mad, she becomes angry with her father for neglecting his responsibilities. Says Kate: ''My father sat, still and silent in his white room, and I was angry with him for asking so much from us.''

Freedom

Kate's fear of madness and dedication to her responsibilities cause her to seek ways of finding freedom, both physically and mentally. Unlike Emmy, ''who had fled, with her boyfriend and 350 tie-dyed T-shirts, to follow the Grateful Dead on tour,'' Kate is unable to leave town. Instead, Kate finds other ways to escape the pressure of her responsibilities. On a daily basis, she hangs out at Mickey's Tavern with a group of artists and slackers, people who live free lives that are entirely different from her own. ''They were young, most of them, but already disenfranchised, known to be odd or mildly crazy or even faintly dangerous.'' Stephen also introduces her to Valium, which becomes another method of escaping the real world. Says Kate: ''I liked the way the edges of things grew undefined, so I was able to rise from my own body, calmly and with perfect grace.'' The ultimate escape, however, comes in the form of skydiving, which Kate has always observed dreamily from her backyard. When Kate hears about the pool bet, where the loser has to go skydiving, Kate says, ''I've always wanted to do that.'' Although she is afraid, she goes through with the skydive, which ends up being the ultimate freeing experience for her.

Style

Metaphor

A metaphor is a figure or speech in which one word, used to mean something literally, is used to

figuratively represent another thing in order to create a new understanding in the mind of (in this case) the reader. This technique is used to give a work of literature more impact, by forcing readers to think about a concept in a different way. In the story, Kate equates falling with madness. Both Kate and readers realize that falling and madness are two separate ideas, but the way Kate describes it, a reader can easily see that the sensation of falling is an appropriate way to figuratively describe madness. Says Kate in the beginning: ''*Take care* I said each time we left my father. . . . And I listened to my own words; I took care, too. That summer, I was afraid of falling.'' Kate starts to hang out more with Stephen after her father goes into the hospital, because she thinks that, with his mental instability, he can help Kate make sense of what it means to be falling. Says Kate, ''I knew that Stephen understood the suspended world between sanity and madness, that he lived his life inside it.'' The metaphor of falling is underscored even more by Kate's decision to go skydiving. By directly confronting her fear of falling, she conquers her fears of mental illness. In fact, at the end, Kate objects to Stephen's use of the word ''falling,'' when he describes how Kate ''disappeared so fast'' out of the plane. Says Kate: ''It was the word he kept using, and it was the wrong one. . . . 'That's the funny thing,' I told him. 'There was no sense of descent. It was more like floating.'' With this change in her perception, Kate is able to abandon the metaphor of falling as madness, and find peace.

Setting

The story takes place in a small town, most likely in upstate New York, where Edwards grew up. Kate initially feels trapped, and says as much when she talks about her friend Emmy, who leaves town to follow the Grateful Dead on tour. Says Kate: ''I was fiercely envious, caught in that small town while the planes traced their daily paths to places I was losing hope of ever seeing.'' However, after her skydiving and the incident with Stephen, she realizes that she is not going to go mad in the small town, and has new confidence in herself. The fact that the small town is near an airplane hangar that offers skydiving lessons is also important. The story would not work in the same way if it were not for this setting.

Suspense

Edwards uses words and pacing that create tension and multiple surprises at the end. When

Kate and Stephen enter the airplane hangar to take their skydiving lessons, the first thing they see is ''a pile of stretchers stacked neatly against the wall'' and a ''hand-lettered sign that warned CASH ONLY.'' These ominous signs of past injuries and danger start to build tension, since readers begin to wonder if Kate and Stephen are going to make it safely to the ground. This feeling grows as Howard explains how some people in the past have lost track of time, ''panicked and pulled their reserve chute even as the first one opened, tangling them both and falling to their deaths.'' Thus, it becomes suspenseful when Kate jumps from the plane, because she loses track of time. Says Kate: ''Three seconds yet? I couldn't tell. My parachute didn't open but the earth came no closer, and I kept my eyes open, too terrified to scream.''

Kate lands safely, and Stephen soon comes up to her, so the reader may think that everything has gone well for both. However, Kate soon finds out from Howard that Stephen did not jump. Says Howard: ''Best in the class, and he didn't even make it to the door.'' When Kate confronts Stephen about this and he suddenly turns dangerous, one wonders once again if anything bad is going to happen to Kate. ''Stephen's breathing was loud against the rising sound of crickets. He looked at me, eyes glittering, and smiled his crazy smile.'' Stephen tells her that ''I could do anything I wanted to you,'' as his hand is on her neck. One wonders if Stephen is going to choke Kate, or something worse. However, all of these issues are resolved by the story's end, when Kate arrives safely home, reconciles with her mother, and enjoys a quiet moment to herself.

Historical Context

The original version of the story was written when Edwards was in college in the late 1970s and early 1980s. However, since she revised the story several times before it was published in the early 1990s, the story's time period is a little ambiguous. In fact, several aspects of the story—including the mention of personal computers—could place the story anywhere in this time period. However, two aspects of the story—the recession that causes Kate's dad to lose his consulting business and the reference to Stephen buying a computer to play chess—seem to indicate that Edwards meant the story to take place in the early 1980s.

In 1980, President Carter signed the controversial Chrysler Loan Guarantee bill, a $1.5 billion relief package to the Chrysler Corporation, which had experienced a $207 million loss in one quarter in the previous year. This unprecedented government bailout was just one of the many signs that the strong industrial base of the United States was weakening. During the 1980s, Many American industries experienced declining profits. The United States had once sold goods to the rest of the world. However, with technology in areas like Japan and Germany rivaling that of the United States, America began to import more goods than it exported. This led to many layoffs and cutbacks in industries, which only increased as some American manufacturers tried to cut costs by opening factories overseas, where they could hire cheaper labor. As businesses downsized or failed, the northeast and north-central states—which were saturated with industrial factories—were hardest hit by recessions. As a result, during the 1980s, America's population shifted from these areas to southern and western regions, where the economy was better.

While southern states offered jobs in many industries such as oil production, the new American west was becoming the center for computer technology. Although computers had been around in various forms for decades, they were usually so expensive and bulky that only government or corporate clients could afford and house them. The first microcomputer—known more commonly as a personal computer—was the Altair, which debuted in 1974. However, since customers had to assemble the computer from a kit, it had limited appeal for anyone other than computer hobbyists and other technologically savvy consumers. Over the next decade, a number of developments from different companies—mainly Apple Computer, International Business Machines (IBM), and Microsoft Corporation—helped to launch the personal computer revolution.

In 1977, Apple Computer, Inc., introduced the Apple II, an inexpensive personal computer which was targeted to individuals, small businesses, schools, and others with limited budgets. Since the Apple II also ran VisiCalc—the first computerized accounting, or spreadsheet, program—it quickly gained popularity. As computer manufacturers began to realize the importance of software programs in making a computer useful for the average person, there were more developments. The IBM Personal Computer, introduced in 1982 and known com-

Compare
&
Contrast

- **1980s:** As personal computers increase in technology and drop in price, they become commonplace in many homes. Application memory, processing speed, and data storage space become three features that are used to sell computers.

  Today: As the Internet offers more options—such as email, online research, shopping, reservations, and e-cards—more people start to use it as part of their daily lives. Connection speed and bandwidth become two features that are used to sell Internet services.

- **1980s:** In certain, industry-rich areas of the United States, recessions occur as America shifts from an export-based to an import-based economy. Manufacturing companies make many cutbacks and layoffs, affecting many workers and related industries.

  Today: Many people from all walks of life are

affected when the information technology boom of the 1990s finally busts, affecting retirement plans and stock portfolios. The massive fall of stock prices creates recessions in several areas of the United States, and workers in many industries are affected by cutbacks and layoffs. The discovery of several corporate financial scandals only makes the stock market more unstable.

- **1980s:** With their limited memory and storage capacity, early computers are only able to handle simple games like chess. However, continuous improvements in computer and gaming technology rapidly improve the quality and complexity of computer games.

  Today: Computers offer three-dimensional, highly realistic games, many of which have plots and characters. Computer games become so popular that their storylines are sometimes adapted into feature films.

---

monly as the IBM PC, was not much faster than the Apple II or other personal computers, but it had several times more memory for running programs. One of these programs, MS-DOS, produced by the Microsoft Corporation, became the standard operating system on IBM PCs.

IBM quickly lost control of its product, however, as Compaq and other computer companies began to make PC clones, which were compatible with IBM PCs, and which also ran MS DOS. This helped to give many companies a foothold in the computer industry, and greatly increased the number of computers available to consumers. However, it was the introduction in 1984 of Apple's Macintosh computer—featuring the first graphical user interface (GUI) and the first computer mouse—that helped to make computers popular and accessible in the average home. As computers became more useful and more powerful, software developers realized that games, such as computer chess, were a huge market, especially when targeted to younger

people with a lot of free time on their hands, like Stephen in the story.

Critical Overview

''The Way It Felt to Be Falling'' was included in Edwards's collection, *The Secrets of a Fire King*, which was published in 1997. This collection received excellent reviews overall. In her review of the book for the *New York Times,* Nina Sonenberg notes that it is an ''accomplished first collection,'' and calls Edwards's stories ''confident.'' Sonenberg also notes that the book captures ''an impressive swath of the world in the book as a whole.'' Other reviewers also comment on the diversity of locations and cultures in the book. The *Publishers Weekly* reviewer claims that the stories are ''noteworthy for the range of their settings—America, Europe, Asia—and for the scope of the author's impressive imagination.'' Likewise, Tom Wilhelmus notes in his review for the *Hudson Review* that the book is "the work of a thoughtful writer with an elegant style and a similarly wide range of cultural, artistic, and intellectual interests." Still, despite this diversity, the *Publishers Weekly* reviewer notes that "the narrative tone remains strangely constant throughout the stories, no matter the setting or the speaker."

The reviewer for *Kirkus Reviews* notes, on a more negative tone, that the stories are marked by "heavy dramatic ironies and polemic," or controversy, and calls Edwards "a talented writer still in search of subjects worthy of her craft." However, this reviewer also notes that Edwards writes with a "clean, fluent style."

Reviewers also comment on the quality of "The Way It Felt to Be Falling," in particular. Sonenberg notes that the stories that "stay close to home," like "The Way It Felt to Be Falling," feature characters who "find new wonder—and terror—in the familiar." In addition, in her review for *Library Journal,* Ellen R. Cohen notes that many of the stories "feature strong, pragmatic women as protagonists, usually motivated by love in its broadest sense." Cohen cites the specific case of Kate in "The Way It Felt to Be Falling," saying that Kate "finds hidden strength after skydiving with an unstable boyfriend." Likewise, Wilhelmus notes that the story "uses skydiving as a metaphor for learning self-sufficiency and freedom in a world in which no values are certain." Finally, the *Publishers Weekly* reviewer analyzes the story in context of the other stories in the collection, noting "Edwards uses the elements (fire, air, water, earth and metal) symbolically to ground her stories as characters move through the various landscapes she has created."

Criticism

Ryan D. Poquette

Poquette has a bachelor's degree in English and specializes in writing about literature. In the following essay, Poquette discusses Edwards's exploration of perception in "The Way It Felt to Be Falling."

"The Way It Felt to Be Falling" is an extremely visual story. Right from the first sentence of the story, Edwards uses language that underscores the idea of perception. Says Kate, the narrator: "The summer I turned nineteen I used to lie in the backyard and watch the planes fly overhead, leaving their clean plumes of jet-stream in a pattern against the sky." Kate is a first-person narrator, meaning that the reader experiences the story from Kate's point of view, seeing the world of the story through her eyes alone. As Kate progresses through the story, the reader gets to know Kate's thoughts about real and perceived reality. Edwards uses the idea of perception to underscore her main theme of fear, by exploring Kate's own fears of madness, her references to colors, and the revelations she has while skydiving.

Kate's greatest fear during the story is that she is going to descend into madness, as her father has. Kate remembers the day that her father was taken away to the hospital. She goes to give him a glass of water, but his eyes are closed. "When he opened his eyes, they were clear and brown, as blank and smooth as the glass in my hand." Kate equates the blankness of her father's eyes with madness, which affects her perceptions about her own mental condition. Several times that summer, she tries to determine whether or not she is going mad, by examining her eyes. "I'd find myself standing in front of mirrors with my heart pounding, searching my eyes for a glimmer of madness." Stephen is the other character in the story who is mentally unstable. As a result, Kate finds herself drawn to him, because she thinks he can help her understand what it is like to be mad. When she describes him, she once again refers to his eyes in conjunction with a delusional madness. As Kate notes, Stephen had "eyes that seemed to look out on some other, more compelling, world." However, although she has romantic notions of Stephen and his mental condition, when he turns violent in the end, her perception of his eyes and mental state suddenly changes: "Stephen's eyes, green, were wild and glittering."

The specific description of Stephen's green eyes is one of many uses of color in the story. Edwards uses colors symbolically in several places to evoke vivid images. In the beginning of the story, Kate notes that even though it is only July, the "grass had a brown fringe and leaves were already falling." For Kate, the brown grass symbolizes the impending death of summer. Her summer has started out badly, since her dad has gone into the hospital, an event that has also sparked Kate's fear of madness. As a result, she can only see the negative implications of the color brown, which are under-

What Do I Read Next?

- In Edwards's story, Stephen says that he is going to skydive because his personal integrity is at stake, and then he backs out at the last minute, although he lies about his jump. In Stephen Carter's *Integrity* (1996), the author poses questions about the degradation of personal integrity in society and offers an eight-principle program for a return to traditional ethics, especially in democracies like the United States.

- John Forbes Nash Jr. is a schizophrenic who is also a Nobel Prize–winning economist. In *A Beautiful Mind: A Biography of John Forbes Nash, Jr.* (1998), Sylvia Nasar gives a thorough overview of Nash's life in mathematics and madness. The book was adapted into an Academy Award–winning film in 2001.

- *Shine,* another biographical film that earned several Oscars, details the story of David Helfgott, a musical prodigy who is driven into a mental breakdown as a child by his father and music teachers. As an adult, David returns to the music scene, to popular acclaim. The 1996 film, which was written by Jan Sardi, was published in script form as *Shine: The Screenplay* in 1997.

- Tom Wolfe, known for decades as a journalist, inspired controversy with his first novel, *The Bonfire of the Vanities* (1987), which uses realism and satire to try to capture the feel of life in 1980s America—particularly New York. In the story, a high-powered investment banker hits a black man while driving through the Bronx. The resulting chain of events takes the reader through a full tour of modern city life in the 1980s.

---

scored even further when she describes her father's "brown" eyes. Likewise, when Emmy sends Kate postcards of the places she has visited, Kate sees "a sky aching blue over the ocean" in one of them. The color blue is given a negative association in Kate's mind at this point, since it evokes the longing and disappointment she feels regarding her being unable to accompany her friends on the Grateful Dead tour. The blue sky in the postcard, like the sky over Kate's backyard—where she watches skydivers and wishes she were up there—represents an escape from Kate's reality. However, in the beginning of the story, she thinks that she will never get to experience the blue sky for herself.

Blue is also the color of Stephen's "plastic bottle of Valium," and the color of the pills themselves. This is appropriate, since Valium represents another form of escape for Kate. She has tried it before, and appreciates the feeling it gives her. Says Kate: "I liked the way the edges of things grew undefined, so I was able to rise from my own body, calmly and with perfect grace." By taking Valium, Kate has learned that she can alter her perception,

escaping from her own reality into someplace where she does not have to worry about her father, her job, or the fact that she is stuck in a small town. In fact, when Kate describes her Valium experience, she says that she likes how "the blue pills slid down [her] throat, dissolving anxiety."

One example in particular illustrates the power of color to evoke ideas. Kate's mother decorates cakes, and is constantly called upon to follow vivid color schemes for the wedding cakes. "This bride's colors were green and lavender, and my mother had dyed the frosting to match swatches from the dresses." Her mother does not understand this obsessive need for color, asking Kate, "Whatever happened to simple white?" Even though her mother's wedding pictures are not in color, Kate knows "that it had been simple, small and elegant, the bridesmaids wearing the palest shade of peach." The use of many colors on the wedding cakes symbolizes the complexity and stress of modern weddings, as opposed to earlier days, when Kate's mother remembers colors—and weddings—as simpler.

The stress of modern weddings is underscored further by Kate's observation about her mother's clients: "That summer, brides and their mothers called us on a regular basis, their voices laced with panic." However, later in the story, Kate implies that this stress is sometimes unwarranted. She thinks about all of the hours her mother "has spent on wedding cakes, building confections as fragile and unsubstantial as the dreams that demanded them." With this statement, Edwards is once again drawing attention to the main theme of the story—fear. The brides are afraid that their weddings will not be perfect, and even after the wedding they will most likely live in fear. Because of this, they may not have the courage to follow their dreams, whether that means staying married or something else, which is why Kate refers to their dreams as "fragile" and "unsubstantial." For these people, the obsessive use of colors masks their own insecurities and fears, whereas Kate's mother, who is described repeatedly as strong, does not need all of these colors; she prefers white, which is more simple.

The greatest exploration of perception comes during Kate's skydiving experience. Throughout the summer, Kate equates madness with the idea of falling. For this reason, even though she is excited about finally being able to go skydiving, she is also terrified of what it will feel like to literally fall through the sky. Kate overcomes this fear and jumps out of the plane. During her freefall, Kate is amazed to find out that her perceptions of falling were wrong. "I knew I must be falling, but the earth stayed the same abstract distance away." Kate loses all sense of time, and is terrified. After her parachute opens, she calms down and looks around at the landscape below her. In this position, far above the ground and apart from the daily struggles of her life, she begins to perceive things differently. "All summer I had felt myself slipping in the quick rush of the world, but here, in clear and steady descent, nothing seemed to move. It was knowledge to marvel at." By conquering her fears of falling, Kate feels a new confidence, and is ready to conquer her fears of madness.

The last incident that changes her perception is the threat from Stephen. After Stephen removes his hand from her neck, Kate looks at him and has her final revelation. "Watching him I thought of my father, all his stubborn silence, all the uneasiness and pain. It made me angry suddenly, a sharp illumination that ended a summer's panic." From this point on until the end of the story, Kate shows that she is a changed woman. She breaks up with

> " . . . Kate achieves self-sufficiency, and realizes that she will not be beaten by her fears, as her father and Stephen have been."

Stephen, realizing that he is not the key to helping her with her fears of madness—he is afraid, just like everybody else. Instead, Kate achieves self-sufficiency, and realizes that she will not be beaten by her fears, as her father and Stephen have been. Says Kate: "Whatever had plunged my father into silence, and Stephen into violence, wouldn't find me. I had a bandaged ankle, but the rest of me was whole and strong." Throughout the story, Kate has been in a constant battle with her fears, like many other characters in the story. However, by surviving the trial of skydiving, she has conquered her fears and has a new perception of life.

Source: Ryan D. Poquette, Critical Essay on "The Way It Felt to Be Falling," in *Short Stories for Students,* Gale, 2003.

Scott Trudell

Trudell is a freelance writer with a bachelor's degree in English literature. In the following essay, Trudell analyzes the feminism and ironic style in Edwards's short story.

The thematic argument of "The Way It Felt to Be Falling" is best understood as a formula for gaining emotional maturity. And, in its simplest reading, the story seems to achieve this goal in a straightforward manner. Kate escapes potential violence, avoids becoming "crazy," and regains a bond with her mother by emerging from a sense of falling. The story seems to reinforce the basic assumption that the crisis of descent is resolved into a stable and safe space within the home.

Before accepting that shiftless complacency is the goal of the story's subtext, it is important to examine Edwards's imagery surrounding the themes of descent, stability, and control. At first glance, the reader takes for granted the cliché connotation of falling out of control and, like Kate, assumes that a rapid movement through the sky is more dangerous than staying lazily in place. On closer examination,

> [Edwards] associates her feminist vision with actual descent, dismissing a shiftless, dangerous, and decaying male world that only pretends to be falling."

however, it is clear that Edwards challenges this assumption until her story, in a number of senses, turns upside down.

Beginning with the introductory images of objects in the sky—"clean plumes of jet-stream" and "discarded paper wings"—Edwards carefully reverses the figurative connotations of descent. "Paper wings," "clean plumes," and a flourishing, descending recession are paradoxical and imply their opposites: that descent is flourishing, clean, and controlled. Indeed, the primary image of the story, that of skydiving in a frightening freefall at the point where the reader might expect Kate to have the least control and emotional stability, is ironically the turning point of her crisis, a moment of silent autonomy over the vast space below: "All summer I had felt myself slipping in the quick rush of the world, but here, in clear and steady descent, nothing seemed to move."

This is a vastly different understanding of her world than ten pages earlier: "I knew: madness was a graceless descent, the abyss beneath a careless step." Here, falling is the worst and most dangerous reaction to Kate's world, although she is certainly fascinated and seduced by a "graceless descent." This is why she is attracted to Stephen; he is supposed to be out of control, master of the "free fall"—just dangerous enough to be exciting, but not too scary.

The reader might ask, then, if descent is actually a good thing, how Kate could have any control or emotional maturity when it comes to the most false, fearful, and dangerous character in the text. Again, it is necessary to look more closely at the ironic paradigm that Edwards has set up. By the time the reader comes to the skydiving scene, Edwards has developed a distinction between actual descent and false, "graceless" falling. It is a dis-

tinction of control. Edwards makes the reader question what actually constitutes descent, and what is merely a superficial seduction that does not move at all. Stephen's version of falling, represented by Valium pills that "slid down [his] throat, dissolving anxiety," is entirely different from the control Kate gains when she jumps from the plane. Imagery of the pale Stephen "able to rise from my own body" proves that he is dangerous in a completely different sense, as Kate will soon find out. The real danger, the "falling" that is not falling at all, is losing control to Stephen's seductive series of lies about himself.

Kate realizes what it really means to fall only when she has jumped out of the plane. It is important that, immediately after her realization, Kate "tugged at the steering toggles." This emblem of control signals that, with her understanding, she has achieved the assertiveness necessary for her final confrontation with Stephen. Skydiving uncovers the myth that letting go and moving oneself forward is an action out of Kate's control, and it also uncovers the facade around Stephen. He could not jump out of the plane, not because he was scared or incapable (he was the "best in the class," after all), but because he is the stationary character without control over his actions. When Stephen says, "The free fall is my natural state of mind," it is another example of the gradually unraveling irony that makes the truth of Kate's world clear both to her and to the reader; Stephen is not falling, or moving, at all. This is made more explicit when Stephen shows his ugly and potentially brutal side during the drive home. The scariest moment in the story is not the rapid and dangerous swerving on the country lane, but the point when he stops the car and Kate cannot move because of her crutches. This stability, underscored by the opposite image to descent, "the rising sound of the crickets," is the thematic danger for Kate.

Kate's parents also, although perhaps less obviously, fit this paradigm of autonomous falling. Her father is introduced as having "retreated into some silent and inaccessible world" instead of following the economic descent into the lower states, and he is completely unresponsive and motionless during the visits of his wife and daughter. Like Stephen, except in his capacity for violent betrayal, Kate's father is characterized by stability and false security. Kate eventually learns that madness like her father's is not "the abyss beneath a careless step"; it is the product, in a sense, of being too afraid to fall out of an airplane.

Her mother, on the other hand, undergoes a similar subplot of emotional descent and control to Kate, beginning with the collapse of her cake. It is no coincidence that this is a wedding cake; the subtle struggle and stress of Kate's mother is an attempt to regain control of her life after the collapse of her marriage. In this sense, Kate's mother emerges as an important marker, if much less explicit to the reader, for the process of attaining emotional maturity. Like her mother, Kate learns to enjoy what has collapsed by eating it. This common search for control and happiness in a new kind of life is what allows for the mother-daughter bond in the closing moments of the story.

Edwards, then, does prescribe a formula for maturity and individual emergence from a potentially violent stability. But the power associated with female control in the story suggests that the reader should look closer still into Edwards's formula to understand its full resonance. Her presentation of an individual quest for control parallels, and is actually dependent on, a wider feminist social struggle.

In the last triumphant and even angelic image, Kate is able to shed her clothes and look outside at the clear starry sky. This is a moment of female control over the domestic space, which Kate's mother underscores by taking a bath (cleansing herself) at the same moment. Edwards's ironic imagery, which inverts the typical associations with negative uncontrollable descent, becomes particularly appropriate when the outward and autonomous triumph occurs indoors. Kate has a bandaged ankle (which connotes the damaged heel of the archetypical masculine hero, Achilles), but she is "whole and strong." She will be able to move outside of the safe domestic space and assert herself, but (as is the case with many feminist texts) this process begins with control over the home.

Edwards is careful to emphasize that this moment is a specifically feminine triumph and distances Kate from the two male characters: "Whatever had plunged my father into silence, and Stephen into violence, wouldn't find me." In its greater implications, "The Way It Felt to Be Falling" is the story of a reversal of male power. To underscore this inversion, Edwards shows Kate in a number of what might be masculine situations in a sexist society: drinking beer, playing pool, jumping out of an airplane, and most importantly, telling Stephen off. It is important that Kate and her mother earn money (unlike Stephen and Kate's father, who are financially useless).

The author associates her feminist vision with actual descent, dismissing a shiftless, dangerous, and decaying male world that only pretends to be falling. With her political subtext, Edwards is interested throughout the story in turning a number of social preconceptions upside down. Kate matures by developing an assertive and broad control over her environment, a genuine control associated with female empowerment, because a more localized version or an emergence dependent on a male character would betray Edwards's greater political understanding. When she remembers "the way it felt to be falling," Kate refers to the process of being betrayed and let down by the men in her life. She does not "remember" the new brand of falling she is experiencing; this is very much in the present and is better described as moving on with self-reliance.

Indeed, the worldview of "The Way It Felt to Be Falling" requires a complete independence from male control. Edwards is so careful to invert imagery and provide an ironic overturning of the male structure because the plot of the story allows no other option. Its feminism is not merely a mild overtone; Edwards is interested in the ways in which an individual struggle interacts with complacent social norms. In this world, men are not only shallow and superficial; they are weak, dangerous, and certainly not a force on which females can or should depend. The story, however much it may seem harmless or easy to fit within a framework of a growing-up tale, has an intense political subtext. In Edwards's formula, only by a greater effort towards social change will an individual female quest for emotional maturity be convincing.

Source: Scott Trudell, Critical Essay on "The Way It Felt to Be Falling," in *Short Stories for Students,* Gale, 2003.

Sources

Cohen, Ellen R., Review of *The Secrets of a Fire King,* in *Library Journal,* Vol. 122, No. 7, April 15, 1997, p. 122.

Edwards, Kim, "The Way It Felt to Be Falling," in *Secrets of a Fire King,* Picador USA, 1998, pp. 93–113.

Review of *The Secrets of a Fire King,* in *Kirkus Reviews,* February 15, 1997.

Review of *The Secrets of a Fire King,* in *Publishers Weekly,* Vol. 244, No. 8, February 24, 1997, pp. 64–65.

Sonenberg, Nina, ''Surprises and Consolation Prizes,'' in the *New York Times Book Review,* April 20, 1997, p. 20.

Wilhelmus, Tom, Review of *The Secrets of a Fire King,* in the *Hudson Review,* Vol. 50, No. 3, Autumn 1997, p. 527.

Further Reading

Breggin, Peter R., *Toxic Psychiatry: Why Therapy, Empathy, and Love Must Replace the Drugs, Electroshock, and Biochemical Theories of the New Psychiatry,* St. Martin's Press, 1994.

> Breggin, a psychiatrist, argues with the popular view that drugs are the best solution for many mental disorders, which are increasingly thought to be caused by chemical imbalances. He advocates alternate, drug-free methods for assisting the mentally ill. He also challenges schoolteachers, parents, and others who seek chemical solutions to behavior problems.

Brick, John, and Carlton K. Erickson, *Drugs, the Brain, and Behavior: The Pharmacology of Abuse and Dependence,* Haworth Press, 1998.

> This book gives an overview of the relationship between the human brain and behavior, with a special emphasis on the effects of mood-altering substances.

Derosalia, John, *Mental Training for Skydiving and Life,* SkyMind Publishers, 2001.

> This book examines the type of mental training that helps skydivers overcome stressful situations. Using this idea as a starting point, the book then applies this type of training to life, showing readers how to overcome weaknesses and fears in general.

Jamison, Kay Redfield, *Night Falls Fast: Understanding Suicide,* Knopf, 1999.

> In the story, Kate talks about her friend, Stephen, who once tried to kill himself. In this book, Jamison, a professor of psychiatry at Johns Hopkins School of Medicine and a person who has attempted suicide, explores the psychology of suicide. The book focuses mainly on people younger than forty and discusses how suicide can be prevented.

Johnson, Erik, *Understanding the Skydive,* Lamplighter Press, 2002.

> Johnson, a skydive instructor, provides a thorough overview of the sport for both novices and experienced skydivers. The book examines the various techniques used in skydiving, risks, weather conditions, competitions, skydiving etiquette, and the psychology of skydiving.

Kallen, Stuart A., ed., *The 1980s,* Cultural History of the United States through the Decades series, Lucent Books, 1999.

> Each book in this series examines a specific decade through theme-based chapters, which place events in a cultural context for students. Among other topics, the 1980s volume discusses the Reagan presidency, the fall of Communism, the rise of Wall Street and corporate power, and the computer revolution. The book also includes a bibliography and a detailed chronology of events.

Glossary of Literary Terms

A

Aestheticism: A literary and artistic movement of the nineteenth century. Followers of the movement believed that art should not be mixed with social, political, or moral teaching. The statement ''art for art's sake'' is a good summary of aestheticism. The movement had its roots in France, but it gained widespread importance in England in the last half of the nineteenth century, where it helped change the Victorian practice of including moral lessons in literature. Edgar Allan Poe is one of the best-known American ''aesthetes.''

Allegory: A narrative technique in which characters representing things or abstract ideas are used to convey a message or teach a lesson. Allegory is typically used to teach moral, ethical, or religious lessons but is sometimes used for satiric or political purposes. Many fairy tales are allegories.

Allusion: A reference to a familiar literary or historical person or event, used to make an idea more easily understood. Joyce Carol Oates's story ''Where Are You Going, Where Have You Been?'' exhibits several allusions to popular music.

Analogy: A comparison of two things made to explain something unfamiliar through its similarities to something familiar, or to prove one point based on the acceptance of another. Similes and metaphors are types of analogies.

Antagonist: The major character in a narrative or drama who works against the hero or protagonist. The Misfit in Flannery O'Connor's story ''A Good Man Is Hard to Find'' serves as the antagonist for the Grandmother.

Anthology: A collection of similar works of literature, art, or music. Zora Neale Hurston's ''The Eatonville Anthology'' is a collection of stories that take place in the same town.

Anthropomorphism: The presentation of animals or objects in human shape or with human characteristics. The term is derived from the Greek word for ''human form.'' The fur necklet in Katherine Mansfield's story ''Miss Brill'' has anthropomorphic characteristics.

Anti-hero: A central character in a work of literature who lacks traditional heroic qualities such as courage, physical prowess, and fortitude. Anti-heroes typically distrust conventional values and are unable to commit themselves to any ideals. They generally feel helpless in a world over which they have no control. Anti-heroes usually accept, and often celebrate, their positions as social outcasts. A well-known anti-hero is Walter Mitty in James Thurber's story ''The Secret Life of Walter Mitty.''

Archetype: The word archetype is commonly used to describe an original pattern or model from which all other things of the same kind are made. Archetypes are the literary images that grow out of the ''collective unconscious,'' a theory proposed by psychologist Carl Jung. They appear in literature as incidents and plots that repeat basic patterns of life. They may also appear as stereotyped characters. The ''schlemiel'' of Yiddish literature is an archetype.

Autobiography: A narrative in which an individual tells his or her life story. Examples include Benjamin Franklin's *Autobiography* and Amy Hempel's story ''In the Cemetery Where Al Jolson Is Buried,'' which has autobiographical characteristics even though it is a work of fiction.

Avant-garde: A literary term that describes new writing that rejects traditional approaches to literature in favor of innovations in style or content. Twentieth-century examples of the literary *avant-garde* include the modernists and the minimalists.

B

Belles-lettres: A French term meaning ''fine letters'' or ''beautiful writing.'' It is often used as a synonym for literature, typically referring to imaginative and artistic rather than scientific or expository writing. Current usage sometimes restricts the meaning to light or humorous writing and appreciative essays about literature. Lewis Carroll's *Alice in Wonderland* epitomizes the realm of belles-lettres.

Bildungsroman: A German word meaning ''novel of development.'' The *bildungsroman* is a study of the maturation of a youthful character, typically brought about through a series of social or sexual encounters that lead to self-awareness. J. D. Salinger's *Catcher in the Rye* is a *bildungsroman*, and Doris Lessing's story ''Through the Tunnel'' exhibits characteristics of a *bildungsroman* as well.

Black Aesthetic Movement: A period of artistic and literary development among African Americans in the 1960s and early 1970s. This was the first major African-American artistic movement since the Harlem Renaissance and was closely paralleled by the civil rights and black power movements. The black aesthetic writers attempted to produce works of art that would be meaningful to the black masses. Key figures in black aesthetics included one of its founders, poet and playwright Amiri Baraka, formerly known as LeRoi Jones; poet and essayist Haki R. Madhubuti, formerly Don L. Lee; poet and playwright Sonia Sanchez; and dramatist Ed Bullins. Works representative of the Black Aesthetic Movement include Amiri Baraka's play *Dutchman,* a 1964 Obie award-winner.

Black Humor: Writing that places grotesque elements side by side with humorous ones in an attempt to shock the reader, forcing him or her to laugh at the horrifying reality of a disordered world. ''Lamb to the Slaughter,'' by Roald Dahl, in which a placid housewife murders her husband and serves the murder weapon to the investigating policemen, is an example of black humor.

C

Catharsis: The release or purging of unwanted emotions—specifically fear and pity—brought about by exposure to art. The term was first used by the Greek philosopher Aristotle in his *Poetics* to refer to the desired effect of tragedy on spectators.

Character: Broadly speaking, a person in a literary work. The actions of characters are what constitute the plot of a story, novel, or poem. There are numerous types of characters, ranging from simple, stereotypical figures to intricate, multifaceted ones. ''Characterization'' is the process by which an author creates vivid, believable characters in a work of art. This may be done in a variety of ways, including (1) direct description of the character by the narrator; (2) the direct presentation of the speech, thoughts, or actions of the character; and (3) the responses of other characters to the character. The term ''character'' also refers to a form originated by the ancient Greek writer Theophrastus that later became popular in the seventeenth and eighteenth centuries. It is a short essay or sketch of a person who prominently displays a specific attribute or quality, such as miserliness or ambition. ''Miss Brill,'' a story by Katherine Mansfield, is an example of a character sketch.

Classical: In its strictest definition in literary criticism, classicism refers to works of ancient Greek or Roman literature. The term may also be used to describe a literary work of recognized importance (a ''classic'') from any time period or literature that exhibits the traits of classicism. Examples of later works and authors now described as classical include French literature of the seventeenth century, Western novels of the nineteenth century, and American fiction of the mid-nineteenth century such as that written by James Fenimore Cooper and Mark Twain.

Climax: The turning point in a narrative, the moment when the conflict is at its most intense. Typically, the structure of stories, novels, and plays is one of rising action, in which tension builds to the climax, followed by falling action, in which tension lessens as the story moves to its conclusion.

Comedy: One of two major types of drama, the other being tragedy. Its aim is to amuse, and it typically ends happily. Comedy assumes many forms, such as farce and burlesque, and uses a variety of techniques, from parody to satire. In a restricted sense the term comedy refers only to dramatic presentations, but in general usage it is commonly applied to nondramatic works as well.

Comic Relief: The use of humor to lighten the mood of a serious or tragic story, especially in plays. The technique is very common in Elizabethan works, and can be an integral part of the plot or simply a brief event designed to break the tension of the scene.

Conflict: The conflict in a work of fiction is the issue to be resolved in the story. It usually occurs between two characters, the protagonist and the antagonist, or between the protagonist and society or the protagonist and himself or herself. The conflict in Washington Irving's story "The Devil and Tom Walker" is that the Devil wants Tom Walker's soul but Tom does not want to go to hell.

Criticism: The systematic study and evaluation of literary works, usually based on a specific method or set of principles. An important part of literary studies since ancient times, the practice of criticism has given rise to numerous theories, methods, and "schools," sometimes producing conflicting, even contradictory, interpretations of literature in general as well as of individual works. Even such basic issues as what constitutes a poem or a novel have been the subject of much criticism over the centuries. Seminal texts of literary criticism include Plato's *Republic,* Aristotle's *Poetics,* Sir Philip Sidney's *The Defence of Poesie,* and John Dryden's *Of Dramatic Poesie.* Contemporary schools of criticism include deconstruction, feminist, psychoanalytic, poststructuralist, new historicist, postcolonialist, and reader-response.

D

Deconstruction: A method of literary criticism characterized by multiple conflicting interpretations of a given work. Deconstructionists consider the impact of the language of a work and suggest that the true meaning of the work is not necessarily the meaning that the author intended.

Deduction: The process of reaching a conclusion through reasoning from general premises to a specific premise. Arthur Conan Doyle's character Sherlock Holmes often used deductive reasoning to solve mysteries.

Denotation: The definition of a word, apart from the impressions or feelings it creates in the reader. The word "apartheid" denotes a political and economic policy of segregation by race, but its connotations—oppression, slavery, inequality—are numerous.

Denouement: A French word meaning "the unknotting." In literature, it denotes the resolution of conflict in fiction or drama. The *denouement* follows the climax and provides an outcome to the primary plot situation as well as an explanation of secondary plot complications. A well-known example of *denouement* is the last scene of the play *As You Like It* by William Shakespeare, in which couples are married, an evildoer repents, the identities of two disguised characters are revealed, and a ruler is restored to power. Also known as "falling action."

Detective Story: A narrative about the solution of a mystery or the identification of a criminal. The conventions of the detective story include the detective's scrupulous use of logic in solving the mystery; incompetent or ineffectual police; a suspect who appears guilty at first but is later proved innocent; and the detective's friend or confidant—often the narrator—whose slowness in interpreting clues emphasizes by contrast the detective's brilliance. Edgar Allan Poe's "Murders in the Rue Morgue" is commonly regarded as the earliest example of this type of story. Other practitioners are Arthur Conan Doyle, Dashiell Hammett, and Agatha Christie.

Dialogue: Dialogue is conversation between people in a literary work. In its most restricted sense, it refers specifically to the speech of characters in a drama. As a specific literary genre, a "dialogue" is a composition in which characters debate an issue or idea.

Didactic: A term used to describe works of literature that aim to teach a moral, religious, political, or practical lesson. Although didactic elements are often found in artistically pleasing works, the term "didactic" usually refers to literature in which the message is more important than the form. The term may also be used to criticize a work that the critic finds "overly didactic," that is, heavy-handed in its delivery of a lesson. An example of didactic literature is John Bunyan's *Pilgrim's Progress.*

Dramatic Irony: Occurs when the reader of a work of literature knows something that a character in the work itself does not know. The irony is in the contrast between the intended meaning of the statements or actions of a character and the additional information understood by the audience.

Dystopia: An imaginary place in a work of fiction where the characters lead dehumanized, fearful lives. George Orwell's *Nineteen Eighty-four,* and Margaret Atwood's *Handmaid's Tale* portray versions of dystopia.

E

Edwardian: Describes cultural conventions identified with the period of the reign of Edward VII of England (1901–1910). Writers of the Edwardian Age typically displayed a strong reaction against the propriety and conservatism of the Victorian Age. Their work often exhibits distrust of authority in religion, politics, and art and expresses strong doubts about the soundness of conventional values. Writers of this era include E. M. Forster, H. G. Wells, and Joseph Conrad.

Empathy: A sense of shared experience, including emotional and physical feelings, with someone or something other than oneself. Empathy is often used to describe the response of a reader to a literary character.

Epilogue: A concluding statement or section of a literary work. In dramas, particularly those of the seventeenth and eighteenth centuries, the epilogue is a closing speech, often in verse, delivered by an actor at the end of a play and spoken directly to the audience.

Epiphany: A sudden revelation of truth inspired by a seemingly trivial incident. The term was widely used by James Joyce in his critical writings, and the stories in Joyce's *Dubliners* are commonly called ''epiphanies.''

Epistolary Novel: A novel in the form of letters. The form was particularly popular in the eighteenth century. The form can also be applied to short stories, as in Edwidge Danticat's ''Children of the Sea.''

Epithet: A word or phrase, often disparaging or abusive, that expresses a character trait of someone or something. ''The Napoleon of crime'' is an epithet applied to Professor Moriarty, arch-rival of Sherlock Holmes in Arthur Conan Doyle's series of detective stories.

Existentialism: A predominantly twentieth-century philosophy concerned with the nature and perception of human existence. There are two major strains of existentialist thought: atheistic and Christian. Followers of atheistic existentialism believe that the individual is alone in a godless universe and that the basic human condition is one of suffering and loneliness. Nevertheless, because there are no fixed values, individuals can create their own characters—indeed, they can shape themselves—through the exercise of free will. The atheistic strain culminates in and is popularly associated with the works of Jean-Paul Sartre. The Christian existentialists, on the other hand, believe that only in God may people find freedom from life's anguish. The two strains hold certain beliefs in common: that existence cannot be fully understood or described through empirical effort; that anguish is a universal element of life; that individuals must bear responsibility for their actions; and that there is no common standard of behavior or perception for religious and ethical matters. Existentialist thought figures prominently in the works of such authors as Franz Kafka, Fyodor Dostoyevsky, and Albert Camus.

Expatriatism: The practice of leaving one's country to live for an extended period in another country. Literary expatriates include Irish author James Joyce who moved to Italy and France, American writers James Baldwin, Ernest Hemingway, Gertrude Stein, and F. Scott Fitzgerald who lived and wrote in Paris, and Polish novelist Joseph Conrad in England.

Exposition: Writing intended to explain the nature of an idea, thing, or theme. Expository writing is often combined with description, narration, or argument.

Expressionism: An indistinct literary term, originally used to describe an early twentieth-century school of German painting. The term applies to almost any mode of unconventional, highly subjective writing that distorts reality in some way. Advocates of Expressionism include Federico Garcia Lorca, Eugene O'Neill, Franz Kafka, and James Joyce.

F

Fable: A prose or verse narrative intended to convey a moral. Animals or inanimate objects with human characteristics often serve as characters in fables. A famous fable is Aesop's "The Tortoise and the Hare."

Fantasy: A literary form related to mythology and folklore. Fantasy literature is typically set in non-existent realms and features supernatural beings. Notable examples of literature with elements of fantasy are Gabriel Garcia Marquez's story "The Handsomest Drowned Man in the World" and Ursula K. LeGuin's "The Ones Who Walk Away from Omelas."

Farce: A type of comedy characterized by broad humor, outlandish incidents, and often vulgar subject matter. Much of the comedy in film and television could more accurately be described as farce.

Fiction: Any story that is the product of imagination rather than a documentation of fact. Characters and events in such narratives may be based in real life but their ultimate form and configuration is a creation of the author.

Figurative Language: A technique in which an author uses figures of speech such as hyperbole, irony, metaphor, or simile for a particular effect. Figurative language is the opposite of literal language, in which every word is truthful, accurate, and free of exaggeration or embellishment.

Flashback: A device used in literature to present action that occurred before the beginning of the story. Flashbacks are often introduced as the dreams or recollections of one or more characters.

Foil: A character in a work of literature whose physical or psychological qualities contrast strongly with, and therefore highlight, the corresponding qualities of another character. In his Sherlock Holmes stories, Arthur Conan Doyle portrayed Dr. Watson as a man of normal habits and intelligence, making him a foil for the eccentric and unusually perceptive Sherlock Holmes.

Folklore: Traditions and myths preserved in a culture or group of people. Typically, these are passed on by word of mouth in various forms—such as legends, songs, and proverbs—or preserved in customs and ceremonies. Washington Irving, in "The Devil and Tom Walker" and many of his other stories, incorporates many elements of the folklore of New England and Germany.

Folktale: A story originating in oral tradition. Folktales fall into a variety of categories, including legends, ghost stories, fairy tales, fables, and anecdotes based on historical figures and events.

Foreshadowing: A device used in literature to create expectation or to set up an explanation of later developments. Edgar Allan Poe uses foreshadowing to create suspense in "The Fall of the House of Usher" when the narrator comments on the crumbling state of disrepair in which he finds the house.

G

Genre: A category of literary work. Genre may refer to both the content of a given work—tragedy, comedy, horror, science fiction—and to its form, such as poetry, novel, or drama.

Gilded Age: A period in American history during the 1870s and after characterized by political corruption and materialism. A number of important novels of social and political criticism were written during this time. Henry James and Kate Chopin are two writers who were prominent during the Gilded Age.

Gothicism: In literature, works characterized by a taste for medieval or morbid characters and situations. A gothic novel prominently features elements of horror, the supernatural, gloom, and violence: clanking chains, terror, ghosts, medieval castles, and unexplained phenomena. The term "gothic novel" is also applied to novels that lack elements of the traditional Gothic setting but that create a similar atmosphere of terror or dread. The term can also be applied to stories, plays, and poems. Mary Shelley's *Frankenstein* and Joyce Carol Oates's *Bellefleur* are both gothic novels.

Grotesque: In literature, a work that is characterized by exaggeration, deformity, freakishness, and disorder. The grotesque often includes an element of comic absurdity. Examples of the grotesque can be found in the works of Edgar Allan Poe, Flannery O'Connor, Joseph Heller, and Shirley Jackson.

H

Harlem Renaissance: The Harlem Renaissance of the 1920s is generally considered the first significant movement of black writers and artists in the United States. During this period, new and established black writers, many of whom lived in the region of New York City known as Harlem, published more fiction and poetry than ever before, the first influential black literary journals were established, and black authors and artists received their first widespread recognition and serious critical appraisal. Among the major writers associated with this period are Countee Cullen, Langston Hughes, Arna Bontemps, and Zora Neale Hurston.

Hero/Heroine: The principal sympathetic character in a literary work. Heroes and heroines typically exhibit admirable traits: idealism, courage, and integrity, for example. Famous heroes and heroines of literature include Charles Dickens's Oliver Twist, Margaret Mitchell's Scarlett O'Hara, and the anonymous narrator in Ralph Ellison's *Invisible Man.*

Hyperbole: Deliberate exaggeration used to achieve an effect. In William Shakespeare's *Macbeth,* Lady Macbeth hyperbolizes when she says, ''All the perfumes of Arabia could not sweeten this little hand.''

I

Image: A concrete representation of an object or sensory experience. Typically, such a representation helps evoke the feelings associated with the object or experience itself. Images are either ''literal'' or ''figurative.'' Literal images are especially concrete and involve little or no extension of the obvious meaning of the words used to express them. Figurative images do not follow the literal meaning of the words exactly. Images in literature are usually visual, but the term ''image'' can also refer to the representation of any sensory experience.

Imagery: The array of images in a literary work. Also used to convey the author's overall use of figurative language in a work.

In medias res: A Latin term meaning ''in the middle of things.'' It refers to the technique of beginning a story at its midpoint and then using various flashback devices to reveal previous action. This technique originated in such epics as Virgil's *Aeneid.*

Interior Monologue: A narrative technique in which characters' thoughts are revealed in a way that appears to be uncontrolled by the author. The interior monologue typically aims to reveal the inner self of a character. It portrays emotional experiences as they occur at both a conscious and unconscious level. One of the best-known interior monologues in English is the Molly Bloom section at the close of James Joyce's *Ulysses.* Katherine Anne Porter's ''The Jilting of Granny Weatherall'' is also told in the form of an interior monologue.

Irony: In literary criticism, the effect of language in which the intended meaning is the opposite of what is stated. The title of Jonathan Swift's ''A Modest Proposal'' is ironic because what Swift proposes in this essay is cannibalism—hardly ''modest.''

J

Jargon: Language that is used or understood only by a select group of people. Jargon may refer to terminology used in a certain profession, such as computer jargon, or it may refer to any nonsensical language that is not understood by most people. Anthony Burgess's *A Clockwork Orange* and James Thurber's ''The Secret Life of Walter Mitty'' both use jargon.

K

Knickerbocker Group: An indistinct group of New York writers of the first half of the nineteenth century. Members of the group were linked only by location and a common theme: New York life. Two famous members of the Knickerbocker Group were Washington Irving and William Cullen Bryant. The group's name derives from Irving's *Knickerbocker's History of New York.*

L

Literal Language: An author uses literal language when he or she writes without exaggerating or embellishing the subject matter and without any tools of figurative language. To say ''He ran very quickly down the street'' is to use literal language, whereas to say ''He ran like a hare down the street'' would be using figurative language.

Literature: Literature is broadly defined as any written or spoken material, but the term most often refers to creative works. Literature includes poetry, drama, fiction, and many kinds of nonfiction writing, as well as oral, dramatic, and broadcast compositions not necessarily preserved in a written format, such as films and television programs.

Lost Generation: A term first used by Gertrude Stein to describe the post-World War I generation of American writers: men and women haunted by a sense of betrayal and emptiness brought about by the destructiveness of the war. The term is commonly applied to Hart Crane, Ernest Hemingway, F. Scott Fitzgerald, and others.

M

Magic Realism: A form of literature that incorporates fantasy elements or supernatural occurrences into the narrative and accepts them as truth. Gabriel Garcia Marquez and Laura Esquivel are two writers known for their works of magic realism.

Metaphor: A figure of speech that expresses an idea through the image of another object. Metaphors suggest the essence of the first object by identifying it with certain qualities of the second object. An example is ''But soft, what light through yonder window breaks?/ It is the east, and Juliet is the sun'' in William Shakespeare's *Romeo and Juliet*. Here, Juliet, the first object, is identified with qualities of the second object, the sun.

Minimalism: A literary style characterized by spare, simple prose with few elaborations. In minimalism, the main theme of the work is often never discussed directly. Amy Hempel and Ernest Hemingway are two writers known for their works of minimalism.

Modernism: Modern literary practices. Also, the principles of a literary school that lasted from roughly the beginning of the twentieth century until the end of World War II. Modernism is defined by its rejection of the literary conventions of the nineteenth century and by its opposition to conventional morality, taste, traditions, and economic values. Many writers are associated with the concepts of modernism, including Albert Camus, D. H. Lawrence, Ernest Hemingway, William Faulkner, Eugene O'Neill, and James Joyce.

Monologue: A composition, written or oral, by a single individual. More specifically, a speech given by a single individual in a drama or other public entertainment. It has no set length, although it is usually several or more lines long. ''I Stand Here Ironing'' by Tillie Olsen is an example of a story written in the form of a monologue.

Mood: The prevailing emotions of a work or of the author in his or her creation of the work. The mood of a work is not always what might be expected based on its subject matter.

Motif: A theme, character type, image, metaphor, or other verbal element that recurs throughout a single work of literature or occurs in a number of different works over a period of time. For example, the color white in Herman Melville's *Moby Dick* is a ''specific'' *motif,* while the trials of star-crossed lovers is a ''conventional'' *motif* from the literature of all periods.

N

Narration: The telling of a series of events, real or invented. A narration may be either a simple narrative, in which the events are recounted chronologically, or a narrative with a plot, in which the account is given in a style reflecting the author's artistic concept of the story. Narration is sometimes used as a synonym for ''storyline.''

Narrative: A verse or prose accounting of an event or sequence of events, real or invented. The term is also used as an adjective in the sense ''method of narration.'' For example, in literary criticism, the expression ''narrative technique'' usually refers to the way the author structures and presents his or her story. Different narrative forms include diaries, travelogues, novels, ballads, epics, short stories, and other fictional forms.

Narrator: The teller of a story. The narrator may be the author or a character in the story through whom the author speaks. Huckleberry Finn is the narrator of Mark Twain's *The Adventures of Huckleberry Finn.*

Novella: An Italian term meaning ''story.'' This term has been especially used to describe fourteenth-century Italian tales, but it also refers to modern short novels. Modern novellas include Leo Tolstoy's *The Death of Ivan Ilich,* Fyodor Dostoyevsky's *Notes from the Underground,* and Joseph Conrad's *Heart of Darkness.*

O

Oedipus Complex: A son's romantic obsession with his mother. The phrase is derived from the story of the ancient Theban hero Oedipus, who unknowingly killed his father and married his mother, and was popularized by Sigmund Freud's theory of psychoanalysis. Literary occurrences of the Oedipus complex include Sophocles' *Oedipus Rex* and D. H. Lawrence's ''The Rocking-Horse Winner.''

Onomatopoeia: The use of words whose sounds express or suggest their meaning. In its simplest sense, onomatopoeia may be represented by words that mimic the sounds they denote such as ''hiss'' or ''meow.'' At a more subtle level, the pattern and rhythm of sounds and rhymes of a line or poem may be onomatopoeic.

Oral Tradition: A process by which songs, ballads, folklore, and other material are transmitted by word of mouth. The tradition of oral transmission predates the written record systems of literate society.

Oral transmission preserves material sometimes over generations, although often with variations. Memory plays a large part in the recitation and preservation of orally transmitted material. Native American myths and legends, and African folktales told by plantation slaves are examples of orally transmitted literature.

P

Parable: A story intended to teach a moral lesson or answer an ethical question. Examples of parables are the stories told by Jesus Christ in the New Testament, notably ''The Prodigal Son,'' but parables also are used in Sufism, rabbinic literature, Hasidism, and Zen Buddhism. Isaac Bashevis Singer's story ''Gimpel the Fool'' exhibits characteristics of a parable.

Paradox: A statement that appears illogical or contradictory at first, but may actually point to an underlying truth. A literary example of a paradox is George Orwell's statement ''All animals are equal, but some animals are more equal than others'' in *Animal Farm.*

Parody: In literature, this term refers to an imitation of a serious literary work or the signature style of a particular author in a ridiculous manner. A typical parody adopts the style of the original and applies it to an inappropriate subject for humorous effect. Parody is a form of satire and could be considered the literary equivalent of a caricature or cartoon. Henry Fielding's *Shamela* is a parody of Samuel Richardson's *Pamela.*

Persona: A Latin term meaning ''mask.'' Personae are the characters in a fictional work of literature. The persona generally functions as a mask through which the author tells a story in a voice other than his or her own. A persona is usually either a character in a story who acts as a narrator or an ''implied author,'' a voice created by the author to act as the narrator for himself or herself. The persona in Charlotte Perkins Gilman's story ''The Yellow Wallpaper'' is the unnamed young mother experiencing a mental breakdown.

Personification: A figure of speech that gives human qualities to abstract ideas, animals, and inanimate objects. To say that ''the sun is smiling'' is to personify the sun.

Plot: The pattern of events in a narrative or drama. In its simplest sense, the plot guides the author in composing the work and helps the reader follow the work. Typically, plots exhibit causality and unity and have a beginning, a middle, and an end. Sometimes, however, a plot may consist of a series of disconnected events, in which case it is known as an ''episodic plot.''

Poetic Justice: An outcome in a literary work, not necessarily a poem, in which the good are rewarded and the evil are punished, especially in ways that particularly fit their virtues or crimes. For example, a murderer may himself be murdered, or a thief will find himself penniless.

Poetic License: Distortions of fact and literary convention made by a writer—not always a poet—for the sake of the effect gained. Poetic license is closely related to the concept of ''artistic freedom.'' An author exercises poetic license by saying that a pile of money ''reaches as high as a mountain'' when the pile is actually only a foot or two high.

Point of View: The narrative perspective from which a literary work is presented to the reader. There are four traditional points of view. The ''third person omniscient'' gives the reader a ''godlike'' perspective, unrestricted by time or place, from which to see actions and look into the minds of characters. This allows the author to comment openly on characters and events in the work. The ''third person'' point of view presents the events of the story from outside of any single character's perception, much like the omniscient point of view, but the reader must understand the action as it takes place and without any special insight into characters' minds or motivations. The ''first person'' or ''personal'' point of view relates events as they are perceived by a single character. The main character ''tells'' the story and may offer opinions about the action and characters which differ from those of the author. Much less common than omniscient, third person, and first person is the ''second person'' point of view, wherein the author tells the story as if it is happening to the reader. James Thurber employs the omniscient point of view in his short story ''The Secret Life of Walter Mitty.'' Ernest Hemingway's ''A Clean, Well-Lighted Place'' is a short story told from the third person point of view. Mark Twain's novel *Huckleberry Finn* is presented from the first person viewpoint. Jay McInerney's *Bright Lights, Big City* is an example of a novel which uses the second person point of view.

Pornography: Writing intended to provoke feelings of lust in the reader. Such works are often condemned by critics and teachers, but those which can be shown to have literary value are viewed less harshly. Literary works that have been described as pornographic include D. H. Lawrence's *Lady Chatterley's Lover* and James Joyce's *Ulysses*.

Post-Aesthetic Movement: An artistic response made by African Americans to the black aesthetic movement of the 1960s and early 1970s. Writers since that time have adopted a somewhat different tone in their work, with less emphasis placed on the disparity between black and white in the United States. In the words of post-aesthetic authors such as Toni Morrison, John Edgar Wideman, and Kristin Hunter, African Americans are portrayed as looking inward for answers to their own questions, rather than always looking to the outside world. Two well-known examples of works produced as part of the post-aesthetic movement are the Pulitzer Prize-winning novels *The Color Purple* by Alice Walker and *Beloved* by Toni Morrison.

Postmodernism: Writing from the 1960s forward characterized by experimentation and application of modernist elements, which include existentialism and alienation. Postmodernists have gone a step further in the rejection of tradition begun with the modernists by also rejecting traditional forms, preferring the anti-novel over the novel and the anti-hero over the hero. Postmodern writers include Thomas Pynchon, Margaret Drabble, and Gabriel Garcia Marquez.

Prologue: An introductory section of a literary work. It often contains information establishing the situation of the characters or presents information about the setting, time period, or action. In drama, the prologue is spoken by a chorus or by one of the principal characters.

Prose: A literary medium that attempts to mirror the language of everyday speech. It is distinguished from poetry by its use of unmetered, unrhymed language consisting of logically related sentences. Prose is usually grouped into paragraphs that form a cohesive whole such as an essay or a novel. The term is sometimes used to mean an author's general writing.

Protagonist: The central character of a story who serves as a focus for its themes and incidents and as the principal rationale for its development. The protagonist is sometimes referred to in discussions of modern literature as the hero or anti-hero. Well-known protagonists are Hamlet in William Shakespeare's *Hamlet* and Jay Gatsby in F. Scott Fitzgerald's *The Great Gatsby*.

R

Realism: A nineteenth-century European literary movement that sought to portray familiar characters, situations, and settings in a realistic manner. This was done primarily by using an objective narrative point of view and through the buildup of accurate detail. The standard for success of any realistic work depends on how faithfully it transfers common experience into fictional forms. The realistic method may be altered or extended, as in stream of consciousness writing, to record highly subjective experience. Contemporary authors who often write in a realistic way include Nadine Gordimer and Grace Paley.

Resolution: The portion of a story following the climax, in which the conflict is resolved. The resolution of Jane Austen's *Northanger Abbey* is neatly summed up in the following sentence: "Henry and Catherine were married, the bells rang and every body smiled."

Rising Action: The part of a drama where the plot becomes increasingly complicated. Rising action leads up to the climax, or turning point, of a drama. The final "chase scene" of an action film is generally the rising action which culminates in the film's climax.

Roman a clef: A French phrase meaning "novel with a key." It refers to a narrative in which real persons are portrayed under fictitious names. Jack Kerouac, for example, portrayed various his friends under fictitious names in the novel *On the Road*. D. H. Lawrence based "The Rocking-Horse Winner" on a family he knew.

Romanticism: This term has two widely accepted meanings. In historical criticism, it refers to a European intellectual and artistic movement of the late eighteenth and early nineteenth centuries that sought greater freedom of personal expression than that allowed by the strict rules of literary form and logic of the eighteenth-century neoclassicists. The Romantics preferred emotional and imaginative expression to rational analysis. They considered the individual to be at the center of all experience and so placed him or her at the center of their art. The Romantics believed that the creative imagination reveals nobler truths—unique feelings and attitudes—than those that could be discovered by logic or by scientific examination. "Romanticism" is also used as a general term to refer to a type of sensibility found in all periods of literary history and usually considered to be in opposition to the principles of classicism. In this sense, Romanticism signifies any work or philosophy in which the exotic or dreamlike figure strongly, or that is devoted to individualistic expression, self-analysis, or a pursuit of a higher realm of knowledge than can be discovered by human reason. Prominent Romantics include Jean-Jacques Rousseau, William Wordsworth, John Keats, Lord Byron, and Johann Wolfgang von Goethe.

S

Satire: A work that uses ridicule, humor, and wit to criticize and provoke change in human nature and institutions. Voltaire's novella *Candide* and Jonathan Swift's essay ''A Modest Proposal'' are both satires. Flannery O'Connor's portrayal of the family in ''A Good Man Is Hard to Find'' is a satire of a modern, Southern, American family.

Science Fiction: A type of narrative based upon real or imagined scientific theories and technology. Science fiction is often peopled with alien creatures and set on other planets or in different dimensions. Popular writers of science fiction are Isaac Asimov, Karel Capek, Ray Bradbury, and Ursula K. Le Guin.

Setting: The time, place, and culture in which the action of a narrative takes place. The elements of setting may include geographic location, characters's physical and mental environments, prevailing cultural attitudes, or the historical time in which the action takes place.

Short Story: A fictional prose narrative shorter and more focused than a novella. The short story usually deals with a single episode and often a single character. The ''tone,'' the author's attitude toward his or her subject and audience, is uniform throughout. The short story frequently also lacks *denouement*, ending instead at its climax.

Signifying Monkey: A popular trickster figure in black folklore, with hundreds of tales about this character documented since the 19th century. Henry Louis Gates Jr. examines the history of the signifying monkey in *The Signifying Monkey: Towards a Theory of Afro-American Literary Criticism,* published in 1988.

Simile: A comparison, usually using ''like'' or ''as,''of two essentially dissimilar things, as in ''coffee as cold as ice'' or ''He sounded like a broken record.'' The title of Ernest Hemingway's ''Hills Like White Elephants'' contains a simile.

Social Realism: The Socialist Realism school of literary theory was proposed by Maxim Gorky and established as a dogma by the first Soviet Congress of Writers. It demanded adherence to a communist worldview in works of literature. Its doctrines required an objective viewpoint comprehensible to the working classes and themes of social struggle featuring strong proletarian heroes. Gabriel Garcia Marquez's stories exhibit some characteristics of Socialist Realism.

Stereotype: A stereotype was originally the name for a duplication made during the printing process; this led to its modern definition as a person or thing that is (or is assumed to be) the same as all others of its type. Common stereotypical characters include the absent-minded professor, the nagging wife, the troublemaking teenager, and the kind-hearted grandmother.

Stream of Consciousness: A narrative technique for rendering the inward experience of a character. This technique is designed to give the impression of an ever-changing series of thoughts, emotions, images, and memories in the spontaneous and seemingly illogical order that they occur in life. The textbook example of stream of consciousness is the last section of James Joyce's *Ulysses.*

Structure: The form taken by a piece of literature. The structure may be made obvious for ease of understanding, as in nonfiction works, or may obscured for artistic purposes, as in some poetry or seemingly ''unstructured'' prose.

Style: A writer's distinctive manner of arranging words to suit his or her ideas and purpose in writing. The unique imprint of the author's personality upon his or her writing, style is the product of an author's way of arranging ideas and his or her use of diction, different sentence structures, rhythm, figures of speech, rhetorical principles, and other elements of composition.

Suspense: A literary device in which the author maintains the audience's attention through the buildup of events, the outcome of which will soon be revealed. Suspense in William Shakespeare's *Hamlet* is sustained throughout by the question of whether or not the Prince will achieve what he has been instructed to do and of what he intends to do.

Symbol: Something that suggests or stands for something else without losing its original identity. In literature, symbols combine their literal meaning with the suggestion of an abstract concept. Literary symbols are of two types: those that carry complex associations of meaning no matter what their contexts, and those that derive their suggestive meaning from their functions in specific literary works. Examples of symbols are sunshine suggesting happiness, rain suggesting sorrow, and storm clouds suggesting despair.

T

Tale: A story told by a narrator with a simple plot and little character development. Tales are usually relatively short and often carry a simple message. Examples of tales can be found in the works of Saki, Anton Chekhov, Guy de Maupassant, and O. Henry.

Tall Tale: A humorous tale told in a straightforward, credible tone but relating absolutely impossible events or feats of the characters. Such tales were commonly told of frontier adventures during the settlement of the west in the United States. Literary use of tall tales can be found in Washington Irving's *History of New York,* Mark Twain's *Life on the Mississippi,* and in the German R. F. Raspe's *Baron Munchausen's Narratives of His Marvellous Travels and Campaigns in Russia.*

Theme: The main point of a work of literature. The term is used interchangeably with thesis. Many works have multiple themes. One of the themes of Nathaniel Hawthorne's ''Young Goodman Brown'' is loss of faith.

Tone: The author's attitude toward his or her audience may be deduced from the tone of the work. A formal tone may create distance or convey politeness, while an informal tone may encourage a friendly, intimate, or intrusive feeling in the reader. The author's attitude toward his or her subject matter may also be deduced from the tone of the words he or she uses in discussing it. The tone of John F. Kennedy's speech which included the appeal to ''ask not what your country can do for you'' was intended to instill feelings of camaraderie and national pride in listeners.

Tragedy: A drama in prose or poetry about a noble, courageous hero of excellent character who, because of some tragic character flaw, brings ruin upon him- or herself. Tragedy treats its subjects in a dignified and serious manner, using poetic language to help evoke pity and fear and bring about catharsis, a purging of these emotions. The tragic form was practiced extensively by the ancient Greeks. The classical form of tragedy was revived in the sixteenth century; it flourished especially on the Elizabethan stage. In modern times, dramatists have attempted to adapt the form to the needs of modern society by drawing their heroes from the ranks of ordinary men and women and defining the nobility of these heroes in terms of spirit rather than exalted social standing. Some contemporary works that are thought of as tragedies include *The Great Gatsby* by F. Scott Fitzgerald, and *The Sound and the Fury* by William Faulkner.

Tragic Flaw: In a tragedy, the quality within the hero or heroine which leads to his or her downfall. Examples of the tragic flaw include Othello's jealousy and Hamlet's indecisiveness, although most great tragedies defy such simple interpretation.

U

Utopia: A fictional perfect place, such as ''paradise'' or ''heaven.'' An early literary utopia was described in Plato's *Republic,* and in modern literature, Ursula K. Le Guin depicts a utopia in ''The Ones Who Walk Away from Omelas.''

V

Victorian: Refers broadly to the reign of Queen Victoria of England (1837–1901) and to anything with qualities typical of that era. For example, the qualities of smug narrow-mindedness, bourgeois materialism, faith in social progress, and priggish morality are often considered Victorian. In literature, the Victorian Period was the great age of the English novel, and the latter part of the era saw the rise of movements such as decadence and symbolism.

Cumulative Author/Title Index

Wunderkind (McCullers): V5

Y

Yamamoto, Hisaye
  The Eskimo Connection: V14
The Yellow Wallpaper (Gilman): V1
Yellow Woman (Silko): V4
Yezierska, Anzia
  America and I: V15
Yoshimoto, Banana
  Kitchen: V16
Young Goodman Brown
    (Hawthorne): V1

Nationality/Ethnicity Index

Subject/Theme Index